Implementing the Americans with Disabilities Act

Implementing the Americans with Disabilities Act

Edited by

Jane West

A Copublication with the Milbank Memorial Fund

First published 1996

Blackwell Publishers, Inc.
238 Main Street
Cambridge, Massachusetts 02142

Blackwell Publishers Ltd.
108 Cowley Road
Oxford OX4 1JF
UK

Library of Congress Cataloging-in-Publication Data
Implementing the Americans with Disabilities Act / edited by Jane West.
    p. cm.
  "A copublication with the Milbank Memorial Fund."
  Includes bibliographical references (p.) and index.
  ISBN 1-55786-867-0 (pbk. : alk. paper)
  1. United States. Americans with Disabilities Act of 1990—Government policy.
2. Handicapped—Legal status, laws, etc.—United States. 3. Discrimination against the handicapped—Law and legislation—United States. 4. Discrimination in employment—Law and legislation—United States. I. West, Jane, 1950–
HV1553.I44   1996
362.4'0973—dc20   95-36574
                                                                        CIP

British Library Cataloguing in Publication Data

A CIP catalogue record for this book is available from the British Library.

Copublished by the Milbank Memorial Fund

Printed in the United States of America

This book is printed on acid-free paper

TABLE OF CONTENTS

IV: Impact on People with Disabilities

FOREWORD

The Milbank Memorial Fund is an endowed national foundation that commissions and makes available the results of nonpartisan analysis, study, and research on significant issues in health policy. The fund disseminates ideas and information about these issues through conferences, pamphlets, books, and a quarterly journal.

In July 1991, a year after the ADA became law, the Fund published *The Americans with Disabilities Act: From Policy to Practice*, a multiauthored work edited by Jane West. As a follow-up to this book, the fund commissioned the authors whose work is presented here to monitor and report on the implementation of the ADA.

Almost six years after its enactment, the ADA is still not well known to many of the people it is intended to benefit. As this book went to press, moreover, the future of the ADA was uncertain. Many people in politics, business, and the media were attacking it as another burdensome unfunded mandate on business, the states, and local government. This book provides information that can inform a debate that has implications for millions of Americans.

Samuel L. Milbank　　　　　*Daniel M. Fox*
Chairman　　　　　　　　　President

ACKNOWLEDGMENTS

Many people contributed to this book through interviews, providing information and ideas, and reviewing manuscripts. The editor particularly thanks the following people, listed with the position they held at the time they provided assistance: Michele Adler, statistician, Office of Disability, Aging, and Long-Term Care Planning, U.S. Department of Health and Human Services; Sherry Arnstein, executive director, American Association of Colleges of Osteopathic Medicine; Robert C. Ashby, deputy assistant, General Counsel for Regulations and Enforcement, U. S. Department of Transportation; Marjorie Baldwin, assistant professor, Department of Economics, East Carolina University; Robert M. Ball, chairman, National Academy of Social Insurance; William Baranowski, director, Office of Fair Employment Practices, U.S. House of Representatives; Andrew Batavia, legislative assistant, office of Senator John McCain; Keith Bateman, associate vice president and director of policy resources, Alliance of American Insurers; Chris Bell, partner, Jackson, Lewis, Schnitzler and Krupman; Monroe Berkowitz, director, Disability and Health Economics Research Section, Bureau of Economics Research, Rutgers University; Peter Blanck, professor of law, senior fellow of Annenberg Program, College of Law, University of Iowa; Janet Blizard, supervising attorney, Public Access Section, U.S. Department of Justice; Barbara Bode, executive director, Council of Better Business Bureaus Foundation; Elizabeth Boggs; Doris Brennan; Charles Bruner, executive director, Child and Family Policy Center; Ed Burke, acting director, National Council on Disability; David Capozzi, director, Office of Technical and Information Services, Architectural and Transportation Barriers Compliance Board; Thomas N. Chirikos, professor of health policy and management, College of Public Health, University of South Florida; Tony Coelho, chairperson, President's Committee on Employment of People with Disabilities; John F. Cosgrove, chairperson, Committee on Insurance, Florida House of Representatives; Maria Cuprill, staff director, House Subcommittee on Select Education and Civil Rights; Justin Dart, Jr., former chairperson, President's Committee on Employment of People with Disabilities; Curtis Decker, executive director, National Association of Protection and Advocacy Systems; Gerben DeJong, director of research, National Rehabilitation Hospital Research Center; Joseph Delfico, director of income security issues, U.S. General Accounting Office; Janet Dorsey, deputy postmaster, U.S. Senate Post Office; Linda Dubroof, acting branch chief, Domestic Services Branch, Domestic Facilities Division, Common Carrier Bureau, Federal Communications Commission; David Esquith, rehabilitation specialist, National Institute on Disability and Rehabilitation Research, U.S. Department of Education; Carolyn Feis, social science analyst, U.S. General Accounting Office; Marty Ford, The Arc; Merrily Friedlander, acting chief, Coordination of Review Section, Civil Rights Division, U.S. Department of Justice; Michael B. Friedman, regional director, New York State Office of Mental Health (Hudson River); Harry C. Goode, vice chairman, Committee on Community Affairs, Florida House of Representatives; Gary Gross, staff attorney, National Association of Protection and Advocacy Systems; Harlan Hahn, professor of political science, University of Southern California; Laura Hall, senior analyst, Biological and Behavioral Program, Office of Technology Assessment, U.S. Congress; Jane L. Hanson, partner, Milbank, Tweed, Hadley & McCloy; Paul Hearne, president, The Dole Foundation for Employment of People with Disabilities; David Helms, president, The Alpha Center; Judy Heumann, assistant secretary, Office of Special Education and Rehabilitative Services, U.S. Department of Education; Ron Honberg, director of legal affairs, National Alliance for the Mentally Ill; H. Allan Hunt, Upjohn Institute; Harriett Jenkins, director, Office of Fair Employment Practices, U.S. Senate; Bill Johnson, School of Health Administration and Policy, College of Business, Arizona State University; Erica Jones, executive director, Pacific Disability Business Technical Assistance Center; Nancy Lee Jones, legislative attorney, Congressional Research Service, Library of Congress; Todd Jones, National Association of Rehabilitation Facilities; Rosalie A. Kane, professor and director, Long-Term Care Resource Center, University of Minnesota, Minneapolis; Evan Kemp, chair, Equal Employment Opportunity Commission; Kathryn G. King, section head, Special Populations, Maryland Department of Health and Mental Hygiene, Medical Care Policy Administration; Stephen Knapp; John Lancaster, executive director, President's Committee on Employment of Persons with Disabilities; Wendy Lechner, legislative representative, National Federation of Independent Businesses; Ruth H. Lusher, ADA technical assistance program manager, Disability Rights Section, Civil Rights Division, U.S. Department of Justice; Gordon Mansfield, executive director, Paralyzed Veterans of America; Paul Marchand, director, governmental affairs, The Arc; Peggy Mastroianni, director, Policy Division, Americans with Disabilities Act Services, Office of Legal Counsel, Equal Employment Opportunity Commission; Arlene Mayerson, directing attorney, Disability Rights Education and Defense Fund; Maureen McCloskey, Paralyzed Veterans of America; Susan Meisinger, vice president of government and public affairs, Society for Human Resource Management; Pat Morrissey, vice president, government and regulatory affairs, Employment Advisory Services, Inc.; Margaret Nosek, Department of Physical Medicine and Rehabilitation, Baylor College of Medicine; Janet Novak, Forbes magazine; Walter Y. Oi, professor, Department of Economics, University of Rochester; Chris K. Olander, executive director, The JM Foundation; Stewart B. Oneglia, former chief, Coordination and Review Section, Civil Rights Division, U.S. Department of Justice; Susan B. Parker, secretary general, Rehabilitation International; Anne Marie Pecht, attorney advisor, U.S. Department of Justice; Mark Pitzer, attorney, Office of Chief Counsel, Internal Revenue Service, Department of Treasury; William F. Raines, Jr., administrative assistant to the architect of the Capitol; Sharon Rennert, attorney advisor, Americans with Disabilities Act Services, Equal Employment Opportunity Commission; Beth Robinson, professional staff member, House Subcommittee on Science; James C. Robinson, associate professor of health policy, School of Public Health, University of California, Berkeley; Thomas D. Romeo, executive in residence, College of Human Sciences and Services, University of Rhode Island; Ron Saunders, chairman, Committee on Community Affairs, Florida House of Representatives; Susan Schruth, acting director, Office of Civil Rights, Federal Transportation Administration, Department of Transportation; Richard Scotch, professor, School of Social Sciences, University of Texas, Dallas; Katherine Seelman, director, National Institute on Disability and Rehabilitation Research, U.S. Department of Education; Kay Shriner, editor, Journal of Disability Policy Studies, Arkansas Research Training Center, University of Arkansas; Robert Silverstein, staff director, U.S. Senate Subcommittee on Disability Policy; Rosalyn Simon, director, Project ACTION, National Easter Seals Society; Mario L. Taylor, staff director, Committee on Community Affairs, Florida House of Representatives; Michael B. Unhjem, president and CEO, Blue Cross/ Blue Shield of North Dakota; Alexander Vachon, legislative assistant, office of Senator Robert Dole; Richard Victor, executive director, Workers' Compensation Research Institute; Sally Weiss, United Cerebral Palsy Association; John Wodatch, chief, Public Access Section, Civil Rights Division, U.S. Department of Justice; Pat Wright, director of governmental affairs, Disability Rights Education and Defense Fund; Irving K. Zola, professor of sociology, Brandeis University; and two anonymous reviewers.

The Americans with Disabilities Act: Early Implementation

Jane West

INTRODUCTION

Implementation of the ADA has proceeded steadily in the first five years since its enactment. The fears of detractors of the ADA – excess cost and litigation – remain unfounded. On the other hand, the hopes of its advocates – significant improvement in the status of people with disabilities – have yet to materialize. The greatest impact of the ADA to date is in two areas: the empowerment claimed by people with disabilities and changes in how our nation's institutions conduct routine business: in stores, on buses, in the office, and in our use of telecommunications. This book presents chapters analyzing the implementation and early impact of the ADA.

The intended audience is those concerned about implementation of public policy in general and the ADA in particular: businesses and state and local governments responsible for compliance, people with disabilities who are protected by the ADA, nonprofit organizations interested in improving the lives of people with disabilities, public officials responsible for implementation and oversight, policy researchers, and those from other lands who look to this law for lessons about proceeding in their countries. The book provides a benchmark for implementation progress and offers policy makers and implementors an assessment of the fruits of their labors. The book assumes that the reader has a basic understanding of the ADA. It is a follow-up volume to *The Americans with Disabilities Act: From Policy to Practice* (J. West, ed. New York: Milbank Memorial Fund, 1991), which describes the requirements and origin of the statute.

In the book, the ADA is examined from the vantage point of business and industry, government, and people with disabilities. The chapters discuss all titles of the statute (employment, public accommodations, state and local government, transportation, and telecommunications relay services) as well as the roles of multiple actors (federal agencies, Congress, the judiciary, covered entities, people with disabilities, nonprofit organizations, private lawyers, professional organizations, and recipients of federal technical assistance funds). Chapters consider the intersection of the ADA with other policy areas, such as health insurance, income maintenance, workers' compensation, and personal assistance services (referred to by the traditional health care community as long-term care). A chapter exclusively examining the implementation of the state and local government requirements was commissioned but it was not completed. However, several authors discuss activities of state and local governments.

Also missing from the book is a chapter dedicated exclusively to the implementation of Title IV of the statute, telecommunications. This omission was purposeful, as this title was well on its way to implementation via state activities even prior to the enactment of the ADA. Its implementation from the federal level is considered in the first chapter, "The Federal Government and Congress."

The ADA mandate is broad and sweeping – to protect the civil rights of the nation's 49 million people with disabilities in virtually all aspects of public life. Elimination of physical and communication barriers is required, in employment, public services, businesses, transportation, and telecommunication. Accommodations for employees in the workplace, such as restructured jobs and flexible schedules, are required. Customers in restaurants, movie theaters, doctor's offices, and retail stores must be provided with auxiliary aids and services, such as sign language interpreters or assistive listening devices. Covered entities must do what they reasonably can to provide an equal opportunity for individuals with disabilities. The goal is the elimination of discrimination against people with disabilities and an increase in their participation in the mainstream of economic and social life.

The ADA is gradually affecting the way our country does business, in virtually every industry and every sector. Employers are changing their job application and interview practices, no longer asking about existing medical conditions or requiring medical exams until after a job offer is made. Businesses are removing architectural barriers and providing services to people with disabilities to make their goods and services accessible, such as motorized shopping carts in grocery stores. Bus operators are calling out stops so passengers who are visually impaired or blind will know where they are. Every telephone user can call or receive calls from a person who is deaf, hard of hearing, or speech impaired by using the relay system, now available across the entire nation. Over 30 philanthropies united to form the Funding Partnership for People with Disabilities and committed over $2.5 million to support projects that promote the goals of the ADA.

People with disabilities have used the ADA to improve their access and opportunities. Because of the ADA, students with learning disabilities can receive additional time to take SAT tests. Applicants for the bar with a history of psychiatric disabilities may not be required to reveal that history. Employees who develop AIDS or other diseases are no longer routinely dismissed, demoted, or provided with diminished insurance coverage. People who are blind or otherwise unable to drive can present identification other than drivers' licenses to cash checks and rent items. People who are blind cannot automatically be barred from jury duty. People who use wheelchairs can gain access to previously inaccessible buildings.

The ADA has made its presence felt in other areas of national policy, notably the provision of health insurance. Employers cannot reject job applicants because they believe their health insurance costs may increase if they hire the applicant. Disability-based distinctions are prohibited in determining the terms of health insurance coverage unless they are demonstrated to be bona fide. The ADA has interjected the antidiscrimination principle into health care reform discussions and policies at both the national and state levels, as demonstrated by the rejection of the Oregon Medicaid waiver request on grounds that it violated the ADA.

The costs of implementing the ADA generally appear manageable. Most accommodations in the workplace cost under $500, with 20 percent costing nothing (President's Committee on Employment of People with Disabilities, 1993). The tax credit available to small businesses may be alleviating some cost burden. Businesses that are removing barriers are not reporting cost burdens. Instead, they often report an increase in business as a result of improved accessibility (U.S. Government Accounting Office, 1993). The telecommunications requirements of the law have generally been well received by common carriers and represent an area of business expansion. The few cases reported of firms claiming that they are going out of business because of the ADA's requirements likely reflect a misunderstanding of the law's requirements, because businesses are protected from excessive costs by expenditure limits on alterations and "undue burden" limits in providing auxiliary aids and services.

Most complaints about cost are coming from state and local governments, which have sometimes included the ADA on their lists of "unfunded federal mandates." Most state and local governments have been covered by ADA requirements since the 1970s under Section 504 of the Rehabilitation Act. Few complaints about expense were voiced during that period. The cost concern is likely prompted by shrinking budgets rather than actual new costs, with the one possible exception of paratransit costs. The ADA has had the unintended effect of increasing paratransit services. Projected costs are estimated to be as high as $1 billion annually when full compliance is achieved.

Litigation is underway, initiated by both the federal government and the public and private bar associations; however, it is not excessive. Out of 850,000 cases in federal court only 650 are ADA cases (Reno and Thornburgh, 1995). There is no evidence that courts are backlogged with frivolous filings. The federal government has filed 35 court actions. Lawrence Gostin reviews over 100 published cases in his chapter in this volume. Issues addressed in litigation are varied, and decisions have been made in favor of both plaintiffs and defendants, gradually fleshing out the parameters of the law's requirements.

Some backlash sentiment has developed in response to complaints and lawsuits as well as media reports. In one community, a series of complaints led the local small business association to claim that such aggressive complaining would bring about repeal of the ADA (LRP Publications, 1994). A groundswell of such sentiment is not evident, but sporadic instances continue.

Although much has been accomplished in removing barriers and increasing opportunities for people with disabilities, much remains to be done. One commentator recently noted that, since the enactment of the ADA in 1990, it has departed from the public imagination and public dialogue (Bennett, 1994). Public awareness of the law is reported at 41 percent for the general public and only 40 percent for people with disabilities. Covered entities actively working to comply remain the exception rather than the rule. Few have been reached by the government's concerted technical assistance efforts. The absence of a national public awareness effort has left "unfunded mandate" campaigns and claims of the ADA as having "gone too far" unrebutted.

It is far too early to assess or predict the long-term impact of the ADA on the lives of people with disabilities. A pre- and post-

ADA measure taken of the status of people with disabilities revealed no change in the employment rate since 1986. Two-thirds of working-age people with disabilities are reported as not working. Most of these continue to want to work (National Organization on Disability, 1994). On the other hand, a dramatic increase in the education level of people with disabilities was reported, across all age groups. Even though this increase is certainly good news, it has not yet been converted into employment or income increases. This lack of conversion suggests that people with disabilities may face a unique array of disincentives and barriers to employment that will not be surmounted either by antidiscrimination measures or increased education. Numerous factors affect whether or not a person with a disability will work – his or her employment history, level of job skills, the availability of support services the person may need such as personal assistance services and assistive technology, the availability of adequate health insurance through employment, and the relative attractiveness of the security of income maintenance accompanied by guaranteed health insurance. The fact that the employment rate of people with disabilities does not appear to have increased cannot be considered a failure of the ADA. The ADA is one of only many policies affecting the employment of people with disabilities. The fact that the ADA may increase the employment life of a person who becomes disabled while working or yield increased promotions for people with disabilities who are already working may be its most significant employment contribution to date.

The following is a distillation of what we know about the early implementation and impact of the ADA, based on information in this book.

- Awareness of the law is increasing although still low.
- Compliance costs are generally manageable. The extent to which businesses are utilizing tax provisions to offset costs is not now known and will likely never be known.
- Litigation is underway, but it is not excessive.
- Systems and procedures for enforcement and implementation are in place and being utilized in federal agencies, but the federal government is not fully utilizing its enforcement authorities.

- The federal government has funded and provided a great deal of technical assistance, though it is reaching only a fraction of involved parties and its effectiveness has not been evaluated.
- Some businesses are gradually altering employment practices, such as preemployment inquiries and reasonable accommodation policies, with little difficulty or disruption.
- Reasonable accommodation extends the working life of employees with disabilities.
- The employment provisions are likely to yield the greatest benefit for people who become disabled while working or people who have disabilities and are already employed, have a good education, and/or are not African Americans. ADA appears unlikely, on its own, to increase the overall employment rate of people with disabilities.
- The ADA is unlikely to deter people from applying for SSI or SSDI benefits or to result in people currently on the rolls leaving to return to work unless those programs are reformed.
- There appears to be an important overlap between workers' compensation and the ADA, but the full impact of this overlap is yet to be determined.
- The ADA is influencing health care reform debate and policy.
- Public accommodations report little if any burden and increased business as a result of complying with the the ADA.
- The ADA is significantly changing the way the transportation industry does business. It has had the unintended consequence of generating an increase in the provision and utilization of paratransit services.
- The 9.6 million people who need personal assistance services are unlikely to reap much benefit from the ADA without an expansion in the availability and comprehensiveness of those services.
- The ADA is becoming an important tool to battle discrimination against people with psychiatric disabilities, although its impact will likely be in the long term.
- It is unlikely that we will know the impact of the ADA over time because no significant efforts are underway or planned to measure changes in the status of people with disabilities or to monitor the implementation of the law.

Many of the chapters in the book end with recommendations for improving implementation and maximizing the likelihood of reaching desired outcomes. I will not attempt to synthesize them here, but I direct the reader to them at the end of several articles. The next few pages, along with the editor's notes that precede each article, provide a summary of the information contained in the book.

SECTION I: AN OVERVIEW OF IMPLEMENTATION

Section I provides a broad look at implementation by examining federal efforts to implement the law and litigation brought under the law. It examines activities by the executive, congressional, and judicial branches of government, including technical assistance, enforcement, research, oversight, internal implementation in Congress, and litigation. It considers these activities conducted under all four titles of the statute: employment, public accommodations, state and local government (including transportation), and telecommunications.

In "The Federal Government and Congress," Jane West concludes that the federal government has done a great deal to implement the ADA in the first four years since its enactment, but it lacks a comprehensive strategic implementation plan that addresses enforcement, technical assistance, and public awareness. Unless changes are made, the ADA is at risk of being accorded a lower priority than it has had.

She examines the efforts of the nine key agencies with the greatest roles in ADA implementation, including the Civil Rights Division of the Department of Justice (DOJ), which is the lead agency with governmentwide responsibility for ADA coordination.

Technical assistance has taken priority over enforcement. Congress has appropriated about $44 million for technical assistance efforts, including the establishment of centers across the country, grants to train people with disabilities about their rights, and grants to help specific industries learn how to comply. Despite large-scale efforts, only a fraction of covered entities and people with disabilities have been reached. The effectiveness of technical assistance has not been evaluated.

Agencies have received over 30,000 complaints under the ADA
– over 80 percent of them related to employment and filed with the
Equal Employment Opportunities Commission (EEOC). Three key
weaknesses of the complaint process are the long time it takes to
process complaints at the EEOC, the fact that the DOJ is not
investigating all the complaints it receives, and the poor tracking
of complaints at the Department of Transportation (DOT). The
federal government has initiated 35 court actions, including one
"pattern or practice" case and 13 friend of the court briefs under
the ADA.

No broad-scale federal public awareness campaign is underway.
Media reports of questionable lawsuits and costly modifications go
unrebutted. National polls indicate that 41 percent of Americans
in general and 40 percent of people with disabilities are aware of
the ADA.

Congress has not held oversight hearings on the ADA. It has,
however, issued five reports about it through the Government
Accounting Office (GAO) and the Office of Technology Assessment
(OTA). Internal implementation is proceeding, yet its progress is
difficult to assess as there is no point of oversight or coordination
in either body.

Research about the effectiveness of implementation activities or
the impact of the law is minimal. No federal agency plans to conduct
routine surveys of people with disabilities to measure changes in
their status. No data collection mechanism is in place to determine
the usage of ADA-related tax code provisions.

In "Litigation Review," Lawrence Gostin examines over 100
court cases that were filed, pending, settled, or decided at the
federal, state, and local levels through the summer of 1994. In the
area of employment, one court ordered injunctive relief while a
jury awarded back pay, compensatory damages, and punitive damages to an employee who was discharged when dying of cancer. The
EEOC settled a case that challenged a $50,000 cap on lifetime
benefits for AIDS while other catastrophic conditions were covered
up to $500,000. The employer provided $100,000 to the estate
of the employee and agreed to amend the health insurance plan
retroactively.

Cases brought under the state and local government title have
found the following. Bar examiners were required to provide a

person with a severe visual disability an extended time period to take the exam, regular breaks, and enlarged type on the exam. Bar examiners in another state were required to provide a person with a learning disability additional time and a private room to take the exam. One court ordered interpreters to be provided for parties with hearing impairments who were in litigation. The DOJ reached settlement in a case against a police department for failure to provide a sign language interpreter in the arrest of a deaf defendant. Another settlement required prison authorities to allow the use of wheelchairs in jail cells. A Massachusetts court rejected ADA claims by homeless people with mental illness who were seeking to require the Department of Mental Health to alter the manner in which it provided housing services. The court upheld a decision of the Alabama Department of Public Health to refuse to license an assisted living facility because two residents had Alzheimer's disease and were unable to self-administer medication or exit safely in an emergency. A university policy prohibiting the assignment of roommates to students who require personal attendant care was rejected by the court. A state program that provides health maintenance to people with physical disabilities was told that it could not exclude from eligibility people who were not "mentally alert." A court held that Medicaid's refusal to pay for heart transplants for people over 21 did not violate the ADA because the limitation was based on age, not heart disease.

Decisions under the public accommodations title include an affirmation of the constitutionality of Title III. A court upheld the denial of admission of a person with a severe hearing impairment to a tractor-trailer driver training program, holding that the accommodations requested would fundamentally alter the nature of the driving school and that the individual posed a direct threat to the safety of others that could not be reduced by reasonable accommodations. A person with a hearing impairment was denied the provision of a computer-aided transcription at a board meeting. The court upheld this denial, noting that the plaintiff was provided with two alternative aids and that the covered entity has discretion as to how to meet the accessibility goal. Several cases related to physical accessibility are pending in areas such as camps, libraries, town halls, night clubs, and school buildings. A court found that a baby with anencephaly could not be denied ventilator services that would keep the baby alive when those life-saving services would otherwise be provided to a baby without disabilities at the parents' request.

Gostin concludes that ADA litigation "shows the fundamental impact of disability law on American law and society." The promise of ADA – to change the way we order society and our institutions – is likely to be kept.

SECTION II: EMPLOYMENT

Concern about the chronic and persistent unemployment and underemployment of people with disabilities was one factor that generated the momentum to enact the ADA. The four articles in this section examine the implementation of the ADA in the employment sector, its potential impact on the employment of people with disabilities, implications for income maintenance policy, and the intersection with workers' compensation policy and practice.

Chai Feldblum considers the implementation of three key employment provisions: the prohibition against preemployment medical inquiries, reasonable accommodation, and employer-based health insurance. Analyzing data from an employer survey, published cases and complaints, and EEOC responses to letters requesting guidance, Feldblum concludes that the ADA is gradually beginning to change the employment landscape.

In response to the ADA prohibition against preemployment medical inquiries, most employers who answered the employer survey had made some modifications to their job application materials. A frequent change was the elimination of questions about the presence of physical limitations, health problems, or previous illnesses. The EEOC filed one suit alleging that an employer inappropriately inquired about an applicant's disability. Several employers have developed or revised job descriptions to include information about physical requirements and essential functions of the job. Several employers have moved required medical exams from the preoffer to the postoffer phase of job application with little disruption to the process reported. The EEOC issued enforcement guidance about preemployment inquiries in May 1994, holding that at the preoffer stage an employer generally may not inquire as to whether an applicant needs reasonable accommodation for the job.

Employers appear to be implementing the reasonable accommodation requirements with little difficulty or expense. Some employers have made workplace modifications without receiving specific requests to do so. Letters to the EEOC about reasonable accommodation have been concerned primarily with how to balance competing interests among coworkers, clients, landlords, and unions. Court cases have concluded that the reasonable accommodation requirement does not require an employer to hire two individuals to do the tasks assigned to one or to declare an entire building smoke free.

The overlay of the ADA on the provision of health insurance has been the subject of much debate and commentary. Although the ADA prohibits an employer from refusing to hire a person because of fear of increased health insurance costs, it does allow for continued underwriting, classifying, and administering of risks so long as a plan is not used as a subterfuge to evade the purposes of the law. EEOC interim guidance on health insurance prohibits disability-based distinctions if they single out particular disabilities. Capping reimbursement for AIDS care at a lower level than reimbursement for care of other physical conditions is prohibited. The EEOC filed an amicus brief arguing that a self-insured employee benefit plan could not exclude coverage for AIDS. A number of cases have been filed challenging limits on health insurance coverage. Feldblum concludes that employers appear to be adjusting to ADA requirements without major disruption.

In "The Potential Impact on the Employment of People with Disabilities," Richard Burkhauser and Mary Daly argue that the ADA is most likely to improve work opportunities for people with good job skills who are working at the time of onset of an impairment. Much more will be needed to find work for the "doubly disadvantaged" – people who have poor job skills, are not currently employed, or are African Americans. The ADA will be least likely to help those currently receiving social security because of their disability to leave the rolls and return to work.

There are 11.5 million people with disabilities of working age or 9.5 percent of the population. Of these, 29.2 percent work full time compared to 60.6 percent of the population without disabilities. However, nearly twice as many people with disabilities have labor earnings as receive income from disability transfer programs (59.2

percent vs. 30.6 percent). Prior to passage of the ADA, a majority of people with disabilities worked at least part time, although their earnings were only about half those of men and women without disabilities. On average, people with disabilities of working age, like people without disabilities of working age, pay more in federal income tax and Social Security contributions than they receive in direct government transfers.

African American men with disabilities have an average before government transfer family income of $9,012, about one-third of that of men who are not African Americans ($27,191). Those with a disability and a poor education have about one-half ($14,514) the before government transfer income of those with a disability and a good education ($28,877).

The degree of impairment alone does not account for differences of economic well-being between those with and without disabilities or within the population of people with disabilities, as evidenced by the dramatic changes in the size and composition of the population of SSI and SSDI recipients over the last two decades. Policy and social environment are influential.

The ADA is intended to promote employment for people with disabilities. Its strategies of antidiscrimination and reasonable accommodation are different from the social welfare strategies of insurance, for disability or unemployment, or welfare.

Data from the 1992 Health and Retirement Survey (HRS) provide a glimpse as to what the impact of the ADA might be in the long term. Those who were accommodated were 44 percent more likely to be working than those who were not accommodated. It is estimated that a worker who is accommodated is likely to continue on the job another 7.5 years whereas a worker who is not accommodated will continue about 2.6 years.

The vast majority of ADA complaints filed with the EEOC were against employers by people with disabilities who are currently working. Only 13.1 percent involved people with disabilities who were seeking new employment. These data support the notion that the ADA is most likely to be used to ensure continued work with a current employer than to obtain new employment.

Strategies to make the government, rather than employers, responsible for financing the costs of accommodation should be explored, according to Burkhauser and Daly. Federal data collection should be enhanced to monitor better the employment status of people with disabilities over the next decade.

Edward Berkowitz examines the Supplemental Security Income (SSI) and Social Security Disability Income (SSDI) programs in light of the ADA in "Implications for Income Maintenance Policy." In 1990, when the ADA was enacted, SSI and SSDI paid about $38 billion to about 6.3 million people with disabilities. In 1993 these programs paid about $54 billion to about 7.4 million people with disabilities (Social Security Administration 1994). The growth trend has been steady since 1982.

Part of the rhetoric surrounding the enactment of the ADA reflected the belief that the statute would result in some people with disabilities leaving the benefit rolls to return to work. It was also intimated that potential beneficiaries might pursue employment instead of benefits. There is no evidence that this is occurring in any proportion.

The ADA and income maintenance policies maintain separate existences, notes Berkowitz. While disability advocates and enforcers at the EEOC work hard to promote the participation of people with disabilities in the labor force, others put equal, if not greater, effort into proving peoples' inability to work so those people can qualify for benefits. "Rising numbers of people seek tickets out of the labor force, just as a major new law is providing a new source of tickets into the labor force," he concludes.

Berkowitz suggests that the ADA needs to serve as a latent screen that keeps people from leaving employment to apply for SSI or SSDI. Given that the overwhelming majority of EEOC complaints are from people currently employed and that half are related to discharge, such an effect may be developing.

Berkowitz recommends changing the SSI and SSDI programs so that intervention occurs before a person enters the rolls. A new "rehabilitation" benefit could be designed for qualifying applicants between ages 18 and 50. Those in rehabilitation status would receive a lifetime entitlement to Medicare or Medicaid and an annual grant for disability-related expenditures that enable the individual to work. Employers who hire individuals in rehabilitation status would be relieved of paying health insurance premiums for these individuals and might receive a rebate on their Social Security payroll taxes.

Berkowitz concludes that reform of SSI and SSDI are essential if improved employment outcomes are the goal.

In "The Intersection with Workers' Compensation," Christopher Bell points out that workers' compensation, like income maintenance policy, is grounded in the assumption that impairments cause work limitations. In contrast, the ADA is grounded in the assumption that people with disabilities can work despite their impairments. Like income maintenance, workers' compensation focuses on inabilities or limitations in order to determine awards while the ADA focuses on abilities and competence – despite impairment – in order to prevent discrimination. Also like income maintenance programs, workers' compensation costs are steadily increasing. Sometimes described as the fastest growing labor cost, they reached $70 billion in 1993.

There is some evidence that the ADA is being used by injured workers to enhance claims against employers. There is also evidence that the ADA is being used to promote speedy recovery and return injured workers to work. Yet, for the most part, the two sets of mandates appear to operate independent of each other. For example, workers' compensation statutes do not require an employer to provide reasonable accommodation, assess a worker's ability to perform the essential functions of a job, or otherwise analyze ADA obligations when determining the ability of an injured worker to resume employment.

Almost 20 percent of ADA complaints filed with the EEOC have come from people with back impairments. The category of "other" (24.6 percent) is also likely to include work-caused disabilities, such as carpal tunnel syndrome. With 50 percent of the claims relating to discharge, it is possible that injured workers could be a significant proportion of those filing ADA claims. The overlay of the ADA onto workers' compensation systems has spurred little activity by the bar and little litigation to date, but it is an area of implementation that bears continued monitoring.

SECTION III: PUBLIC ACCOMMODATIONS AND TRANSPORTATION

In "Public Accommodations," Andrew Batavia reviews the requirements of the public accommodations provisions (Title III) and examines implementation efforts of the federal government, the disability community, and regulated businesses.

Perhaps the most far-reaching public access requirements in history, the Title III provisions require accessibility in an estimated 5 million restaurants, theaters, hotels, grocery stores, shopping malls, banks, dry cleaners, gas stations, professional offices, amusement parks, private schools, day-care centers, health spas, and other public accommodations. Batavia finds a story of "considerable, though mixed success . . . involving both investigatory discretion and rigorous enforcement by government agencies, innovative accommodation and stubborn resistance by the business community, and gentle prodding and hardball negotiating by the disability community."

The federal government provides technical assistance and enforces Title III through the Department of Justice's Division of Civil Rights, Public Access Section. In the technical assistance arena, the DOJ has produced handbooks, manuals, and fact sheets; responded to thousands of calls on its information hotline; and awarded $6.5 million in technical assistance grants.In the enforcement arena, the Public Access Section has received over 1,200 complaints – 65 percent in the area of barrier removal; 25 percent related to policies and procedures, and 15 percent related to auxiliary aids and services. The DOJ is not investigating all the complaints it receives due to lack of enough staff. Most lawsuits filed by the DOJ have been in the area of state and local government rather than public accommodations. However, the DOJ has negotiated a number of consent decrees with such entities as discount department stores, parking lots and garages, restaurants, dentists, hotels, and the Empire State Building. One notable lawsuit determined that Little League Baseball could not ban little league coaches in wheelchairs from sitting in the coaches' box.

The National Institute on Disability and Rehabilitation Research provides ADA technical assistance through its regional centers. Some centers report that most of their inquiries are related to Title III. Problematic areas include removal of communication barriers in offices of doctors, attorneys, and bankers; a lack of understanding about why particular technical requirements are necessary; a belief that the requirements apply only if the business has a certain number of employees (a Title I provision); a "wait and see" attitude toward compliance; and a general lack of awareness about the law.

The GAO studies requested by Congress suggest that both facility accessibility and knowledge of the ADA had increased during the 15-month period of the study. Although businesses have begun to respond to the ADA, the continued presence of barriers and lack of plans to remove them and the inappropriateness of some barrier removal plans suggest the need for continued education and outreach, the GAO concludes. United Cerebral Palsy Association conducted a public accommodation access survey in 11 cities just prior to the effective implementation date and gave almost all surveyed cities a rating of B – basically barrier free. The Building Owners and Managers Association noted that, after 18 months of the ADA, much confusion continued about questions of interpretation, implementation, and enforcement – much of it generated by self-professed ADA "experts."

Batavia recommends that state and local governments and organizations undertake joint efforts to assess compliance throughout the country and that federal enforcement target obstinate industries and businesses.

In her article on the implementation of the transportation requirements, Rosalyn Simon reviews the ADA requirements, including the provision of both accessible fixed route service (e.g., buses and subways) and complementary paratransit service (door to door service in vans or taxis) for those whose disabilities prevent them from using accessible fixed route service.

Bus fleet accessibility has increased since the passage of the ADA from 36 percent in 1989 to 50 percent in 1994. Expenditures for accessible fixed route bus service are generally in line with projections. Lift and securement systems on buses add between 6 and 8 percent to the total cost of the bus. Annual capital expenditures for purchase of accessible buses is about $50 million nationwide. Use of accessible fixed route bus service by people with disabilities appears minimal. Some people with disabilities appear to prefer paratransit over fixed route service, because they encounter a lack of predictable and consistent accessibility in fixed route services. Some bus operators are resisting DOT service delivery requirements – failing to announce stops and passing up people in wheelchairs at bus stops. Operational and safety problems are reported, such as malfunctioning and nonworking lifts, difficulty securing motorized scooters, and the safety of standees on lifts.

Though intended to serve as a safety net for people whose disabilities prevent them from using accessible fixed route service, paratransit services are continuing to increase in response to increased demand. Ridership increased 13 percent from 1990 to 1992 with people with disabilities accounting for 54 percent of the ridership in 1990 and 58 percent of the ridership in 1992. Riders accompanying people with disabilities – personal care attendants or companions – accounted for about 14 percent of the ridership in both 1990 and 1992. Reasons for this increase include lenient certification for eligibility, improved service, clients "dumped" from transportation services previously provided by human services agencies, and consumer reluctance to use accessible fixed route service. Costs for full compliance may be $1 billion annually. Some transit systems report that their paratransit operating budgets will need to triple to meet full compliance in the next few years.

Nationwide, 708 railway stations have been designated as "key stations," which are obligated to comply with accessibility requirements. Forty percent of key station plans missed accessibility deadlines. Of 399 requested time extensions, 284 were granted by the DOT. Lack of capital funds is the greatest obstacle. The requirement for detectible warnings (tactile strips bordering platform edges of subways) has been controversial, prompting at least one metro system to request and receive a time extension to explore alternative technology to meet the requirement.

Simon recommends the development of funding mechanisms to help transit systems come into compliance, enhanced technical assistance for transit systems, increased removal of pedestrian barriers that prevent use of fixed route services, education for people with disabilities about the requirements of the law, and improved data collection to monitor ridership on fixed route systems.

SECTION IV: IMPACT ON PEOPLE WITH DISABILITIES

The last section of the book comprises two chapters considering the impact of the ADA on two groups of people with disabilities that are frequently overlooked: people with psychiatric disabilities and people whose impairments require the assistance of other people to perform activities of daily living. Although they are protected by the ADA, these two groups are at risk of gaining minimum benefit from the law.

In his article on people with psychiatric disabilities, Leonard Rubenstein concludes that the ADA is gradually becoming a vehicle to challenge conventional attitudes toward people with psychiatric disabilities, which have accepted discrimination as natural, reasonable, and just. Employers are removing questions from their employment applications like "Are you now or have your ever been in mental health treatment?" Practices of medical and legal licensing agencies that inquire about psychiatric history have been questioned. The DOJ filed a brief challenging the practice of requiring physicians seeking medical license renewal to disclose psychiatric illness that resulted in a termination or a leave of absence.

Compared to what we know about people with physical disabilities, our knowledge base about accommodating people with mental disabilities in the workplace is scant. Some employers remain unaware that people with psychiatric disabilities are covered by the ADA even though 10 percent of charges of employment discrimination filed with the EEOC are from people with psychiatric disabilities. The ADA has prompted research efforts about psychiatric disability and employment by the U.S. Congress's Office of Technology Assessment, the National Institute on Disability and Rehabilitation Research, the Washington Business Group on Health, and the John D. and Catherine T. MacArthur Foundation.

Although the ADA does not prohibit a disparity of health insurance coverage for physical and mental conditions, it does prohibit "disability-based distinctions" and the use of health insurance limitations as "subterfuges" to evade the purpose of the ADA. Rubenstein believes that in time the ADA will be used to challenge limitations and exclusions of mental health coverage.

The ADA has been used to promote the integration of people with psychiatric disabilities into community life through lawsuits challenging continued reliance on institutionalization of people with psychiatric disabilities; the failure to provide community-based mental health services for people with mental illness who are on parole; and refusal of attendant care to people with mental disabilities.

Rubenstein concludes that the accomplishments of the ADA on behalf of people with psychiatric disabilities have been modest, but "when measured against the depth of an entrenched prejudice that will work to defeat everything the ADA stands for, . . . the impact of the law must be considered significant."

In her article on personal assistance services, Simi Litvak asserts that the 9.6 million people with disabilities who need personal assistance services (PAS) are unlikely to be able to exercise their civil rights fully unless they have access to a comprehensive system of PAS. PAS refers to assistance provided by another person in activities of daily living such as dressing, toileting, and eating. People with sensory, cognitive, psychiatric, or communication disabilities may need PAS.

Only about 2 million of the 7.8 million people living in the community who need PAS are receiving it from a government-funded program. Most people rely on relatives to meet their PAS needs. If relatives are not available, the individual usually lives in a nursing home.

The ADA includes the provision of PAS as a reasonable accommodation for an employee when the functions for which the employee receives PAS are job related. The ADA may require PAS to be provided on overnight business trips. The provision of PAS for toileting, feeding, and dressing is not explicitly addressed for the employment setting; however, it is explicitly exempted for public accommodations except under special circumstances such as in custodial or correctional facilities.

Although there are no reports of ADA complaints or lawsuits regarding PAS, anecdotal evidence indicates that employees are pursuing the provision of such services with employers. Employees are reticent to confront the issue too intently for fear of losing their jobs; employers see PAS as a potentially costly accommodation. Unresolved issues include the following: If universities provide assistance such as typists and dictaphones, are they required to provide assistance with toileting, feeding, or pushing a wheelchair? If a personal assistant needs to live in the dorm with a student who needs PAS, who pays for the assistant's living expenses? Should personal assistants be admitted to events (e.g., baseball games) free of charge? Who is ultimately responsible for paying for PAS?

Some employers have hired staff members to serve as both a personal assistant and a secretary. Some organizations employ a staff member whose primary job is to provide PAS to all persons who need it. One employee with a visual disability is provided transportation to and from work by a driver. Another employee negotiated a full-time assistant as a condition of her job.

Some employees hire their own personal assistants and deduct costs using the "impairment-related work expenses" provision of the tax code. Some employees engage coworkers to assist them and pay them "under the table." Some coworkers volunteer to provide assistance. Some people with disabilities simply go without eating or toileting during work hours.

The PAS system is fragmented, inconsistent, complex, and uncoordinated. It does not provide enough services to meet the needs of consumers. Long-term care legislation, such as that proposed by President Clinton as part of his health care reform package, would increase the availability of PAS. However, even with health care reform and the civil rights protections of the ADA, most people with significant disabilities will continue to face major barriers to independent living because of the inadequacy of PAS. The ADA offers one more tool to utilize in efforts to increase the availability of PAS, Litvak concludes. The full impact of the ADA will not be felt for generations. Gradual increased opportunity for people with disabilities ideally will raise their expectations as well as their level of independence. Increased exposure of people with disabilities to people without disabilities ideally will lead to greater acceptance and lessening discrimination as their presence and participation changes from the unusual to the routine. The tenets of the ADA ideally will be embraced by ongoing social policy reformers as the goal of full participation gains broader acceptance by the general public. Implementation of this landmark law is off to a solid start after four years. The challenge is to sustain and enhance it over the long haul.

REFERENCES

Bennett, E. B. 1994. "We Are Afraid to Talk about Disability." *Baltimore Sun* (September 1): 27A.

LRP Publications, Inc. 1994. "Bowling Center Complies with ADA under Justice Department Orders." *Disability Compliance Bulletin* 4, no.15:10.

National Organization on Disability. 1994. *NOD/Harris Survey of Americans with Disabilities*. Washington, D.C.: Author.

President's Committee on Employment of People with Disabilities. 1993. *JAN Quarterly Report, April 1–June 30, 1993*. Washington, D.C.: Author.

Reno, J. and D. Thornburgh. July 26, 1995. "ADA – Not a Disabling Mandate." *Wall Street Journal*: A12.

Social Security Administration. 1994. *Developing a World-Class Employment Strategy for People with Disabilities*. Baltimore: Author.

U.S. General Accounting Office. 1993. *Americans with Disabilities Act Initial Accessibility Good but Important Barriers Remain*. Washington, D.C.: Author.

West, J. In press. *Closing the Gap: Highlights of the 1994 NOD/Harris Survey of Americans with Disabilities*. Washington, D.C.: National Organization on Disability.

I:
An Overview of Implementation

The Federal Government and Congress

Jane West

EDITOR'S NOTE

The federal government made significant progress in implementing the ADA between 1991 and 1994 – particularly when compared to its efforts to implement ADA's predecessor legislation, Section 504 of the Rehabilitation Act. However, it lacks an overall strategy and approach to implementation. Over nine federal agencies are significantly involved in implementation – providing technical assistance, investigating complaints, litigating, approving plans, and funding research. The federal government has yet to utilize fully its enforcement authority; for example, the DOJ is not investigating all the complaints it receives. There is some evidence of a public backlash against the ADA as "having gone too far." Without a public awareness and education effort underway, such sentiments remain uncontested. West calls for the development of a strategic implementation plan including strong enforcement, technical assistance and an aggressive public awareness campaign, modeled after the government's HIV/AIDS campaign. Research should be undertaken to determine effective implementation strategies and monitor the impact of the law over time.

Jane West is a consultant in the Washington, D.C., area. She served as staff director for the U.S. Senate Subcommittee on Disability Policy under the chairmanship of then Senator Lowell P. Weicker of Connecticut and as senior policy analyst on the Presidential Commission on the HIV Epidemic chaired by Admiral James Watkins (Ret.). She has provided consultation to numerous federal and nonprofit agencies to analyze and improve disability policy. West has advised members of Parliament in the United Kingdom, who are considering the enactment of legislation similar to the ADA. She edited The Americans with Disabilities Act: From Policy to Practice *for the Milbank Memorial Fund and served as a program officer of the fund during the project that culminated in this book. West received her Ph.D. from the University of Maryland in special education and disability policy studies.*

A more detailed version of this chapter has been published by the Milbank Memorial Fund as a report entitled Federal Implementation of the Americans with Disabilities Act, 1991–1994.

4

INTRODUCTION

When President Bush signed into law the Americans with Disabilities Act (ADA) on the White House lawn on 26 July 1990, he said, "Let the shameful wall of exclusion finally come tumbling down" (Bush, 1990). Senator Tom Harkin (D-Iowa), chief Senate sponsor of the act, called it the "emancipation proclamation" for people with disabilities.

But many listeners knew that passing a law would not eliminate discrimination against people with disabilities. "We must fight to make sure that the words in the law . . . become reality," said Congressman Steny Hoyer (D-Md.), chief House sponsor of the ADA (Hoyer, 1990). Justin Dart, then chairman of the President's Committee on Employment of People with Disabilities (PCEPD), called the ADA "a promise to be kept" (Dart, 1993).

The politics of health care reform has dominated the life of the ADA in the first two years of the Clinton administration. President Clinton, celebrating the administration's fourth anniversary in 1994, said that health care reform would finish the business of the ADA. A more cynical observer commented, "The administration won't aggressively enforce the ADA in the midst of courting the business community for support on health care reform" (Anonymous, 1994).

Achievement of the ADA goals has also been caught in the politics of "unfunded mandates" on business and in state and local government. In April 1994 Senator Harkin warned that the ADA and other disability rights laws faced "unprecedented attacks" from the public and private sectors (Harkin, 1994).

On the other hand, disability policy is a source of bipartisan pride. Commemorating the 25th anniversary of Senator Robert Dole's first speech in Congress on disability policy, President Clinton declared in the spring of 1994, "For all our differences there is a common chord that unites us when we all are at our best." Dole noted that disability is "one area where there has been no politics, just people doing the right thing" (Dole, 1994).

The ADA was the most controversial disability legislation ever enacted. The first four years of its enactment have been much less contentious. Disability groups and covered entities have been waiting for the federal government to establish implementation

5

mechanisms and an enforcement posture, and they are also listening to discern public opinion. Meanwhile, disability interest groups, especially in Washington, have moved on to other priorities, most notably health care reform. Of people with disabilities who were aware of the ADA, 50 percent expect it to make no difference (or a negative difference) in their lives (Louis Harris and Associates, Inc., 1994).

The most highly publicized national confrontation in the ADA's first four years of existence centered on an application for a Medicaid waiver submitted to the federal government by the state of Oregon in 1991. Disability interest groups denounced the waiver as discriminatory; Louis Sullivan, then secretary of Health and Human Services, rejected the waiver because it was "based in substantial part on the premise that the value of life of a person with a disability is less than the value of life of a person without a disability" (Bureau of National Affairs [BNA], 1992b). The Clinton administration, under strong pressure from the Oregon congressional delegation, quickly negotiated a compromise that satisfied both the state and national disability interest groups.

PUBLIC AWARENESS AND PUBLIC OPINION

Public awareness of the ADA is growing, but it remains limited. A 1991 poll commissioned by the National Organization on Disability and conducted by Louis Harris and Associates, Inc., found that only 18 percent of Americans were aware of the Americans with Disabilities Act (NOD, 1991). A 1992 Gallup poll found that 17 percent of businesses were not at all familiar with the ADA, 25 percent were familiar in name only, and 44 percent were somewhat familiar (Gallup, 1992). A 1993 Harris poll determined that 41 percent of Americans were aware of the law (Louis Harris, 1993). According to studies by GAO in 1993 and 1994, awareness of the ADA among business owners and managers increased considerably in just 15 months. Whereas the 1993 report found that 69 percent were familiar with the ADA, the 1994 report found that 92 percent knew about it. Of those who were informed about the ADA, the percentage who reported that they knew they were expected to remove barriers before the effective date of 26 January 1992 increased from 77 percent in January 1992 to 88 percent in April

6

1993 (GAO, 1993). A 1991 survey by Louis Harris revealed that only 16 percent of people with disabilities were aware of the ADA; this figure increased to 40 percent in the firm's 1994 survey (NOD, 1993). The higher the education level, the more likely there was to be individual awareness of the ADA.

Public opinion about the ADA is mixed. For example, 92 percent believed more people with disabilities should have paid jobs (NOD, 1993). Fifty-six percent agreed that some expenditures were required to make the country more accessible (NOD, 1991). At the same time, there is some public sentiment that the ADA has "gone too far" (NBC, 1991; Associated Press, 1994; "Was Closing of S.F. Diner over Disabled Access Unreasonable?," 1994).

TECHNICAL ASSISTANCE: WHAT THE AGENCIES DO

Each of nine agencies in the executive branch provides technical assistance, but only four agencies have received specific appropriations to do so: National Institute on Disability and Rehabilitation Research (NIDRR), Equal Employment Opportunity Commission (EEOC), Department of Justice (DOJ), and Department of Transportation (DOT). The EEOC and DOJ have funded technical assistance through grants and contracts, in many cases by providing the services of their own staffs. The DOT has provided technical assistance primarily through Project Action of the National Easter Seal Society. From the time the law was enacted through fiscal year 1994, federal expenditures on technical assistance totaled almost $44 million. The DOJ and NIDRR have each spent about $17 million; EEOC, $5 million; and DOT, about $6 million dollars.

Agencies define technical assistance broadly. Federal agencies and recipients of their funds are developing and disseminating materials, running toll-free 800 numbers, providing training, advising individual problem solving, making referrals to other agencies, and promoting public awareness through publications, press releases, and public service announcements. Federal funds have supported the production of videotapes and the development of resource libraries, public forums, and curriculum modules.

The volume of technical assistance activities provided by federal agencies has been considerable. The Department of Justice disseminated over 6,000 documents electronically in 1993. The DOJ has also sent mailings to 5.9 million businesses through the IRS. A mailing in the fall of 1994 informed these businesses of the DOJ's toll-free ADA Information Line. The ADA Information Line currently receives more than 80,000 calls a year. Through a grant, the DOJ has created an ADA information file containing 33 ADA publications, which will be provided to 15,000 libraries around the country. The DOJ has placed ADA brochures in 7,600 grocery stores throughout the country serving about 120 million customers weekly. In addition, the agency has funded 35 organizations to provide technical assistance and in July 1994 solicited proposals to assist architects and other design professionals, contractors, tradespeople, building inspectors, state and local historic preservation groups, staffs of legal services and public interest law centers, and professional mediators.

The EEOC speakers bureau has delivered over 2,300 speeches on the ADA, has distributed technical assistance manuals to 125,000 organizations and individuals, has written and disseminated more than 1 million brochures, and like the DOJ, has conducted a mailing to employers via the IRS. The EEOC and DOJ jointly funded a $1.4 million contract to train 400 people with disabilities, who in turn will instruct others about their rights under the ADA.

The NIDRR funds 10 regional technical assistance centers, 2 national peer training projects to educate associates and volunteers at independent living centers, and individuals with disabilities and their families about the ADA. Three materials development projects create and test technical assistance and training materials and programs for use by the centers and the training projects. The organizations that carry out these projects and run the centers include six disability organizations, five business organizations, four universities, one labor union, and one state agency (Abt Associates, 1993).

Most of the projects funded by the DOJ and NIDRR are run by groups representing either people with disabilities or organizations covered by the act. Some of the grants from the DOJ went to disability organizations that worked to secure the enactment of the law. Many projects, particularly the NIDRR centers, are the result of partnerships between disability and business organizations. The DOT's major externally funded technical assistance effort, Project Action, works with disability community and public transportation interest groups. Project Action funds local demonstration projects and provides technical assistance and training under a $2 million annual cooperative agreement with DOT.

Unlike the other agencies that enforce the ADA, the DOT transfers a great deal of money to agencies of state and local government. Some argue that this offers more opportunities to provide technical assistance to covered entities. In September 1992, one week after the publication of its final ADA rule, the Federal Transit Administration (FTA) issued the *Paratransit Plan Implementation Handbook*. The FTA has also published procurement guides for accessible vehicles and sponsors research on accessibility systems that could be applied for use in transit. In 1993, the DOT published *Americans with Disabilities Act Paratransit Eligibility Manual* in conjunction with a nationwide training program. In the fall of 1994, the DOT will offer an updated paratransit manual and training course, and in the spring of 1995, a manual and training on public participation.

The Federal Communications Commission (FCC) has undertaken considerably less direct technical assistance than other enforcement agencies, in part because its enforcement responsibility is straightforward: to establish a national relay system. However, the FCC requires common carriers and relay service providers to offer technical assistance in their service areas. The FCC published a *Handbook of State Telecommunications Relay Services* in January 1992 and issued a second edition, *The TRS Directory*, in October 1993.

The Access Board prepares technical manuals, technical bulletins, videos, and an Americans with Disabilities Act Accessibility Guidelines (ADAAG) checklist. Between 1991 and the middle of fiscal year 1993, it had responded to more than 50,000 phone calls, mailed out over 30,000 packages of information, and provided 188 training sessions.

The Job Accommodation Network (JAN) of the University of West Virginia receives about half of its total budget, $2 million, from PCEPD. Before the ADA was enacted, the JAN advised employers about workplace accommodations. Since enactment, it has added two more toll-free numbers to assist employers in complying with Title I of the ADA. The JAN currently answers about 7,000 calls per month, twice the number it received before the ADA.

HOW EFFECTIVE IS TECHNICAL ASSISTANCE?

According to Robert Silverstein, former staff director of the Senate Subcommittee on Disability Policy, the amount of technical assistance available is inadequate. Only a small fraction of the 666,000 businesses, the 5 million places of public accommodation, the 80,000 state and local government entities, and the 49 million people with disabilities are aware of the agencies' technical assistance initiatives. A director of one NIDRR-funded center reported that, in 1994, his staff still encountered businesses, nonprofit organizations, agencies, and state and local government agencies that were unaware of their ADA obligations (Jones, 1994). The federal government's major training effort targeted to people with disabilities – the $1.4 million contract to the Disability Rights and Education Defense Fund (DREDF) from the EEOC and DOJ – instructed 400 people to work as trainers. As of July 1994, they had taught a total of 137,000 people – 40,000 of them people with disabilities. This is only a small fraction of people protected by the statute.

Many people who have sought technical assistance from enforcement agencies report that they did not receive it promptly. They complain about spending long periods on the toll-free ADA phone lines whose hours of operation are limited and waiting a long time to receive answers to their inquiries. A February 1994 study found that the DOJ took an average of 98 days to respond to a letter requesting assistance. The quickest response time was 2 days and the longest was 456 days (BNA, 1994b). In the summer of 1994, the DOJ increased both the hours of daily on-line services and the number of ADA specialists responding to calls. An increase in the number of calls may occur after promotion of the DOJ's phone number through public service announcements in the summer of 1994, followed by an IRS mailing to 5.9 million businesses.

The DOT has been criticized for providing only minimal technical assistance. Susan Schruth, acting director of the Office of Civil Rights of the Federal Transit Administration, described the ADA as a "momentous overlay" on the transportation industry. "It is a new way of doing business," she said, adding that it has been difficult to convey the idea that the ADA is a set of civil rights requirements, not an engineering code.

Robert Ashby of the DOT, in contrast, says that the daily interaction between FTA and transit providers "provides probably the most thorough . . . technical assistance relationship between any Federal agency and any industry concerning the ADA'' (Ashby, 1994). He notes, however, that technical assistance is lacking for the private sector of the industry, especially in response to frequent requests from over-the-road buses and companies providing taxi and shuttle services.

The task of providing technical assistance is complicated by misinformation about the ADA. According to Robert Silverstein, ''People still don't understand how flexible the law is. . . . If I get phone calls from 150 people concerned about the requirements of the ADA, 149 of them are comfortable about the law's requirements after we finish talking.'' Barbara Bode of the Council of Better Business Bureaus Foundation reported fear-mongering by people promoting themselves as ''certified ADA consultants,'' capitalizing on fears among businesses about the requirements of the law (BNA, 1992a). Paul Marchand of The Arc described a ''mini-industry of people providing training in how to avoid compliance with the law.''

Some business organizations report their members' reluctance to pursue technical assistance from agencies that enforce the law. Susan Meisinger of the Society for Human Resources Management (SHRM) noted businesses' ''real fear of talking to someone affiliated with the government. There is a sense that every government office can determine your identification and keep tabs on your performance.''

Technical assistance occurs most effectively between peers, some experts argue. A number of the DOJ grants were based on this concept. For example, the agency funded the Building Owners and Managers Association (BOMA) to educate its members about the law. The Council of Better Business Bureaus received DOJ funds to promote voluntary compliance by working with businesses and disability organizations.

The extent to which businesses are aware of and utilizing the tax code provisions for the ADA is unknown. The access credit (Section 44 of the IRS code), enacted shortly after the ADA, allows small businesses credit against tax for 50 percent of eligible expenditures that exceed $250 but are not greater than $10,250. It is estimated that over 16 million firms are eligible to use the credit. At the time that the credit was enacted, the Section 190 deduction, available to businesses since 1976, was amended. The amount of the deduction allowed was lowered from $35,000 to $15,000 to offset potential new tax expenditures under the access credit. An IRS official noted that the Section 190 deduction was virtually unknown until the ADA was enacted. PCEPD has developed a brochure about the tax provisions of the ADA and the technical assistance centers offer tax information. The IRS enclosed DOJ and EEOC brochures about the ADA in three mailings to small businesses, but the agency has done no mailings to inform businesses of the access credit.

The business community has persistently raised concerns about the vagueness of the law and has sought technical assistance for particular industries on applications of the law (National Council on Disability [NCD], 1993). Lechner reported that her members were often frustrated with the DOJ responses. "Our members need more practical information, but what they get is formal responses," she said (Lechner, 1992). David Capozzi of the Access Board noted: "Everyone knew there would be a learning curve, but we didn't anticipate the great desire for certainty. Covered entities want to do the right thing, but they are having a hard time getting specific timely answers" (personal interview, 1994).

Some information about persistent problems of complying with the law can be deduced from the questions most frequently asked of providers of technical assistance. An analysis of queries received by the DOJ noted that most questions concerned the availability of interpreters, particularly in medical settings such as doctors' offices (BNA, 1994a). Other concerns were the use of modems on emergency telephone (dial 911) systems, parking, bathrooms, compliance by residential buildings, enforcement of the act, and signage (BNA, 1994a).

John Wodatch of the DOJ listed a number of "particularly troublesome" problems: "failure of doctors to provide appropriate auxiliary aids, the denial by restaurants of access to persons using service animals, the refusal of dentists to treat individuals with HIV, physical barriers to access at courthouses and town halls, and the failure by public entities to provide effective 911 emergency telephone service to TTY users" (Wodatch, 1994).

An emphasis on federal technical assistance could create the perception that the government is more interested in technical assistance than in strong enforcement. Curtis Decker, executive director of the National Association of Protection and Advocacy Systems, worries about this situation. The appearance of imbalance may be aggravated when a major source of technical assistance is the lead enforcement agency, the Department of Justice. John Dunne, assistant attorney general for civil rights in the Bush administration, described the department's approach to the ADA as "educate and negotiate, and litigate only when compliance is refused" (Dunne, 1992). Advocates are concerned that covered entities may hear only the first part of that slogan. Despite the claims by James Turner, acting assistant attorney general, in 1993 that "jawboning as the main enforcement tool is coming to an end" (BNA, 1993a), the DOJ has not fully used its enforcement authority.

One contractor for a DOJ technical assistance project, Barbara Bode of the Council of Better Business Bureaus Foundation, reported hearing business leaders claim that they were not complying because they believe the law would never be enforced. John Wodatch of the DOJ also cited a "wait and see" attitude as a main obstacle to ADA compliance (Wodatch, 1994).

Federal agencies hope that technical assistance will decrease the likelihood of complaints and litigation. Disability rights activist Pat Wright of the Disability Rights and Education Defense Fund notes that "as the technical assistance funds dry up, litigation will increase."

WHO IS COMPLAINING?

During the first 22 months of enforcement, the EEOC and DOJ received the bulk of complaints. From 26 July 1992 to 31 May 1994, the EEOC received approximately 28,000 complaints under Title I. In the first two and a half years of enforcement for public accommodations, from January 1992 to July 1994, the DOJ received almost 3,000 complaints. In the first two and a half years of enforcement for state and local government, from January 1992 to July 1994, the DOJ received just under 3,000 complaints.

Considerably fewer complaints have been filed with the FCC and DOT. As of 1 June 1994, the FCC had received only four. As of 21 July 1994, the DOT reported receiving a total of 363 complaints; however, the DOJ reported having referred 414 complaints to the DOT.

The EEOC has undertaken the most detailed ADA complaint analysis. Back impairments constitute the largest category of persons making complaints, at 20 percent, followed by neurological impairments at 13 percent, emotional/psychiatric impairments at 11 percent, and impairment of extremities at 6 percent. Other disability categories represent 5 percent or less of received complaints (EEOC, 1994).

The ADA violation most often cited in the complaints (50 percent) is inappropriate discharge. Others alleged, in rank order, are failure to provide reasonable accommodation (25 percent), discrimination in hiring (12 percent), harassment (10 percent), employer discipline (7 percent), and layoff (5 percent). Additional categories comprise less than 5 percent of the complaints filed (EEOC, 1994).

Employment complaints have been filed from every state in the union. Kansas tops the list with 40.9 complaints per 100,000 members of the civilian labor force, followed by the District of Columbia (36.2), New Mexico (30.7), Colorado (22.8), and Arkansas (17.1) (BNA, 1993b).

Back impairments top the list of the disability categories, and about half of the complaints are made at the point of firing, leading some advocates to worry that the ADA is not being sufficiently used by the "truly disabled." Furthermore, they claim, the ADA does not appear to be alleviating the situation of persons who are not currently working and may make it even harder for those with significant disabilities to find employment.

By the end of July 1994, the DOJ had received 2,649 complaints under public accommodations and 2,722 complaints under state and local government (DOJ, 1994). The DOJ categorizes public accommodations complaints as follows: 62 percent are related to barrier removal; 23 percent to policies and procedures; and 11 percent to auxiliary aids and services, with 4 percent classified as "other."

Of the 2,722 state and local government complaints the DOJ received as of 26 July 1994, it referred 1,490 (55 percent) to other agencies, retaining 1,232 for its own investigation. Of the latter groups, the largest category was inaccessible facilities, which logged 250 complaints, or 33 percent, followed by employment (160, or 21 percent), auxiliary aids (140, or 18 percent), and policies and practices (110, or 14 percent).

Table 1
Disposition of Complaints to the EEOC

Disposition	Percent
Administrative closures	45
No cause	34
Withdrawal of complaint with benefit	11
Settlements	7
Unsuccessful conciliation	2
Conciliation	1

Source: EEOC, 1994.

Therefore, the EEOC has received 10 times the number of complaints filed with the DOJ. The reasons for the disparity are not clear. Perhaps persons whose employment is threatened feel a greater incentive to complain than those who cannot enter a movie theater or use a dry cleaner. Perhaps most state and local governments, after 20 years of responsibility for complying with Section 504, stimulate fewer complaints. According to John Wodatch of the DOJ, "State and local governments in general have . . . shown a surprising lack of awareness of the ADA's requirements and how to implement them" (Wodatch, 1994). People with disabilities may have lost faith in state and local government facilities and services ever becoming accessible, and thus do not bother to file complaints. Moreover, because complainants against state and local governments and public accommodations can go directly to court, they may be turning less often to DOJ.

WHAT HAS HAPPENED TO COMPLAINTS?

As of 30 June 1994, EEOC had resolved 12,830 of the 29,720 ADA complaints received, or 43 percent of the total. Table 1 shows a breakdown of how the EEOC disposes of the complaints.

About 80 percent of the complaints resolved are either closed for administrative reasons or because "no cause" of discrimination was found. (Administrative reasons include lack of jurisdiction, failure of the charging party to qualify as a person with a disability or to cooperate, or the issuance of a requested "right-to-sue" letter.) A "no cause" determination does not prevent the complainant from proceeding to court. Sometimes the "no cause" findings stem from a lack of time or staff to undertake an extensive investigation that could lead to a different finding. Charging parties sometimes request a "right-to-sue" letter after initiating a complaint rather than wait for a possibly lengthy investigation. Backlogs of complaints at the EEOC have been problematic for years and are increasing. The EEOC's inventory of pending charges grew to 85,212 through March 1994, 21,547 more than the previous year. The average time to process a charge rose from 274 days to 293 days in the same period (EEOC, 1994). Cases that result in "unsuccessful conciliation" (2 percent) may be taken up by the EEOC for litigation.

EEOC commissioners are authorized to bring charges themselves against covered entities, usually when they discover a discriminatory pattern or practice in a business. As of July 1994, EEOC had initiated only one ADA charge.

The DOJ refers most of its incoming complaints against state and local governments to other federal agencies with jurisdiction. Of the 2,722 complaints it had received by late July 1994, over half (1,490) were referred to seven other federal agencies for investigation: Department of Education (456); Department of Transportation (414); Department of Health and Human Services (321); Department of the Interior (116); Department of Housing and Urban Development (86); Department of Labor (86); Department of Agriculture (11).

Of the 1,232 complaints against state and local government retained by the DOJ as of July 1994, 77 percent were under investigation and 23 percent had been resolved as shown in Table 2.

The DOJ received 2,649 complaints by July 1994 under the public accommodations title of the ADA. Half of these were either never opened or were closed for administrative reasons (such as lack of jurisdiction or because the individual alleging discrimination did not have a disability). Less than 1 percent of complaints received to date have resulted in the individual with a disability obtaining relief. The DOJ cites insufficient investigatory staff as the reason for not opening 40 percent of those complaints. Instead, the DOJ staff have recommended that complainants proceed directly to

Table 2	
Disposition of Complaints to the DOJ	
Resolution	Number
Closed (for both administrative and substantive reasons)	285
Letters of findings	37
Issues resolved	73
Formal settlement letters	16
Referred for litigation	1

Source: DOJ, 1994.

court. The DOJ defines its primary ADA enforcement role as litigation to establish precedents and clarify the limits the ADA (DOJ, 1994).

Of the 4 complaints received by the FCC, two were resolved and two were still under investigation in February 1994. The DOT was not able readily to provide information about the status of the complaints it had received. The DOT does not appear to have an internal mechanism in place for tracking the status of complaints.

HOW EFFECTIVE IS THE COMPLAINT PROCESS?

Critics charge that the complaint processes are complex, time consuming, bureaucratic, and frustrating. Anecdotal evidence includes the case of a teacher with multiple sclerosis who complained about lack of accessibility in his school. After 17 months of letters and phone calls to more than 11 federal, state, and local agencies, the complainant began to question the usefulness of the law (Matthew, 1993). According to a recent letter sent to Attorney General Janet Reno by the Consortium for Citizens with Disabilities (CCD) and National Organization Responding to AIDS (NORA) Civil Rights Task Forces, "Reports from around the country indicate that DOJ is turning away complaints under ADA on a daily basis" (CCD and NORA Civil Rights Task Forces, 1993).

The EEOC reports that the average complaint takes about 293 days. Each EEOC investigator currently has a caseload of 108 complaints, more than twice the level of four years ago. This situation has likely worsened since 24 July 1994, when ADA coverage was extended to small businesses with more than 15 employees (it had been 25). To add to the frustration of advocates, only a small percentage of complaints has resulted in relief for complainants. EEOC data indicate that 11 percent of charges resulted in withdrawal of complaint with benefit, 7 percent of charges resulted in settlements, 2 percent in unsuccessful conciliation, and 1 percent in successful conciliation. Less than 11 percent of the DOJ state and local government cases ended in resolution, and .6 percent of public accommodations cases resulted in relief being obtained.

If the EEOC and DOJ continue to reject complaints or to process them slowly, more complainants may pursue remedies through the courts. Such a transfer of enforcement demand to the court system would increase the backlog in courts and be costly for everyone involved. Increased recourse to litigation, moreover, would relegate the EEOC and DOJ to secondary roles in ADA-related enforcement and policy development. On the other hand, people with disabilities, already disheartened by the sluggish response of federal agencies, may not file more lawsuits, either because they lack the funds or attorneys with ADA expertise.

LITIGATION

The federal government had filed or joined a lawsuit in 35 court actions under the ADA, 23 by the EEOC and 12 by the DOJ, and participated as a friend of the court in an additional 13 cases (3 by the EEOC and 10 by the DOJ) as of July 1994. These cases constitute a tiny fraction of ADA litigation currently before the courts. The EEOC and DOJ, however, have initiated and entered cases that raise important issues. The EEOC, for example, has participated in cases concerning the provision of health insurance and other benefits to persons with HIV infection, discriminatory discharge from employment, failure to provide reasonable accommodation, and withdrawal of a job offer after a disability was revealed.

Issues in cases filed or joined by the DOJ include accommodations for an individual with a learning disability when taking a state bar examination, the requirement of a psychological history before a candidate could receive medical licensing, readmission to graduate school by an individual with Tourette syndrome, the mandatory provision of auxiliary aids to students with hearing impairments when taking a national certified public accountant exam, the exclusion of persons who are blind from serving on juries, the refusal of dentists to treat persons with HIV, and the constitutionality of ADA itself. The DOJ filed its first "pattern or practice discrimination" suit in December 1993. The DOJ suit challenges state statutes in Illinois that deny, on the basis of disability, eligibility for police or firefighter pension funds mandated by the state of Illinois. The DOJ alleges that the ADA is violated by the denial of admission to the Illinois pension system of a police officer with diabetes who is employed by the City of Aurora Police Department and who has been performing his job successfully for eight years (Wodatch, 1994).

Successful litigants have received substantial relief. The EEOC estimates that, from July 1992 to October 1993, monetary benefits rendered under the ADA totaled approximately $7.1 million. This figure includes settlements, charges that were withdrawn with benefit, and conciliation agreements. In *EEOC et al. v. AIC Investigations, Ltd. et al.*, the jury awarded the plaintiffs $22,000 in back pay and $50,000 in compensatory damages. Both defendants were ordered to pay $250,000 in punitive damages; however, the court reduced the punitive damages to $150,000. Similar data are not available from the DOJ. However, settlements have involved financial payments; a hotel, for example, agreed to pay a complainant $10,000 in damages. Remedies in other settlements took the form of changes in the physical environment such as construction of ramps, posting of signs, training of staff, physical modification of hotel rooms, installation of accessible bathrooms, and changes in policies and procedures.

OTHER ENFORCEMENT METHODS

Federal compliance reviews are another enforcement mechanism. In December 1992, the DOJ undertook a compliance monitoring effort targeted to construction projects. The DOJ notified contractors and architects in 15 states of the ADA's specifications for alterations and its construction requirements, and it has reviewed as well selected architectural plans from building projects across the country.

The DOJ may certify that state or local laws or building codes meet or exceed the ADA's minimum accessibility requirements. As of July 1994, the DOJ had received only six requests for certification: from Washington state, New Hampshire, New Mexico, Utah, Florida, and New York City.

Approval of plans, or program certification, is required in three areas of the ADA: telecommunications relay services, key stations for mass transit, and paratransit. All state programs for relay services were certified by November 1993.

To receive federal funds under the Federal Transit Act, transit authorities must submit to the DOT plans to make key stations accessible and to provide paratransit. The Federal Transit Administration contracted out the review process for determining the acceptability of plans. Several were initially disapproved, and some had to be resubmitted two or three times before receiving approval.

An alternative to lawsuits authorized by Section 513 of the ADA is alternative dispute resolution (ADR). ADR includes settlement negotiations, conciliation, facilitation, mediation, fact finding, minitrials, and arbitration. In 1990, Congress enacted the Administrative Dispute Resolution Act (P.L. 101-552), which encouraged federal agencies to utilize consensual methods. This law was prompted in part by the ongoing backlog of complaints at the EEOC and in part by concern that administrative proceedings had become too formal and lengthy ("EEOC Seeks Comments," 1993).

Little information exists on the extent to which consensual methods are being utilized to resolve ADA complaints. DREDF, in a training project jointly funded by the EEOC, reported that it attempted 748 ADR negotiations to resolve ADA-related disputes. According to the DOJ officials, 400 of these negotiations led to successful resolutions (DOJ, 1994).

Finally, the Protection and Advocacy (P & A) System, established in 1975 to assist people with developmental and other disabilities, has formed the basis of an aggressive ADA compliance campaign in a number of states. In phase 1 of its campaign in Texas, for example, Advocacy Inc. filed 53 lawsuits alleging ADA violations under Titles I, II, and III. These suits targeted health care providers, convenience stores, attorneys' offices, retail stores, theaters, restaurants, banks, and day care centers. Sixty-eight businesses voluntarily complied.

Covered entities have repeatedly expressed concerns about federal compliance mechanisms. They want to know the exact requirements for compliance and when they can be certain they have attained it (NCD, 1993). Because the ADA is a civil rights law, enforced when individuals complain, there is no mechanism to provide them with such security. Although parts of the ADA resemble a building code, for instance, the statute is enforced for the most part by investigation of complaints. State or local building-code officials do not have the authority to certify that a building's plans are in compliance (Building Owners and Managers Association [BOMA], 1994).

CONGRESS PARTIALLY APPLIES THE ADA TO ITSELF

Breaking the tradition of not applying civil rights statutes to itself, Section 509 of the statute directs its implementation within Congress, but with only partial application. The 21,000 congressional employees are not entitled equally to the remedies and enforcement procedures of employees of covered entities but, rather, to remedies and procedures established by Congress itself.

Implementation activities have taken place in both bodies. The House and the Senate Offices of Fair Employment Practices have received inquiries and complaints under the ADA, but the number is not available. In the Senate, the Office of the Sergeant at Arms has established a policy to provide and pay for reasonable accommodations for employees with disabilities. In the House, the Committee on House Administration has established a procedure for providing reasonable accommodations.

Other activities designed to promote ADA compliance have occurred in both bodies. In the House, for example, the Office of the Clerk offers braille and large-print capabilities for its members to use when communicating with constituents. The House of Representatives provides closed captioning for floor proceedings and offers a closed-caption monitor in its gallery to assist visitors who may be hearing-impaired or deaf.

The architect of the Capitol conducted an accessibility survey in 1993 that yielded 2,053 ADA violations in 532 public and restricted spaces. The cost of rectifying these violations was estimated to be $4.4 million, although some may be exempt from ADA regulations because the Capitol is a historic building. Some implementation activities may have been inspired by Senator John McCain (R-Ariz.), who took the floor to assail the Senate's lack of compliance with the ADA on 3 March 1992 (McCain, 1992). He particularly noted the lack of parking spaces for people with disabilities and the inaccessibility of congressional special services offices in the Capitol.

WHAT ADVOCATES SAY ABOUT ENFORCEMENT

Some advocates say the Clinton administration is equivocal about enforcing the ADA. "We lost a year with the ADA because President Clinton did not make ADA political appointments," noted Pat Wright. One key position with responsibility for enforcement of the ADA, the assistant attorney general for civil rights, was filled in the spring of 1994. Another key post, EEOC chairperson, was not filled until the fall of 1994.[1]

Other disability rights leaders worry that aggressive enforcement may engender a backlash by businesses that would perhaps attract public sympathy. Recent reports of two restaurants closing because of the unmanageable cost of meeting accessibility requirements have increased what some view as the backlash potential.

Most disability rights activists do not have high expectations of the federal government. Paul Marchand says, "The federal government will never fully enforce this law, and we really can't expect them to." Pat Wright of DREDF says she "didn't ever think the federal government could accomplish full enforcement of the ADA, especially with the current fiscal situation." Both believe that there will never be enough staff to enforce the law fully. Wright says that even when adequate staff were available, other civil rights laws were not fully enforced: "We had to sue the Department of Health,

---

1. In 1995, as a part of the "Contract with America," Congress enacted legislation that fully applies the ADA and other civil rights laws internally.

Education and Welfare to have the *Adams Order* (a school desegregation mandate) enforced. The result was a time frame for processing complaints." "Even if we tripled enforcement staff," notes Paul Marchand of The Arc, "there will always be backlogs and many cases that will never see the light of day." Marchand and Wright believe that full enforcement of the law will come when all parties are fully participating: people with disabilities, publicly funded legal services, and the private bar.

EVALUATING THE IMPLEMENTATION OF ADA

There has been little systematic assessment of either implementation of the ADA or its impact. Disability interest groups have generally opposed funding for ADA-related research, preferring to see scarce resources targeted to technical assistance and enforcement rather than to the "evaluation" of civil rights. Statistics are, however, readily available about progress in such related areas as voting rights for racial minorities (Scher and Button, 1984), desegregation in schools (Bullock, 1984), and equal employment for racial minorities (Rodgers, 1984). The EEOC regularly surveys businesses to measure national progress in equal employment for women, racial and ethnic minorities, and elderly people. Yet there are no surveys to measure the changes in employment among people with disabilities.

Five studies about the ADA have been conducted by agencies of Congress, three by the General Accounting Office (GAO), two by the Office of Technology Assessment (OTA). In May 1993, the GAO issued its first report and, in June 1994, its second report in response to a request from Congressman Owens to evaluate the long-term impact of the ADA. The 1993 study concluded that although most business and government facilities were accessible, a number of important barriers remained, including business owners' ignorance of the law (GAO, 1993). The 1994 study noted steady improvement in both accessibility and awareness during the initial 15 months following passage of the ADA but recommended continuing educational outreach and technical assistance, as well as regular monitoring by Congress (GAO, 1994b). A third report by GAO estimated that the cost of conforming to the paratransit requirements in the ADA would be approximately $920 million per year through 1996 (GAO, 1994a).

Currently no federal agency routinely gathers population-based information about the impact of the ADA. Data about disability and employment status can, however, be culled from surveys designed for other purposes (e.g., the Current Population Survey [CPS] and the National Health Interview Survey [NHIS]). The NHIS is adding a supplement for 1994 and 1995 that will ask comprehensive questions on disability of approximately 250,000 people nationwide, but it represents a one-time effort.

The Job Accommodation Network routinely collects information from users of the service to evaluate its effectiveness. When completing the question on the JAN survey about the cost of accommodation, respondents consistently report the amount to be less than $500 for most employees with disabilities. The 1993 GAO study of public accommodations found few businesses reporting burdens and many reporting benefits associated with barrier removal.

The federal government through NIDRR has funded $400,000 worth of ADA-related research. Grants include an exploratory analysis of factors affecting its implementation and a project to design an enhanced technical assistance program to provide companies with information and activities that will lead to ADA compliance.

The ADA, in sum, is a major civil rights law with broad implications for the social and economic life of our country, but its effects will not be known, at least not at the current level of research.

The author recommends the following actions on the basis of the information summarized in this report.

CONGRESS

1. Retain the current statute without amendment.

2. Establish minimal enforcement standards, including timeliness for complaint process and closure. Adequate resources should be allocated to the EEOC, DOJ, and DOT to enable them to comply with these standards.

3. Appropriate funds to the Civil Rights Division of the DOJ for a comprehensive ADA public awareness/education campaign. The campaign should be developed and coordinated with the EEOC,

DOT, FCC, Access Board, NIDRR, NCD, PCEPD, and other relevant federal agencies.

4. Designate an internal ADA coordinator for each body and provide for an independent assessment of progress.

THE ADMINISTRATION

1. Devise and execute a comprehensive plan to fulfill ADA requirements that includes strong enforcement, technical assistance, and an aggressive public awareness campaign.

EXECUTIVE AGENCIES

1. Ensure that the comprehensive plan is effectively achieved across the federal government.

2. Appoint an ADA coordinator in the DOT to ensure internal coordination and accomplishment of ADA responsibilities and effective communication with other agencies and the public.

3. Evaluate all government funded and conducted technical assistance efforts and then develop a second generation of technical assistance to be part of the comprehensive implementation plan.

4. Devise a research agenda to (a) determine effective implementation techniques and strategies and (b) monitor the changes in status of people with disabilities.

5. Assign the U.S. Commission on Civil Rights or the National Council on Disability to monitor implementation of the ADA and routinely report to the president and the Congress.

REFERENCES

Abt Associates. 1993. *The Second Year (FY 1993) of the NIDRR ADA Technical Assistance Initiative: Promoting Implementation of the Americans with Disabilities Act of 1990*. April. Washington, DC: U.S. Department of Education, Office of Special Education and Rehabilitative Services, National Institute on Disability and Rehabilitation Research.

Building Owners and Managers Association. 1994. *The ADA: An Update on Key Issues*. Washington, DC: Author.

Bullock, C. 1984. "Equal Education Opportunity." In *Implementation of Civil Rights Policy*, ed. C. Bullock and C. Lamb. Monterey, CA: Brookes/Cole Publishing Co.

Bureau of National Affairs. 1992a. "Businesses Advised to Watch out for ADA 'Consultants'." *BNA's ADA Manual* (February): 9.

————. 1992b. "Disability Bias Cited in HHS Delay on Oregon Medicaid Plan." *BNA's ADA Manual* (August): 48.

————. 1993a. "Justice to Step up ADA Enforcement." *BNA's ADA Manual* (August): 1.

————. 1993b. "ADA Charges per Capita, by State: June 1993." *BNA's ADA Manual* (September): 60.

————. 1994a. "Charges of Disability Discrimination Boost EEOC Intake by 22 Percent in Fiscal '93." *Daily Labor Report* (13 January): 1–2.

————. 1994b. "DOJ Takes Months to Answer Technical Assistance Queries; Accommodating Deaf Persons Is Top Issue, BNA Study Finds." *BNA's ADA Manual* (February): 9–12.

Bush, G. 1990. "Statement by the President of the United States at the Signing of the Americans with Disabilities Act of 1990." (26 July.) Washington, DC: The White House.

Consortium for Citizens with Disabilities Rights Task Force and National Organizations Responding to AIDS Civil Rights Task Force. 1993. "Letter to Janet Reno." (8 December.) Washington, DC: Author.

Dart, J. 1993. "Introduction: A Promise to Be Kept." In H. Beyer and L. Gostin, *Implementing the ADA: Rights and Responsibilities of All Americans*, p. xxi. Baltimore: Paul Brookes Publishing Co.

Dole, R. 1990. Statement by Senator Robert Dole at the Commemoration of the 25th Anniversary of Senate Majority Leader Robert Dole's First Disability Speech in Congress. (14 April.) Washington, DC: U.S. Capitol.

Dunne, J. 1992. "Testimony of John R. Dunne at a Public Hearing on the Americans with Disabilities Act." (15 June.) Washington, DC: National Council on Disabilities – ADA Watch.

"EEOC Seeks Comments on Use of Alternative Dispute Resolution." 1993. *Disability Compliance Bulletin* 4, no. 4 (1 September).

Gallup Organization. 1992. *Baseline Study to Determine Business' Attitudes, Awareness, and Reaction to the ADA. A Study Conducted for the Electronics Industry Foundation.* Washington, DC: Author.

General Accounting Office, U.S. Congress. 1993. *Americans with Disabilities Act: Initial Accessibility Good but Important Barriers Remain.* (May.) Washington, DC: Author.

————. 1994a. *The Americans with Disabilities Act: Challenges Faced by Transit Agencies in Complying with the Act's Requirements.* (March.) Washington, DC: Author.

————. 1994b. *Americans with Disabilities Act: Effects of the Law on Access to Goods and Services.* (June.) Washington, DC: Author.

Harkin, T. 1993. "Current Trends in Disability Policy: Interviews with Senators Tom Harkin and Orrin G. Hatch." *Focus* [National Council on Disability] (Summer): 3–7.

Hoyer, S. 1990. "ADA: The Advocates." *Worklife* [President's Committee on Employment of People with Disabilities] (Fall): 13

Lechner, W. 1992. *ADA Watch Hearing Transcripts.* (16 June.) Washington: National Council on Disability.

Louis Harris and Associates, Inc. 1994. *N.O.D/Harris Survey of Americans with Disabilities.* Washington: National Organization on Disability.

Matthew, J. 1993. "Having Doubts about Disabilities Act." *The Washington Post* (6 December): A21.

McCain, J. 1992. *McCain Criticizes Senate Adherence to ADA; Calls for Hearing.* (3 March.) Washington, DC: Office of Senator John McCain.

National Broadcasting Company. 1994. *NBC Nightly News* (16 May).

National Council on Disability. 1993. *ADA Watch – Year One: A Report to the President and the Congress on Progress in Implementing the Americans with Disabilities Act.* (5 April.) Washington, DC: Author.

National Organization of Disability. 1993. "New Survey Shows People with Disabilities Not Well Informed on ADA." *NOD Report* (Summer).

————. 1991. *Willing to Act: Highlights of the 1991 Louis Harris Survey of Americans' Attitudes toward People with Disabilities.* Washington, DC: Author.

Rodgers, H. R. 1984. "Fair Employment Laws for Minorities: An Evaluation of Federal Implementation." In *Implementation of Civil Rights Policy*, ed. C. Bullock and C. Lamb, pp. 93–117. Monterey, CA: Brookes/Cole Publishing Company.

Scher, R., and J. Button, 1984. Voting Rights Act: Implementation and Impact. In *Implementation of Civil Rights Policy*, ed. C. Bullock and C. Lamb. Monterey, CA: Brookes/Cole Publishing Company.

"Was Closing of S.F. Diner over Disabled Access Unreasonable?" 1994. *Hokubei Maipichi* [San Francisco] (5 March).

Wodatch, J. 1994. "Testimony before the U.S. Commission on Civil Rights." (6 May.) Washington, DC.

Litigation Review*

Lawrence O. Gostin

Author's Note: Since this article was completed, many ADA cases have been decided by the courts. Readers should conduct an up-to-date search of the relevant case law before drawing conclusions about the current state of the law.

EDITOR'S NOTE

One of the business community's greatest fears during congressional consideration of the ADA was the potential for an avalanche of costly litigation related to "vague" legal requirements. To date, less than 1/100th of a percent of cases in federal court are ADA cases. Although Gostin's review of ADA litigation shows "the fundamental impact of disability law on American law and society," it does not provide evidence of litigation excess. The issues addressed by the 100 cases reviewed are many. Can a smoke-free workplace be required as a reasonable accommodation? Can obesity be considered a disability? Can health insurance policies cap coverage for a particular condition? Can universities deny roommates to students with disabilities who use personal attendants? Can wheelchair users be Little League coaches? Can people with vision impairments be categorically excluded from jury duty? Can medical treatment be required for infants born with anencephaly? Just as antidiscrimination legislation on the basis of sex and race have pervaded how we order our society and our institutions, so too will disability antidiscrimination law, Gostin predicts.

Lawrence O. Gostin is professor of law, Georgetown University Law Center, and professor of public health at the Johns Hopkins School of Hygiene and Public Health. He is co-director of the Johns Hopkins/Georgetown University Program on Law and Public Health and a fellow of the Kennedy Institute of Ethics of Georgetown University. Gostin is editor of the law and medicine section of the Journal of the American Medical Association (JAMA). *He is on the Advisory Committee for the Prevention of HIV Infection of the U.S. Centers for Disease Control and advisory committees of the World Health Organization and the Council of International Organization for Medical Sciences. Gostin was a member of President Clinton's Task Force on National Health Care Reform. In Great Britain, Gostin served as chief executive of the National Council for Civil Liberties, Legal Director of the National Association of Mental Health and was on the faculty at Oxford University. In 1994, Gostin was awarded an Honorary Doctor of Laws Degrees by the Board of Trustees of the State University of New York.*

INTRODUCTION

A central finding of Congress in enacting the Americans with Disabilities Act of 1990 (ADA) was that individuals with disabilities are "a discrete and insular minority who have been faced with restrictions and limitations, subjected to a history of purposeful unequal treatment, and relegated to a position of political powerlessness in our society . . ." (42 USC 12101(a)(7)).

Irving Zola (1993), however, observed that the "empirical reality is that everyone, unless they experience sudden death, will in fact acquire one or more disabilities with all their consequences. This is the reality on which future conceptualization, measurement, and policy must be based – truly the sleeping giant in our midst."

Congress took a broad view of the forms of discrimination that would be proscribed in the ADA, including intentional exclusion; the discriminatory effects of architectural, transportation, and communication barriers; overprotective rules and policies; failure to make modifications to existing facilities and practices; exclusionary qualification standards; segregation; and relegation to lesser services, programs, activities, benefits, jobs, or other opportunities (42 U.S.C. 12101 (a)(5)). The ADA prohibits discrimination in employment (Title I), public services including public transportation (Title II), public accommodations (Title III), and telecommunications (Title IV). Although beyond the scope of this chapter, the Fair Housing Amendments Act (FHAA), the Individuals with Disabilities Education Act (IDEA), and the Rehabilitation Act of 1973 cover discrimination against persons with disabilities in housing, education, federal employment, and by entities that receive federal financial assistance. These acts coexist with, and supplement, the ADA. Similarly, the ADA does not completely supplant state laws prohibiting discrimination against persons with disabilities.[1] The ADA expressly provides that "nothing in this chapter shall be construed to invalidate or limit the remedies, rights, and procedures of any Federal law or law of any State . . ." (42 U.S.C. at 12202(b)). The ADA also explicitly abrogates the 11th amendment, so there is no sovereign immunity conferred in ADA litigation (sovereign immunity is a judicial doctrine that precludes bringing suit against the government without its consent).

The ADA attempts to reconcile the equal treatment/special treatment paradox inherent in all civil rights legislation. On one level, the ADA treats persons with disabilities as if their disability did not matter by requiring covered entities not to discriminate. This concept of equal treatment is powerfully articulated in the law. At the same time, the ADA also requires special treatment. The law requires reasonable accommodations or modifications designed to promote inclusion of persons with disabilities in society. However, Feldblum (1993) thoughtfully observes that the ADA does not take the special treatment principle to its logical extension. The act requires only accommodations or modifications that are "reasonable" and do not impose "undue" hardships or burdens. Nor does the ADA allocate significant public resources for special treatment.

Given the broad scope of the ADA, together with the reality that most of the population will at some point experience a covered disability, the courts are likely to adjudicate an innumerable number of legal claims. As of July 1994 (the date of writing), the ADA had been in effect for two and one half years or less. Accordingly, many cases are as yet undecided by the courts. This chapter reviews over 100 court cases that were filed, pending, settled, or decided at the federal, state, or local level through the summer of 1994. Statistics from the Department of Justice (DOJ) and the Equal Employment Opportunity Commission (EEOC) show a combined number of 35,110 complaints filed as of 30 June 1994 (EEOC, 1993a; 1994a; 1994b; personal communication from DOJ). The EEOC has already filed 23 actions in court, and more are likely as complaints continue to be processed. The large number of cases and complaints, so early after the implementation of the ADA, is probably due to several factors, including the large number of people with disabilities in America, the still prevalent discrimination and disparate treatment of persons with disabilities, and the growing understanding of legal remedies by persons with disabilities and their advocates.

The cases demonstrate the courts' and agencies' ongoing attempts to delineate the boundaries of the ADA, and the struggle with the equal treatment/special treatment dilemma inherent in the act. Moreover, the facts and issues in each case reflect the conflicting values that the courts must seek to resolve as they continue to develop the corpus of disability law. This survey of judicial cases, therefore, should serve as a valuable tool for assessing preliminary trends in the law, and observing the social transformation of disability rights in America.

SOURCES

This investigation constitutes a broad search of the LEXIS and NEXIS databases, American Medical News, and primary disability law reporters including the *AIDS Litigation Reporter, Disability Advocates Bulletin, Mental and Physical Disability Law Reporter*, and *National Disability Law Reporter*. Many more cases on the ADA are likely to have been filed than was revealed in this search.

SCOPE OF ADA

Although the ADA is designed as expansive antidiscrimination legislation, the courts have identified certain claims as outside the mandate of the statute. Such invalid claims refer to either discrimination occurring before the ADA's effective date or seek protection for rights, services, or disabilities not covered by the statute.

Effective Dates of the ADA: Nonretroactivity

The effective date for the public services and public accommodations titles was 26 January 1992; the effective date under the employment title for twenty-five or more employees was 26 July 1992; and the effective date under the employment title for entities with fifteen to twenty-four employees is 26 July 1994. Any discrimination that occurred prior to the ADA's effective date of implementation is not eligible for protection under the statute.[2] In *Raya v. Maryatt Industries*[3] the court refused to allow a plaintiff to amend a complaint to include a claim under the ADA when the discrimination took place in 1987. The court noted: "The ADA itself and its legislative history mention nothing about retroactive application" (p. 1173). The court reasoned that it is inappropriate to apply a statute retroactively when it is not merely remedial and instead "bestows new substantive rights upon those the statute is designed to protect" (p. 1174). Further, the fact that Title II applies to existing places of public accommodation does not render the statute retroactive. Congress routinely regulates existing businesses and programs, imposing new requirements that reflect changing social and environmental standards. To do so is clearly constitutional.[4]

Other courts that agreed with the holding in *Raya* have, nonetheless, involved interesting fact patterns that would have been decided under the ADA had they occurred after the effective date of implementation. These included the dismissal of a temporary automotive worker because of her speech impairment and physical disabilities,[5] the demotion of an attorney with a hearing impairment,[6] and the capitation of lifetime benefits for HIV-related diseases by a self-funded group medical insurance plan.[7]

The courts can separate instances of discrimination in the same action falling before and after the ADA's effective date into valid and invalid claims. A claim for failure to accommodate a law student with epilepsy who graduated from law school in 1992 was dismissed because the alleged discrimination occurred prior to the 26 January 1992 effective date. However, the court found that the law school dean's critical letter to the Illinois bar, written after the effective date, might constitute a valid claim under the ADA. The court noted that such letters of recommendation are services that all law students expect to receive.[8]

Substantive Rights Not Covered in the Statute

The ADA does not address substantive rights of persons with disabilities that do not fall within the four titles of the statute. For example, a newspaper's editorial decision not to review a book on the history of civil rights of persons with disabilities by a plaintiff with a disability was not deemed a public "accommodation" or "service" within the meaning of ADA. Newspapers are not public accommodations; none of the facilities described in Title III is comparable to a newspaper column. Further, an editorial decision to publish a particular book review is not a "service" within the meaning of Title II, despite the plaintiff's claim that the newspaper had published similar book reviews by authors who were not persons with disabilities. Another court found a person with hearing impairments could not use the ADA to claim exemption from a state's mandatory helmet law. The court said that the ADA does not address the operation of motor vehicles or road safety standards.[9] Similarly, a state's failure to exempt guide dogs from animal quarantine regulations is not a violation of ADA, since a public health measure is neither a service or benefit furnished by the state.[10]

Definition of Person with a "Disability": Disabilities Not Covered in the Statute

The ADA defines the term *disability* to mean (a) a physical or mental impairment that substantially limits one or more of the major life activities, (b) a record of such an impairment, or (c) being regarded as having such an impairment (Sec. 3(2)).[11] The Tenth Circuit's interpretation of the term disability suggested that an impairment that affects performance in only one job is not covered under the Rehabilitation Act.[12] Following this decision, one federal district court held that the plaintiff has the burden of demonstrating that he is "disabled in some more general sense transcending his specific job, that his limitations substantially impaired a major life activity . . ."[13]

The ADA specifically excludes certain statuses and conditions from the definition of *disability*, including homosexuality and bisexuality, compulsive gambling, kleptomania or pyromania, a number of gender identity disorders, and psychoactive substance use disorders resulting from current illegal use of drugs (Section 511).

Courts have begun to delineate the scope of disabilities covered under the ADA. A wide number of physical and mental conditions have been accepted by the courts as covered disabilities under the ADA ranging from visual[14] or hearing[15] impairments, cancer,[16] and HIV/AIDS,[17] to seizure disorders[18] ("*State Sides*," 1992), mental illness,[19] developmental disabilities,[20] and learning disabilities.[21] Cases pending include a worker with a severe stuttering disability who was dismissed. ("*Pennsylvania Man*," 1993).

However, several claims that a status or condition was a covered disability were rejected. A federal Court of Appeals set aside an arbitrator's reinstatement of an Exxon process technician who had tested positive for cocaine. Because Congress explicitly refused to include current drug users in the protective ambit of the ADA, the dismissal of the employee was not unlawful. The court further found that it is against public policy to reinstate an employee who uses drugs in a safety-sensitive position.[22]

The EEOC *Technical Assistance Manual* (8.5) notes that "a person who casually used drugs illegally in the past, but did not become addicted, is not an individual with a disability based on past drug use." It was on this basis that one federal district court held that a former musician who unsuccessfully applied for a position in the police department was not eligible for protection under Title I. In the employment application, the musician said he had been only a casual user of drugs. To the extent that he now claims a more serious drug problem, he may not be "qualified" because he showed "insufficient candor" in the job application. The court also observed that "in addition to the general qualification regarding honesty, a police department could well require a law abiding history as a specific qualification for employment."[23]

A federal district court dismissed a claim that placement of a pregnant woman on a disability leave violated the ADA. The definition of the word "impairment" does not include conditions such as pregnancy that are not the result of physiological disorders.[24] Later, the plaintiff's counsel was held liable for Rule 11 sanctions because it should have been clear that the plaintiff had no cause of action under the ADA. The attorney was ordered to attend practice sessions on either general federal practice or Title VII/federal discrimination law.[25]

Sometimes the borderline between behavior that is not covered by the ADA and a physical or mental impairment that is covered is not apparent. For example, a former Florida appeals court judge, removed from the bench by the state supreme court after being charged with shoplifting, is trying to regain his seat. He alleges that he was discriminated against because of a severe depression ("Ex-Judge Claims Disability," 1993).

Many innovative and important claims involving the definition of disability remain to be determined by the courts. Prior to the ADA, at least one federal[26] and one state[27] court found that an adverse employment decision based on a person's obesity could constitute unlawful discrimination under disability law. The First Circuit Court of Appeals held that the "mutability" of the plaintiff's condition is relevant only in determining the substantiality of the limitation flowing from the impairment; mutability precludes from protection of the act only those conditions that the individual can easily and quickly reverse by behavioral alteration. Morbid obesity that affects or is seen to affect a person's musculoskeletal and cardiovascular systems, therefore, may be a disability under the ADA.[28] However, a federal district court held that a decision of an airline company not to allow an overweight woman to work as a flight attendant was not unlawful under the ADA. The court found that the airline did not regard her weight as a physical impairment that substantially limited a major life activity. "Working as a flight attendant is just one particular job with defendant, and thus does not qualify as a substantial limitation . . ."[29] Additional ADA cases brought by overweight individuals are pending (Swisher, 1994).

TITLE I: EMPLOYMENT DISCRIMINATION

Section 102 of the ADA prescribes that "no covered entity shall discriminate against a qualified individual with a disability because of the disability of such individual in regard to job application procedures, the hiring, advancement, or discharge of employees, employee compensation, job training, and other terms, conditions, and privileges of employment" (42 U.S.C. 12112).

Title I requires an employer to treat qualified workers with and without disabilities equitably in terms of the conditions and privileges of employment. Title I, however, does not require employers to provide special treatment for persons with disabilities; that is, "to somehow compensate a disabled worker for his or her disability."[30] Citing *Alexander v. Choate*,[31] one federal district court rejected the notion that all disparate-impact showings constitute prima facie showings of discrimination. To constitute discrimination, the grantee of a benefit must deny a qualified individual with a disability equal and meaningful access to a benefit offered by that grantee. If the individual has access to a benefit, but decides not to choose it, there is no violation of Title I.[32]

Covered Entities

Covered entities include private employers, state and local governments, employment agencies, and labor unions (Section 101(2)). Claims of employment discrimination sometimes hinge on the definition of *employer*. Federal circuit courts are divided on the issue of individual and supervisors' liability under Title VII.[33] The ADA's definition of "employer" mirrors Title VII's definition (42 U.S.C. @ 12111(5)), and the early court decisions under the ADA appear equally unsettled.[34]

Qualified Individuals

"Qualified individuals" are persons with disabilities who, with or without reasonable accommodation, can perform the essential functions of the employment position (Sec. 101(8)). If the disability prevents an individual from performing essential functions of the job, he or she is not qualified for purposes of the ADA.[35] Qualified individuals need not be current employees. Title I does not use the term *employee*, but rather refers to an *individual*; in order to maintain a suit under Title I there must be an "employment relationship." In *Northen, Markham and McCarthy* v. *City of Chicago*,[36] the court held that the ADA covers retired police officers who claimed that an alteration of their retirement benefits violated Title I. Retirement benefits are within the "compensation, terms, conditions, or privileges of employment," even though the person is no longer employed.

The ADA uses the concept of "direct threat" as a qualification standard under Title I. Persons who pose a significant risk of substantial harm are not qualified for the job, unless the risk can be reduced through reasonable accommodations.[37] Even though courts have yet to carefully examine this standard under the ADA, several recent Rehabilitation Act cases have done so.[38] In *Roe* v. *District of Columbia*, a court struck down a requirement preventing a fire fighter infected with hepatitis B virus (HBV) from performing mouth-to-mouth resuscitation. The court concluded that, because the risk of transmission of HBV through saliva was only "theoretical," there had never been a documented case where it had occurred, and the fire department did not screen for HBV, the "direct threat" standard had not been met.[39]

Reasonable Accommodation

Reasonable accommodation may include, but is not limited to, making existing facilities readily accessible to and usable by persons with disabilities; job restructuring, modifying work schedules, reassignment to a vacant position; acquiring or modifying equipment or devices; adjusting or modifying examinations, training manuals, or policies; and providing qualified readers or interpreters (Sec. 101(9)).

Many ADA cases turn on the issue of reasonable accommodation. For example, a worker filed suit against the Walt Disney Company when, as a result of a permanent knee injury, he was given a medical restriction. He asked to be made an "area mechanic"; Disney refused his request and instead reduced his work schedule to 32 hours a week, which affected his access to both benefits and workers' compensation (Burnett and Hagstrom, 1993).

Little precedent on the meaning of "reasonable accommodation" exists under the ADA, but cases under the Rehabilitation Act suggest that employers are not obligated "to provide plaintiff with every accommodation he may request, but only with reasonable accommodation as is necessary to enable him to perform his essential functions."[40] The individual is not entitled to absolute accommodation if he or she can safely perform the essential functions of the job with lesser forms of accommodation. For example, in *Harmer* v. *Virginia Electric and Power Co.*, a federal district court rejected a claim by an employee with a pulmonary disability who requested that his employer provide a smoke-free environment. Under the accommodation already provided (e.g., smokeless ashtrays and relocation of two smokers from his work space), plaintiff was unable to demonstrate that he could not perform the essential functions of his job (he received satisfactory evaluations) or that the environment posed a significant risk to his health.[41] Similarly, in *Davis* v. *York International Inc.*, the court held that when the job responsibilities of an employee with muscular sclerosis "were constantly changing in response to changes in her physical condition," the employer's actions surpassed the required minimum of reasonable accommodation.[42]

Some Rehabilitation Act case law suggests that a reasonable accommodation does not include reassigning tasks in a manner inconsistent with the collective bargaining agreement.[43] Similarly, in an ADA case, a court held that a request to use a person's annual leave for sick time was a reasonable accommodation because it did not require the employer to reassign tasks or otherwise affect the rights of other workers.[44]

Undue Hardship

An employer is required to make an accommodation to the known disability of a qualified applicant or employee if it would not impose an "undue hardship" on the operation of the employer's business. *Undue hardship* is defined as an action requiring significant difficulty or expense when considered in light of factors such as an employer's size, financial resources, and the nature and structure of its operation (Sec. 101(10)).

Retaliation

The ADA provides that "No person shall discriminate against any individual because such individual has opposed any act or practice made unlawful by this Act . . ." (42 U.S.C. @ 12203(a)).[45] To prevail on a retaliation claim, a person with a disability must first establish a prima facie case by a preponderance of the evidence. To establish a prima facie case, the plaintiff must prove that (1) he engaged in protected activity; (2) his employer took an adverse employment action against him; and (3) a causal connection exists between the protected activity and the adverse action. If a prima facie case is made, the employer must articulate a legitimate nonretaliatory reason for its action. Then, the plaintiff has the burden of proving by a preponderance of evidence that the articulated reason is unbelievable or not the real reason for the action.[46] The court found no retaliation in *Harmer*. Although Harmer did not receive a promotion he expected, the court found that he never, in fact, applied for the position.[47]

Harassment

The proscription in Title I against discrimination in job advancement, employee compensation and "other terms, conditions, and privileges of employment" (42 U.S.C @12112(a)) includes complaints of harassment. In July 1993 the EEOC issued "Proposed Guidelines on Harassment Based on Race, Color, Religion, Gender, National Origin, Age or Disability."[48] An employer has a duty to maintain a harassment-free workplace. The proposed rules define *harassment* as verbal or physical conduct that has the purpose or effect of creating an intimidating, hostile, or abusive work environment. The standard is whether the actions unreasonably interfere with a person's job performance or otherwise adversely affects an individual's employment opportunities. The conduct will be evaluated from the perspective of a reasonable person with a disability. No additional showing of psychological harm is necessary. Although each case is evaluated on the totality of the circumstances, one court refused to dismiss a harassment claim from an employee with multiple sclerosis who alleged that his speech and gait were mimicked and ridiculed at work, which perpetuated and enhanced myths about MS.[49]

Enforcement: Exhaustion of Administrative Remedies, "Right-to-Sue" Letters, and Preliminary Injunctions

The employment provisions of the ADA are enforced under the same procedures applicable to race, color, sex, national origin, and religious discrimination under Title VII of the Civil Rights Act of 1964, as amended, and the Civil Rights Act of 1991 (Section 107).[50] Complaints may be filed with the EEOC or a designated state human rights agency. Available remedies include hiring, reinstatement, promotion, back pay, front pay, restored benefits, reasonable accommodation, attorneys' fees, and court costs. Compensatory and punitive damages also may be available in cases of intentional discrimination or where an employer fails to make a good faith effort to provide a reasonable accommodation.

In *EEOC* v. *AIC Security*,[51] a federal district court entered a judgment for $222,000 and injunctive relief where a company discharged a top executive while he was dying of cancer. This followed a verdict of $572,000 returned by a jury, composed of $22,000 in back pay, $50,000 in compensatory damages, and $500,000 in punitive damages. The District Court held that the Civil Rights Act of 1991 (42 U.S.C. @1981a(b)(3)(C)) requires that the compensatory and punitive damages awarded by the jury be limited to a total of $200,000 based on the size of the employer (200–500 employees), in addition to the back pay of $22,000. The jury's compensatory damages award was reasonable in view of the evidence that his life was his work; the jury had the right to consider the emotional impact of termination on a person faced with the simultaneous burdens of impending death and the inability to continue to provide for his family.

Prior to bringing civil litigation pursuant to Title I of the ADA, plaintiffs must exhaust their administrative remedies, including the need to obtain a notice of right to sue from the EEOC.[52] Courts will dismiss Title I claims in the absence of a "right-to-sue" letter from the EEOC.[53] In the interests of justice, courts will grant leave for the plaintiff to amend the complaint to reflect the exhaustion of administrative remedies.[54] In *Kent* v. *Missouri Department of Elementary and Secondary Education and Division of Vocational Rehabilitation*, the district court dismissed an ADA action without prejudice because Kent had not received a right-to-sue letter. When Kent received the letter, he had exhausted his administrative remedies and his action was reinstated by the Court of Appeal.[55]

Federal courts, however, can enjoin an employer from discriminating against a person who has not yet obtained a right-to-sue letter.[56] In considering a request for a preliminary injunction, the courts will require the plaintiff to show he or she will suffer irreparable harm, the defendant would not be significantly harmed, he or she is likely to succeed on the merits, and it is in the public interest.[57] In *Altman* v. *New York City Health and Hospitals Corporation*,[58] the chief of the Department of Medicine in a public hospital sought a preliminary injunction to compel reinstatement after being fired because of an alcohol problem. A federal district court denied the preliminary injunction in light of the fact that he was offered a position at the hospital at a substantially similar salary.

DISABILITY-BASED DISTINCTIONS IN EMPLOYEE BENEFITS

In late 1992 the Supreme Court decided not to accept an appeal, by the executor of the estate of John McGann, from a lower court judgment, which allowed an employer to reduce health care benefits radically for one of its employees. After Mr. McGann began to make health insurance claims seeking to be reimbursed for HIV-related medical expenses, his employer terminated the company's existing group insurance plan. The plan had provided health care benefits of up to $1 million for all diseases. Subsequently, the employer established a risk retention plan (commonly known as self-insurance arrangements) providing benefits of up to $1 million for all diseases except AIDS, which was limited to a lifetime maximum of $5,000. The courts found no discrimination under the Employee Retirement and Income Security Act (ERISA).[59] The amicus curiae brief for the United States urged the Supreme Court not to review the McGann case because discrimination under the terms of employee benefit plans is addressed under the ADA (Gostin and Widiss, 1993).[60]

Certainly, under Title I, an adverse *employment* decision cannot be taken against a person with a disability because of the effect the person may have on the benefits plan. Thus, even if the employer could demonstrate with sound actuarial data that an employee with a costly, chronic disability would undermine the financial stability of the employee health insurance plan, it could not dismiss or demote the individual. For example, the EEOC filed an action against H. Hirschfield Sons Co. for refusing to reinstate an employee returning to work from a disability leave. The employee offered, but was denied, the opportunity to demonstrate his ability to perform the essential functions of his job. The EEOC properly argued that the employer's claim that it would experience difficulty with its insurance coverage was not an adequate justification for the employment discrimination under the ADA.[61]

Although an adverse employment decision cannot be made based upon a person's effect on the benefits plan, it remains unclear to what extent the plan itself can be structured in ways that may discriminate against the employee. The ADA (Section 501) affords insurers and entities that administer benefit plans the same opportunities to underwrite, classify, and administer risks that existed before the statute was enacted. Employers may establish and change the terms of a bona fide benefit plan based on sound actuarial data.

Equal Employment Opportunity Commission Regulations state that employees with disabilities must be accorded "equal access to whatever health insurance coverage the employer provides to other employees." Employers, however, are permitted to offer policies with preexisting condition clauses and caps or limitations on coverage provided they are not used as a subterfuge to evade the purposes of the ADA (29 CFR @1630.5).

On 8 June 1993 the EEOC issued interim enforcement guidance on the application of the ADA to disability-based provisions of employer-provided health insurance. The guidance states that decisions about *employment* cannot be motivated by concerns about the impact on the health plan of the disability of the employee or the disability of someone with whom that person has a relationship. Further, employees with disabilities must be accorded equal access to whatever health insurance is provided.

Disability-based distinctions single out a particular disability or discrete group of disabilities, or a procedure or treatment of a particular disability or discrete group of disabilities (e.g., exclusion of a drug used only to treat AIDS). The employer has the burden to prove, based on risk assessment, actuarial, or claims data that a disability-based distinction is bona fide (and, if it is not a risk retention plan, that it is consistent with state law) and is not being used as a subterfuge to evade the purposes of the act. If an employer asserts that the distinction is necessary to prevent the occurrence of an unacceptable change in coverage or premiums or to assure the fiscal soundness of the plan, the evidence should include non-disability-based options for modifying the plan that were considered and the reasons for the rejection of these options.

To demonstrate that a distinction such as a cap on benefits is not a subterfuge, the employer must show that it has a business or insurance justification. For example, a disability-based distinction can be imposed if the plan applies equally to all similar medical conditions. Disparate treatment can also be justified by actuarial data showing that conditions with comparable costs are treated similarly (Health Lawyer, 1993).

On 9 June 1993, the day following the issuance of its interim enforcement guidance, the EEOC filed a lawsuit in federal district court claiming that a health insurance plan amendment by a union trust fund violates the ADA by excluding coverage for treatment of conditions resulting from HIV infection.[62] The Union Trust Fund later moved for a summary judgment in its lawsuit, seeking a declaration that the HIV exclusion is a lawful exercise of discretion by the fund's trustees. The EEOC argued that the cost of treating HIV disease is comparable to the cost of treating other chronic costly diseases such as cancer and heart disease (Hellinger, 1992; 1993).

A number of similar cases are pending (O'Connor, 1993; UPI, 1993).[63]

On 21 December 1993 the EEOC announced that it had settled an ADA case challenging an AIDS cap in a health benefit plan. The lawsuit alleged that a health benefit plan for union workers violated the ADA because the plan provided only $50,000 in lifetime benefits for AIDS, while insuring other catastrophic medical conditions for up to $500,000. The AIDS limitation, however, was adopted in 1987 before any plan participant had been diagnosed with HIV infection and before the date the ADA became effective. The EEOC argued that it was irrelevant when the cap was adopted or whether the action was intentionally discriminatory; all that was relevant was that the cap was in place and not actuarially supportable when the ADA became effective. The case was settled under a consent decree that provided $100,000 to the estate of the employee; the employer also agreed to amend the plan retroactively (EEOC, 1993b).

TITLE II: PUBLIC SERVICES, STATE AND LOCAL GOVERNMENT

Section 202 of the ADA states that ''no qualified individual with a disability shall, by reason of such disability, be excluded from participation in or be denied the benefits of the services, programs, or activities of a public entity, or be subjected to discrimination by any such entity'' (42 U.S.C. 12132; 28 CFR @35.130).

A public entity cannot apply eligibility criteria that screen out or tend to screen out any class of individuals with disabilities from the full and equal enjoyment of a service, program, or activity unless the criteria are necessary for the provision of the service, program, or activity being offered (28 CFR 35.130(b)(8)).

A ''qualified individual with a disability'' is ''an individual with a disability who, with or without reasonable modifications to rules, policies or practices, the removal of architectural, communication, or transportation barriers, or the provision of auxiliary aids and services, meets the essential eligibility requirements for the receipt of services or the participation in programs or activities provided by a public entity'' (42 USC 112131).

A "public entity" is any state or local government; any department, agency, or other instrumentality of a state or local government (such as school, water, and housing authorities); and Amtrak and certain commuter rail agencies.[64]

Broadly speaking, Title II covers the following kinds of activities, programs, and practices by public entities: (1) employment; (2) contact with the general public such as communication through telephone, office walk-ins, and use of public facilities; (3) activities administered by state and local government such as the electoral and judicial systems, zoning authority, professional and other licensing, and police and fire services; and (4) benefits provided by state and local government such as Medicaid (Kilb, 1993).

The equal treatment/special treatment dilemma emerges with particular force in Title II because of the traditional role of state and local governments in providing benefits, services, and programs that strongly affect the lives of many persons with disabilities. The ADA does not require government to provide special benefits or programs for persons with disabilities. However, if the government does offer services to its citizens, it cannot discriminate against qualified persons with disabilities.

Employment

Department of Justice regulations make it clear that Title II discrimination by public entities includes employment discrimination (28 CFR @35.140). Unlike Title I, all state and local governments are prohibited from employment discrimination under Title II, irrespective of the size of their work force. The DOJ regulations cross-reference Title I and EEOC regulations in setting the standards for employment discrimination under Title II (see later for a discussion of exhaustion of administrative remedies before bringing an employment discrimination lawsuit under Title II).

Nowhere in Title II is the requirement that the "public entity" must be the employer of the individual making the claim of employment discrimination. Only in Title I is the term *covered entity* defined as an "employer, employment agency, labor organization, or joint labor-management committee" (42 USC 12111(2)). In a Title II case brought against the retirement board of the city of Chicago for reinstatement to an active position with the fire service, the court found that the board was an instrumentality of a local government; the board was statutorily created and administered money for the benefit of public employees. The board is thus an entity to which Title II applies.[65]

Contact with the General Public

State and local government services for the general public must be provided on a nondiscriminatory basis to persons with disabilities. For example, one court ordered the City of New York to make its 911 emergency services system directly accessible to persons with hearing impairments.[66] The system at the time of the lawsuit required TDD users to dial an 800 number to contact a relay service which then notified the authorities. The complaint alleged that the system caused unreasonable delay and had in fact resulted in the death of some persons with hearing impairments. The court referred to a House of Representatives (1990) report stating that local governments must provide individuals with hearing and speech impairments a direct line to 911 emergency services.

Government Activities: Licensing

A public entity may not administer a licensing or certification program in a manner that subjects qualified individuals with disabilities to discrimination on the basis of a disability (28 CFR 35.130(b)(3)(i)). In *Medical Society of New Jersey* v. *Jacobs and the New Jersey State Board of Medical Examiners*,[67] a federal district court struck down certain questions on the application and renewal forms for a medical license that inquired about the physician's disabilities (e.g., "Have you ever been dependent on alcohol, controlled dangerous substances, treated for alcohol abuse, drug abuse or mental illness? Do you have any uncorrected physical handicap which causes substantial limitation on your ability to practice medicine?"). The court found that the questions placed added burdens on persons with disabilities. "The essential problem with the present questions is that they substitute an impermissible inquiry into the status of disabled applicants for the proper, indeed necessary, inquiry into the applicants' behavior . . . An individual's status cannot be used to make generalizations about that individual's behavior." The court, however, stressed that it is not the questions themselves that are discriminatory but the extra investigations of qualified applicants who answer "yes."

In a similar case involving the Connecticut bar, the application asked whether the person has been treated for mental illness (Megan, 1993). In Maine, the state supreme court ruled that since questions about mental health were not limited to addressing behavior affecting the practice of law, denial of admission to two applicants who refused to answer the questions violated Title II.[68]

Frequently, licensing requirements include testing applicants for the requisite skills and knowledge in a field. Several cases have been brought against state bar examiners by individuals with disabilities. For example, a federal district court required the bar examiners to provide a person with a severe visual disability a requested accommodation of a four-day testing schedule consisting of six hours of testing per day plus a one-hour lunch break each day. This was in addition to enlarged type on the exam, which the board previously agreed to provide. The court reasoned that the most important factor that the board must consider in determining reasonable accommodations is the nature and extent of the person's disability.[69]

The Massachusetts Supreme Judicial Court similarly required bar examiners to provide additional time and a private room for a person with dyslexia, attention deficit disorder, and learning disabilities that prevented him from finishing the exam within the normally allotted time.[70] One court ordered the state bar of board examiners to issue a certificate of admission due to its manifest unfairness of denying extra time to a person with a learning disability.[71]

The question arose in *Rothman* v. *Emory University*[72] whether furnishing potentially discriminatory information to a state bar committee concerning a law student with disabilities was privileged. The court suggested that, if the student could demonstrate that he was discriminated against because of his disability, he could sustain a claim under the ADA despite the privileged nature of the communication.

States must also issue marriage licenses on a nondiscriminatory basis. In 1987, the Utah legislature enacted a statute banning (and annulling) marriages if one of the partners was HIV infected. A suit was filed on behalf of two couples and their children, who would be illegitimate if the marriages had been voided.[73] The state agreed to repeal the statute (AP, 1993).

Systems of Government: Judicial

The judicial, electoral, and other systems of government must make all of their services, programs, and activities accessible to qualified individuals with disabilities. Several federal and state courts have applied this principle to the jury selection process. A policy of categorically excluding all persons who are visually impaired from juries violates the Rehabilitation Act and the ADA.[74] A court cannot exclude a juror unless he or she could not, with reasonable modifications, fulfill the functions of a juror in the case. As a reasonable modification for a juror with visual impairments in one case, the court moved her seat closer, had all evidence read into the record, and provided an enlarged print version of a transcript.[75]

Other cases involving the judicial system have been brought under the ADA. One court ordered interpreters for parties in litigation with hearing impairments ("Making the Courtroom Come to Life," 1993). In another case, a nurse who contracted HIV infection from a contaminated needle challenged a state law that allows the state to pay her $5.4 million verdict over a period of years. She fears she will die of AIDS before she collects the full award, and filed suit in federal court under the ADA ("Today's News Update," 1992).

Systems of Government: Corrections

Corrections officials have a duty to reasonably modify facilities in prisons and jails to accommodate the needs of inmates. The Department of Justice reached a settlement in a case against a police department for failure to provide a sign language interpreter in the arrest of a deaf defendant.[76] Federal courts, for example, refused to dismiss law suits by prisoners who claimed failure to accommodate morbid obesity[77] and semi-quadriplegia.[78] A settlement agreement in one case required prison authorities to allow the use of wheelchairs in jail cells (Baughman, 1993). In some cases the disability may be so severe as to require transfer to a facility that provides adequate health or nursing services.[79] Courts, however, will not allow prisoners to utilize the ADA for trivial claims, such as when a person in a wheelchair argued that the vehicle was traveling too fast while transporting him to the county jail.[80]

Housing

The federal Fair Housing Amendments Act of 1988 added a new class – persons with disabilities – to Title VIII of the Civil Rights Act of 1968 (the Fair Housing Act), which prohibits discrimination on the basis of race, religion, sex, or national origin in the sale or rental of private housing (42 USC 3601–3619). The FHAA prohibits housing discrimination against persons who have a disability or associate with a person with a disability. The FHAA also requires housing providers to make reasonable accommodations in rules, policies, practices, or services, when necessary, to give persons with disabilities an equal opportunity to use and enjoy housing. The act also states that persons with disabilities cannot be prohibited from making reasonable modifications in a dwelling at their own expense if necessary for the full enjoyment of the premises.

Unlike the FHAA, the ADA does not cover all types of housing. However, where the laws do overlap, the ADA's statutory language and legislative history often "articulate the promise of equal opportunity and community integration with greater specificity" (Milstein and Hitov, 1993). Both Title II and Title III (Public Accommodations, see later) cover housing discrimination in certain circumstances. Title II includes all housing created, developed, managed, leased, owned, and planned by every state, county, and local public entity. Therefore, when housing discrimination was alleged in the provision of apartments and condominiums built as part of a program for urban renewal, the court found that, although they were not public accommodations under Title III, they were public services within the meaning of Title II.[81]

Martin et al. v. *Voinovich*[82] provides a detailed and interesting examination of the application of the Rehabilitation Act and Title II of the ADA to housing discrimination. Plaintiffs represented a class consisting of all persons in Ohio with mental retardation or developmental disabilities who are or will be in need of community housing and services that are normalized, homelike, and integrated.

Plaintiffs contended that they could not find places to live in the community because the state failed to create housing options in sufficient numbers to meet the needs of the class. Plaintiffs argued they are now living in institutions or other large facilities when they should be living in the community or they are not receiving the services they require to remain in the community. Citing the decision of the Supreme Court in *Southeastern Community College* v. *Davis*,[83] the state argued that the Rehabilitation Act and the ADA do not create an affirmative duty to provide services. *Davis* held that a nursing college was not required to make major adjustments to its program to accommodate a person with a hearing impairment because it would have required the school to substantially lower its standards and divert from its educational purposes. In this case, however, the plaintiffs sought inclusion in an existing program that arguably does not impede the purpose of the program. The court felt it was premature to say whether it might order the expansion or creation of housing or simply require the existing housing programs to be administered in a nondiscriminatory manner.

Citing the Supreme Court case of *Traynor* v. *Turnage*,[84] the state also contended that the Rehabilitation Act and the ADA do not provide relief when the discrimination is between persons with different disabilities, as opposed to between persons with and without disabilities.[85] The court, however, rejected the notion that "because others served by defendants' programs also happen to be mentally retarded, discrimination suffered by plaintiffs . . . is not actionable. . . . It would be manifestly unfair to view plaintiffs differently from people who are not mentally retarded in determining whether they have a claim." The plaintiffs' claim that, although they are qualified for community residential services, they are denied opportunities to participate in those services to the same extent as persons with less severe disabilities. The court, accordingly, declined to dismiss the complaint.

In *Williams* v. *Secretary of the Executive Office of Human Services*, the Massachusetts Supreme Judicial Court rejected ADA claims by homeless persons with mental illness who were seeking to require the Department of Mental Health (DMH) to modify the manner in which it provided housing services. The plaintiffs argued, first, that DMH did not provide sufficient integrated supported housing. Plaintiffs observed that nearly 65 percent of persons offered DMH housing were required to accept residences occupied only by other people with disabilities. The court reasoned that the ADA did not require that a specific proportion of housing placements provided by a public entity be in "integrated" settings.

Plaintiffs argued, second, that DMH unlawfully discriminated against individuals who suffer from a combination of substance abuse and mental disabilities (dually diagnosed) in the operation of its services. The plaintiffs observed that DMH policies result in dually diagnosed individuals being disproportionately denied residential placements and discharged in a disproportionately high ratio to streets and shelters. The court found that the DOJ specifically provides that government may confer special benefits, beyond those required by the nondiscrimination requirements of the ADA, to certain individuals with disabilities without incurring additional responsibilities to persons without disabilities or other classes of persons with disabilities. The focus of the ADA is on addressing discrimination between persons with and without disabilities, rather than eliminating differences among persons with varying types of disabilities.[86]

It is apparent, given the somewhat different holdings in *Martin* and *Williams*, that courts will need to develop clearer guidance on the extent to which government can exclude persons with more severe or different kinds of disabilities from services designed for a class of persons with disabilities.

Zoning

Local government cannot discriminate against persons with disabilities in exercising its zoning powers. However, although such discrimination may be unlawful under the Fair Housing Act, several courts have ruled that the ADA does not exempt operators of group homes for persons recovering from substance abuse from a city zoning ordinance that prohibited four or more nonrelated persons from living together.[87]

In another case, a residential home for women recovering from drug dependence requested a zoning change so that it could be run as a community facility. The parishioners of the church that owned the building supported the zoning change, but some neighbors opposed the plan. The church sued the town asking for an injunction to bar eviction of the women, claiming the town's action was based on bias and prejudice. The town argued that its decisions were based purely on traditional zoning principles, pointing out that the use is not compatible with a residential neighborhood. The suit has been filed under the ADA, the Fair Housing Act, and state law (Herbeck, 1993). The DOJ and HUD have warned another local zoning board that it may have violated the ADA and the Fair Housing Act by rejecting a proposal by the United Cerebral Palsy Foundation to build a group home for persons with physical impairments (Hacker, 1993).

In *O'Neal and Thrailkill* v. *Alabama Department of Public Health,* the court observed that health departments may be caught between the competing goals of state and federal law. The ADA and FHAA seek to end the isolation and segregation of individuals with disabilities by ensuring them equal treatment. State law, however, requires health departments to promote the public health, safety, and welfare by establishing standards for the treatment and care of individuals in institutions and group homes. The Alabama Department of Public Health refused to license an assisted living facility because two of the residents had Alzheimer's disease. They were unable to self-administer medication and could not safely exit the facility in an emergency. The court observed differences in judicial approach in resolving conflicts between state safety requirements and disability law.[88] Ultimately, courts must be guided by the reasonableness of the state regulations: the extent of the restriction on the rights of persons with disabilities balanced against the need for safety measures. Where the safety requirements are unnecessary and ill-suited to the needs of residents, they may be struck down as based upon "false and overprotective assumptions."[89]

Education

Prior to the ADA, the major federal statute addressing the educational needs of children with disabilities was the Education for All Handicapped Children Act of 1975 (EAHCA), now called the Individuals with Disabilities Education Act (IDEA) (20 USC 1232, 1401, 1405–1420, 1453). IDEA provides federal grants to state and local education authorities that meet extensive procedural and substantive requirements designed to promote appropriate, high-quality education programs for all children with disabilities – principally, a free appropriate public education and an individualized education program to meet the education needs of all children with a disability in the least restrictive environment.

In the postsecondary education context, a qualified individual with a disability is a person who meets the academic and technical standards requisite to admission or participation in the program (45 CFR 84.3(k)(3)). *Technical standards* refer to all nonacademic admissions criteria that are essential to participation in the program.

In *Coleman* v. *Zatechka*,[90] the University of Nebraska had a rule that prohibited the assignment of roommates to students with disabilities who required personal attendant care. The university argued that persons in wheelchairs would utilize more than half the space in the dormitory room and that personal attendant visits would interfere with the roommate's privacy. The court held that these eligibility criteria unlawfully screened out persons with disabilities and were not "necessary" for the provision of the service being offered (see discussion of 28 CFR 35.130(b)(8) previously). The university's assumption about persons who use wheelchairs and their personal care attendants "falls far short of the individualized assessment that is required by the ADA."[91] The policy of requiring students with disabilities to live in single rooms may have been adopted as an accommodation to students who were uncomfortable having a roommate present during attendant care visits. However, nothing in the ADA requires persons with disabilities to accept such accommodations (28 CFR 35.130(e)(1)). "Even when separate programs are permitted, individuals with disabilities cannot be denied the opportunity to participate in programs that are not separate or different . . . Separate, special or different programs . . . cannot be used to restrict the participation of persons with disabilities in general, integrated activities." Modified participation for persons with disabilities must be a choice, not a requirement.

The regulations implementing the ADA require a public entity to furnish appropriate auxiliary aids and services where necessary to afford an individual with a disability an equal opportunity to participate in and enjoy the benefits of a service, program, or activity. In determining the type of auxiliary aid or service necessary, a public entity must give primary consideration to the requests of the person with disabilities. The public entity must honor the expressed choice unless it can demonstrate that another effective means exists (28 CFR 35.160(b)). In *Petersen*,[92] plaintiffs with hearing impairments alleged that their school must provide them with their chosen sign language, strict SEE-II. The court found that the principal purpose of the ADA is circumvented if only an "effective" auxiliary aid is needed when a requested aid is vastly superior. "To truly end discrimination against persons with disabilities, some type of equally effective means of communication must be provided if the disabled person's choice of auxiliary aid is denied." In this case, the aid offered by the school was a "less-than-equally-effective signing system than that which [the plaintiffs] have requested."

Government Benefits and Programs

As stated earlier, government has no obligation to provide special benefits and programs for persons with disabilities. However, once it offers a program it must not discriminate against qualified individuals with a disability or use improper eligibility criteria to screen out qualified individuals with a disability. In *Easley* v. *Snider*, a federal district court held that a state program that provides health maintenance and other ancillary services to individuals with physical disabilities could not exclude from eligibility persons who are not "mentally alert." The court found that the eligibility criterion of "mental alertness" was improper because those individuals could equally benefit from the program. The court observed that it could not rely on the state's characterization of the program, the qualifications of the plaintiffs, or the legitimacy of the eligibility criteria. Rather, the court must make an independent inquiry about the "essential nature of the program" and whether the eligibility criteria are "necessary for the provision of the service, program, or activity being offered."[93]

The nondiscrimination principle in Title II becomes more complex when the government is acting as an insurer because of the protections provided to entities that underwrite, classify, or administer risks provided under Section 501(c) of the ADA (42 USC 12201(c)) (see the discussion under Title I previously). In an intriguing case, the American Civil Liberties Union filed suit against the

Insurance Risk Pool of South Carolina. The pool provides insurance to any South Carolina resident whose age, income, and assets make him or her ineligible for other government programs such as Medicaid or Medicare. However, unlike the risk pools in some 20 other states, South Carolina excludes persons with HIV infection from participating. HIV infection is the only disqualifying disease. The case is pending ("Insurance," 1993).

The application of the ADA to government benefits programs is markedly complex. Consider the decision of the Bush administration in August 1992 to reject Oregon's Medicaid health care rationing plan on the grounds that it violated the ADA. The Oregon program would increase the number of people eligible for Medicaid but would restrict certain medical services. These categories of restriction – such as highly expensive treatments for incurable cancer, the final stages of AIDS, or premature infants with virtually no chance of survival – would present a disproportionate impact on persons with disabilities that potentially could be invalidated under the ADA. The act might prevent the state from denying care simply because the treatment is expensive or because of the person's quality of life (Pear, 1992).

In March 1993 the Clinton administration approved Oregon's Medicaid waiver subject to conditions. Before implementing the plan, Oregon must rerank the services provided without reference to data it used previously that rated the quality of life of persons with disabilities lower than that of persons with less severe, or no, disabilities ("Health Care," 1993).

James Alderman filed a suit in federal district court alleging that Medicaid's refusal to pay for heart transplants for patients older than 21 violates the ADA. The state pays for transplants of other vital organs for those over 21 (including more costly liver transplants) but sets an age cap for heart transplants. Plaintiff would die shortly if he did not receive the transplant. The court held that the ADA does not apply to the case because the state's decision was based on the plaintiff's age and not his heart disease ("Judge," 1992).

Exhaustion of Administrative Remedies

Unlike Title I, which adopts the procedures set forth in Title VII of the Civil Rights Act requiring exhaustion of administrative remedies, Title II adopts the remedies, rights, and procedures of Section 505 of the Rehabilitation Act of 1973, which does not require exhaustion of administrative remedies. Title II allows a plaintiff to go directly to court without obtaining a right-to-sue letter or filing an administrative claim with the EEOC (42 USC 12133).[94]

The question arises whether, if a plaintiff could have made a claim of *employment* discrimination under Title I, does he or she have to exhaust administrative remedies before bringing litigation? In *Petersen* v. *University of Wisconsin Bd. of Regents*,[95] defendant argued that the court should not allow the brief employment section in Title II to create an exception to the elaborate employment provisions in Title I requiring exhaustion of administrative remedies. On the basis of the ambiguity in the statute and the deference to DOJ's interpretation, the court concluded that no exhaustion of remedies is required under Title II in an employment discrimination claim. Another federal court made the same decision in a case involving the medical director of a county hospital who alleged she was forced to resign her position because of her efforts to provide health care services for patients with AIDS.[96]

TITLE III: PUBLIC ACCOMMODATIONS

The general nondiscrimination rule in Title III is that ''no individual shall be discriminated against on the basis of disability in the full and equal enjoyment of the goods, services, facilities, privileges, advantages, or accommodations of any place of public accommodation by any person who owns, leases (or leases to), or operates a place of public accommodation'' (42 USC 12182(a)).

The ADA provides a comprehensive list of private entities that are considered public accommodations for the purposes of Title III. The ADA's list of public accommodations effectively covers most places that are open to business or contact with the general public, including places of lodging, establishments serving food or drink, places of public gathering, service establishments, places of recreation, places of education, and social services establishments (42 USC 12181(7)). *Public accommodations* are defined to include only private entities affecting commerce; buildings owned by state and local governments are covered under Title II. Private clubs and religious organizations are exempted from coverage, as are private housing and residences (Burgdorf, 1992).

In *Aikens, California Association of the Deaf* v. *St. Helene Hospital, James Lies*, the court held that Title III does not apply to a doctor on the staff of a hospital because he does not own, lease, or operate the accommodation. The preamble to the regulations notes that the ADA places obligations on public accommodations rather than on persons or places of public accommodation (36 CFR App. B @ 35.201(a)). The use of language relating to ownership or operation implies a requirement of control over the place providing services that does not occur with a doctor on the staff of a hospital.[97]

Title III's general prohibition against discrimination uses the phrase *full and equal enjoyment*. The statute enumerates categories of actions that constitute such discrimination. It is discriminatory to subject an individual or class of individuals on the basis of a disability to denial of the opportunity to participate in or benefit from the goods or services of a public accommodation; to participate in an unequal benefit; or to participate in a different or separate benefit, unless it is necessary to provide the individual(s) with goods or services that are as effective as those provided to others (although the person cannot be denied the opportunity to participate in programs or activities that are not separate or different). Public accommodations must be afforded to individuals with a disability in the most integrated setting appropriate to the person's needs (42 USC 12182(b)). The legislative history explains that full and equal enjoyment does not encompass the notion that persons with disabilities must achieve the identical result or level of achievement of nondisabled persons but does mean that persons with disabilities must be afforded equal opportunity to obtain the same result (Senate Report, at 60).[98] The ADA also sets out specific prohibitions against discrimination, including (1) the application of eligibility criteria that screen out or tend to screen out persons with disabilities; (2) the failure to make reasonable modifications in policies, practices, or procedures when necessary unless it would fundamentally alter the nature of the accommodations; (3) the failure to take steps as necessary to ensure that no individual with a disability is denied services, segregated, or otherwise treated differently than others because of the absence of auxiliary aids and services, unless it would fundamentally alter the nature of the accommodation or would result in an undue burden; (4) failure to remove architectural barriers, and communication barriers that are structural in nature, in existing facilities where such removal is readily achievable; (5) and where an entity can demonstrate that the removal of a barrier is not readily achievable, a failure to make accommodations available through alternative methods if readily achievable (42 USC 12182(b)(2)).

Constitutionality of Title III

Title III places significant responsibilities on owners of public accommodations that can be costly. It may not be surprising, therefore, that the first serious constitutional challenge to the ADA came in the context of Title III. In *Pinnock* v. *International House of Pancakes Franchisee*,[99] the court held that Title III represents an appropriate exercise of congressional power pursuant to the commerce clause; it is not unconstitutionally vague; promulgation of DOJ regulations is not an unconstitutional delegation of authority by Congress; its required alterations to property is not an unconstitutional taking without just compensation; and it does not intrude upon state sovereignty in violation of the 10th Amendment.

Readily Achievable Barrier Removal

The concept of "readily achievable barrier removal" for existing places of public accommodation is defined as "easily accomplishable and able to be carried out without much difficulty or expense" (42 USC 12181(9)). The statute enumerates four factors to consider when determining whether a modification is readily achievable, and the DOJ regulations and legislative history list examples of the types of barrier removal that Congress believes are readily achievable, including rearranging tables and chairs, repositioning shelves and telephones, and installing small ramps and grab bars in restrooms (28 CFR 36.104, 36.304). Similarly, the legislative history and the regulations provide specific examples of appropriate alternatives to barrier removal. These include providing curb service or home delivery, coming to the door of the facility to handle transactions, serving beverages at a table where a bar is inaccessible, providing assistance to retrieve items from inaccessible shelves, and relocating services and activities to accessible locations (Senate Report at 66; 28 CFR 36.305(b)).

Requirement to Provide Auxiliary Aids and Services: Fundamental Alteration and Undue Burden

The requirement to provide auxiliary aids and services unless it would fundamentally alter the nature of the accommodation or would impose an undue burden is construed in the DOJ regulations and case law. *Undue burden* is defined in the regulations as a "significant difficulty or expense." The regulations list factors for determining whether a particular action will create an undue burden. These are the same factors as those provided for assessing whether an action is "readily achievable." The preamble, however, clarifies that; "Readily achievable" is a lower standard than "undue burden" in that it requires a lower level of effort on the part of the public accommodation.

The term *fundamentally alter* was used by the Supreme Court in *Southeastern Community College* v. *Davis* in construing Section 504. The Court found that a nursing school did not illegally discriminate against a nursing applicant who could communicate only by reading lips and sign language by refusing to modify its program in such a way as to "dispense with the need for effective oral communication" with a nursing instructor. Justice Powell said that the Rehabilitation Act "imposes no requirement upon an educational institution to lower or to effect substantial modifications of standards to accommodate a handicapped person."[100]

In *Breece* v. *Alliance Tractor-Trailer Training II, Inc.*, a person with a severe hearing impairment was denied admission to a training program that was known for its special emphasis on having students drive on public roads. The plaintiff requested accommodations such as a driving simulator, more instruction before taking the wheel, and a sign language interpreter in the truck cab. The court held that the accommodations would fundamentally alter the nature of the driving school. It found that the person with disabilities posed a direct threat to the safety of others (42 USC 12182(b)(3)) that could not be reduced sufficiently by the reasonable accommodations.[101]

In *Dobard* v. *San Francisco Bay Area Rapid Transit District*,[102] a hearing-impaired person claimed he was denied access to a board meeting open to the public because the defendant failed to provide a computer aided transcription (CAT) auxiliary aid. The plaintiff was provided two alternative aids for persons with hearing impairments, sign language interpreters and assistive listening devices. The court held that the individual is not entitled to auxiliary aids or services absolutely but rather that the public meeting is made accessible. The covered entity has discretion in determining how to achieve that goal. Further, the use of the most advanced technology is not required. "A public accommodation can choose among various alternatives as long as the result is effective communication" (28 CFR 36.303(c), App. B).

Equal Access

Persons with disabilities are claiming access to, and equal treatment in, a wide range of public accommodations. Approximately 70 percent of DOJ complaints concern physical access (Kessler, 1993). Many cases have been filed in court, but are undecided, under Title III. For example, after a lengthy process of negotiation, the French company Decaux, which manufactures public toilets, agreed that each of the units will be large enough to accommodate wheelchairs. The Department of Justice has not yet ruled on whether the units are permanent structures that are required to be accessible (Adams, 1993). Other cases involve claims for accessibility to school buildings ("Seven Disabled Students," 1993; Breckenridge, 1993), camp facilities run by the Girl Scouts,[103] libraries,[104] the Orange Bowl in Miami ("Sports Digest," 1993), town halls (Koff, 1993; Moore, 1993), night clubs (Kessler, 1993), and even upper mountain facilities for skiers who use wheelchairs (Ehrlich, 1993). However, Title III's prohibition on discrimination in public accommodations probably does not apply where there is no physical facility.[105]

Individualized Determinations

Determinations under the ADA must be made on an individualized basis. Thus, Little League baseball could not exclude all coaches in wheelchairs from being on the playing field. There must be an individual assessment of the nature, duration, and severity of the risk, probability that potential injury could actually result, and whether the reasonable modifications of policies, practices, or procedures would mitigate the risk.[106] In another case involving Little League baseball, persons with developmental disabilities sued when their team was not given uniforms, caps, or insignias and were treated like "bush leaguers" (Simon, 1993).

The ADA and the Health Care System

The ADA specifically defines *public accommodations* to include a professional office of a health care provider, hospital, or other service establishment (42 USC 12181(7)). Health care providers, therefore, have a duty to provide nondiscriminatory health care services. This requires medical or dental practitioners and hospitals to provide equivalent services to all patients consistent with their medical needs and irrespective of their disabilities. A plaintiff is not required to prove discriminatory intent to establish prima facie case; he or she need only show the health care provider denied treatment "under circumstances which give rise to an inference that the denial is based solely on the handicap."[107]

Several cases have been filed, but not decided, by persons with HIV infection who claimed they were not given medical or dental treatment because of their serological status (Peller, 1993).[108] Predicting the outcome of these cases is difficult because the ADA does not completely clarify the distinction between the genuine exercise of clinical judgment and unlawful discrimination. The statute certainly prohibits a refusal to treat based upon prejudice or irrational fear, but health care decisions and practices may be far more nuanced (Gostin, 1992).

The most difficult cases arise when the disability is directly related to the condition being treated (Parmet, 1990). An intriguing illustration of this dilemma is the Baby K case.[109] A hospital sought to discontinue ventilator treatment against the wishes of the mother for an infant born with anencephaly, a congenital defect in which the brain stem is present but the cerebral cortex is rudimentary or absent. Baby K was permanently unconscious. The district court found that, under Section 504, Baby K is a person with a disability[110] who is "qualified" to receive ventilator treatment, and such treatment was being denied because of an unjustified consideration of the infant's disability. The court distinguished the judgments of two federal courts that allowed the withdrawal of treatment to disabled neonates on the ground that in both cases the parents consented.[111] The Baby K court rejected the contention that ventilator treatment could be withheld because the infant's recurring breathing troubles are intrinsically related to her disability. The court made an analogy to a person with AIDS: "Just as an AIDS patient seeking ear surgery is 'otherwise qualified' to receive treatment despite poor long term prospects of living, Baby K is 'otherwise qualified' to receive ventilator treatment despite similarly dismal health prospects." A person with AIDS, however, could benefit from the treatment in terms of living a conscious and interactive life, whereas the permanently comatose neonate could not.

The court also found a violation of the ADA and noted there is no qualification standard under Title III. The court rejected the hospital's argument that the treatment was "futile." The court found that the plain language of the act does not permit denial of ventilator services that would keep alive an anencephalic baby, when those lifesaving services would otherwise be provided to a baby without disabilities at the parent's request.[112] [Author's Note: The Baby K case was affirmed on appeal, but on grounds not relating to the ADA.]

CONCLUSION

Examination of ADA litigation shows the fundamental impact of disability law on American law and society. The litigation effectuates the two primary purposes of the act: prohibiting discrimination in civil society and dismantling barriers to full participation. It also has the potential to do much more, affecting the structure of government benefits programs, the regulation of public health and safety (Gostin, 1991), and the provision of health care services in society.

This is as it should be. Just as nondiscrimination legislation on the basis of race and sex has pervaded the way we order our society and our major institutions, so too will disability law require fundamental change. That is the promise of the ADA, and early litigation suggests its impact will be no less than predicted by persons with disabilities and advocates during passage of the act.

ACKNOWLEDGMENTS

The author is grateful to Barbara Looney, M.P.H., J.D. (Georgetown/Johns Hopkins Program in Law and Public Health), and Kathleen Flaherty, J.D. (Harvard Law School) for their able research assistance.

REFERENCES

Adams, J. M. 1993. "San Francisco Disabled Groups Win Toilet Access Fight." *Sacramento Bee* (July 8): A2.

AP. 1993. "Lawsuit Challenges AIDS Marriage Ban." *Times-Picayune* (July 16): A3; "AIDS Marriage Ban to Be Lifted." *Times-Picayune* (August 19): A9.

Baughman, A. 1993. "Salazar v. Inham." *The Recorder* (February 25): 5.

BNA. 1993. "Panelists Discuss Workplace Impact of ADA." *BNA Pension and Benefits Reporter* 20, no. 31 (August 2): 1646.

Breckenridge, T. 1993. "Parents Want Son, 11, to Stay with Peer Group." *Cleveland Plain Dealer* (March 4): 6B.

Burgdorf, R. L. 1992. "Equal Access to Public Accommodations." In *The Americans with Disabilities Act: From Policy to Practice*, ed. J. West, pp. 183–213. New York: Milbank Memorial Fund.

Burnett, R., and S. Hagstrom, 1993. "Disney Lawsuit in Central Florida Federal Court." *Orlando Sentinel* (July 26): 19.

EEOC. 1993a. "EEOC Marks First Year of Enforcing the Americans with Disabilities Act in the Workplace." News release, July 23.

———. 1993b. "EEOC Intervenes as Plaintiff and Settles Controversial ADA Case Challenging AIDS-Cap in Health Benefit Plan." News release, December 21.

———. 1994a. "EEOC Reports Discrimination Charges Surged in FY 1993." News release, January 12.

———. 1994b. "Total Number of ADA Charges Received by EEOC, June 26, 1992–June 30, 1994." News release, July.

————. 1994c. "EEOC ADA Cases in Litigation or Resolved." News release, July 1.

Ehrlich, R. 1993. "Squaw Valley Is Test Case for Disabilities Act." *Christian Science Monitor* (June 28): 12.

"Ex-Judge Claims Disability Bias in Trying to Reclaim Seat." 1993. *The Recorder* (March 5): 4.

Feldblum, C. R. 1993. "Antidiscrimination Requirements of the ADA." In *Implementing the Americans with Disabilities Act: Rights and Responsibilities of All Americans*, ed. L. O. Gostin and H. A. Beyer, pp. 35–54. Baltimore: Paul H. Brookes Publishing Co.

Golden, M. 1993. "Title II – Public Services, Subtitle B: Public Transportation." In *Implementing the Americans with Disabilities Act: Rights and Responsibilities of All Americans*, ed. L. O. Gostin and H. A. Beyer, pp. 109–121.Baltimore: Paul H. Brookes Publishing Co.

Gostin, L. O. 1991. "Public Health Powers: The Imminence of Radical Change." In *The Americans with Disabilities Act: From Policy to Practice*, ed. J. West, pp. 268–290. New York: Milbank Memorial Fund.

————. 1992. "The Americans with Disabilities Act and the U.S. Health System." *Health Affairs* 11: 248–257.

Gostin, L. O., and A. I. Widiss. 1993. "What's Wrong with the ERISA Vacuum? Employers' Freedom to Limit Health Care Coverage Provided by Risk Retention Plans." *JAMA* 269: 2527–2532.

Hacker, W. 1993. "Shorewood Board Again Says No to Group Home Despite Warnings." *Chicago Tribune* (July 28): 4.

Hartzel, T. 1993. "Suits Filed over Access for Disabled." *Dallas Morning News* (July 30): 31A.

"Health Care; Oregon Request for Medicaid Waiver Approved by HHS with Conditions." 1993. *BNA Daily Report for Executives* (March 22): 53.

Health Lawyer. 1993. "Employers Face a Difficult Burden of Proof When Attempting to Enforce a Disability-Based Distinction in Employee Benefits." *ABA Forum on Health Law* 7: 4.

Hellinger, F. 1992. "Forecasts of the Costs of Medical Care for Persons with HIV: 1992–1995." *Inquiry* 29: 356 (average HIV treatment costs are $38,300 per year and $102,000 lifetime).

———. 1993. "The Lifetime Cost of Treating a Person with HIV." *JAMA* 270: 474–478 (estimated lifetime cost of treatment is $119,000).

Herbeck, D. 1993. "Canaan House Sues to Avoid Eviction: Recovering Addicts' Home Claims Bias in Cheektowaga Zoning Denial." *Buffalo News* (August 11).

House of Representatives. 1990. *H.R. Report* No. 485, Part 2, 101st Cong., 2d Sess., pp. 84–85.

"Insurance." 1993. *AIDS Law and Litigation Reporter Monthly Review* (May–June).

"Judge: Medicaid Needn't Pay for Heart Transplant." 1992. *Miami Herald* (October 2).

Katzmann, R. A. 1992. "Transportation Policy." In *The Americans with Disabilities Act: From Policy to Practice*, ed. J. West. New York: Milbank Memorial Fund.

Kessler, B. 1993. "Woman Fighting for Breathing Space." *Dallas Morning News* (May 1): 1A.

Kilb, L. 1993. "Title II – Public Services, Subtitle A: State and Local Governments' Role." In *Implementing the Americans with Disabilities Act: Rights and Responsibilities of All Americans*, ed. L. O. Gostin and H. A. Beyer, pp. 87–108. Baltimore: Paul H. Brookes Publishing Co.

Koff, S. 1993. "Disabled Woman Sues Township; Wants No Meetings until Ramp Is Built." *Cleveland Plain Dealer* (April 28): 1B.

"Making the Courtroom Come to Life for a Deaf Defendant." 1993. *Philadelphia Inquirer* (April 28): 51.

Megan, K. 1993. "Would-Be Lawyer Objects to Bar Queries and Sues." *Hartford Courant* (May 27): C1.

Milstein, B., and S. Hitov. 1993. "Housing and the ADA." In *Implementing the Americans with Disabilities Act: Rights and*

Responsibilities of All Americans, ed. L. O. Gostin and H. A. Beyer, pp. 137–153. Baltimore: Paul H. Brookes Publishing Co.

Moore, B. A. 1993. "City Hall off Limits to Disabled? East Point Yet To Satisfy Law." *Atlanta Journal and Constitution* (August 19): K1.

O'Connor, M. O. 1993. "Cop with Diabetes Sues for Benefits." *Chicago Tribune* (February 10): D2 (police officer suing city of Aurora, Ill., in federal court claiming discrimination in being denied pension benefits because he has diabetes).

Parmet, W. E. 1990. "Discrimination and Disability: The Challenges of the ADA." *Law, Medicine and Health Care* 18: 331–344.

Pear, R. 1992. "Plan to Ration Health Care Is Rejected by Government." *New York Times* (August 4): A8.

Peller, R. 1993. "Suit Claims HIV Status Ended Care; Man with Virus Says Dentists Refused Him." *Houston Chronicle* (February 24): A13.

"Pennsylvania Man Who Stutters Sues over Firing." 1993. *Liability Week* 8, no. 18 (May 3).

"Seven Disabled Students Sue Penn State." 1993. *Philadelphia Inquirer* (July 2): B4.

Simon, E. 1993. "Separate but Unequal? Disabled Challengers Challenge Little League in ADA Suit." *Ct. Law Tribune* (July 12): 6.

"Sports Digest." 1993. *St. Petersburg Times* (June 24): 2C.

"State Sides." 1992. *Houston Chronicle* (October 4): 2.

"Today's News Update." 1992. *New York Law Journal* (September 28): 1.

Swisher, K. 1994. "Overweight Workers Battle Bias on the Job: Looks Discrimination Called Common, but Hard to Prove." *Washington Post* (January 24): A1. ("There are many negative stereotypes for the overweight: They are in poor physical shape, or are unclean, or lazy, or either very happy or depressed.")

UPI. 1993. "Union Local Sued for Limiting Coverage to Member Who Died of AIDS." March 17 (estate of Mark Kadinger field suit in federal court claiming that Local 110 of IBEW and its health plan discriminated against him by capping the benefits for AIDS treatments).

Vaughan, V. 1993. "Lawsuits Expected to Be an Offshoot of Disabilities Act; One Year after Its Implementation, the Act Continues to Have Big Influence on Businesses." *Orlando Sentinel* (July 25): F1 (derived from BNA statistics).

Zola, I. K. 1993. "The Sleeping Giant in Our Midst: Redefining 'Persons with Disabilities'." In *Implementing the Americans with Disabilities Act: Rights and Responsibilities of All Americans.* ed. L. O. Gostin and H. A. Beyer, pp. xvii–xx. Baltimore: Paul H. Brookes Publishing Co.

NOTES

1. Beaumont v. EXXON Corporation, 1994 U.S. Dist. LEXIS 50 (E.D.La. Jan. 4, 1994). See Hartzel (1993) for a story about Advocacy, Inc., of Texas, which has embarked on a campaign to ensure compliance with the ADA; as of April 1993, 10 percent of complaints filed with EEOC were from the state of Texas.
2. Santiago Aramburu v. Boeing Co., 1993 U.S. Dist. LEXIS 18620 (D.Kan. Dec. 29, 1993); Dean v. Thompson, 1993 U.S. Dist. LEXIS 10746 (N.D.Ill. July 9, 1993); Barraclough v. ADP Automotive Claims Services, 818 F. Supp. 1310 (N.D.Cal. 1993); Davis v. York International, 1993 U.S. Dist. LEXIS 17649 (D.Md. Nov. 22, 1993); Major v. Southeastern Pa. Transp. Authority, 1993 WL 21212 (E.D.Pa. Jan. 22, 1993).
3. Raya v. Maryatt Industries, 829 F. Supp. 1169 (N.D.Cal. 1993).
4. Pinnock v. International House of Pancakes Franchisee, 1993 U.S. Dist. LEXIS 16399 (S.D. Cal. Nov. 8, 1993).
5. Barraclough v. ADP Automotive Claims Services, 818 F. Supp. 1310 (N.D.Cal. 1993).
6. Post v. Kansas Gas & Electric Co., 1993 U.S. Dist. LEXIS 9702 (D.Kan. June 14, 1993).

7. Westhoven v. State of Indiana Civil Rights Commission v. Lincoln Foodservice Products, Inc., 616 N.E.2d 778 (Ind. Ct. App. 1993).

8. Rothman v. Emory University, 828 F. Supp. 537 (N.D.Ill. 1993).

9. Buhl v. Hannigan, 16 Cal. App. 4th 1612 (1993).

10. Crowder v. Kitagawa, 842 F. Supp. 1257 (D.Hawaii 1994).

11. Equal Employment Opportunity Commission. Regulations to Implement the Equal Employment Provisions of the Americans with Disabilities Act, 29 CFR Part 1630.2.

12. Welsh v. City of Tulsa, 977 F.2d 1415 (10th Cir. 1992).

13. Bolton v. Scrivner, 836 F. Supp. 783 (W.D.Okla. 1993).

14. Galloway v. Superior Court, 816 F. Supp. 12 (D.D.C. 1993).

15. Chatoff v. City of New York, 3 NDLR, p. 80 (1992).

16. U.S. EEOC v. AIC Sec. Investigations Ltd, 823 F. Supp. 571 (N.D.Ill. 1993) (motion for new trial denied 1993 U.S. LEXIS 15025 (Oct. 30, 1993).

17. Fineley v. Giacobbe, 827 F. Supp. 215 (S.D.N.Y. 1993).

18. Rothman v. Emory University, 828 F. Supp. 537 (N.D.Ill. 1993).

19. Williams v. Secretary of the Executive Office of Human Services, 414 Mass. 551 (SJC, Mass. 1993).

20. Martin v. Voinovich, 1993 U.S. Dist. LEXIS 18468 (S.D.Ohio, Dec. 14, 1993).

21. D'Amico v. New York State Bar Examiners, 813 F. Supp. 217 (W.D.N.Y. 1993); Weintraub v. Board of Bar Examiners, *Mass. Lawyers Weekly*, September 21, 1992, p.11 (SJC); Rosenthal v. New York State Board, 92 Civ. 1100 (1992).

22. Gulf Coast Industrial Workers Union v. Exxon, 991 F.2d 244 (5th Cir. 1993). Accord, Welsh and Welsh v. Boy Scouts of America, 993 F.2d 1267 (7th Cir. 1993).

23. Hartman v. City of Petaluma, Petaluma Police Department, 1994 U.S. Dist. LEXIS 257 (N.D. Cal. 1994).

24. Byerly v. Herr Foods, 1993 U.S. Dist. LEXIS 4253, April 6, 1993.

25. Byerly v. Herr Foods, 1993 U.S. Dist. LEXIS 8271, June 10, 1993.

26. Cook v. State of Rhode Island, 10 F.3d 17 (1st Cir. 1993).

27. State Div. of Human Rights v. Xerox Corp., 480 N.E.2d 695 (N.Y. 1985).

28. Cook v. State of Rhode Island, 10 F.3d 17 (1st Cir. 1993). In a brief filed with the 1st Circuit Court of Appeals, the EEOC argued that obesity is protected if it is "of sufficient duration and has a significant impact on major life activities." "EEOC Pushes to Label Obesity as a Disability," *Washington Times* (1 March 1994): A7.

29. Horton v. Delta, 1993 U.S. Dist. LEXIS 12865 (N.D.Cal. Sept. 3, 1993).

30. Felde v. City of San Jose, 1994 U.S. Dist. LEXIS 109 (N.D.Cal. Jan. 6, 1994).

31. 469 U.S. 287 (1985).

32. Felde v. City of San Jose, 1994 U.S. Dist. LEXIS 109 (N.D.Cal. Jan. 6, 1994).

33. Compare Paroline v. Unisys Corp., 879 F.2d 100 (4th Cir. 1989) (supervisor may be individually liable as "employer" under Title VII) with Miller v. Maxwell's Int'l, Inc., 991 F.2d 583 (9th Cir. 1993) (agent not individually liable under Title VII and ADEA).

34. See Thompson v. City of Arlington, Texas, 1993 U.S. Dist. LEXIS 17093 (N.D.Tex. Nov. 17, 1993) (only when a person is working in his or her official capacity can the official be an agent of the employer under the ADA); Janopoulos v. Walner & Associates, LTD and Walner, 835 F. Supp. 459 (N.D.Ill. 1993) (upholding associate's liability under the ADA because he or she has "authority and responsibility"); Carparts Distribution Center, Inc. v. Automobile Wholesaler's Association of New England, 826 F.Supp. 583 (D.N.M, 1993) (Title I of ADA does not apply to defendant who sponsored a health benefit plan that provided group health coverage for employees because it was not the "employer").

35. Johnston v. Morrison, Inc., 849 F. Supp. 777 (N.D.Ala. 1994).

36. 1993 U.S. Dist. LEXIS 14311 (N.D.Ill. Oct. 12, 1993) (claiming violation of Title I when city changed the terms of retirement benefits plan to require retirees to pay for their own health insurance).

37. School Board of Nassau County v. Arline, 480 U.S. 273, 288 (1987).

38. See, generally, Bradley v. University of Texas M.D. Anderson Cancer Ctr., 3 F.3d 922, 924 (5th Cir. 1993); Doe v. District of Columbia, 796 F. Supp. 559, 567–68 (D.D.C. 1992); Doe v. Washington University, 780 F. Supp. 628, 632 (E.D.Mo. 1991).

39. Roe v. District of Columbia, Civil Action No. 93-0164 (JHG), (D.D.C. Dec. 21, 1993).

40. Carter v. Bennett, 840 F.2d 63, 67 (D.C. Cir. 1988). See also Langon v. HHS, 959 F.2d 1053, 1057 (D.C. Cir. 1992).

41. Harmer v. Virginia Electric and Power Co., 831 F. Supp. 1300 (E.D.Va. 1993).

42. Davis v. York International Inc., 1993 U.S. Dist. LEXIS 17649 (D.Md. Nov. 22, 1993).

43. Jasany v. United States Postal Service, 755 F.2d 1244 (6th Cir. 1986).

44. Eisfelder v. State of Michigan Department of Natural Resources, 1993 U.S. Dist. LEXIS 17520 (W.D.Mich. Nov. 15, 1993).

45. See Melton v. Community for Creative Non-violence, U.S. Dist. LEXIS 12235 (DDC, Aug. 31, 1993) (no retaliation if plaintiff cannot show that the reason for the eviction was the person's disability).

46. See McDonnell Douglas Corp. v. Green, 411 U.S. 792 (1973) (employment discrimination action brought under Title VII of the Civil Rights Act of 1964); Ross v. Communications Satellite Corp., 759 F.2d 355, 365 (4th Cir. 1985).

47. Harmer v. Virginia Electric and Power Co., 831 F. Supp. 1300 (E.D.Va. 1993).

48. 58 Fed. Reg. 51266 (Oct. 1, 1993).

49. Davis v. International Inc., 1993 U.S. Dist. LEXIS 17649 (D.Md. Nov. 22, 1993).

50. Fasone, Relator v. Clinton Township, 1993 Ohio LEXIS 5589 (Court of Appeals of Ohio, 10th appellate district, Nov. 18, 1993).

51. EEOC v. AIC Security, 823 F. Supp. 571 (N.D.Ill. 1993).

52. Dutton v. Board of County Commissioners of Johnson County, Kansas, 1993 U.S. Dist. LEXIS 12169 (D.Kan. Aug. 18, 1993).

53. Post v. Kansas Gas & Electric Company, 1993 U.S. Dist. LEXIS 9702 (D.Kan. June 14, 1993).

54. James v. Texas Department of Human Services, 818 F. Supp. 987 (1983).
55. Kent v. Missouri Department of Elementary and Secondary Education and Division of Vocational Rehabilitation, 989 F.2d 505 (8th Cir. 1993), citing Jones v. American State Bank, 857 F.2d 494, 499–500 (8th Cir. 1988) (receiving a right to sue letter is not a jurisdictional prerequisite to filing an action but, rather, is a condition precedent curable after the action has commenced).
56. Sheehan v. Purolator Courier Corporation, 676 F.2d 877 (2d Cir. 1981).
57. L.J. v. Massinga, 838 F.2d 118, at 120 (4th Cir. 1988).
58. Altman v. New York City Health and Hospitals Corporation, 1993 U.S. Dist. LEXIS 4228, aff'd without opinion 999 F.2d 537 (2d Cir. 1993).
59. McGann v. H & H Music Company, 946 F.2d 401 (5th Cir. 1991), *cert. denied sub nom,* Greenberg v. H & H Music Company, 113 S.Ct. 482 (1992). See Owens v. Storehouse, U.S. App. 1993 LEXIS 3066 (11th Cir. 1993).
60. In the Supreme Court of the United States, October Term 1992, No. 91-1285, Greenburg, Executor of Estate of John W. McGann v. H & H Music Company, brief for the United States as amicus curiae, Kenneth W. Starr, solicitor general.
61. U.S. EEOC v. H. Hirschfield Sons Co., EEOC news release, Sept. 3, 1993.
62. U.S. EEOC v. Mason Tenders District Council Welfare Fund, U.S. District Court, No. 93-3865 (S.D.N.Y. June 9, 1993).
63. John Doe v. Victory Van Corp., Civil Action No. 93-1173A (E.D.Va. Sept. 14, 1993) (moving and storage company seeking to enjoin Victory Van from enforcing a cap on AIDS treatment reimbursement claims); U.S. EEOC v. Allied Services Division, Sept. 28, 1993 (cap on insurance plan to bar coverage for HIV).
Subtitle B of Title II and Title IV are not covered in this article. There has been relatively little litigation on public transportation. (But see, Kinney v. Yerusalim, 812 F. Supp. 547, *aff'd* 1993 U.S. App. LEXIS 30167 (3d Cir. Pa. 1993); Hardin v. Southeastern Pennsylvania Transportation

Authority, C.A. No. 91-CV-7434 (U.S.D.C.,E.D.Pa., amended complaint filed 2/24/92). For a discussion of public transportation and the ADA, see Golden, 1993; Katzmann, 1992; and Simon article in this volume.

64. See, e.g., Coleman v. Zatechka, 824 F. Supp. 1360 (D. Neb., 1993) (university established by the state legislature as a state institution is a "public entity"); Petersen v. University of Wisconsin Board of Regents, 818 F. Supp. 1276 (W.D.Wis. 1993) (same); Treanor v. Washington Post Co., 826 F. Supp. 568 (D.D.C. 1993)(private newspaper is not a public entity and is not a "service").

65. Bell v. The Retirement Board of the Firemen's Annuity and Benefit Fund of Chicago and the City of Chicago, 1993 U.S. Dist. LEXIS 14020 (N.D.Ill. Sept. 27, 1993).

66. Chatoff v. City of New York, 3 NDLR at 80 (1992).

67. Medical Society of New Jersey v. Jacobs and the New Jersey State Board of Medical Examiners, 1993 U.S. Dist. LEXIS 14294 (D.N.J. Oct. 5, 1993).

68. In re application of Underwood, No. BAR-93-21 (Me.Sup.-Jud.Ct. Dec. 7, 1993).

69. D'Amico v. New York State Board of Bar Examiners, 813 F. Supp. 217 (W.D.N.Y. 1993).

70. Weintraub v. Board of Bar Examiners, Massachusetts Lawyers Weekly, Sept. 21, 1992. See Rosenthal v. New York State Board, 92 Civ. 1100 (1992) (plaintiff with dyslexia and attention deficit disorder withdrew motion for an injunction in return for being allowed two extra days and a separate room to take the exam; a damages suit is still pending).

71. Petition of Rubenstein, 637 A.2d 1131 (Del.Supr. 1994).

72. Rothman v. Emory University, 1993 U.S. Dist. LEXIS 15190 (N.D.Ill. Oct. 27, 1993).

73. T.E.P. v. Leavit, No. 93-C-653A (D.Utah Sept. 17, 1993).

74. Galloway v. Superior Court, 816 F. Supp. 12 (D.D.C. 1993); DeLong v. Commonwealth of Pennsylvania, 703 F. Supp. 399 (W.D.Pa. 1989); People of the State of New York v. Caldwell, 603 N.Y.S.2d 713 (1993).

75. People of the State of New York v. Caldwell, 603 N.Y.S.2d 713 (1993).

76. U.S. v. Clearwater Police Dep't, DOJ 204-17M-20 (U.S. DOJ June 29, 1993).
77. Torcasio v. Murray, 1993 U.S. App. LEXIS 29548 (4th Cir, Nov. 15, 1993).
78. Noland v. Wheatley, 835 F. Supp. 476 (N.D.Ind. 1993).
79. Noland v. Wheatley, 835 F. Supp. 476 (N.D.Ind. 1993).
80. Tomey v. Gissy, 832 F. Supp. 172 (N.D.W.Va. 1993). The application of Title III to housing is limited because the definition of *commercial facilities* excludes those covered or exempted from coverage under the Fair Housing Act of 1968 (42 USC 12181). The ADA, however, does cover housing discrimination in places of public accommodation such as places of lodging including inns, hotels, homeless shelters, substance abuse treatment centers, rape crisis centers, and halfway houses (Milstein and Hitov, 1993).
81. Independent Housing Services of San Francisco v. Fillmore Center Associates, 1993 U.S. Dist. LEXIS 18343, Dec. 27, 1993.
82. Martin et al. v. Voinovich, 1993 U.S. Dist. LEXIS 18468 (S.D.Ohio, Dec. 14, 1993).
83. Southeastern Community College v. Davis, 442 U.S. 397, 410–411 (1979).
84. Traynor v. Turnage, 485 U.S. 535 (1988).
85. See also Chiari v. City of League City, 920 F.2d 311, 315 (5th Cir. 1991); P.C. v. McLaughlin, 913 F.2d 1033 (2d Cir. 1990) (Section 504 does not apply between different categories of persons with disabilities).
86. Williams v. Secretary of the Executive Office of Human Services, 414 Mass. 551, 1993 Mass. LEXIS 122 (SJC, Mar. 11, 1993).
87. Oxford House, Inc. v. City of Virginia Beach, 825 F. Supp. 1251 (E.D.Va. 1993); see also Oxford House, Inc. v. City of Albany, 819 F. Supp. 1168 (N.D.N.Y. 1993); Burnham v. City of Rohnert Park, 1992 U.S. Dist. LEXIS 8540 (N.D.Cal. May 18, 1992); Moyer v. Lower Oxford Township, 1993 WL 5489 (E.D.Pa. Jan. 6, 1993).
88. Compare Marbrunak, Inc. v. City of Stow, 974 F.2d 43 (6th Cir. 1992) with Familystyle of St. Paul v. City of St. Paul, 728 F. Supp. 1396 (D.Minn. 1990) (state licensing requirement

governing administration of homes for mentally disabled did not violate act, even though they restricted ability of disabled to live where they chose).

89. Marbrunak, Inc. v. City of Stow, 974 F.2d 43, 47–48 (6th Cir. 1992).

90. Coleman v. Zatechka, 824 F. Supp. 1360 (D.Neb. 1993).

91. See also Anderson v. Little League Baseball, Inc., 794 F. Supp. 342 (D.Ariz. 1992) (blanket policy of prohibiting coaches in wheelchairs from being on the field violates the ADA; baseball league needs to make individualized assessments).

92. Petersen v. University of Wisconsin Board of Regents, 818 F. Supp. 1276 (W.D.Wis. 1993).

93. Easley v. Snider, 1993 U.S. Dist. LEXIS 18021 (E.D.Pa. Dec. 21, 1993); see also Concerned Parents to Save Dreher Park Center v. City of West Palm Beach, No. 93-8532-CIV-RYSKAMP, 1994 U.S. Dist. LEXIS 7153 (S.D.Fla. May 26, 1994) (entry of consent judgment that closure of leisure services program at center for persons with mental and physical disabilities violated Title II of ADA).

94. Smith v. Barton, 914 F.2d 1330, 1338 (9th Cir. 1990, *cert denied*, 111 S. Ct. 2825 (1991) (outlining enforcement provisions of Title I and Title II, respectively); Finlely v. Giacobbe, 827 F. Supp. 215, 219 n.3 (S.D.N.Y. 1993); Noland v. Wheatley, 835 F. Supp. 476 (N.D.Ind. 1993) (semi-quadriplegic did not have to exhaust administrative procedures before suing prison under Title II); Bell v. Retirement Bd. of the Firemen's Annuity and Benefit Fund of Chicago, No. 92-C-5197, 1993 U.S. Dist. LEXIS 14020 (N.D.Ill. Sept. 27, 1993); Bechtel v. East Penn School District, No. 93-4898, 1994 U.S. Dist. LEXIS 1327 (E.D.Pa. Jan. 4, 1994).

95. Petersen v. University of Wisconsin Bd. of Regents, 818 F. Supp. 1276 (W.D.Wis. 1993).

96. See, Finley v. Giacobbe, 827 F. Supp. 215, 219 (S.D.N.Y. 1993).

97. Aikens, California Association of the Deaf v. St. Helene Hospital, James Lies, 1994 U.S. Dist. LEXIS 1644, Feb. 2, 1994.

98. Dobard v. San Francisco Bay Area Rapid Transit District, 1993 U.S. Dist. LEXIS 13677 (N.D.Cal. Sept. 7, 1993).

99. Pinnock v. International House of Pancakes Franchisee, 1993 U.S. Dist. LEXIS 16399 (S.D. Cal. Nov. 8, 1993). DOJ regulations under Title II maintain the distinction between existing facilities (28 CFR 35.159) and new construction and alterations (28 CFR 35.151). With limited exceptions, the regulations do not require public entities to retrofit existing facilities immediately and completely. In contrast, when a public entity engages in new construction or alterations it must, to the maximum extent feasible, do so in a manner that is readily accessible. The court in *Kinney, et al.* v. *Yerusalim*, et al., 1993 U.S. App. LEXIS 30167 (3rd Cir, Nov. 23, 1993) found that resurfacing city streets is an "alteration" requiring the installation of curb ramps, and the "undue burden" defense is limited to existing facilities, not alterations.

100. Southeastern Community College v. Davis, 442 U.S. 397, 409, 413 (1979). See Kohl by Kohl v. Woodhaven Learning Center, 865 F.2d 930, 938 (8th Cir), cert. denied, 493 U.S. 892 (1989).

101. Breece v. Alliance Tractor-Trailer Training II, Inc., 824 F. Supp. 576 (E.D.Va. 1993).

102. Dobard v. San Francisco Bay Area Rapid Transit District, 1993 U.S. Dist. LEXIS 13677 (N.D.Cal. Sept. 7, 1993).

103. Willow v. Freedom Valley Girl Scout Council, 92-CV-0652; NLJ, Mar. 16, 1992.

104. Town of Seekonk (MA), 3 NDLR at 87 (ED Reg. I OCR, Complaint No. 01-92-4005, LOF dated 7/2/92, reported 10/14/92).

105. See Welsh v. Boy Scouts of America, 993 F.2d 1267 (7th Cir. 1993), *cert. denied* 114 S.Ct. 602 (however, this case was decided under Title II of the Civil Rights Act of 1964, which has narrower restrictions on places of public accommodation; the ADA's more expansive definition of *a place of public accommodation* may not necessarily yield a similar result).

106. Anderson v. Little League Baseball, Inc., 794 F. Supp. 342 (D.Ariz. 1992).

107. Mayberry v. Von Valtier, 843 F.Supp. 1160 (health care provider indicated that she no longer wished to provide treatment to patient because of extra cost of sign-language interpreter needed to communicate with patient).

108. Fuentes v. Reich, AIDS Law & Litigation Rptr., March/April 1992, at 15–16; Toney v. U.S. Healthcare, 1993 U.S. Dist. LEXIS 18365 (E.D.Pa. Dec. 30, 1993) (plaintiff's claim time barred). See also Doe v. Mercy Health Corporation of Southeastern Pennsylvania, 150 F.R.D. 83; 1993 U.S. Dist. LEXIS 6942 (E.D.Pa. May 25, 1993) (summary judgment denied in case where orthopedic surgeon infected with HIV had surgical privileges restricted); U.S. v. Morvant, 843 F. Supp. 1092 (E.D.La. 1994) (government sued dentist for failure to treat patients with AIDS; government can ask for award on behalf of deceased patient and also for "other persons aggrieved" even though not specifically identified).

109. In re Baby "K", 832 F. Supp. 1022 (E.D.Va. 1993).

110. See Bowen v. American Hospital Association, 476 U.S. 610, 624 (1986) (a "handicapped individual" under the Rehabilitation Act "includes an infant who is born with a congenital defect").

111. United States v. University Hospital, 729 F.2d 144, 157 (2d Cir. 1984); Johnson v. Thompson, 971 F.2d 1487, 1493 (10th Cir. 1992), *cert denied*, 113 S. Ct. 1255 (1993).

112. The case was affirmed on appeal, 16 F.3d 590 (4th Cir. 1994), but the appeals court based its decision on the Emergency Medical Treatment and Active Labor Act's (EMTALA's) requirement to provide that level of treatment necessary to prevent material deterioration in the patient's condition. The appellate court did not address the issue of a violation under the ADA.

II:
Employment

The Employment Sector

Chai R. Feldblum

EDITOR'S NOTE

Utilizing data from an employer survey, published cases and complaints, and EEOC responses to letters requesting guidance, Feldblum examines the impact of three key ADA provisions on the employment sector: the prohibition of medical inquiries and exams at the preoffer stage of employment, the duty to provide reasonable accommodations to enable employees with disabilities to perform the essential functions of the job, and nondiscrimination requirements related to the provision of health insurance by employers. Three of these areas of implementation – medical inquiries, health insurance, and definition of disability – have been the subject of one of the only guidances issued by the federal government on the ADA since the regulations in 1991. Although aspects of implementation remain somewhat problematic or unclear, such as an employer's inquiry about an applicant's need for reasonable accommodation at the preoffer stage and the notion of "disability-based distinctions" in determining terms of health insurance coverage, implementation in all of these areas is, in general, proceeding smoothly. Requests for reasonable accommodations have not been excessive nor has the provision of such accommodations been costly. Feldblum documents a gradual evolution of implementation in each of the areas, "not an earthquake, but a slow rolling wave."

Chai R. Feldblum is associate professor of law at Georgetown University Law Center in Washington, D.C., and director of the center's Federal Legislation Clinic. A leading expert on disability and AIDS law, Feldblum helped draft the original ADA introduced in the 101st Congress and served as principal legal advisor to the disability, AIDS, and civil rights communities during the two-year negotiations on the ADA. Feldblum received her J.D. from Harvard Law School, where she was an editor of the Harvard Law Review. *She clerked for Justice Harry A. Blackmun on the U.S. Supreme Court and served as legislative counsel with the American Civil Liberties Union in Washington, D.C. Feldblum has spoken and written widely on disability and AIDS issues. Her articles include "Employment Protections of the ADA" in* The Americans with Disabilities Act: From Policy to Practice *(ed. J. West, Milbank Memorial Fund, 1991) and "Antidiscrimination Requirements of the ADA," in* Implementing the Americans with Disabilites Act: Rights and Responsibilities of All Americans *(ed. L. Gostin and H. Beyer, Paul H. Brookes Publishing Co., 1992)*.

INTRODUCTION[1]

The Americans with Disabilities Act (ADA) was signed into law, with much fanfare, on 26 July 1990. After a two-year phase-in period, the employment provisions of the law became effective on 26 July 1992, for employers with 25 or more employees. After an additional two years, on 26 July 1994, the employment provisions of the law became effective for employers with 15 or more employees.

The years following passage of the ADA was a fertile period for the holding of conferences and seminars and for the production of law review articles, business articles, and general media articles on the ADA and its implications.[2]

Most of the law review articles dealt with legal issues that were either interesting, complicated, or simply the subject of much debate. Issues that engendered the most comment in the employment arena included: the ADA's requirement that employers provide reasonable accommodations;[3] the ADA's impact on employee health benefits;[4] and the ADA's effect on collective bargaining agreements.[5] The great majority of the law review articles attempt primarily to describe the requirements of the law. Approximately half of these articles describe the law as a whole;[6] the other half describe the employment provisions of the law.[7]

This chapter considers the implementation of the ADA in the employment sector with regard to medical examinations and inquiries, reasonable accommodation, and the provision of health insurance benefits in the employment sector. The ADA requirements with regard to medical examinations and inquiries are, relatively speaking, the least ambiguous obligations in the law.[8] Therefore, it is an area in which immediate changes in practice on the part of employers may have occurred. The obligation of reasonable accommodation, by contrast, was an area that elicited intense and vociferous concern on the part of employers during passage of the ADA. These concerns revolved primarily around the potentially high cost of providing accommodations and the flexible and "non-bright line" nature of the undue hardship determination.[9] Both disability advocates and business people should be interested in whether these concerns have, in fact, materialized in the case law and in employer experiences. Finally, the issue of restrictions on employer-provided insurance was one that various commentators noted would need clarification from the agencies and the courts.[10] It is interesting to explore what guidance has been provided thus far by those sources.

The description and analysis in this chapter are derived from three sources. The first source is published cases arising under the employment title of the ADA, and complaints under the ADA employment title that have been published in various ADA newsletters and reporters.[11] Although it would have been particularly useful to have access to the charges filed with the Equal Employment Opportunity Commission (EEOC), the substance of those charges cannot be made public.[12]

The second source is responses from the EEOC to 142 letters requesting guidance on the ADA.[13] These letters span the period of 24 April 1991 to 26 March 1993. The EEOC letters do not constitute legally binding guidance, but they are interesting in providing a snapshot of the issues concerning employers and people with disabilities.[14]

The third source is responses to a survey distributed by the Society for Human Resource Management (SHRM) to 500 randomly selected members in the summer of 1993. This survey dealt primarily with the issues of medical examinations and inquiries and reasonable accommodation.[15] The SHRM membership consists of human resources managers working at a variety of companies. Unfortunately, only 42 surveys were returned and analyzed. Therefore, although the survey responses may be used as interesting anecdotal evidence, they cannot support statistically valid conclusions.

MEDICAL EXAMINATIONS AND INQUIRIES

Introduction

The requirements of the ADA with regard to medical examinations and inquiries are designed to accommodate two concerns. The first concern is that of people with disabilities: to get a fair chance to demonstrate their abilities for a particular job before an employer is informed about a disability that is irrelevant to a job. The second concern is that of employers: to be allowed to assess whether an applicant or employee is qualified for a job that needs to get done.

The ADA accommodates these two concerns through a two-stage process. In the initial application stage, an employer may not administer medical examinations or require applicants to respond to medical inquiries. The employer remains free, however, to determine through the use of inquiries or through requested demonstrations, whether the applicant is able to perform job-related functions.[16]

If the employer wishes to hire the applicant, the employer must then extend to the applicant a conditional job offer. At that point, the employer may require the applicant to undergo a medical examination or to respond to medical inquiries and may condition the final offer of employment on the results of those medical tests or inquiries.[17]

This two-step process is derived directly from a similar process established in regulations issued under Section 504 of the Rehabilitation Act of 1973.[18] It is unclear how much of a practical impact those regulations actually had on the application processes of employers covered under the law. There was certainly no significant litigation with regard to medical examinations and inquiries. A review of Section 504 cases up to September 1991 found one case in which an employer's use of a preemployment disability question was challenged.[19]

This lack of litigation should not be particularly surprising. Most people with disabilities were probably not aware of the scope of Section 504 in general or the specific prohibitions on preemployment medical examinations and inquiries imposed by the regulations to Section 504. Therefore, even if an employer covered under Section 504 had violated those requirements, it is unlikely the violation would have been challenged.

The situation is somewhat different under the ADA. There is a greater understanding among people with disabilities of the ADA's requirements. In addition, many lawyers and personnel managers within the business community have made a substantial effort to educate their clients about the requirements of the law. Finally, the EEOC has produced extensive guidance on various aspects of the ADA, including specifically on medical examinations and inquiries.[20]

Even though we do not have extensive empirical data on employer actions in the area of medical examinations and inquiries, it seems intuitively true that a significant number of employers would review their application procedures and voluntarily correct any violations. If an employer were violating the law by requiring a medical examination or including a medical inquiry prior to a conditional job offer, that employer would be a "sitting duck" if a lawsuit were filed. The plaintiff's proof in such a case, in which the plaintiff wished to get the application process changed, would be easy; and there would be no clear defense in the law for employers to hide behind. On a simple cost–benefit analysis, it makes more sense for employers to fix these violations voluntarily.

Although the SHRM survey responses cannot be the basis for statistically valid conclusions, they do highlight a number of the major issues that have arisen in the implementation of the medical examinations and inquiries requirements of the ADA. As anecdotal evidence, these survey responses give us a general sense of the landscape and a framework in which to address implementation issues.

Modifications in the Application Process

In General Approximately two-thirds of employers responding to the SHRM survey had made some changes in their application materials. The remaining third stated that no modifications were made because their written application materials were already in compliance with ADA requirements.[21]

A common, and certainly the easiest, change was to delete questions that clearly violated the ADA's prohibition on preemployment inquiries. For example, 9 out of 42 employers eliminated questions dealing with the presence of physical limitations, health problems, or previous illnesses.

One employer noted it had removed a question concerning the number of days the applicant had missed from work in previous jobs. The employer was correct, as a legal matter, to remove a question asking how many *sick* days an applicant had used in previous jobs. As the EEOC notes in its May 1994 "Enforcement Guidance," asking for an accounting of sick days missed in the past is tantamount to identifying whether the applicant had previously

86

experienced a significant medical problem.[22] An employer may, however, continue to ask whether an applicant is able to perform the function of coming to work without significant absenteeism. The best approach for the employer, at the preconditional offer stage, is to focus on the job function (i.e., ability to come to work without significant absenteeism) and then use an inquiry or medical examination post offer to confirm that the applicant does not, in fact, have a current, serious medical condition that would cause significant absenteeism.[23]

The same employer noted it had also removed a question about whether the applicant had filed workers' compensation claims. Again, this employer acted appropriately. In the EEOC's *Technical Assistance Manual*, the agency notes that questions regarding workers' compensation may be asked of an applicant *after* a conditional job offer has been extended to the individual.[24] The EEOC repeats this guidance in several Opinion Letters[25] and in its official enforcement guidance notice of May 1994.[26] The rationale is that a question regarding an individual's workers' compensation history is essentially a proxy for obtaining information about a preexisting disability of the individual – something that an employer could not ask about directly.[27]

Only one employer responding to the survey stated it had removed questions regarding workers' compensation or use of sick days. It is possible none of the other employers responding to the survey had such questions to delete. It may also be possible that some employers have not yet realized that such questions need to be deleted and have focused, thus far, on questions that directly ask about the existence or severity of a disability.

The EEOC has filed some suits in the area of medical examinations. In *EEOC* v. *Community Coffee*, the EEOC alleged that the employer inappropriately inquired about an applicant's disability. The applicant, Timothy Burke, did not have control over some facial muscles and one of his eyes did not blink and was sewn halfway shut.[28] The complaint alleges the employer's practices included "making inquiries of Timothy Burke regarding the nature or severity of his perceived disabilities during a preoffer interview." The complaint further alleged that "during a preoffer interview, Timothy Burke was asked about his disability and, among other things, to describe the nature of his disability and whether store managers had a problem dealing with him because of his impairment.''[29]

Physical Requirements and Essential Functions The most common change made by employers in their application materials is a change not directly mandated by the law. Twelve employers noted they revised their materials to set forth the physical requirements of the job at issue.[30] In addition, 10 employers revised their materials to set forth the functions of the job or to include a revised job description or both.

It may well be useful, for purposes of compliance with the ADA, to determine the essential functions of a job before interviewing applicants for a job. As a legal matter, however, the ADA does not mandate that employers develop written job descriptions or written essential functions. Rather, the ADA provides that an employer may not refuse to *hire* an individual because the person's disability prevents him or her from performing a nonessential job function. If employers choose to do so, they may wait until they are faced with a particular applicant who cannot perform a function of a job because of his or her disability. The employer may then assess whether that function which the applicant cannot perform is an ''essential'' job function.

The effort of many employers to develop extensive and detailed job descriptions is probably because the ADA states that ''if an employer has prepared a written job description before advertising or interviewing applicants for the job, this description shall be considered evidence of the essential functions of the job.''[31] But this provision may be having more of an impact than is legally required.

Even if a job description is prepared by an employer after hiring an applicant, the description will still be considered by a court as evidence of essential functions. The ADA provision at issue was inserted in the law solely as an alternative to an amendment that would have given job descriptions prepared *before* interviewing applicants *determinative* weight in assessing the essential functions of the job. That would have significantly altered the state of the law under Section 504 and would have given employers significant power to control the essential function determination.

The provision ultimately accepted as a compromise was a simple restatement of existing Section 504 law; that is, everything, including job descriptions prepared either before or after interviewing applicants, is to be considered "evidence" of essential functions. The provision was not intended to elevate job descriptions prepared before interviewing applicants above all other pieces of information.[32]

As a practical matter, employers may wish to prepare job descriptions prior to the application process for the purpose of engaging supervisors and managers in clarifying the actual functions and goals of a job. But, even if it is useful to develop a list of such functions prior to interviewing, it is not clear it is equally useful to expend significant time and energy determining the exact physical and mental qualifications traditionally used to achieve those goals.

One of the survey returns illustrates this point well. A county government employer returned with its survey response a copy of a "Work Conditions/Physical Abilities Assessment Candidate Questionnaire" it had developed. The questionnaire, four pages long and incredibly detailed, represents significant work on the part of the entity that prepared it and will require yet additional work on the part of those who will fill it out.

Part I of the questionnaire is a "Work Conditions Analysis," "designed to find out about the working conditions that may affect an individual's ability to perform his/her job." The analysis asks about work conditions such as the following: inside (protected from weather); outside (exposed to weather); wetness (contact with water); slippery walking surface; risk of bodily injury; close proximity to coworkers (less than 3 feet); confined spaces and/or cramped bodily conditions; and heights. In each case, the county department official filling out the analysis must state whether these conditions are present a great deal, moderately, occasionally, or never. The analysis also lists 16 types of workplace exposures and asks the department official to rate the amount of such exposures, in categories of never, little, moderate, and great.

Part II of the analysis is a "Physical Abilities Assessment." The department is asked to evaluate, with regard to the essential job duties of a position, the number of hours in a normal workday that the employee is required to sit, stand, walk, and drive. The department official must also evaluate the frequency with which an employee performs various activities such as bending, stooping, lifting, and carrying.

Each applicant is provided the Work Conditions/Physical Abilities Assessment Form, as completed by the department official for the particular position. The applicant is provided the following Candidate Instructions:

> As part of the interview process for the position listed above you will be provided with a copy of the *Work Conditions/ Physical Abilities Assessment Form* for the position. This form describes the working condition and physical requirements of the position. You are asked to review the information on the form and complete this questionnaire. The Unified Personnel System of County Government is using this procedure to ensure compliance with the Americans with Disabilities Act of 1990. Review the *Work Conditions/Physical Abilities Assessment Form* and complete the bottom portion of this questionnaire by checking the single most appropriate box and singing [sic] the questionnaire in the space provided.
>
> *(Note: This section completed by interviewed candidate.)*
>
> I have read (or had read to me) the *Work Conditions/Physical Abilities Assessment Form* for this position and
>
> _____ **Option 1** – I am capable of performing the duties of this position/job as described.
>
> _____ **Option 2** – I am capable of performing the duties of this position/job with the following accommodations:
>
> _____
>
> _____
>
> _____
>
> _____ **Option 3** – I am not capable of performing the duties of this position/job.

I hereby certify that my answers are true and correct to the best of my knowledge.

Signature   Date

The county government may well have developed this form to "assure compliance" with the ADA. However, a form of such complexity and detail may actually be counterproductive for complying with the ADA.

First, there is a danger the county supervisor might become tied too literally to the stated requirements. For example, assume an office has a stack of file cabinets and a secretary in the office currently spends approximately 30 percent of his or her time in a normal workday reaching above shoulder level to get to the files on the top level. A supervisor estimating the overall amount of time the employees spent performing certain physical activities would dutifully note on the form that the secretary's position included reaching above shoulder level 30 percent of the time.

Assume the supervisor is now looking for a new secretary. A candidate with limited upper body mobility, who cannot reach above shoulder level, might apply, read the form, and answering the County Government-type questionnaire truthfully, check Option 3 on the questionnaire: "I am not capable of performing the duties of this position/job." Seeing that box checked, the supervisor may well decide not to interview the candidate.[33]

A candidate who is a person sophisticated in disability law and understands what an "accommodation" means may check Option 2 ("I am capable of performing the duties of this position/job with the following accommodations") and state on the provided lines: "I have limited mobility in my arms and cannot reach above arm level. However, if whatever is above shoulder level is moved down, or if whatever is above shoulder level is something I can reach with a stepstool, then I can perform the duties of this job." Most applicants, of course, are not that versed in the requirements of the ADA or that aware of the scope of the term *accommodation*.

This entire problem could have been averted if the secretary's job had been described as including requiring "ability to file" instead of requiring "reaching above shoulder level 30 percent of the time." In other words, the goals of the ADA are better achieved if the employer focuses on the *job function* that must be performed, rather than on the *physical manner* in which the job function has traditionally been achieved by incumbents in the job. A person with limited upper body mobility could still perform the filing functions of the secretary's job with the simple accommodation of having a stepstool near the filing cabinet.

In its May 1994 guidance on medical examinations and inquiries, the EEOC appears to have focused to some extent on this concern. The EEOC guidance recommends that employers not ask general questions about an applicant's ability to perform major life activities because such questions are "likely to elicit information about a disability," and broad questions about the ability to perform major life activities are unlikely to be considered "specifically about the ability to perform job functions."[34] Rather, the agency recommends that questions about an applicant's ability to perform some major life activity be tied directly to some specific job function of the position.[35]

Setting out the physical requirements of a job may be counterproductive for a second reason. It may force applicants to disclose the presence of a disability by requiring them to ask for a reasonable accommodation prior to a conditional job offer. This issue is discussed in the next subsection.

Questions during the Application Process Regarding Need for Reasonable Accommodation A significant number of employers responding to the surveys (8 out of 42) set forth the physical requirements of the job in the application process and presumably ask applicants if they are able to perform these requirements. An additional six employers specifically ask whether the applicant needs a reasonable accommodation to perform the job.

This trend could be problematic and counter to the goals of the ADA. Even if an employer does not specifically ask whether an applicant needs a reasonable accommodation to perform a physical job requirement, the fact that the employer has framed the application question in terms of the physical *manner* in which a job function is performed – rather than in terms of the applicant's ability to perform the job *function* itself – will inevitably lead to a disclosure of the need for an accommodation as soon as the concept of accommodation is explained to the applicant.

Similarly, an employer who directly asks whether an applicant needs a reasonable accommodation effectively forces that applicant to disclose his or her disability in the course of discussing the need for a reasonable accommodation. Such a discussion should not have to occur before a conditional job offer is extended.

Let us return to the example of the secretary's job. A candidate who understood what an "accommodation" was may have checked Option 2 ("I am capable of performing the duties of this position/ job with the following accommodations") and stated that although limited in upper body mobility in his or her arms and not able to reach above shoulder level, he or she could nevertheless perform the job with an accommodation, such as using a stepstool. The problem with this resolution is that the employer is now aware – prior to extending a conditional job offer – that the applicant has limited upper body mobility. An employer who was inclined to deny such a person the job could do so and hide behind a number of reasons for the job rejection other than the person's limited mobility. In other words, an employer can effectively evade the purpose of the two-stage process with regard to medical inquiries by eliciting information from the applicant regarding a needed reasonable accommodation.

In the initial application stage, the employer may ask candidates whether they can perform the functions of the job, which, as noted, includes filing. A candidate with limited mobility in his or her arms should be allowed to answer a simple "yes" to the question of whether he or she can perform the function of filing. Even the candidate who knows from experience that many filing cabinets are above arm reach should not be required, at this stage of the application process, to inform the employer that he or she can perform the job function of filing only if provided with the accommodation of a stepstool. This type of accommodation is simple enough, and inexpensive enough, that there is no need for extensive conversation with the employer. The fact that the applicant *can* perform the job function of filing is all he or she should be required to tell the employer at the initial application stage.

Assume the employer offers the candidate the job. In some situations, such an offer may be conditioned on a medical exam; in others, it will not. In any event, once a job offer (conditional or otherwise) is extended to the candidate, it is at *that* point that he or she may inform the employer about the limited upper body mobility and the need for a reasonable accommodation. If an effective accommodation is, indeed, feasible (hence "reasonable") and if the effective accommodation does not cause the employer a significant difficulty or expense (hence is not an "undue hardship"), the employer should make that accommodation. Conversely, if no accommodation is effective and feasible (for example, assume the filing cabinets are so high that the current secretary already uses a ladder and still has to reach above shoulder length) or if the accommodation would impose an undue hardship on the employer, then the employer can withdraw the job offer (conditional or not) because the applicant is not able to perform the job function.

By contrast, there are circumstances in which an employer and an applicant should be permitted to discuss the specifics of a reasonable accommodation before a conditional job offer because such a discussion would benefit both parties. For example, if an applicant has a manifest disability that clearly would require an accommodation or if the applicant has volunteered the fact that he or she has a disability that would clearly require an accommodation, the employer and the applicant should be allowed to discuss the type of accommodation that would meet the needs of the applicant and would be consistent with the resources of the employer. Precluding such a discussion would mean employers would have to guess about the type and cost of accommodations required by applicants with manifest disabilities. In practical terms, that may well result in employers assiduously avoiding discussions about reasonable accommodations – but also assiduously avoiding the hiring of applicants with disabilities because of the resulting lack of information. The EEOC enforcement guidance of May 1994 appears to be both overinclusive and underinclusive in its treatment of discussions of reasonable accommodations in the preoffer stage. The guidance sets forth three rules for discussions regarding reasonable accommodation at the preoffer stage:

1. An employer may ask an applicant if he or she can perform specified job-related functions with or without reasonable accommodation and may ask an applicant to describe or dem-

onstrate how he or she would perform job-related functions, with or without reasonable accommodation.[36]

2. At the preoffer stage, an employer may not generally inquire whether the applicant needs a reasonable accommodation for the job. For example, an employer may not ask: "would you need a reasonable accommodation to perform this specific function?"[37]

3. If an applicant voluntarily discloses that he or she would need a reasonable accommodation to perform the job, the employer still may not make inquiries at the preoffer stage about the *type* of required reasonable accommodation (except where the applicant has requested reasonable accommodation as part of a required preoffer job demonstration).[38]

This last rule has concerned employer groups about the scope of permitted discussions regarding reasonable accommodation.[39] In truth, both the first and the third rule presented by EEOC probably need review and modification. When the EEOC initially articulated the first rule in its regulations and interpretive guidance, the agency cited three congressional reports.[40] None of the cited reports, however, stated that applicants may be asked about their need for reasonable accommodations. To the contrary, the reports stated that "[e]mployers may ask questions which relate to the ability to perform job-related functions, but may not ask questions in terms of disability."[41] There is no reference in any of these congressional reports that indicate it is permissible to ask an applicant about a potential need for a reasonable accommodation to perform the job functions.

Therefore, the EEOC's first rule is arguably too expansive, in that it may inadvertently elicit information about disabilities that is not necessary for the employer to know at the preoffer stage. The example noted previously of the secretary and the filing function falls into that category. By contrast, the EEOC's third rule is arguably too restrictive, in that it does not allow discussions that could benefit both applicants with disabilities and employers when the applicant has a manifest disability or has volunteered information about his or her disability. Although the second rule is probably appropriate, an explanation of how that rule fits logically with the other two rules is necessary.

As a general matter, the May 1994 guidance issued by the EEOC in the area of medical examinations and inquiries will be of tremendous assistance in the implementation of the ADA in this area. Given the particular concerns raised with regard to reasonable accommodation questions, however, it is possible the EEOC will modify its guidance on that particular issue.

Provision of Reasonable Accommodations in the Application Process Several employers indicated they had reviewed their application processes to ensure that reasonable accommodations were available for applicants who needed such accommodations. One employer noted it was reviewing its testing procedures, including required use of a keyboard, to determine what changes could be made if necessary. A second employer stated that instructions for the application process were available in alternative formats for applicants with vision or hearing impairments. A third employer noted it had lowered postings on boards for easier viewing by people who use wheelchairs and had bought a TDD (telecommunications device for the deaf) for telephone inquiries from applicants with hearing impairments.

The "EEOC Enforcement Guidelines" discusses reasonable accommodations in the application process.[42] Employers are required to ensure that their application procedures are accessible to applicants with disabilities through the provision of reasonable accommodations that do not impose an undue hardship. If an applicant needs a reasonable accommodation to apply, it is better for the applicant to disclose his or her disability and receive the accommodation than to keep the disability confidential.

As with any reasonable accommodation, an applicant generally must request the accommodation before the employer's duty to provide the accommodation is triggered. Nevertheless, it behooves an employer to anticipate the types of accommodations that may be requested, such as application instructions in an alternate format or job postings that can be viewed by people who use wheelchairs or people of short stature. Some of these accommodations should be in place ahead of time, such as application instructions in alternative formats. Other accommodations that do not impose an undue hardship should be available in an expeditious manner once they are requested.

Use of Medical Examinations

In General The majority of the employers responding to the survey (27 out of 42) require medical examinations as part of their application process. Fifteen employers already administered their medical examinations postoffer and therefore had no need to make any changes in their process as a result of the ADA. Twelve employers moved their examinations postoffer to comply with the ADA.

In response to the question "Have you experienced any difficulty with [moving your medical examinations postoffer]?" only three employers answered in the affirmative. One employer stated it had experienced "minimal difficulty" because of "some delay in hiring." A second employer stated it was "more cumbersome" and that it would probably eliminate the physical exams altogether. A third employer stated the process was more expensive now because its drug tests were still being administered preoffer and there were now two steps in the medical examination process.[43]

It is interesting to note that the placement of medical examinations at the postoffer stage has not seemed to cause much disruption in the application process. Although one employer found the change to be cumbersome, a significant number of employers were already offering their exams postoffer. Because this apparently was not done in response to the ADA, one can only assume these employers had found some utility in having the exams placed at that stage.[44] In addition, as noted, other employers who made the switch did not experience any difficulty with the change.

One employer applied quite literally the ADA requirement that, if medical examinations are required, the exam must be given to "all entering employees."[45] This employer noted it had "formerly required medical exams only for drivers under DOT for [the] mobile medical portion of [its] services," but now "required medical exams for all incoming employees because of the ADA."

This employer is correct that the literal words of the ADA require the same medical exam to be given to "all entering employees," but the legislative history of the ADA and the EEOC regulations clarify that the same medical examination must be given to all employees entering *the same job category*, not to *all* employees entering the business.[46] Thus, the employer at issue could have continued to require a medical exam solely of its drivers and not of all its personnel.

Role of Physicians in the Medical Exam Process Respondents to the survey were asked whether the personnel who perform their medical examinations had "expressed any difficulty or discomfort" in complying with ADA requirements and what interaction, if any, they had with these medical personnel.

Twenty-one employers responded that their medical personnel had expressed no difficulty or discomfort with the ADA requirements regarding medical examinations. Of these, 13 employers were silent on the issue of their interaction with medical personnel and 4 employers stated they had no interaction with the medical personnel. Five employers responded they had significant interaction with the medical personnel; two of these employers noted their medical personnel had attended ADA seminars or trainings.

Three employers responded that their medical personnel had expressed difficulty. One employer stated that, because the medical personnel were unfamiliar with every aspect of the operation, they were "hesitant to say that an applicant was unfit for employment." This employer noted that the medical personnel had been sent copies of the employees' job descriptions. A second employer responded that there "has been a change in the willingness of medical personnel to commit to someone's lack of ability to perform the essential job functions." A third employer responded that the company physician went to an ADA seminar and was "uncomfortable with the liability aspect."

It is unclear how much can be extrapolated from these responses. On one hand, it is not a bad consequence that physicians may be more circumspect now in concluding whether an applicant cannot perform a job. Historically, applicants with even minor disabilities, who could perform the essential functions of the job, were screened out by company physicians seeking to keep workers' compensations costs as low as possible. The ADA creates a direct counterincentive to this practice by imposing liability on employers who allow their physicians to engage in such practices.

On the other hand, physicians should not recommend an applicant for a job that the applicant cannot, in fact, perform. The solution for employers may be to expend some time and money educating medical personnel about the nature of the jobs and the types of reasonable accommodations that may be available. In most cases, sending job descriptions to the medical personnel should be sufficient. In some cases, however, more direct interaction may be necessary.

Employers and medical personnel should be aware that liability under the ADA for discrimination falls on the employer not on the medical personnel. It is the employer's obligation to inform the medical personnel about the nature of the job, the functions that need to be achieved, and the physical manner in which those functions have ordinarily been performed. The medical personnel administer the medical examination or inquiry and relay their findings back to the employer.[47] If the medical personnel conclude that an applicant cannot perform the job, the responsibility shifts back to the employer to determine whether a reasonable accommodation would enable the applicant to perform the job and would not be an undue hardship. Although the employer may want to consult with the medical personnel in this analysis, the key person for the employer to talk to at this stage is the applicant. Ultimately, the decision as to whether an accommodation is feasible and not an undue hardship rests with the employer not the applicant.[48] Of course, as a final matter, the determination rests with a court.

Similar responsibility on the part of the employer exists if the medical personnel conclude an applicant would pose a direct threat to his or her own health or safety or to the health or safety of others. Once the medical personnel make this decision, it is the employer's responsibility to ensure the physician's determination is not speculative and no reasonable accommodation exists to mitigate the risk. If a court decides there was no direct threat, liability for that decision will rest with the employer, not with the medical personnel.

Drug Tests Although questions regarding drug tests tend to abound during ADA seminars, not much discussion of such tests was reported in the survey responses. As noted, one employer stated the medical examination process was more expensive now because drug tests were administered preoffer and the rest of the medical exam was administered postoffer. Another employer, however, noted that both its drug test and medical exam were offered postoffer. A third employer stated it had deleted the medical questionnaire from its application process but had retained its drug test "preemployment."[49]

One employer included the consent and release form it uses for its "preemployment drug screen." The form requires applicants to list all the drugs and medications they are taking. Applicants are asked for the name of the drug, the condition they are taking the drug for, and the name of their prescribing physician.

These questions are presumably asked by the employer to provide a valid explanation for an applicant whose drug test result is positive as a result of legally prescribed medications. It is illegal under the ADA, however, to ask these questions pre offer as a general matter – as they are tantamount to asking the individual if he or she has a disability.[50]

The EEOC, in its "Enforcement Guidelines," presents a new solution to the problem of applicants whose drug test results are positive as a result of legally prescribed medications. In its Interpretative Guidance to the regulations, the EEOC had recommended that if employers receive information from a drug test about an individual's medical condition, beyond whether the individual is currently engaging in the illegal use of drugs, that additional information should be treated as confidential.[51] In the "Enforcement Guidelines," the EEOC goes further and provides that only if an applicant tests positive for the illegal use of drugs may an employer validate the test results by inquiring as to lawful drug use or other biomedical explanations for the positive result.[52]

This recommendation from the EEOC may well be challenged by plaintiff lawyers in the future. The Committee Reports to the ADA take a different approach to the dilemma posed by drug tests that identify the presence of legally prescribed medication pre offer. The House Education and Labor Report suggests that, to resolve the dilemma, all drug tests should be either given post offer or be strictly restricted to the screening of illegal use of drugs.[53] Although these solutions may seem unduly burdensome to employers, it is worth noting the conflict between the EEOC's approach and that of the ADA's legislative history.

Even when an employer administers a *postoffer* drug test to applicants, it may be prudent for employers not to ask applicants broad-ranging questions about medications the applicants are taking. Instead, an employer may be well advised to wait until a drug test result is actually positive before asking an applicant to list the legally prescribed medications he or she is taking.

For example, a drug test will not show a positive response because an applicant is taking psychotropic drugs, such as Prozac or Zoloft, if the employer does not ask the laboratory to screen for those drugs. If the employer, nevertheless, asks the applicant to list *all* medications he or she is taking and the applicant discloses use of a psychotropic drug, the employer will then be in possession of information that the employer must keep confidential. If that sensitive information is later disclosed in violation of the ADA's confidentiality requirements, the employer will be liable.[54] If the drug test would not show up positive as a result of those drugs in any event, there is no reason for the employer to ask such a broad-based question.

REASONABLE ACCOMMODATIONS

A key component of the ADA is the requirement that employers provide reasonable accommodations to a person with a disability, if such accommodations are necessary to enable the person to perform a job. This requirement may be described as follows:

> The second component of a "qualified person with a disability" is that of reasonable accommodation. A person with a disability is often qualified to perform a job – if some adjustment is first made in the structure, schedule, physical layout, or equipment [of the job]. For example, a person who uses a wheelchair may need a table adjusted for height or may need a ramp built to allow access. Persons with varying degrees of hearing impairments may need a telephone amplifier or an interpreter. Someone with a chronic physical condition may need some time off each week for medical treatments. If these adjustments or modifications – which are called "reasonable accommodations" – are made, a person with a disability might then be qualified for the particular job he or she seeks.[55]

The ADA sets a limit on an employer's obligation to provide a reasonable accommodation. An accommodation need not be provided if doing so would impose an "undue hardship" on the employer. The law defines an *undue hardship* as something that would result in a "significant difficulty or expense" for the employer.[56]

The reasonable accommodation requirement was the subject of much debate during passage of the ADA. Despite the "undue hardship" limitation, employers feared they would be required to spend a significant amount of money on reasonable accommodations. Moreover, employers were concerned they would not be able to discern the types of reasonable accommodations they would need to provide and would not be able to judge accurately when an accommodation would be considered an undue hardship.

Employers' concerns with the reasonable accommodation requirement led to a number of alternatives being proposed during passage of the ADA for an approach that would provide more certainty for employers.[57] In the final analysis, Congress chose to continue a flexible approach that takes into account various factors, including the size of the business and the cost of the accommodation.[58]

It is interesting to use the SHRM survey results as anecdotal evidence of employer experiences with reasonable accommodation.[59] Employers were asked for the following information:

1.   Whether, in the past six months, the company had received a request from an applicant or employee with a disability for a reasonable accommodation;
2.   How the accommodation requests were resolved and whether there were financial or operational costs in resolving the requests;
3.   Whether workplace modifications to make the company more accessible had been made without a request for an accommodation; and
4.   What difficulties the employer foresaw in providing reasonable accommodations as required by the ADA.

Sixteen employers responded they had received one or more requests for a reasonable accommodation. Twenty employers responded they had not received any requests. Of those 20, 11 noted they had made workplace modifications in the absence of any requests.[60]

The ADA sets forth seven types of reasonable accommodations that might be required by people with disabilities. These include modifying the physical layout of a job facility, restructuring a job, establishing modified work schedules, moving a person to a vacant position, acquiring or modifying equipment or devices, modifying policies, and providing readers or interpreters.[61]

The provision of a reasonable accommodation is tied to the specific, unique needs of an individual with a disability:

> The basic characteristic of a reasonable accommodation is that it is designed to address the unique needs of a person with a particular disability. Thus, an accommodation for one person might be one that falls within one of the above categories, or it might be a different type of accommodation personally identified by the person with a disability or by the employer. The underlying goal is to identify aspects of the disability that make it difficult or impossible for the person with a disability to perform certain aspects of a job, and then to determine if there are any modifications or adjustments to the job environment or structure that will enable the person to perform the job.[62]

As might be expected, there was no "common" reasonable accommodation in the survey responses. Rather, the accommodations provided reflect the particular needs of different employees and applicants.[63]

Four modifications dealt with modifying the physical layout of a workstation. One employer made workplace modifications at "modest costs";[64] a second employer installed a wheelchair lift; and a third employer repositioned a workstation so as to cut down on noise for an employee with a hearing impairment. A fourth employer moved an employee to a different location to deal with a sight problem.

Two modifications fell into the category of restructuring the manner in which jobs were performed. One employer added additional people to assist in "patient lifting," and a second employer stated it had "redeveloped" some jobs.[65]

Three modifications dealt with modifying work schedules. One employer changed shifts for employees; a second employer established "different time limits"; and a third employer allowed an employee with diabetes additional break time.

Two modifications fell into the category of reassignment. One employer reassigned a nurse to a different department, and a second employer assigned an employee to light duty work.

Five modifications dealt with the provision of equipment and devices. One employer bought various equipment, including computers and CCTVs; a second employer bought a TDD for a deaf employee; a third employer bought a trackball mouse for a computer for an employee with limited hand mobility; and two employers bought a phone headset and a speaker phone, respectively, for employees with hearing impairments.

No modifications dealt with changing policies or training materials.[66] Two accommodations consisted of providing interpreters – one to an employee and one to an applicant.

Almost all employers noted that provision of the accommodations had cost them either nothing or a minimal amount. The winner in the high cost category for reasonable accommodations was an employer who bought various equipment, including computers and CCTVs. This employer noted the cost for its accommodations ranged from $0 to $6,000. The employer also noted that state agencies or insurance companies or both had helped to pay for the more expensive items.

Again, it is important to emphasize that these SHRM survey results serve primarily as anecdotal evidence; they do not represent statistically valid conclusions. Nevertheless, the survey results are consistent with the findings of a more extensive survey undertaken by the Job Accommodation Network (JAN) during the 1 April–30 June 1993 period. In that survey response of 111 employers, JAN found that 19 percent of the accommodations cost nothing; 50 percent cost under $500 and 12 percent cost between $501 and $1,000.[67]

A significant number of employers had made workplace modifications without receiving a specific request for a reasonable accommodation. Thirteen employers responded they had made such modifications but provided no details. For the various modifications for which details were provided, all concerned making the physical layout of the workplace more accessible. They included bathroom renovations, provision of designated parking spaces, automatic door openers, office partitions, accessible drinking fountains, and ergonomic workstations. One human resources manager replied she had requested that her office be made accessible "just in case" it was necessary.

Human resource managers were asked in the survey: "What difficulties do you foresee in providing reasonable accommodations as required by the ADA?" Seventeen employers responded they did not foresee any difficulties in providing reasonable accommodations. Of these, 8 employers had actually received and responded to a reasonable accommodation request; 13 employers had made some workplace modifications in the absence of a request; and only 2 employers had neither received a request nor made any modifications voluntarily.

Of the employers who responded they did foresee difficulties, fear of cost took the lead. Eight employers responded they could foresee difficulties in the cost of complying with the ADA's reasonable accommodation requirements. Of this group, four employers had never received or responded to a request for a reasonable accommodation and three of those four employers had also not made any voluntary modifications. The remaining four employers had received and responded to a request for a reasonable accommodation.

What is interesting in this difference between the two categories of employers – that is, between those who had responded to an actual request for a reasonable accommodation and those who had not – was the way in which the employers' concerns were framed. The four employers who had neither received nor responded to a reasonable accommodation request simply stated flatly they were afraid of "cost." By contrast, the employers who had actually received a request for an accommodation had more nuanced comments. One employer noted a foreseeable difficulty was "possibly costs"; a second employer noted there might be future costs in modifying the methods used by its packagers; a third employer, who had provided an interpreter, noted it might be difficult to define the limits of the requirement; and a fourth employer noted the definition of *reasonable* might be difficult.[68]

The next leading contender for future difficulties was that the law was ambiguous and difficult to interpret. What is most interesting about this response is that only four employers responded with this concern. This is in striking contrast to the period of time when the ADA was being enacted, during which this concern was voiced repeatedly. It is perhaps also instructive to note that, of these four employers, none had received or responded to a request for a reasonable accommodation and only one of the four had made any voluntary modifications.

Three employers stated they could foresee difficulties in the reaction of coworkers, with two of the three specifically mentioning potential conflicts with union workers. Of these three employers, two had never responded to a reasonable accommodation request or made voluntary modifications. One employer had responded to a reasonable accommodation request and had made voluntary modifications.

Like the survey responses, letters from employers to the EEOC requesting guidance on reasonable accommodation do not focus primarily on concerns regarding costs. Although two letters asked about financial concerns,[69] far more common were questions evidencing concern about how to balance competing interests among coworkers, clients, landlords, and unions.

For example, a number of letters asked about the obligation to provide accommodations that would affect the entire workplace – such as smoke-free work environments for employees sensitive to smoke, special allowances for smokers, and fragrance-free environments for employees with chemical sensitivity.[70] One letter asked whether service animals must be allowed in the workplace to accommodate an employee with a disability. Presumably, the employer was concerned that the service animal would be disruptive to other employees or to customers.[71] Another letter, inquiring about restroom modifications, was concerned with the fact that the building owner leasing to the employer had objected to the modifications.[72] Finally, one letter inquired about how to reassign an employee to a vacant position without conflicting with a collective bargaining agreement.[73]

As can be seen from these letters, a major concern on the part of employers is how to balance different interests among coworkers, clients, and people with disabilities. This is often a key aspect of reasonable accommodation. Ensuring that an accommodation works equally well for a person with a disability, that person's coworkers, and that person's employer usually requires a commitment on the part of the employer to create a "team effort" for the provision of the accommodation.[74]

Published cases regarding reasonable accommodation provide another glimpse of the type of issues facing employers and people with disabilities in this area. Of course, the cases that have proceeded to trial and have resulted in judicial opinions presumably reflect only a small percentage of the actual number of accommodation requests that have been made and resolved in the employment setting.

Many of the cases under the ADA concerning reasonable accommodation reflect points of law already established in cases brought under Section 504 of the Rehabilitation Act of 1973. For example, a federal district court in *Reigel* v. *Kaiser Foundation Health Plan of North Carolina*[75] ruled that the ADA's reasonable accommodation obligation did not require an employer to make fundamental or substantial modifications in its operations and did not require an employer to hire two individuals to do the tasks ordinarily assigned to one.[76] Similarly, in *Larkins* v. *CIBA Vision Corp.*,[77] a federal district court ruled that an employer had not violated its reasonable accommodation obligations when the only effective accommodation for the employee with the disability would have been to eliminate the essential function of handling customer telephone calls.[78]

A number of interesting cases have concerned the issue of reasonable accommodation and absenteeism. Thus far, the published cases appear to strike the balance desired by Congress. In cases where an employer has made serious efforts to accommodate an employee with a disability, but an employee's absenteeism as a result of his or her disability continues to seriously affect workplace production, the courts have upheld the rights of an employer to fire such an individual.[79] By contrast, courts have required that employers make an effort to accommodate an employee's need for a flexible work schedule when that accommodation would not unduly burden the employer's workplace operations.[80]

It is not unusual to find, among the published cases, situations in which courts determine that employers have made all the accommodations that could reasonably be expected of an employer and that the further demands of the employee are not required by the ADA. One example can be found in *Harmer* v. *Virginia Electric and Power Co.*[81] In that case, Robert Harmer, an employee with bronchial asthma requested that his employer, Virginia Power, declare the entire building smoke free to accommodate his disability.[82]

Virginia Power had provided several accommodations for Harmer in the building, such as fans, smokeless ashtrays, and air purifiers. It had also moved smoking employees away from Harmer and had barred smoking in the rest rooms, conference rooms, and hallways on Harmer's floor, limiting smoking to the smokers' cubicles. It had prohibited smoking in elevators, cashier and service lines, and cafeterias (except for designated smoking areas), auditoriums, stairways, and hallways, and had authorized individual managers to adopt additional smoking restrictions if needed.[83] Finally, Virginia Power had announced it would bar smoking in all facilities, except in specially constructed smoking rooms, but wished first to weigh the benefits of this further accommodation against the potential effects on the morale and productivity of smoking employees.[84]

The court ruled against Harmer, concluding the ADA did not require Virginia Power to declare the building smoke free. The court concluded that Harmer had not shown that the accommodations made by Virginia Power were insufficient and had not shown that a smoke-free building was necessary to enable him to perform the essential functions of his job.[85]

On the other side of the spectrum are situations in which an employee with a disability claims an employer has attempted to force him or her out of employment by deliberately not making accommodations. For example, a complaint filed in the case of *Smith* v. *South Carolina Budget and Control Bd.*[86] alleges that the supervisor of an employee with multiple sclerosis deliberately changed her duties to make it more difficult for her to function at her job. Smith was employed as a data management and research analyst, with duties involving no significant moving, walking, or other physical activity. Eight days after she notified her employer that she was diagnosed with multiple sclerosis, Smith's supervisor removed her from her private office and relocated her work station to a reception area. Her duties were changed to include strenuous physical activities such as running errands, walking long distances, and mailing packages. One month later, Smith's supervisor suggested she take medical retirement. The supervisor refused to give Smith back her old job and duties. Smith's doctor gave written notice to the employer that Smith was capable of performing her original duties as a research analyst, that disability retirement was not justified, that continuing work would be therapeutic, and that her new duties would worsen her condition. Despite this recommendation, the employer did not change Smith's duties. After a year, Smith resigned.[87]

Despite these extremes of activity on the part of both employees and employers, most requests for reasonable accommodation are probably dealt with by employers in a considerate manner. The key is for employers to overcome their initial fears that the ADA obligation will overwhelm them financially and operationally. As one employer expressed it in the survey response, in response to the question: "What difficulties do you foresee in providing reasonable accommodations as required by the ADA?":

> None really. At first, the entire issue was a little scary but as you get into it, you find that they aren't asking for the world, but rather minor, relatively inexpensive renovations that are easily enough done. We also have a great source of support here in our area in terms of people who can offer good sound advice about how to accommodate something.

HEALTH INSURANCE

The issue of what the ADA requires in the area of health insurance has been the subject of much debate and commentary.[88] There is universal agreement that the ADA prohibits an employer from refusing to hire a person with a disability because of fear of increased health insurance costs.[89] The more complicated question, however, is what measures an employer may legitimately take under the ADA to restrain overall health care costs in its health plan after it hires individuals who may require extensive health care.

Prohibition of Discrimination in Employment Benefits

Title I of the ADA contains several provisions governing an employer's obligations with regard to the provision of health care benefits to its employees. The title's general rule provides that: "No covered entity shall discriminate against a qualified person with a disability because of the disability of such individual in regard to job application procedures, the hiring, advancement, or discharge of employees, employee compensation, job training, *and other terms, conditions, and privileges of employment.''*[90]

Unlike the Age Discrimination in Employment Act, in which the Supreme Court concluded that the phrase "other terms, conditions, and privileges of employment" referred solely to non-fringe benefit terms and conditions of employment,[91] the ADA clearly envisioned that fringe benefits would be covered under the statute's antidiscrimination provision. In the "construction" section immediately following the general rule, the statute provides that: "[T]he term 'discriminate' includes . . . participating in a contractual or other arrangement or relationship that has the effect of subjecting a covered entity's qualified applicant or employee with a disability to the discrimination prohibited by this title (*such relation includes a relationship with . . . an organization providing fringe benefits to an employee of the covered entity. . . .)*''[92]

The "construction" section of the ADA also provides that: "[T]he term discriminate includes . . . limiting, segregating, or classifying a job applicant or employee in a way that adversely affects the opportunities or status of such applicant or employee because of the disability of such applicant or employee.''[93] This provision is used by both the Committee Reports to the ADA and by the EEOC regulations as another source of the prohibition against discrimination in health benefits. The rationale is that restrictions in health insurance plans may inappropriately "classify" employees in a way that adversely affects their employment opportunities or status.

Absent any other provision in the ADA, the reasonable implication from these provisions would be that any "covered entity"[94] under Title I may not provide health insurance benefits to its employees that discriminate in any form against employees with disabilities. That, in fact, is not the case under the ADA. A separate insurance exception in the ADA allows covered entities to take actions in their benefit plans that have an adverse impact on people with disabilities.[95] Nevertheless, these provisions of Title I are the starting point for any analysis regarding discrimination in the provision of health benefits.

Prohibition of Discrimination by Insurance Companies

Although this chapter focuses on the provision of insurance in the employment context, it is important to note that insurance companies are covered independently under Title III of the ADA, the public accommodations title. Public accommodations, as defined in the ADA, include any private service establishment whose operations affect commerce.[96] Insurance offices are explicitly mentioned in the ADA as an example of a covered service establishment.[97]

The general rule of Title III provides that "No individual shall be discriminated against on the basis of disability in the full and equal enjoyment of the goods, services, privileges, advantages or accommodations of any place of public accommodation by any person who owns, leases (or leases to) or operates a place of public accommodation."[98]

The "construction" section of the ADA explains that the discrimination prohibited by the general rule includes "subject[ing] an individual or class of individuals on the basis of disability . . . directly or through contractual, licensing or other arrangements, to a *denial of the opportunity* of the individual or class to participate in or benefit from the goods, services, facilities, privileges, advantages, or accommodations of an entity."[99]

The "construction" section also notes that the discrimination prohibited by the general rule includes "afford[ing] an individual or class of individuals on the basis of disability . . . directly or through contractual, licensing, or other arrangements with the opportunity to participate in or benefit from a good, service, privilege, advantage, or accommodation that is *not equal to* that afforded to other individuals."[100]

Again, absent the insurance exception in the ADA described later, the reasonable implication from these provisions would be that an insurance company could not, under Title III, refuse to provide health insurance benefits to a customer based on his or her disability or provide unequal health insurance coverage based on a customer's disability. In fact, insurance companies do have leeway because of the ADA's insurance exception. Nevertheless, as with employment, these provisions of Title III are the starting point for any analysis regarding discrimination on the part of insurance companies.

The Insurance Exception

A Brief Introduction The insurance exception in the ADA is far from a model of legislative clarity. It was, nevertheless, the final result of a series of negotiations between the disability community, the insurance companies, and Senate sponsors of the ADA.

The ADA, as first introduced in the 101st Congress, did not include an insurance exception.[101] Lawyers for the insurance industry, however, were quick to discern the implications of the Title I and Title III provisions. Without some modification, the statutory language could easily be interpreted as requiring major and significant changes in the way the insurance industry operated. Any differential treatment based on disability could be called into question. The use of limitations based on preexisting conditions, the use of annual and lifetime caps, and the use of limitations on reimbursement of medical treatments and procedures were all time-honored insurance practices that have a disparate impact on people with disabilities.[102] Absent some clarification, argued lawyers for the insurance industry, the ADA could undermine the entire practice of insurance.

The disability community did not have enough political clout to achieve the goal of completely restructuring the private insurance industry. It did have sufficient clout, however, to negotiate language that would achieve some protection against unjustified insurance discrimination targeted at selected, vulnerable disabilities.

The final language of the insurance exception was as follows:

> Titles I through IV of this Act shall not be construed to prohibit or restrict —
> (1) an insurer, hospital or medical service company, health maintenance organization, or any agent, or entity that administers benefit plans, or similar organizations from underwriting risks, classifying risks, or administering such risks that are based on or not inconsistent with State law; or
> (2) a person or organization covered by this chapter from establishing, sponsoring, observing or administering the terms of a bona fide benefit plan that are based on underwriting risks, classifying risks, or administering such risks that are based on or not inconsistent with State law; or
> (3) a person or organization covered by this Act from establishing, sponsoring, observing or administering the terms of a bona

fide benefit plan that is not subject to State laws that regulate insurance.
Paragraphs (1), (2), and (3) shall not be used as a subterfuge to evade the purposes of subchapters I and III.[103]

Paragraphs 1, 2, and 3 were developed primarily by the insurance companies, with some minor tinkering by lawyers for the disability community and by Senate staff.[104] The language of these provisions therefore reflects the lingo and terminology of the insurance industry. The basic requirements of these provisions are not onerous: insurance plans have to be bona fide and have to be consistent either with state laws governing the plans or with requirements of the Employee Retirement and Income Security Act (ERISA).

The last sentence of the provision – that insurance plans could not be used as a subterfuge to evade the purposes of the ADA – was written jointly by insurance industry lawyers, Senate staff, and disability community lawyers. In addition, Senate Labor Committee report language explaining the meaning of the subterfuge provision was negotiated, line by line, among all parties.[105]

The key purpose of this legislative history was to lay out the parameters of what the negotiating parties accepted as legitimate and illegitimate insurance practices under the ADA. For example, courts could have broadly interpreted the antisubterfuge provision as prohibiting the use of any preexisting condition clauses or prohibiting the imposition of low annual caps for all medical conditions, because such insurance provisions make an overall employment package less attractive to individuals with disabilities and could be seen as a subterfuge against hiring such individuals. At the other end of the spectrum, subterfuge could have been given a cramped interpretation by the courts, so as to prohibit almost no discriminatory insurance practices. The role of the committee reports, therefore, was to provide examples to explicate the antisubterfuge provision as understood by the parties to the negotiation.[106]

The sections that follow analyze the various practices that were viewed as legitimate or illegitimate by the legislative committees. The position of the EEOC and DOJ, as set forth in their regulations, technical assistance manuals, and official guidance, is also included with regard to each practice. Finally, to the extent litigation has begun with regard to these practices, that litigation is described.

Refusal to Hire and Decision to Fire Under the ADA, an employer may not refuse to hire an applicant with a disability because that person's disability might increase the employer's health insurance costs. Nor may an employer fire, or otherwise penalize, an employee with a disability because health care for that person's disability increases costs for the employer.

These requirements regarding hiring and firing were set out in each of the three committee reports dealing with the issue. The Senate Labor and Human Resources Committee states: "[A]n employer could not deny a qualified applicant a job because the employer's current insurance plan does not cover the person's disability or because of the increased costs of the insurance."[107]

The EEOC spells out this requirement as well. In its section on "defenses," the EEOC regulations provide "It may be a defense to a charge of disparate treatment brought under [the ADA] that the challenged action is justified by a legitimate, nondiscriminatory reason."[108] In its Interpretive Guidance to this regulation, the EEOC explains "The fact that an individual's disability is not covered by the employer's current insurance plan or would cause the employer's insurance premiums or workers' compensation costs to increase, would not be a legitimate nondiscriminatory reason justifying disparate treatment of an individual with a disability."[109]

This requirement makes sense. A person with a disability, defined in the ADA as a person with a physical or mental impairment that substantially limits one or more major life activities, is more likely on average to incur greater health care costs than a person without a disability. If employers could refuse to hire applicants with disabilities or could fire employees who develop disabilities simply because of an anticipated or real increase in health care costs, a huge loophole would be created in the ADA's employment protection for people with disabilities.

The employer's obligation not to discriminate against an individual with a disability because of a possible increase in health care costs also extends to a possible increase in health care costs as a result of the disability of an individual's dependent.[110] This obligation is derived from the provision of the ADA that prohibits "excluding or otherwise denying equal jobs or benefits to a qualified individual because of the known disability of an individual with whom the qualified individual is known to have a relationship or association."[111]

Obviously, it is difficult for an applicant with a manifest disability, such as a person missing a limb or a person who is blind, to prove he or she was not hired because the employer feared increased health insurance costs. Even if that is the determining factor, an intelligent employer will proffer any number of seemingly legitimate nondiscriminatory reasons for the failure to hire a particular applicant among a large pool. Only a "smoking gun" proving the employer's illegitimate motivation could enable the applicant to prevail in court.

For an applicant with a nonmanifest disability, however, such as HIV infection, diabetes, a heart condition, or a bad back, the two-step process of medical examinations and inquiries may enable the person to pinpoint if the disability was a motivating factor in the failure to hire.[112] In such cases, it may be easier to prove that the employer inappropriately took into account the health care costs that the disability might generate.

One of the cases filed in federal court, *Gifford* v. *Spartan Tool and Manufacturing Inc.*,[113] alleged that an employee was penalized in the terms and conditions of employment, and then constructively discharged, because of health insurance costs generated by his disability. Bruce Gifford worked for Spartan Tool, a parts manufacturer for the aircraft and defense industry, for 14 years, ultimately working his way up to the position of vice president. Gifford's work consistently received praise and he was informed he would take over the company when the present president left.

One year before his promotion to vice president, Gifford developed sinus lymphoma, a form of cancer. Three years later, Gifford developed sarcoma of the sinus, also a form of cancer. Eight months after finding out about Gifford's sarcoma, the president reduced Gifford's weekly salary from $1,250 per week to $670. According to the complaint, the president claimed that Gifford's cancer was causing high health insurance costs for the company, because only one insurance company would cover Gifford.

One month later, the president raised Gifford's salary to $900 per week. In the intervening month, Spartan Tool had been named a "preferred supplier" by one of its principal clients, Pratt and Whitney, a designation important to the company's business. In a letter informing Spartan Tool of the designation, Pratt and Whitney specifically mentioned its appreciation of the work performed by Gifford.

Approximately seven months later, Gifford underwent surgery related to his cancer. Gifford's doctor cleared him to return to work, stating that Gifford was able to perform all of his prior duties. The president, however, informed Gifford that he was being "granted" a leave of absence for six months and that Gifford's pay would be reduced to $400 per week during this period. In addition, $93.45 would be deducted every week from the $400 to pay premiums for Gifford's share of medical insurance. The president also demanded a written authorization from Gifford to release all of his medical records to the company.[114]

If the facts alleged in the complaint are true, Spartan Tool has violated the ADA. An employee with a disability who remains qualified for his or her job may not be fired or placed on involuntary leave because of the employer's concern regarding increased health insurance costs. Moreover, an employee with a disability may not be required to pay for his or her health insurance in a manner different from other employees. Although an employer may make overall changes in a health insurance plan to reduce costs,[115] an employer may not provide unequal access to the company's health insurance for a person with a disability. Deducting additional money from an employee's salary to pay health insurance premiums is equivalent to providing "unequal access" to the employer's health insurance plan.[116] As of this writing, two other cases have been filed in federal court.[117]

Use of Preexisting Condition Clauses One of the basic means used by employers to keep health insurance costs down is that of time-limited preexisting condition clauses.[118] These clauses vary from contract to contract. Ordinarily, an insurance plan will not reimburse for the treatment costs of a medical condition that a person either had before being covered by the plan or for which a person received treatment within a set period of time before being covered by the plan. The length of the exclusion for reimbursement varies from 6 to 18 months.

All three committee reports specifically provide that preexisting condition clauses in health insurance plans remain valid under the ADA. As noted previously, even time-limited preexisting condition clauses could have been viewed as a subterfuge for evading the purposes of the law because they make an employment opportunity less attractive to a person with a disability affected by that exclusion. To counter that interpretation, each committee report contains a sentence along the following lines:

> The ADA does not, however, affect pre-existing condition clauses included in insurance policies offered by employers. Thus, employers may continue to offer policies that contain pre-existing condition exclusions, even though such exclusions adversely affect persons with disabilities, so long as such clauses are not used as a subterfuge to evade the purposes of this legislation.[119]

Thus, the use of uniform preexisting condition clauses that limit coverage for a specified period of time are not considered a subterfuge under the ADA. The type of preexisting clauses that may run afoul of the subterfuge limitation are those that exclude coverage for only one disability or for a class of disabilities, either for a limited time period or for the entire length of the insurance plan coverage.[120]

Limitations on Treatments and Procedures Another basic technique used by employers to restrain health insurance costs is to limit coverage for certain procedures or limit coverage for particular treatments to a specified number per year. As with preexisting condition clauses, these limitations could have been viewed as a subterfuge for evading the purposes of the law because they, like preexisting condition clauses, make an employment opportunity less attractive to a person with a disability affected by those limitations. All three committee reports state, however, that such limitations are not invalidated by the ADA.[121] The restrictions, however, must be uniformly applied to all insured individuals.[122]

Differential Treatment of One Disability or Class of Disabilities During negotiations on the ADA, disability lawyers, including myself, recognized that basic insurance practices, such as uniform preexisting condition clauses or uniform limitations on treatments and procedures, could not realistically be invalidated. Although such limitations adversely affect people with disabilities, outlawing such practices would require a major overhaul of insurance industry practices.

There were certain insurance practices, however, that disability lawyers were interested in outlawing under the ADA. These were practices that singled out one disability, or a class of disabilities, for discriminatory treatment – without any justification for treating that disability, or class of disabilities, differently from other disabilities.

The key sentence, finally agreed to by all parties to the negotiation, and placed in each committee report in the section explaining the meaning of *subterfuge*, was the following:

> [W]hile a plan which limits certain kinds of coverage based on classification of risks would be allowed under this section, the plan may not refuse to insure, or refuse to continue to insure, or limit the amount, extent, or kind of coverage available to an individual, or charge a different rate for the same coverage solely because of a physical or mental impairment, except where the refusal, limitation, or rate differential is based on sound actuarial principles or is related to actual or reasonably anticipated experience.[123]

In other words, although limits on treatments and procedures applied uniformly to people with all disabilities were to be allowed, an employer would not be allowed to deny coverage completely for one disability or to treat that disability differently from others, unless that "refusal, limitation, or rate differential is based on sound actuarial principles or is related to actual or reasonably anticipated experience."[124]

The Interpretive Guidance to the EEOC regulations, and the EEOC Technical Assistance Manual repeated most of the major points of the legislative history without further explication.[125] Finally, in response to repeated requests for additional guidance, the EEOC issued an official notice on 8 June 1993, titled "Interim Enforcement Guidance on the Application of the Americans with Disabilities Act of 1990 to Disability-Based Distinctions in Employer

Provided Health Insurance" ("Enforcement Guidance"). This "Enforcement Guidance" set forth, for the first time, a clear statement of the EEOC's position on employer obligations with regard to the provision of health insurance.[126]

The EEOC set forth a two-part framework for analyzing whether a challenged provision of an employer-provided health plan violates the ADA. First, the EEOC would determine whether the challenged provision included a "disability-based distinction."[127] Second, if the provision included such a distinction, the EEOC would determine whether the provision fell within the protective ambit of the ADA's insurance exception based on a nonexclusive list of potential business or insurance justifications.[128]

The fact that a challenged provision must include a disability-based distinction to violate the ADA is a matter of common sense. The only thing the ADA prohibits are actions that discriminate on the basis of disability. Consider, for example, a law firm that decides to offer better health insurance benefits to lawyers born in California and Oregon. Although some might consider this a strange and inappropriate policy, it would not violate the ADA. People with disabilities are born in California and Oregon – and in the rest of the United States. This is not a disability-based distinction.

What is interesting, however, is the EEOC's definition of a disability-based distinction. According to the "Enforcement Guidance," "broad distinctions, which apply to the treatment of a multitude of dissimilar conditions and which constrain individuals both *with and without disabilities*, are not distinctions based on disability."[129] The EEOC offers two examples of non-disability-based distinctions: (1) a plan in which lower benefits are provided for the treatment of mental or nervous conditions than are provided for the treatment of physical conditions; and (2) a plan that provides fewer benefits for "eye care" than for other physical conditions.[130]

Although the EEOC does not provide any further explication of why these are not disability-based distinctions, the agency's rationale appears to be as follows. First, a provision providing lesser benefits for mental disorders covers a "multitude of dissimilar conditions." In addition, restrictions on mental health coverage affect *both* people with disabilities (i.e., people with mental impairments that limit some life activity) and people without disabilities (i.e., people with mental stress who do not have limitations in their life activities). For example, people who enter marriage counseling may have mental stress in their relationship but are not substantially limited in their life activities. Similarly, although restrictions on general eye care would affect people with disabilities (i.e., people whose eye impairments, uncorrected, significantly limit the major life activity of seeing), it presumably also affects people without disabilities (i.e., people without eye impairments who go for general eye check-ups and people whose eye impairments, uncorrected, are sufficiently minor so not to significantly limit their major life activity of seeing).

The EEOC's approach in this regard seems more a prudent response to the political winds than a persuasive legal document. Most people who enter mental health therapy probably experience some limitation in their daily activities. People often suffer either depression or anxiety, the most common forms of mental impairments, for years but may enter treatment only when they experience some limitation in their daily lives. Of even greater importance, if a differential limitation is applied to coverage of in-hospital psychiatric care than to coverage of in-hospital physical care, that differential limitation on mental health care clearly affects only people whose mental impairments substantially limit them in a major life activity.[131]

The EEOC, however, was clearly sensitive to political realities. The fact is most health insurance plans currently provide lesser benefits for mental health care and for eye care. Such differential treatment may, in fact, not be justified under the ADA. But the EEOC clearly did not want to throw those practices into doubt. Hence, the agency developed a strained, if not totally implausible, distinction for these practices. There may be good reason to let this distinction stand for the moment. Employers should be aware, however, that the EEOC's analysis will likely be subject to legal challenge in the future.

The EEOC sets forth other examples of disability-based distinctions and non-disability-based distinctions that are consistent with the legislative history. For example, the "Enforcement Guidance" states that "blanket preexisting condition clauses" that do not distinguish among disabilities are not "distinctions based on disability" and hence do not violate the ADA.[132] Similarly, "universal limits or exclusions from coverage of all experimental drugs and/or treatment, or of all 'elective surgery' " are likewise not distinctions based on disability.[133] A plan that limits the benefits provided for the treatment of any physical condition to $25,000 does not include a disability-based distinction.[134]

By contrast, a provision is disability based if "it singles out a particular disability (e.g., deafness, AIDS, schizophrenia), a discrete group of disabilities (e.g., cancers, muscular dystrophies, kidney diseases), or disability in general (e.g., noncoverage of all conditions that substantially limit a major life activity)." The EEOC offers two examples of disability-based distinctions: (1) a plan that places a cap of $5,000 for reimbursement of AIDS care while placing a cap of $100,000 for reimbursement of care for all other physical conditions,[135] and (2) a plan that excludes from coverage treatment for any preexisting blood disorders for a period of 18 months, but does not exclude the treatment of any other preexisting conditions.[136]

If an employer's health insurance plan contains a challenged disability-based distinction, the employer must then prove the provision falls within the protective ambit of the insurance exception.[137] There are two elements to this proof. The first element is easy. The employer must prove its health insurance plan falls within the requirements of either paragraph 2 or paragraph 3 of the insurance exception.[138]

An employer will use paragraph 2 if it is an "insured" plan; that is, if it purchases its insurance from an insurance company or other organization, such as an HMO. To meet the requirements of paragraph 2, the employer must prove its health plan is "bona fide"[139] and contains terms that are not inconsistent with applicable state law.[140] An employer will use paragraph 3 if it is a "self-insured" plan; that is, if it directly assumes the liability of an insurer. To meet the requirements of paragraph 3, the employer must prove its health plan is "bona fide."[141] Because self-insured plans are not governed by state insurance laws, as a result of preemption under ERISA, the second requirement is inapplicable.

The second element of proof is the difficult one. This element derives from the employer's obligation not to use disability-based distinctions as a "subterfuge" to evade the purposes of the law. The EEOC explains that: " 'Subterfuge' refers to disability-based disparate treatment that is not justified by the risks or costs associated with the disability."[142]

The agency presents five ways in which an employer may prove there is a "business/insurance justification" for the disability-based distinction and hence prove it is not using the distinctions as a subterfuge. Even though the EEOC notes this is a "nonexhaustive" list of possible defenses, it appears to this author that the EEOC has covered all possible available defenses.

The first defense rebuts the conclusion that a true disability-based distinction has occurred. For example, assume an employee asserts that a $50,000 cap for the coverage of heart disease under the employer's plan is discriminatory. If the employer can prove that its plan places a $50,000 cap on *all* similar catastrophic conditions, then the plan does not include a disability-based distinction.[143]

The second defense is that the disability-based distinction "is justified by legitimate actuarial data or by actual or reasonably anticipated experience" and that "conditions with comparable actuarial data and/or experience are treated in the same fashion."[144] In cases in which an employer relies on an actuarial defense, the employer must provide to the EEOC investigator "a detailed explanation of the rationale underlying the disability-based distinction, including the actuarial conclusions arrived at, the actuarial assumptions relied upon to reach those conclusions, and the factual data that supports the assumptions and/or conclusions."[145] It is doubtful that most employers who create disability-based distinctions, such as lower caps for AIDS treatment, have undertaken such a detailed analysis. Nor would such an analysis, if it were undertaken, be likely to justify treating AIDS differently from other catastrophic conditions.[146]

The third defense is that the disparate treatment is "necessary" – that is, there is no non-disability-based health insurance plan change that could be made – to ensure the plan meets legal standards of fiscal soundness. For example, an employer may limit coverage for a discrete group of disabilities if continued, unlimited coverage would be so expensive that the health insurance plan would become financially insolvent. The employer may do so, however, only if there is no *non-disability*-based health insurance change that could be made to avert insolvency.[147]

The rocketing costs of health care today may enable an employer to prove that its plan would actually become insolvent absent sweeping and radical changes to a health care plan. It would be rare, however, for there to be no non-disability-based changes that could be made to reduce costs instead. For example, the employer probably could place a lower cap on *all* physical conditions covered by the plan, rather than just a lower cap on a discrete group of disabilities, and save an equivalent amount of money.

If an employer offers the defense that the disability-based distinction was necessary to assure the fiscal soundness of the plan, the employer must provide the EEOC investigator with "evidence of the non-disability-based options for modifying the health insurance plan that were considered and the reason(s) for the rejection of these options."[148]

A related defense is that the disability-based distinction was necessary to prevent an "unacceptable change" in the plan. An unacceptable change includes a drastic increase in premium payments, copayments, or deductibles or a drastic alteration in the scope of coverage or level of benefits provided. These changes must be so drastic that (1) the health insurance plan effectively becomes unavailable to a significant number of employees; (2) the health insurance plan becomes so unattractive that significant adverse selection occurs (i.e., healthy employees choose to opt out of the plan and obtain their insurance elsewhere); or (3) the health insurance plan becomes so unattractive that the employer cannot compete in recruiting and maintaining qualified workers. Again, the requirement of necessity means there must be no non-disability-based changes possible that would have averted these results.[149]

The level of disaster required by the EEOC is so high it is doubtful most employers could justify a disability-based distinction on these grounds. Moreover, as in the third defense, it is unlikely that there would have been no non-disability-based distinctions the employer could have used instead.[150]

The fifth defense is that the disability-based treatment for which coverage is being denied "does not provide *any* benefit (*i.e.*, has no medical value)."[151] Under this defense, the employer must prove, by reliable scientific evidence, "that the disability-specific treatment does not cure the condition, slow the degeneration/deterioration or harm attributable to the condition, alleviate the symptoms of the condition, or maintain the current health status of individuals with the disability who receive the treatment."[152]

The EEOC's "Enforcement Guidance" clearly lays out the significant hurdles that an employer must overcome before it can justify a disability-based distinction. In fact, as noted previously, the individuals who negotiated the insurance exception did not intend that distinctions among disabilities be easily allowed under the ADA. Employers and insurers were basically given a free hand in reducing costs through uniform and across-the-board reductions and changes, even though such changes adversely impact people with disabilities. They were not given a free hand, however, to reduce such costs on the backs of selected and vulnerable disability groups.

In the case of *Mason Tenders District Council Welfare Fund v. Donaghey*,[153] the EEOC filed an amicus brief setting forth its arguments against a disability-specific exclusion. In that case, the Mason Tenders Welfare Fund, a self-insured employee benefit plan, instituted a blanket exclusion for coverage of AIDS under its plan. The EEOC argued the fund had failed to demonstrate that its exclusion of AIDS-related conditions was not a subterfuge to evade the requirements of the ADA. According to the EEOC, the plan's exclusion of AIDS-related conditions could not be justified as consistent with the principles of insurance risk classification, because the plan used no insurance risk classification principles in deciding on the AIDS exclusion.

Summary judgment for the plan was denied on 22 November 1993, and the case is proceeding to trial.[154]

As of this writing, two other ADA challenges to AIDS caps have been brought in federal court.[155] Health insurance coverage for other types of disabilities has also generated litigation under the ADA.[156]

CONCLUSION

Passage of the Americans with Disabilities Act is a significant step in the advancement of civil rights for people with disabilities. But passage of a law is only the first step. The law must be manageable for those who are subject to it. It must be capable of being understood and applied without significant difficulty. Both employers and people with disabilities benefit from a law that is neither feared nor misused.

Despite extensive fears regarding implementation of the ADA in the employment sector, those fears do not appear to have materialized to the degree expected. Although some members of the business community continue to voice general and vague concerns about the ADA and some academic writers continue to repeat the same concerns about the law, employers appear to be adjusting to ADA requirements without major disruption.

Most employers appear to have instituted the necessary changes in their application processes and in the application of their medical examinations and inquiries. The EEOC's "Enforcement Guidelines" in this area, issued in May 1994, is a useful addition to the technical assistance available to people with disabilities and to employers. Although some issues remain to be worked out, the requirements of medical examinations and inquiries will, one hopes, continue to be implemented in the business sector without major disruption.

The area of reasonable accommodations will continue to evolve over time. The provision of reasonable accommodations is, by definition, an individual process, geared to an individual with a disability, a job, and an employer. Ideally, as the body of experience with reasonable accommodations grows, more employers will become aware that the provision of a reasonable accommodation can be easy and inexpensive. Litigation in this area will obviously continue, but the number of successful accommodations that will be worked out before the courtroom door is reached should far outweigh the number of cases that come to trial.

The area of employer-provided health insurance has been clarified considerably through the issuance of the EEOC's "Interim Guidance." The overall issue of how employers will manage with the rising costs of health care, however, remains one of the critical issues of the day. The current debate over health care reform indicates that policy makers are aware that changes in the current system are necessary. The restrictions placed on employers by the ADA might only hasten efforts toward reform. As a result of the ADA, employers may not reduce their health insurance costs on the backs of selected, targeted groups of individuals. Cost-saving measures must be applied across the board; otherwise, employers must have a valid, actuarial justification for their actions. As the pinch of achieving health care savings is felt across the board by all employees, perhaps the effort toward universal health care coverage will be hastened.

The Americans with Disabilities Act has begun to change the landscape of employment in this country for people with disabilities. It is not an earthquake. But it is a slow rolling wave, ideally bringing a better day behind it.

NOTES

1. I would like to thank Jennifer Mathis, GULC '94, and Jennifer McMahon, GULC '94, for their tireless and careful work in preparing background memos for this piece. I could not have asked for better research assistants.
2. The WESTLAW database file of law review and academic journal articles contains 164 articles about the ADA and 896 articles that reference the ADA. A NEXIS search of general media articles recovered 9193 news stories referencing the ADA written over the past two years.
3. See, e.g., Barbara Lee, "Reasonable Accommodation under the ADA: The Limitations of Rehabilitation Act Precedent," *Berkeley Journal of Employment and Labor Law* 14 (1993): 201; David Harger, Comment, "Drawing the Line between Reasonable Accommodation and Undue Hardship under the Americans with Disabilities Act: Reducing the Effects of Ambiguity on Small Businesses," *Kansas Law Review* 41 (1993): 783; Loretta K. Haggard, Note, "Reasonable Accommodation of Individuals with Mental Disabilities and Psychoactive Substance Use Disorders under Title I of the Americans with Disabilities Act," *Washington University Journal of Urban and Contemporary Law* 43 (1993): 343; Louis Rabaut, "The Americans with Disabilities Act and the Duty of Reasonable Accommodation," *University of Detroit Mercy Law Review* (1993): 721; Margaret E. Stine, Comment, "Reasonable Accommodation and Undue Hardship under the Americans with Disabilities Act of 1990," *South Dakota Law Review* 37 (1992): 97; Albert S. Miles et al., "The Reasonable Accommodations Provision of the Americans with Disabilities Act," *Educational Law Report* 69 (1991): 1; Rosalie K. Murphy, Note, "Reasonable Accommo-

dation and Employment Discrimination under Title I of the Americans with Disabilities Act," *Southern California Law Review* 64 (1991): 1607; Lawrence P. Postol and David D. Kadue, "An Employer's Guide to the Americans with Disabilities Act: From Job Qualifications to Reasonable Accommodations," *John Marshall Law Review* 24 (1991): 693; Jeffrey O. Cooper, Comment, "Overcoming Barriers to Employment: The Meaning of Reasonable Accommodation and Undue Hardship in the Americans with Disabilities Act," *University of Pennsylvania Law Review* 139 (1991): 1423; Steven F. Stuhlberg, Comment, "Reasonable Accommodation under the Americans with Disabilities Act: How Much Must One Do before Hardship Turns Undue?" *University of Cincinnati Law Review* 59 (1991): 1311; Gregory S. Crespi, "Efficiency Rejected: Evaluating 'Undue Hardship' Claims Under the Americans with Disabilities Act," Tulsa Law Journal 26 (1990): 1; Julie Brandfield, "Undue Hardship: Title I of the Americans with Disabilities Act," *Fordham Law Review* 59 (1990): 113.

4. See, e.g., Terry A.M. Mumford et al., "Coordinating Employee Benefits with the Americans with Disabilities Act," in *Employee Retirement and Welfare Plans of Tax Exempt and Governmental Employers* 19 (ALI-ABA Course of Study No. C840, 1993); Leon E. Irish, "The Impact of the Americans with Disabilities Act of 1990 on Employee Benefit Plans," in *Qualified Plans, PCs, and Welfare Benefits* 445 (ALI-ABA Course of Study No. C796, 1993); Sondra M. Lopez-Aguado, Note, "The Americans with Disabilities Act: The Undue Hardship Defense and Insurance Costs," *Review of Litigation* 12 (1992): 249; Kimberley A. Ackourey, Comment, "Insuring Americans with Disabilities: How Far Can Congress Go to Protect Traditional Practices?" *Emory Law Journal* 40 (1991): 1183; Eric C. Sohlgren, Comment, "Group Health Benefits Discrimination against AIDS Victims: Falling through the Gaps of Federal Law – ERISA, the Rehabilitation Act and the Americans with Disabilities Act," *Loyola of Los Angeles Law Review* 24 (1991): 1247.

5. See, e.g., Jerry M. Hunter, "Potential Conflicts between Obligations Imposed on Employers and Unions by the

National Labor Relations Act and the Americans with Disabilities Act," *Northern Illinois University Law Review* 13 (1993): 207; Erika F. Rottenberg, Comment, "The Americans with Disabilities Act: Erosion of Collective Rights?" *Berkeley Journal Employment and Labor Law* 14 (1993): 179; R. Bales, "Title I of the Americans with Disabilities Act: Conflicts between Reasonable Accommodation and Collective Bargaining," *Cornell Law Journal and Pubic Policy* 2 (1992): 161; Barbara Kamenir Frankel, Comment, "The Impact of the Americans with Disabilities Act of 1990 on Collective Bargaining Agreements," *Southwestern Law Review* 22 (1992): 257; David S. Doty, Comment, "The Impact of Federal Labor Policy on the Americans with Disabilities Act of 1990: Collective Bargaining Agreements in a New Era of Civil Rights," *Brigham Young University Law Review* 1992 (1992): 1055; Joanne Jocha Ervin, "Reasonable Accommodation and the Collective Bargaining Agreement under the Americans with Disabilities Act of 1990," *Detroit College of Law Review* 1991 (1991): 925.

6. See, e.g., Brent Edward Kidwell, "The Americans with Disabilities Act of 1990: Overview and Analysis," Indiana Law Review 26 (1992): 707; Charles D. Goldman, "Commentary: Americans with Disabilities Act: Dispelling the Myths, a Practical Guide to EEOC's Voodoo Civil Rights and Wrongs," University of Richmond Law Review 27 (1992): 73; Robert F. Stewart, Jr., "The Americans with Disabilities Act: Coming to Grips with the Law," *Delaware Law Review* (Summer 1992): 34; James Kratovil, "Americans with Disabilities Act," *West Virginia Law Review* (July 1992): 18; Amy Scott Lowndes, Note, "The Americans with Disabilities Act of 1990: A Congressional Mandate for Heightened Judicial Protection of Disabled Persons," *Florida Law Review* 44 (1992): 417; Jack M. Rolls, Jr., "The Americans with Disabilities Act of 1990," *Haw. Bar Journal* (June 1992): 18; Bonnie P. Tucker, "The Americans with Disabilities Act of 1990: An Overview," *New Mexico Law Review* 22 (1992): 13; Larry M. Schumaker, "The Americans with Disabilities Act of 1990," *Journal of the Missouri Bar* 47 (1991): 542; David L. Ryan, "Americans with Disabilities: The Legal Revolution,"

Journal of the Kansas Bar Association (Nov. 1991): 13; Jeffrey Higginbotham, "The Americans with Disabilities Act," *Hamline Journal of Public Law and Policy* 12 (1991): 217; Robert L. Burgdorf, Jr., "The Americans with Disabilities Act: Analysis and Implications of a Second-Generation Civil Rights Statute," *Harvard Civil Rights–Civil Liberties Law Review* 26 (1991): 413; Timothy M. Cook, "The Americans with Disabilities Act: The Move to Integration," *Temple Law Review* 64 (1991): 393; Nancy Lee Jones, "Overview and Essential Requirements of the Americans with Disabilities Act," Temple Law Review 64 (1991): 471; Michael M. Johnson, "New Rights for the Disabled," *California Lawyer* (June 1991): 63; Edmund V. Ludwig, "New Promises to Keep: The Americans with Disabilities Act of 1990," *Pennsylvania Lawyer* (Jan. 1991): 15; George J. Tichy, II, "The Americans with Disabilities Act of 1990," *Catholic Lawyer* 34 (1991): 343; Randy Chapman, "The Americans with Disabilities Act: Civil Rights for Persons with Disabilities," *Colorado Lawyer* 19 (1990): 2233.

7. See, e.g., John Albrecht, "A Guide to Employment Discrimination Cases under the Americans with Disabilities Act," *Nevada Lawyer* (Feb. 1993): 20; Chai R. Feldblum, "Americans with Disabilities Act: Selected Employment Requirements," in *Americans with Disabilities Act* (ALI-ABA Course of Study No. Q217, 1992), p. 29; Thomas H. Christopher and Charles M. Rice, "The Americans with Disabilities Act: An Overview of the Employment Provisions," *South Texas Law Review* 33 (1992): 759; Michael G. Pfefferkorn, Employment Discrimination in the Americans with Disabilities Act, *Journal of the Missouri Bar* 48 (1992) 335; D. Todd Arney, Note, "Survey of the Americans with Disabilities Act, Title I: With the Final Regulations in, Are the Criticisms Out?" *Washburn Law Journal* 31 (1992): 522; G. William Davenport, "The Americans with Disabilities Act: An Appraisal of the Major Employment-Related Compliance and Litigation Issues," *Alabama Law Review* 43 (1992): 307; Peter David Blanck, "Empirical Study of the Employment Provisions of the Americans with Disabilities Act: Methods, Preliminary Findings, and Implications," *New Mexico Law Review* 22

(1992): 119; Matthew B. Schiff and David L. Miller, " The Americans with Disabilities Act: A New Challenge for Employers," *Tort and Insurance Law Journal* 27 (1991): 44; Peter David Blanck, "The Emerging Workforce: Empirical Study of the Americans with Disabilities Act," *Journal of Corporate Law* 16 (1991): 693; Jeffrey T. Johnson, "The Americans with Disabilities Act: A Primer for Employers," *Colorado Lawyer* 20 (1991): 473; Mary T. Gannon, Comment, "Employment Law – The Americans with Disabilities Act of 1990 and Its Effect upon Employment Law," *Journal of Corporate Law* 16 (1991): 315; Robin Andrews, Comment, "The Americans with Disabilities Act of 1990: New Legislation Creates Expansive Rights for the Disabled and Uncertainties for Employers," *Cumberland Law Review* 21 (1990–91): 629; Thomas H. Barnard, "The Americans with Disabilities Act: Nightmare for Employers and Dream for Lawyers," *St. John's Law Review* 64 (1990): 229.

8. See Chai R. Feldblum, "Medical Examinations and Inquiries under the Americans with Disabilities Act: A View from the Inside," *Temple Law Review* 64 (1991): 521, 534–540 (describing the ADA's requirements) (hereinafter Feldblum, "Medical Examinations").

9. See Chai R. Feldblum, "Employment Protections," in *The Americans with Disabilities Act: From Policy to Practice*, pp. 81, 95 (ed. J. West, 1991) (describing employer concerns regarding reasonable accommodation and undue hardship) (hereinafter "Employment Protections").

10. See, e.g., ibid., pp. 100–102; Sondra M. Lopez-Aguado, Note, "The Americans with Disabilities Act: The Undue Hardship Defense and Insurance Costs," *Review of Litigation* 12 (1992): 249, 268–269; Eric C. Sohlgren, Comment, "Group Health Benefits Discrimination Against AIDS Victims: Falling through the Gaps of Federal Law – ERISA, the Rehabilitation Act and the Americans with Disabilities Act," *Loyola of Los Angeles Law Review* 24 (1991): 1247, 1298; Chai Feldblum, "Workplace Issues: HIV and Discrimination," in *AIDS Agenda: Emerging Issues in Civil Rights*, ed. B. Rubenstein and N. Hunter (1992), pp. 274, 284.

11. The following newsletters and reporters were surveyed: the Bureau of National Affairs (BNA) *Americans with Disabilities Act Manual, the National Disability Law Reporter,* and the *Disability Advocates Bulletin.* The LEXIS database was also surveyed. A separate memo providing a synopsis of these cases and complaints was prepared for the Milbank Memorial Fund and is available from the author.

12. See 29 C.F.R. §1601.22. The Equal Employment Opportunity Commission (EEOC) does disclose the aggregate number of charges it receives, as well as a breakdown of the type of complaints and type of disabilities alleged.

13. These letters were received through a Freedom of Information Request to the EEOC. The names of the individuals or entities that submitted the letters were redacted from the copies by the EEOC before release.

14. A separate analysis of the EEOC letters was prepared for the Milbank Memorial Fund and is available from the author.

15. The survey was developed by the author and appears at the end of this chapter. Work on the survey was supported by the Milbank Memorial Fund.

16. 42 U.S.C. §12112 (c)(2) (Supp. IV 1992).

17. Ibid. §12112 (c)(3)(4). See also Feldblum, ''Medical Examinations,'' p. 537.

18. See 45 C.F.R. §84.14 (1990).

19. The case, *Doe* v. *Syracuse School District,* 508 F. Supp. 333 (N.D.N.Y. 1981), concerned a job application form that asked whether the applicant ''had experienced, or had ever been treated for any 'migraine, neuralgia, nervous breakdown, or psychiatric treatment.' '' ibid., p. 335. The plaintiff answered the question in the affirmative, explaining he had suffered a nervous breakdown while in the Air Force. The plaintiff was subsequently rejected for the position of a teacher's assistant and substitute teacher.

The district court concluded that the school district's application form violated ''both the letter and the spirit'' of the Section 504 regulations issued by then-Department of Health, Education and Welfare and enjoined the school district from continuing such inquiries. *Id.* at 337-38.

20. In May 1994, the EEOC issued enforcement guidance on medical examinations and inquiries. See Equal Employment Opportunity Commission Notice 915.002, "Enforcement Guidance: Preemployment Disability-Related Inquiries and Medical Examinations under the Americans with Disabilities Act of 1990" (May 19, 1994) hereinafter "EEOC Enforcement Guidance." This is the second topic area in which the EEOC issued guidance subsequent to issuance of its regulations and technical assistance manual, it has issued guidance in only these topic areas thus far.

21. Thirteen out of 42 employers stated that no modifications were necessary because their application materials already complied with the ADA. Prior to passage of the ADA, many states had already passed anti-disability discrimination statutes patterned on Section 504. Therefore, many management lawyers were already counseling their clients to remove potentially illegal questions from their applications.

22. See "EEOC Enforcement Guidance," pp. 18–19. In one opinion letter, the EEOC explained that the ADA does not prohibit an employer from asking generally how many days an applicant was absent from work during the past year, as this would not be an inquiry about the existence, nature, or severity of a disability. However, an employer may not ask how many days an applicant missed due to illness, as this question might reveal a disability. See Opinion Letter dated Dec. 3, 1991.

23. See "EEOC Enforcement Guidance," pp. 18–19.

24. See EEOC *Technical Assistance Manual*, §9.3, p. IX-3 ("After making a conditional job offer, an employer may inquire about a person's workers' compensation history in a medical inquiry or examination that is required of all applicants in the same job category.").

25. See, e.g., EEOC letter dated Aug. 28, 1991 responding to a writer who "raised several issues regarding the effect of the ADA on state workers' compensation claims proceedings." With regard to questioning, the EEOC explained: "There are two stages during which employers may obtain information about an employee's workers' compensation history. First, such inquiries may be made of all selectees in the same job

category during the post-offer stage of the hiring process. Second, an employer may make such inquiries of an incumbent employee while investigating or defending against the employee's claim before a Workers' Compensation Appeals Board." Letter, p. 3.

26. "EEOC Enforcement Guidance," pp. 19–20.

27. In its Opinion Letters, the EEOC also sought to alleviate concerns from employers and state workers' compensation programs that this requirement would have an adverse impact on such programs. The EEOC explained that information regarding workers' compensation claims and preexisting disabilities could be obtained by the employer before an individual actually entered employment and could be relayed to state workers' compensation offices and to second injury funds in accordance with state workers' compensation laws. See Opinion Letter dated Aug. 28, 1991, p. 3.

28. Government Suit: "Employee Asked about Disability during Job Interview," *National Disability Law Reporter* (May 11, 1994):1, 8.

29. EEOC v. Community Coffee, Civ. No. H-94-1061, complaint at 3 (S.D.Tex. filed Mar. 30, 1994). EEOC also filed suit in EEOC v. Herzog Stone Products, Civ. No. 94-2016, (W.D.Ark., filed Jan. 31, 1994). The complaint alleged that the employer failed to hire Paul Jones, a qualified individual with a disability, because the employer regarded Jones as having a disability. In addition, the complaint alleged the employer "required a medical examination and asked medical questions as a part of the employment application process" (ibid., p. 3). The suit was resolved through a consent decree in February 1994. With regard to the medical examinations issue, the decree stated simply that "the defendant . . . shall not make medical inquiries of applicants for employment prior to making an offer of employment to the applicant" (ibid., consent decree, p. 3).

30. One employer noted it sets forth the physical and mental requirements of the job.

31. 42 U.S.C. §12111(8) (Supp. III 1991).

32. This provides a good example of how offering amendments to a bill often results in unexpected legislative outcomes. On

its face, the statutory language could be read to mean that job descriptions prepared *after* interviewing applicants for a job *would not* be considered as evidence of essential functions. That result would clearly be adverse to employer interests, given that some employers may, in good faith, not develop such descriptions prior to interviewing applicants.

There is no limitation in the Section 504 case law on using job descriptions prepared after an individual is on the job. Such a limitation should not apply to the ADA either, unless there is evidence the employer prepared the description specifically to disqualify a specific individual with a disability, or a class of individuals with disabilities, from a job.

The irony is that the original amendment was offered to advance employer interests by making job descriptions prepared before interviewing applicants determinative. In truth, the compromise provision should not have been accepted by the employer advocates without a proviso in the legislative history that the amendment should not be read to impact adversely on job descriptions prepared, in good faith, after an individual is on the job. While such a proviso was not included, most courts would probably read such a provision into the law and not construe the statutory language strictly against employer interests.

33. Obviously, some supervisors may ask the applicant why he or she cannot perform the job. Many supervisors, however, will simply not interview the candidate.

34. "EEOC Enforcement Guidance," p. 11.

35. Ibid., pp. 11–12.

36. "EEOC Enforcement Guidance," p. 16. This is similar to the rule the EEOC set forth previously in its regulations and interpretive guidance. See 29 C.F.R. §1630.14(a) ("A covered entity may make pre-employment inquiries into the ability of an applicant to perform job-related functions, and/or may ask an applicant to describe or to demonstrate how, *with or without reasonable accommodation*, the applicant will be able to perform job-related functions") (emphasis added); Interpretive Guidance to 29 C.F.R. §1630.14(a) ("The employer may describe or demonstrate the job function and inquire whether or not the applicant can perform

that function *with or without reasonable accommodation*")
(emphasis added).

37. "EEOC Enforcement Guidance," p. 16.
38. Ibid.
39. See letter from Jeffrey A. Norris, president, Equal Employment Advisory Council, to Tony E. Gallegos, chairman, EEOC, May 25, 1994; letter from Susan R. Meisinger, vice president, Government and Public Affairs, Society for Human Resources Management, to Tony E. Gallegos, chairman, EEOC, June 10, 1994.
40. The EEOC cited the Senate Report, p. 39; the House Labor Report, p. 73; and the House Judiciary Report, p. 43.
41. Senate Labor and Human Resources Report, p. 39. The Senate Report goes on to say: "For example, an employer may ask whether the applicant has a driver's license, if driving is an essential job function, but may not ask whether the applicant has a visual disability. This prohibition against inquiries regarding disability is critical to ensure that bias does not enter the selection process."

    The House Education and Labor Report follows the Senate Report language exactly. House Labor Report at 73. The House Judiciary Report states simply: "Employers may not conduct a medical examination or make inquiries of a job applicant as to whether the applicant is disabled or as to the nature or severity of a disability. An employer may make inquiry into the ability of an applicant to perform job-related functions." House Judiciary Report, at 43.
42. "EEOC Enforcement Guidelines," pp. 15–16.
43. This employer could, of course, choose to administer its drug exams post offer as well. See later in this section.
44. I say this "apparently" was not done in response to the ADA because it is possible some employers made the change during the two-year grace period before the ADA became effective but in anticipation nevertheless of the ADA's requirements. Many employers, of course, have always placed their medical exams post offer as a means of conserving money by giving the exam to fewer applicants.
45. 42 U.S.C. §12112(c)(3)(A).

46. See Feldblum, "Medical Examinations," p. 541 (explaining why the clarification of this provision was relegated to the committee reports, rather than set forth in the statute).

47. One management lawyer advises her clients who require medical examinations to describe to the physician the position the applicant has been offered and request that the physician advise the employer *only* if there is an impediment to the applicant performing the position. Thus, if the examination discloses a medical condition that has no bearing on the applicant's performance, the employer will not be in the position of acquiring information that the employer cannot lawfully use. See correspondence from Jane L. Hanson, Milbank, Tweed, Hadley and McCloy, to Jane West, May 10, 1994.

48. See *EEOC Technical Assistance Manual*, pp. VI-9 to VI-11.

49. It was not clear from this survey response whether this pre-employment status denoted a preoffer or postoffer drug test.

50. See "EEOC Enforcement Guidelines," pp. 20–21, 35–36.

51. See EEOC Interpretive Guidance to 29 C.F.R. § 1630.16(c).

52. "EEOC Enforcement Guidelines," p. 21.

53. *See* House Education and Labor Report at 79-80. The House Judiciary Report makes the same suggestions. *See* House Judiciary Report at 47.

54. The employer is also precluded from using that information to withdraw a conditional job offer unless the employer proves that the use of such a drug makes the applicant not qualified for the job.

55. Feldblum, "Employment Protections," pp. 89–90. I discuss the jurisprudential justifications for this requirement as a civil right of people with disabilities in Feldblum, "Antidiscrimination Requirements of the ADA," in *Implementing the Americans with Disabilities Act: Rights and Responsibilities of All Americans* (ed. L. Gostin and H. Beyer, 1992), pp. 36–37.

56. 42 U.S.C. §1211 (10)(A) (Supp. IV 1992).

57. Some examples included a requirement that employers spend up to 10 percent of their gross income on reasonable accommodations, a requirement that employers spend up to 10 percent of their net income on reasonable accommodations,

or a requirement that limited the accommodation cost to 10 percent of an employee's salary. See Feldblum, "Employment Protections," p. 95. Only the last alternative received serious attention in the form of an amendment offered during consideration of the ADA by the House of Representatives. That amendment was defeated.

58. See ibid., p. 94.
59. As noted in the introduction to this chapter, the SHRM survey results cannot be used to arrive at statistically valid conclusions.
60. Four employers left this section of the survey blank.
61. 42 U.S.C. §12111(9). See also Feldblum, "Employment Protections," pp. 93–94 (describing accommodations and the accommodation process).
62. Feldblum, ibid., pp. 93–94.
63. The survey responses describe 18 modifications made as a result of requests for reasonable accommodations.
64. The employer gave no further details on the type of workplace modifications that were made.
65. My ability to explain some of these modifications is necessarily limited by the amount of information provided by the employers in the surveys.
66. Some modifications in testing and application materials were made and are described in the preceding section on medical examinations and inquiries.
67. *JAN Quarterly Report* (April 1–June 30, 1993), President's Committee on Employment of People with Disabilities, Washington, D.C.
68. This last employer actually seemed to be referring to more than just financial difficulty. The comment was: "Only the definition of reasonable – who decides, and how reasonable are the parties involved. If everyone *wants* to make it work – it usually can."
69. One letter asked if a store must install an elevator to afford an employee with a disability access to another floor. A second letter asked if accommodations may be phased in over time.
70. The EEOC typically responded that these questions must be decided on a case-by-case basis.

71. The EEOC responded that allowing the use of service animals on the job is a form of reasonable accommodation that may be required of employers.
72. The EEOC noted if the employer was barred from making structural changes under the lease terms, such terms might constitute an undue hardship. However, the building owner might be in violation of Title III for refusing to allow structural changes.
73. The EEOC stated that, according to its Interpretive Guidance, collective bargaining agreements may be taken into consideration in determining undue hardship. The answer to this question is actually quite complicated and requires an analysis of the interaction between the ADA and the National Labor Relations Act.
74. A good example of employers recognizing the need to establish a "team effort" for accommodation can be found in the various workplace education programs regarding workers with HIV and AIDS. As Jane West points out in her analysis of effective employer assistance programs accommodating people with AIDS: "Providing accommodation to employees with HIV infection or AIDS is a team effort with impact on a company's workforce, managers, and policies. . . . A fearful work environment is not a productive work environment. A useful supplement to effective accommodation of employees with HIV infection or AIDS is addressing coworker attitudes." National Leadership Coalition on AIDS, *Accommodating Employees with HIV Infection and AIDS: Case Studies of Employer Assistance*, p. 7 (1994).
75. 859 F. Supp. 963 (E.D.N.C. 1994).
76. Ibid., p. 973.
77. 858 F. Supp. 1572 (N.D. Ga. 1994).
78. Ibid., p. 1584. A more complicated question is whether courts deciding ADA claims are inappropriately ignoring the ADA's explicit inclusion of "transfer to a vacant position" as a form of reasonable accommodation. The district court in the *Reigel* case used Section 504 case law to reject a claim for such a transfer. See *Reigel*, 859 F. Supp., p. 972. The court should have analyzed that claim based on the ADA language

and regulations, which are different from Section 504 with regard to transfers.

79. In Tyndall v. National Educ. Ctrs., Inc., 31 F.3d 209 (4th Cir. 1994), the court of appeals upheld a grant of summary judgment from the district court in favor of the employer. (A *summary judgment grant* means the employer was not required to proceed to a trial on the plaintiff's claim because the court ruled, as a matter of law, that the employer had not violated the ADA.) In this case, the employer had made serious efforts to accommodate an employee with lupus erythematosus, but her absences from her teaching position were seriously disrupting the operations of the school for both her students and coworkers. Moreover, in this case, the employee required a significant amount of time off not for her own disability but to care for her son who also had a serious disability. The court noted that the reasonable accommodation requirement does not extend to providing time off to care for a family member with a disability.

In Zande v. State of Wisconsin Dept. of Administration, 851 F. Supp. 353 (W.D.Wis. 1994), the federal district court granted summary judgment to an employer on the grounds that it did not violate the ADA when it required an employee with paraplegia, who had requested to work at home, to go to part-time status once there was not sufficient work for the employee to do at home. In fact, the employer provided sufficient work to cover 95% of the employee's hours at home. This case was upheld on appeal, although the court's interpretation of the term "reasonable accommodation" in that opinion is directly contrary to the ADA's legislative history and Section 504 precedent. See 44 F. 3d 538 (7th Cir. 1995).

80. For example, in Dutton v. Johnson Cty. Bd. of Cty. Commrs, 859 F. Supp. 498 (D.Kan. 1994), the court noted that "for an accommodation to be reasonable, it must be effective in permitting a disabled worker to perform the essential job functions." Ibid., p. 507. In that case, the court concluded that the employer's proposed accommodation for an employee whose severe migraine headaches required absences that could not be scheduled in advance would not

be effective in allowing the employee to perform his job satisfactorily. (The employer's proposed accommodations were establishment of a part-time work schedule or a flexible prescheduled full-time schedule.) By contrast, the court found that the accommodation requested by the employee – the right to use his vacation time for unscheduled absences – had not been proven by the employer to be unreasonable or to impose an undue hardship. The employer remained free to prove these elements at trial.

81. 831 F. Supp. 1300 (E.D.Va. 1993).
82. Virginia Power actually banned smoking in all of its facilities except in designated smoking rooms the month before the court's decision was rendered, but the plaintiff contended that a declaration and injunction were necessary to prevent Virginia Power from altering this policy. The court exercised jurisdiction to decide the case, noting that voluntary cessation of allegedly illegal conduct does not make a case moot.
83. Ibid., pp. 1303–1304.
84. Ibid., p. 1304.
85. Ibid., pp. 1306–1307.
86. No. 3:93-1493-OBC (D.S.C. filed June 17, 1993). The facts in the text are derived solely from the allegations in the complaint and do not reflect the employer's "side of the story."
87. A similar situation existed in the complaint filed in the case of Brown v. Roadway Express, Inc., No. 3-93-0019 (M.D.Tenn. filed Jan. 7, 1993). The complaint charges that an employer deliberately moved its parking spaces for people with disabilities further from a building used by Brown, an employee with a disability, after Brown complained that employees without disabilities were using the spaces. The complaint also charges that Roadway Express failed to give Brown new trucks that his doctor recommended he be given because of his spinal arthritis, even when such trucks were available. This case was settled in December 1993.
88. See note 4.
89. See EEOC Interpretive Guidance to 29 C.F.R. §1630.15.
90. 42 U.S.C. §12112(a) (emphasis added).

91. In Ohio Pub. Employees Retirement System v. Betts, 492 U.S. 158 (1989), the Supreme Court was faced with a challenge to a benefits system under the Age Discrimination in Employment Act (ADEA). The general rule against employment discrimination in the ADEA provided that employers could not "fail or refuse to hire or discharge any individual or otherwise discriminate against any individual with respect to his compensation, *terms, conditions or privileges of employment* because of such individual's age." 29 U.S.C. §623(a)(1) (emphasis added). The ADEA also had an explicit provision that exempted from the general rule against age-based discrimination "any bona fide employment benefit plan, such as a retirement, pension, or insurance plan which is not a subterfuge to evade the purposes of the Act." 29 U.S.C. §623(f)(2). The Court concluded that the only way to make sense of the two provisions was to interpret the general rule as covering only "hiring and firing, wages and salaries, and other *non-fringe benefit terms and conditions of employment.*" 492 U.S. at 177 (emphasis added).

92. 42 U.S.C. §12112(b)(2) (emphasis added).

93. 42 U.S.C. §12112(b)(1).

94. The Title I provisions govern a *covered entity*, defined in the statute as "an employer, employment agency, labor organization, or joint labor-management committee." Some jointly administered, multiemployer trust funds have argued that they are not covered entities for purposes of Title I of the ADA. See, e.g., Mason Tenders District Council Welfare Fund v. Donaghey, No. 93 Civ. 1154 (S.D.N.Y. 1993). This argument has been rejected thus far in the *Mason Tenders* case and was explicitly rejected by the First Circuit Court of Appeals in Carparts Distribution Ctr. v. Automotive Wholesaler's Assn. of New England, Inc. 37 F.3d 12 (1st Cir. 1994).

95. See the section on insurance exemption later.

96. 42 U.S.C. §12181(7)(F) (Supp. III 1991). The requirement that the operations of the service establishment "affect commerce" is included to provide the constitutional basis for the law. The federal government is allowed to make laws reaching businesses within the various states as long as the

operations of those businesses affect interstate commerce. U.S. Constitution, Article I, §8, cl. 3 provides that Congress shall have the power to "regulate Commerce with foreign Nations, and among the several States." Under Supreme Court case law, the requirement that operations affect commerce has been interpreted broadly to include any activity in which goods or services may have crossed interstate lines. See, e.g., Stafford v. Wallace, 258 U.S. 495 (1922). In today's economy, this encompasses almost every business in this country.

97.   42 U.S.C. §12181(7)(F) (Supp. III 1991). In Carparts Distribution Ctr. v. Automotive Wholesaler's Assn. of New England, Inc. 37 F.3d 12 (1st Cir. 1994), the Court of Appeals for the First Circuit ruled it was not necessary for an insurance plan to have a physical facility to be covered under Title III of the ADA.

98.   42 U.S.C. §12182(a) (Supp. III 1991).

99.   42 U.S.C. §12182(b)(1)(A)(i) (Supp. III 1991) (emphasis added).

100.   42 U.S.C. §12182(b)(1)(A)(ii) (Supp. III 1991) (emphasis added).

101.   *Congressional Record* 135 (1989): 8509–8513.

102.   *Disparate impact* refers to a practice that, although neutral in appearance, has a disproportionate adverse impact on a protected group. For example, an annual cap of $50,000 on all medical treatments, or a limitation of 30 days of in-hospital care, may sound neutral. In practice, however, such limitations will have more of an adverse impact on people with disabilities (who, on average, require more medical care) than on people without disabilities.

The ADA explicitly prohibits practices that have an adverse impact on people with disabilities. See 42 U.S.C. §12112(b)(3)(A) and (b)(6) (Title I) and 42 U.S.C. §12182(b)(1)(D)(i) (Title III). In Alexander v. Choate, 469 U.S. 287 (1985), the Supreme Court ruled that Section 504 included an implicit disparate impact prohibition, but that the prohibition did not invalidate limitations on the number of reimbursable in-hospital care days under a state Medicaid plan. There was no assurance, however, that the ADA would necessarily be interpreted in a similar manner. While the statutory language of Section 504 does not include an explicit disparate impact provision, the ADA does.

103. 42 U.S.C. §12201(c) (Supp. III 1991). Through pure oversight on the part of the drafters of the ADA, Title II was not referenced in this last phrase. Drafters of the ADA, including myself, tended to think of Title II primarily in terms of transportation. Although much of Title II is, indeed, devoted to detailed issues of transportation, the title of course covers all state and local activities. Those activities were intended to be referenced in this section.

104. Paragraphs 1 and 2 were developed before the Senate Labor and Human Resources Committee considered the ADA. They were therefore included in the substitute bill passed by the committee and were addressed in the Senate Labor Committee report. Paragraph 3 was written the day before the full Senate considered the ADA. That language was adopted as a technical amendment by the Senate. *Congressional Record* 135 (1989): 19830. Report language explaining that provision appears, therefore, only in the House Education and Labor report and the House Judiciary report. The House of Representatives took up the ADA subsequent to Senate passage and essentially used the ADA, as passed by the Senate, as its starting point. See Feldblum, "Medical Examinations," pp. 529–530.

105. Three committee reports address the issue of insurance: the Senate Labor and Human Resources Committee report; the House Education and Labor Committee report; and the House Judiciary Committee report. Report language concerning insurance appears in two places in each of these committee reports. The most lengthy discussion appears, as would be expected, in the part of each report explaining Section 501(c), the insurance exception. Discussion also appears in the part of each report explicating Section 102(b)(1), which deals with the classification of employees resulting in adverse employment status.

106. The intricate legislative compromises made by the different interest groups (in this case, the disability community, the insurance industry, and the business community) reflect, in

this author's mind, the type of compromises contemplated by Judge Richard Posner in his analysis of statutory interpretatism. *See, e.g.,* Richard A. Posner, *The Federal Courts: Crisis and Reform,* pp. 286–293 (1985).

107. Senate Labor and Human Resources Committee report, p. 85. Identical language appears in the House Education and Labor Committee report, p. 136, and almost identical language appears in the House Judiciary report, p. 71. The House Judiciary report notes an employer may not deny a qualified applicant a job because of "the anticipated increase in the costs of the insurance."

108. 29 C.F.R. §1630.15(a) (1990). "Disparate treatment" occurs when an employer explicitly discriminates on the basis of disability.

109. Interpretive Guidance to 29 C.F.R. §1630.15, *ADA Handbook,* p. I-77. The same obligation is repeated in the EEOC's *Technical Assistance Manual,* §7.9 (1991).

110. See EEOC *Technical Assistance Manual,* §7.9 ("An employer cannot fire or refuse to hire an individual [whether or not that individual has a disability] because the individual has a family member or dependent with a disability that is not covered by the employer's current health insurance plan, or that may increase the employer's future health care costs.")

111. 42 U.S.C. §12112(b)(4) (Supp. III 1991).

112. Feldblum, "Medical Examinations," pp. 531–534, and the introduction to the earlier section on medical examinations and inquiries.

113. Civ. Action No. 3:93CV-629(JAC), filed March 26, 1993, U.S. District Court, District of Connecticut, reprinted in BNA's *Americans with Disabilities Act Manual,* p. 60:0581. The summary of the case appearing in the text is derived solely from the complaint.

114. Complaint, ibid., p. 60:0582.

115. The two subsections that follow this one describe various valid cost-saving modifications to health insurance plans.

116. The committee reports consistently note that "[a]ll people with disabilities must have equal access to the health insurance coverage that is provided by the employer to all employ-

ees." Senate Labor report, p. 29; House Labor report, p. 59; House Judiciary report at 38. In its Interpretive Guidance to 29 C.F.R. §1630.16(f), ADA *Handbook*, p. I-87, the EEOC notes that: "an employer or other covered entity cannot deny a qualified individual with a disability equal access to insurance or subject a qualified individual with a disability to different terms or conditions of insurance based on disability alone, if the disability does not pose increased risks." Because the facts of this case are derived solely from the plaintiff's complaint, it is difficult to know if Spartan Tool engaged in an analysis to determine whether Gifford's type of cancer posed a risk of financial cost greater than all other disabilities covered under the plan. See, generally, the subsection on the differential treatment of one disability or class of disabilities, detailing burden of proof employers must meet before imposing different terms or conditions.

The *Gifford* case was settled in August 1993. The settlement terms are confidential. Gifford died one month after the complaint was filed.

117.   The plaintiffs in both of these cases claimed they were terminated because of their employer's fears that their disabilities would increase health insurance costs. One of the plaintiffs had chronic heart disease. See Finley v. Cowles Business Media, No. 93 Civ. 5051 (PKL), 1994 U.S. Dist. LEXIS 8205 (S.D.N.Y. June 20, 1994). The other plaintiff had multiple sclerosis. DeLuca v. Winer Indus., No. 93 C. 6535, 1994 U.S. Dist. LEXIS 9467 (N.D.Ill. July 6, 1994). The *DeLuca* court granted summary judgment for the employer because the plaintiff did not allege sufficient facts to establish discriminatory intent and did not dispute his employer's contention that the insurance costs would not in fact have risen. Ibid., pp. *10–11. The *Finley* court refused to grant summary judgment for the employer, noting that the employee's failure to produce direct evidence was not fatal to his claim. Ibid., p. *9. Finley's complaint was based on the facts that he was fired only a few weeks after submitting an insurance application indicating his heart condition and only one month after starting employment.

118. Employers with very large work forces often have no preexisting condition clauses. For example, the health insurance plans offered by federal government have no such limitations.

119. Senate Labor report, p. 29; see also House Labor report, p. 59; House Judiciary report, p. 38. The EEOC Interpretive Guidance to the regulations and the EEOC *Technical Assistance Manual* repeat the assurance that "employers may continue to offer policies that contain preexisting condition exclusions, even if they adversely affect individuals with disabilities, so long as the clauses are not used as a subterfuge to evade the purposes of [the regulations]." EEOC Interpretive Guidance to 29 C.F.R. §1630.5, ADA *Handbook*, p. I-53; EEOC *Technical Assistance Manual*, §7.9.

120. See the subsection on differential treatment, for an analysis of such limitations.

121. Senate report, p. 29; House Labor report, p. 59; House Judiciary report, p. 39.

122. Ibid.; see also EEOC Interpretive Guidance to 29 C.F.R. §1630.5, ADA *Handbook*, p. I-54; EEOC *Technical Assistance Manual*, §7.9. The same rule applies to limits on reimbursements for types of drugs. For example, an employer may offer a health insurance plan that does not cover experimental drugs, as long as this restriction is applied to all insured individuals and all experimental drugs. EEOC *Technical Assistance Manual*, §7.9.

123. Senate Labor report, p. 85; House Labor report, pp. 136–137; House Judiciary report, p. 71.

124. The House Judiciary report also explicitly noted the following: "[I]t is permissible for an employer to offer insurance policies that limit coverage for certain procedures or treatments (e.g., a limit on the extent of kidney dialysis or whether dialysis will be covered at all, or a limit on the amount of blood transfusions or whether transfusions will be covered). It would not be permissible, however, to deny coverage to individuals, such as persons with kidney disease or hemophilia, who are affected by these limits on coverage for procedures or treatments, for other procedures or treatments connected with their disability" (House Judiciary report, p. 38).

In other words, limits on certain treatments and procedures that, at least on their face, applied uniformly to people with all types of disabilities would be allowed. However, an employer could not use this particular allowance to combine denials of coverage such that coverage for all treatments and procedures specific to one disability would be denied. That would effectively constitute denial of coverage for that disability and would have to be justified on the grounds that the "refusal, limitation, or rate differential is based on sound actuarial principles or is related to actual or reasonably anticipated experience" (Senate Labor report, p. 85; House Labor report, pp. 136–137; House Judiciary report, p. 71).

125. EEOC Interpretive Guidance to 29 C.F.R. §1630.16(f), ADA *Handbook*, p. I-87 and 29 C.F.R. §1630.5, ADA *Handbook*, p. I-54; EEOC *Technical Assistance Manual*, §7.9.

The Department of Justice provided more guidance in its regulations than did the EEOC. DOJ explained: "Congress intended to reach insurance practices by prohibiting differential treatment of individuals with disabilities in insurance offered by public accommodations unless the differences are justified. 'Under the ADA, a person with a disability cannot be denied insurance or be subject to different terms or conditions of insurance based on disability alone, if the disability does not pose increased risks.' " (citing Senate Labor Report at 84 and House Labor Report at 136.) This meant that the " 'standards used are based on sound actuarial data and not on speculation.' " (citing House Judiciary Report.) DOJ Interpretive Guidance 36 C.F.R. §36.212, ADA Handbook at III-66-77.

The Department of Justice refuted the concerns raised by insurance companies that they would be required to provide a copy of the actuarial data on which their actions were based whenever requested by the applicant. The Guidance noted the following, however: "Because the legislative history of the ADA clarifies that different treatment of individuals with disabilities may be justified by sound actuarial data, such actuarial data will be critical to any potential litigation on this issue. This information would presumably be obtainable in a court proceeding where the insurer's actuarial data was the basis for different treatment of persons with disabilities." DOJ Guidance to 36 C.F.R. §36.212, ADA Handbook at III-68.

The Department of Justice Technical Assistance Manual makes the same points. DOJ T.A. Manual at 18-19 (1992).

126. Although the notice was titled "interim" guidance, the agency did not set an expiration date for it. Rather, the agency stated that "this Notice will remain in effect until rescinded or superseded."

127. "Enforcement Guidance," pp. 3–4.

128. Ibid., pp. 4, 11.

129. Ibid., p. 6 (emphasis added).

130. Ibid., p. 6.

131. In addition, restrictions on mental health coverage or on eye care clearly have a disparate impact on people with mental disabilities and eye disabilities. Although the EEOC states in its guidance that it accepts the same limitations on disparate impact theory that the Supreme Court imposed on Section 504 in the case of Alexander v. Choate, 469 U.S. 287 (1985), that limitation applies only to *non-disability-specific restrictions* on health coverage that have an overall disparate impact on people with *all* disabilities. By contrast, there is no reason to assume that a disparate impact analysis would not remain valid when it affects only *one* particular disability.

132. "Enforcement Guidance," p. 7.

133. Ibid.

134. Ibid.

135. Ibid., p. 8.

136. Ibid.

137. Ibid., p. 9. The EEOC notes that requiring the employer to bear the burden of proof is "consistent with the well-established principle that the burden of proof should rest with the party who has the greatest access to the relevant facts" (ibid.). In the health insurance context, the employer (and/or the employer's insurer) alone has access to the risk assessment, actuarial, or claims data on which the employer relied in adopting the disability-based distinction (ibid., p. 10).

138. 42 U.S.C. §12201(c)(2)–(3). Paragraph 1 of the insurance exception applies to insurers, hospital and medical service companies, and health maintenance organizations that are governed by the obligations of Title III.
139. According to the EEOC, a "bona fide" plan is one that "exists and pays benefits and its terms have been accurately communicated to eligible employees" (ibid., p. 10).
140. Ibid.
141. Ibid., p. 11.
142. Ibid., p. 11.
143. Ibid., p. 11. In reality, this seems to fit better in the first step of the analysis, in which an employer demonstrates that no disability-based distinction exists. The EEOC probably placed it as the first defense, however, to deal with situations in which the agency erroneously concludes that a disability-based distinction does exist – and the employer then rebuts that conclusion.
144. Ibid., pp. 11–12.
145. Ibid., p. 15.
146. An employer who relies on the defense that the disability-based distinction is justified by actual or reasonably anticipated experience must provide the EEOC investigator with "evidence about the [employer's] insurance claims experience, and the way in which the [employer] has reacted to similar previous experience situations." Ibid., p. 15.
147. Ibid., p. 12.
148. Ibid., p. 15.
149. Ibid., p. 12–13.
150. Indeed, an employer whose plan is so fiscally unsound as to require such drastic changes would probably never save sufficient money through using just disability-based distinctions. Across-the-board cuts would probably be required in those circumstances in any event.
151. Ibid., p. 13 (emphasis in original).
152. Ibid., p. 13.
153. No. 93 Civ. 1154 (S.D.N.Y. 1993).
154. This case is in an odd posture. The plan was sued by two beneficiaries with AIDS on the grounds the plan violated the ADA. The plan then sued in court asking for a declaratory

judgment that the plan was not subject to the ADA or, in the alternative, had not violated the ADA. The latter case is the one proceeding to trial.

155. One of these cases involved allegations by the estate of a deceased employee, Timothy Bourgeois, that Bourgeois's employer terminated him to avoid paying AIDS-related insurance claims under an employer-sponsored group welfare benefit plan. The complaint also charged that after Bourgeois was terminated, the employer amended the plan to limit AIDS-related treatment costs to $10,000 annually with a lifetime maximum of $40,000; all other physical ailments continued to be covered up to a lifetime maximum of $1 million with no annual limit. Gonzales v. Garner Food Servs., 855 F. Supp. 371 at 372 (N.D.Ga. 1994). No ADA challenge to the discharge was brought because it occurred prior to the effective date of the ADA. The challenge to the AIDS cap amendment was dismissed because Bourgeois was no longer an employee at the time of the amendment and hence was not covered by Title I of the ADA. Ibid., p. 374.

In another case, a complaint was filed challenging total exclusion of coverage for AIDS-related treatment in a joint management/union health and pension fund. EEOC v. Monroe Foods, Inc., Civ. No. 93-2925 (D.Md. filed Oct. 7, 1993). The fund does not exclude payment for treatment of any other "high cost" disease. "EEOC Sues Maryland Fund That Allegedly Excludes AIDS Coverage," *National Disability Law Reporter* (Dec. 8, 1993): 9. Cross motions for summary judgment have been denied, and the case is set for trial on December 5, 1994.

In one of the early cases, an ADA claim was brought by the estate of Mark Kadinger, a member of IBEW Local 110 who died of AIDS. Estate of Mark Kadinger v. International Brotherhood of Electrical Workers, Local 110, No. 3-93-159 (D.Minn. filed Mar. 17, 1993). The estate brought suit against the IBEW and against the St. Paul Electrical Construction Medical Reimbursement Plan. Kadinger's medical benefits had been covered by the plan until he reached the plan's cap of $50,000 on AIDS-related health care coverage. The plan's cap for all other illnesses was $500,000.

The Kadinger case was settled on December 21, 1993. As part of the settlement, the lower AIDS-specific cap was removed.

156. In one case, a registered nurse at Bethesda Hospital brought suit challenging the denial of family health insurance coverage for her husband, who has hypertension, and her son, a paraplegic who uses a wheelchair. See Pappas v. Bethesda Hosp. Ass'n., 861 F. Supp. 616 (S.D.Ohio June 29, 1994). The court dismissed the plaintiff's claim against the insurer under Title I of the ADA, finding that the insurer was not her employer. Ibid., p. 619. The plaintiff's Title III claims against both the hospital and the insurer were also dismissed, as the court found that neither defendant was a public accommodation under Title III. Ibid., p. 620.

The EEOC is currently investigating claims that Blue Cross/Blue Shield of Missouri is unlawfully denying insurance coverage for certain disabilities. Three complaints have been filed with the EEOC alleging that Blue Cross of Missouri refused to cover costs for high-dosage chemotherapy treatment. Two of the complainants have breast cancer and one has multiple myeloma. "U.S. Investigates Missouri Blue Cross for Alleged Disability-Based Exclusion," *National Disability Law Reporter* (Aug. 3, 1994): 1.

The Potential Impact on the Employment of People with Disabilities

Richard V. Burkhauser
Mary C. Daly

EDITOR'S NOTE

The ADA is more likely to have an impact on the employment of individuals with disabilities who are currently employed than those who are not, Burkhauser and Daly argue. A person with a disability who is accommodated in his or her workplace is 44 percent more likely to be working than an individual who is not accommodated. An accommodated worker is likely to continue working a longer period of time than a worker who is not accommodated. However, those with disabilities who are out of the work force, black, or have less than a high school education – the "doubly disadvantaged" – are not likely to reap much employment benefit from the ADA. One factor is the relative attractiveness of alternatives to employment – income transfer payments, unemployment subsidies, and welfare. Incentives in policies promoting and supporting employment, such as accommodations and rehabilitation, appear weaker for employers and potential employees alike than social welfare alternatives. Burkhauser and Daly urge consideration of direct government subsidies to employers for workplace accommodations, an expansion of tax credits for people with disabilities, and required evaluation for rehabilitation during application for SSI or SSDI. They call for the collection of a new generation of data on people with disabilities over time.

Richard V. Burkhauser is professor of economics and associate director of the Aging Studies Program, Center for Policy Research at Syracuse University. He is a member of the Disability Panel of the National Academy of Social Insurance and has written widely on issues related to disability policy. His books include Public Policy toward Disabled Workers: A Cross-National Analysis of Economic Impacts *with Robert H. Haveman and Victor Halberstadt and* Disability and Work: The Economics of American Policy *with Robert H. Haveman. Mary C. Daly is a National Institute of Aging post-doctoral fellow and adjunct professor of economics at Syracuse University. Her research includes cross-national comparisons of American and German working-age men with disabilities.*

EMPLOYING PEOPLE WITH DISABILITIES: WHAT TO EXPECT FROM THE AMERICANS WITH DISABILITIES ACT[1]

To evaluate the employment impact of the Americans with Disabilities Act of 1990 (ADA), it is necessary to look behind the disability label and identify the socio-economic characteristics of the working-age population it was meant to protect; to place the ADA's influence within a broader context of current social welfare policy; and to predict who, within the population with disabilities, the ADA will most likely help and who will need additional help to be fully integrated into the work force.

In this chapter we argue that the ADA will never be the work panacea hoped for by its most ardent supporters. It is most likely to improve work opportunities, following the onset of a work-limiting health condition, for people who are employed and have good job skills. This is the subgroup among those with disabilities who were most successfully integrated into the work force prior to their disability and who had the greatest resources to offset the negative effects of work disabilities in the absence of the ADA. But much more will be needed to secure a place in the work force for the "doubly disadvantaged," those with functional impairments and poor job skills, as well as those not currently employed. And the ADA will be least likely to help those already on traditional disability transfer programs – Social Security Disability Insurance and Supplemental Security Income (SSI) – to leave the rolls of the permanent disability transfer population and return to work.

Work Activities and Economic Well-Being among the Working-Age Population with Disabilities

Evaluation of the population with disabilities must start with a definition of that population. Disability is a more complex concept to either define or measure than age, race, or gender. Reno (1994) argues that the appropriateness of any definition of *disability* depends on the purpose for which it is used and documents over 20 definitions of disability used for purposes of entitlement to public or private income transfers, government services, or statistical analysis (see Table A-1 in the appendix).

In the Americans with Disabilities Act, *disability* is defined as a physical or mental impairment that substantially limits one or more major life activities, a record of such an impairment, or being regarded as having such an impairment. LaPlante (1991) provides a useful discussion of alternative definitions that can be used to estimate this population. The measure used here builds on the methodology developed by Nagi (1965, 1969, 1991), which distinguishes three components of disability. The first component is the presence of a pathology – a physical or mental malfunction or the interruption of a normal process or both. This leads to the second component, an impairment, which Nagi defines as a physiological, anatomical, or mental loss or abnormality that limits a person's capacity and level of function. The final component of disability is then defined as an inability to perform or limitation in performing roles and tasks that are socially expected. For men and, increasingly, for women of working age, market work is a socially expected role.

What is most controversial about Nagi's definition is the relative importance of pathology and environment in determining how a given pathology results in an impairment that then leads to disability. Less controversial is the recognition the definition gives to *disability* as a dynamic process in which individual pathology and the socioeconomic environment interact. What is limiting about this definition of *disability* with respect to the ADA is that it both ignores the broader "population with disabilities" who have successfully integrated into society and hence are not "disabled" under the Nagi definition and those who are not integrated because of perceptions concerning an impairment that does not exist.

In evaluating the importance of Title I of the ADA on employment, we will concentrate on the working-age population with disabilities. But, unlike past empirical studies of the population with disabilities that defined the "disabled" by what they cannot do, we will include the portion of the population with disabilities that is successfully integrated into the work force.

AN EMPIRICAL ESTIMATE OF THE WORKING-AGE POPULATION WITH DISABILITIES

In most surveys of income and employment the data available on health come from a small set of questions that ask respondents to assess whether their health limits the kind or amount of work they can perform. Others ask respondents to rate their health relative to individuals in their age group. Researchers have been suspicious of these measures for a number of reasons. First, self-evaluated health is a subjective measure that may not be comparable across respondents. Second, these measures may not be independent of the observed variables one wants to explain – such as economic well-being, employment status, or family structure (Chirikos and Nestel, 1984; Chirikos, 1991). Third, because social pressures make it undesirable to retire before certain ages, reasonably healthy individuals who wish to exit the labor force prematurely may use health as their excuse (Parsons, 1980; 1982; Bazzoli, 1985). Finally, in the United States, federal disability transfer benefits are available only to those judged unable to perform any substantial gainful activity, so individuals with some health problems may have a financial incentive to identify themselves as incapable of work because of their health. Misclassification based on self-reported health can overestimate both the true number of persons who suffer from a particular condition and the negative effects of health on economic well-being.

Although the problems inherent in disability measures based on self-evaluated health have led some researchers (Myers, 1982; 1983) to conclude that no useful information can be gained from self-evaluated health data, objective measures of health, which are much less available, also suffer from inherent biases (Bound, 1991). Moreover, as Bound and Waidman (1992) argue, even when a clear relationship between changes in public policy and changes in disability prevalence rates is demonstrated, it does not imply that those who come under the disability classification are erroneously classified. Although the information available in most microdata sources does not allow us to determine the extent to which changes in pathology have contributed to changes in the prevalence of disability, it is possible to inform the policy debate about the relationship between health, employment, and public policy by applying a consistent definition of disability and being cautious when interpreting the results.

In the Panel Study of Income Dynamics, which will be used here, the population with disabilities is identified using a survey question that asks respondents, "Do you have any physical or nervous condition that limits the type or the amount of work that you can do?'' To eliminate those individuals whose health limitations are short term from our analysis, only individuals who report a limitation for two consecutive years are included in the sample. In this way the analysis is restricted to the population with disabilities whose impairment is long-term.

In Table 1 we use data from the 1989 response-nonresponse file of the Panel Study of Income Dynamics (PSID) to measure labor force participation and disability transfer receipt of people with disabilities prior to the passage of the ADA.

Using our definition of disability, we find 11.5 million people (or 9.5 percent of the population) aged 18 to 61 with disabilities in 1988.[2] In general, we find prevalence rates similar to those found in other studies. Our prevalence rate for the entire working-age population is slightly higher than those found by Burkhauser, Haveman, and Wolfe (1993) or Bennefield and McNeil (1989) using the Current Population Survey (CPS), but nearly identical to that reported by McNeil (1993) using the Survey of Income and Program Participation.[3]

Bennefield and McNeil (1989), using a definition similar to ours, find that in 1988, 8.6 percent of those aged 16 to 64 had a disability. Our estimate is slightly higher, 9.6 percent, but most of this difference is attributable to our higher estimates of the prevalence of disability among women. Our estimates of the percentage of working-age men with a disability are closer to those found in the CPS. We find that 8.9 percent of working-age men had a disability in 1988; Bennefield and McNeil find a prevalence rate of 8.7 percent. When we restrict our sample to those with health conditions who work less than full time we obtain similar results to those reported by Burkhauser, Haveman, and Wolfe (1993). Their results suggest that in 1987 approximately 6.2 percent of the working-age population worked less than full time because of health.[4] Our estimate of the prevalence of health-constrained work among the working-age population in 1988 is 6.8 percent. Again, the primary difference between our estimates from the PSID and those from the CPS relates to the prevalence of disability among women.

To understand the impact of the ADA on the diverse population with disabilities, it is important to see how successfully people of working age with disabilities were integrated into the labor force

Table 1

Labor Force Participation and Transfer Receipt of People with and without Disabilities of Working Age in 1988* (Aged 18 to 61)

	People with Disabilities[b]			People Without Disabilities		
	Total	Men	Women	Total	Men	Women
Number of persons	11,517,670	4,877,616	6,640,053	109,275,703	49,841,805	59,433,897
Percent of total population	9.5	8.9	10.0	90.5	91.1	90.0
Percent receiving disability transfers	30.6	37.3	25.7	3.7	2.9	4.4
Percent working	60.7	68.1	55.2	88.8	97.5	81.5
Labor Force Activity						
Full-time work[c]	29.2	43.0	19.0	60.6	82.8	42.0
Receive disability transfers[d]	13.7	15.6	10.7	2.7	2.5	3.1
Part-time work[e]	31.5	25.0	36.3	28.2	14.8	39.5
Receive disability transfers[d]	17.4	29.0	11.4	4.5	4.1	4.7
No work[f]	39.3	33.4	44.8	11.2	2.5	18.5
Receive disability transfers[d]	53.7	72.9	43.6	6.9	9.0	6.7

[a]Population is limited to those aged 18 to 61 who are either household heads or spouses and were so in both the 1988 and 1989 PSID surveys.
[b]People who report a physical or nervous condition that limits the type of work or the amount of work they can do in 1988 and 1989.
[c]People who worked at least 1,820 hours in 1988 (35 hours per week).
[d]People who received disability-based transfers: Social Security Disability Insurance; Supplemental Security Income; Veterans Disability Benefits; Workers'
Compensation.
[e]People who worked at least one hour but no more than 1,820 hours in 1988.
[f]People who did not work in 1988.
Source: 1989 Response-Nonresponse File of the Panel Study on Income Dynamics.

prior to its passage. Past studies of the "disabled" population have concentrated on that part of the population with disabilities who received Social Security benefits or were working less than full-time because of a health-related impairment. (See, for example, Haveman and Wolfe, 1990; Burkhauser, Haveman, and Wolfe, 1993.) Table 1 shows that in 1988, this definition would have excluded the quarter of the population with disabilities who worked full-time and received no disability-related transfers (29.2 × (1 − .137)). Although full-time work is far lower among the population with disabilities than among those without disabilities (29.2 percent versus 60.6 percent), it is still an extremely important activity. Nearly twice as many people with disabilities have labor earnings as receive income from disability transfer programs (59.2 percent versus 30.6 percent). This belies the notion that people with disabilities cannot work.

Among working-age men with disabilities, two of every three worked in the labor market and 43.0 percent worked full-time in 1988. Only 37.3 percent of these men received a disability transfer payment. The patterns are similar for women. In 1988 more than one-half of women with disabilities worked. Comparing those with and without disabilities, we verify that work limitations mean less work, but prior to the passage of the ADA, a majority of people with disabilities worked at least part time and a large fraction worked full-time (Table 1).

However, the fact that a majority of men and women with disabilities work does not suggest that pathologies cannot result in serious work limitations or that health never prevents work. Nearly one-third of men and about one-half of women with a disability had no labor earnings in 1988. Among this subgroup of the population with disabilities, nearly 70 percent of men and 42 percent of women received a disability transfer payment in that year. The economic consequences of disability depend heavily on whether or not individuals continue working.

In Table 2 we look more closely at the variation within the population of those with disabilities and examine the relationship between work and economic well-being for those with disabilities. We find that the experiences of men and women with disabilities vary dramatically across race and education. As can be seen in columns 1 and 2, while more than twice as many nonblack men

Table 2

Source of Income and Economic Well-Being of People with Disabilities in 1988[a,b]

Population with Disabilities	Receive Labor Earnings (percentage) (1)	Receive Disability Transfer Income[c] (percentage) (2)	Labor Economics[d] Mean (dollars) (3)	Labor Economics Relative to Those Without Disabilities[f] (4)	Before-Government Income Mean[e] (dollars) (5)	Before-Government Income Relative to Those Without Disabilities[f] (6)	After-Government Income Mean[e] (dollars) (7)	After-Government Income Relative to Those Without Disabilities[f] (8)
All Men[a]	68.1	37.3	17,850	0.47	25,019	0.66	23,818	0.75
Black	32.9	71.7	4,964	0.22	9,012	0.42	12,633	0.67
Nonblack	72.8	32.6	19,599	0.49	27,191	0.68	25,336	0.76
With less than high school education	40.9	63.3	6,211	0.29	14,514	0.65	17,213	0.88
With at least a high school education	78.0	27.7	22,125	0.54	28,877	0.71	26,244	0.79
All women	55.2	25.7	7,674	0.50	23,589	0.68	22,744	0.77
Black	43.7	37.2	5,935	0.48	13,195	0.77	14,079	0.88
Nonblack	57.7	23.2	8,051	0.51	25,842	0.69	24,623	0.77
With less than a high school education	35.3	37.8	2,354	0.30	12,600	0.63	14,371	0.76
With at least a high school education	63.1	20.9	9,796	0.59	27,972	0.75	26,084	0.83

[a]Population is limited to those aged 18 to 61 who are either household heads or spouses and were so in both the 1988 and 1989 PSID surveys.

[b]People who report a physical or nervous condition that limits the type of work or the amount of work they can do in 1988 and 1989.

[c]People who received disability-based transfers: Social Security Disability Insurance; Supplemental Security Income; Veterans Disability Benefits; Workers' Compensation.

[d]Mean labor earnings include 0 earnings. Reported in 1991 dollars.

[e]Before- and After-Government incomes are adjusted for household size using the equivalence scale implied by the United States poverty line.

[f]Ratios of income for those with and without disabilities are computed relative to the same demographic group (e.g., mean labor earnings of blacks with disabilities/mean labor earnings of blacks without disabilities).

Source: 1989 Response-Nonresponse File of the Panel Study on Income Dynamics.

with disabilities received labor earnings as received transfers, the opposite was the case for black men with disabilities. Men with at least a high school education who have disabilities were almost three times as likely to have worked in 1988 as to have received a disability transfer. Men with a disability but less than a high school education were almost 55 percent more likely to receive a transfer than work [(63.3 − 40.9)/40.9]. Among women with disabilities the relative importance of labor earnings and transfer income varies by race and education in a similar way. Black women and women with poor education work less and are more likely to receive disability transfers.

This great diversity in work and transfer experience results in an even greater diversity in labor earnings and economic well-being. As can be seen in column 3, the average labor earnings of all men with disabilities, which includes those who work full time as well as those who work part time or not at all, was $17,850 in 1988. But this average masks large differences across race and education groups. Among men with disabilities, blacks and those with a poor education receive only a small fraction, 25 percent ($4,964) and 28 percent ($6,211), respectively, of the labor earnings of non-blacks ($19,599) and those with at least a high school education ($22,125). The pattern is similar for women with disabilities, although the difference in labor earnings between black women and nonblack women is smaller ($5,935 versus $8,051) than between other groups.

The wide differences in economic well-being implied by the gaps in labor earnings within the population with disabilities are reduced once the earnings of other family members, other private family income, and government tax and transfers are considered. But blacks and those with poor education continue to have substantially fewer economic resources than other members of the population with disabilities.

As can be seen in column 5, in the absence of government intervention (before-tax family income from all sources except government transfers) the average size-adjusted family income of all men with disabilities was $25,019 in 1988.[5] Looking behind this average we find that the average black man with a disability had before-government family income of just $9,012, one-third of the family income of a nonblack man with a disability ($27,191). Men with a disability and a poor education ($14,514) had one-half the before-government income of those with a disability and a good education ($28,877).

In column 7 we show the importance of government tax and transfer policy on the population with disabilities. Note that on average mean after-government family income falls to $23,818. On average, working-age people with disabilities of working age, like other working-age people, pay more in federal income tax and Social Security contributions than they receive in direct government transfers. This should come as no surprise once it is recognized that the typical person of working age with a disability in the United States works! Tax and transfer policy is propoor, so the gaps in economic well-being across race and education narrow. Black men with disabilities have one-half the after-government income of non-blacks with disabilities, and men with poor education and a disability have about two-thirds the income of men with good education and a disability. The pattern is the same for women with disabilities.

Columns 3, 5, and 7 of Table 2 show the dramatic differences in labor earnings and in economic well-being within the population with disabilities. It suggests that people with a disability who are also black or have a poor education are "doubly disadvantaged." Hence, it is critical when evaluating the effects of public policy to go beyond asking how a given policy will affect the average person with disabilities to ask how that policy will affect each segment of this diverse population.

Because we believe it is critical to understand the diversity in work experience and economic well-being within the population with disabilities and because few studies have documented this diversity, we have concentrated on differences within the population with disabilities in Table 2. But there are also differences in work and economic well-being between those with and without disabilities. Burkhauser, Haveman, and Wolfe (1993), Bennefield and McNeil (1989), and McNeil (1993) have documented these differences in the 1980s. In Table 2 we also show differences in labor earnings and economic well-being between those with and without disabilities.

Although a majority of men and women with disabilities work, column 4 of Table 2 shows that the labor earnings of men and women with disabilities were only around one-half those of men and women without disabilities. When we compare subgroups of

163

the population with disabilities to their counterparts without disabilities, we find that all groups with disabilities do worse, but the doubly disadvantaged do much worse. Hence, with respect to labor earnings the doubly disadvantaged are far behind both other groups with disabilities and their nondisabled racial or educational peers.

As can be seen in column 6, other private sources of income narrow the difference in income between those with disabilities and those without disabilities from about one-half to about two-thirds, but once again the ratio varies across subgroups. With the exception of black women, the "doubly disadvantaged" do much worse.

Column 8 shows that government tax and transfer policies narrow the gap in economic well-being further so the average person with a disability lives in a family with about three-quarters of the family size-adjusted income of those without a disability. Even though all subgroups of this population do worse than their counterparts without disabilities, the gap for black women and those without a high school education are relatively smaller than for nonblack women and those with a good education. Nonetheless, on an absolute scale, the "doubly disadvantaged" are substantially below all other groups in the working-age population.

PLACING DISABILITY POLICY IN THE CONTEXT OF GENERAL SOCIAL WELFARE POLICY

Even though those with disabilities work less, earn less, and have lower levels of economic well-being than those without disabilities, it is too simplistic to argue either that pathology alone accounts for these differences or that the severity of pathology within the population with disabilities alone explains who does or does not work. The startling changes in the size and composition of the long-term disabled transfer population in the United States – those receiving disability transfer benefits from either Social Security Disability Insurance or SSI – as well as in the labor force participation of the population with disabilities over the last two decades, make it clear that the transition out of work and onto the rolls of those permanent disability programs is also influenced by the social environment faced by those with disabilities. (See Daly, 1994, for a 20-year measure of these patterns.)

The road to long-term disability transfer status begins with a pathology, but whether a person remains on the job or moves onto the disability transfer rolls is influenced by the socio-economic characteristics of the individual as well as by the government policies and labor market conditions the worker faces. The Americans with Disabilities Act was championed by those who believe that mandated changes in the social environment, including the workplace, are critical to the integration of people with disabilities into the mainstream of American society. In what follows we put the ADA in the context of overall social policy and discuss how it is likely to affect the work experience of the population with disabilities described in Tables 1 and 2. We argue that the ADA will provide assistance to part of the population with disabilities but that the doubly disadvantaged – blacks, those with low job skills, those not currently working, and those already on the long-term disability transfer rolls – are least likely to be helped by the ADA.

Figure 1 conceptualizes government policies to ameliorate job loss caused by economic or health factors as a series of paths that workers take as they move from full-time work to traditional retirement. For workers who remain on the job over their work life, the path to retirement is a straightforward one. It is not until they reach early retirement age that they must choose between retirement and continued work. But for a significant number of workers, job separation before normal retirement is a reality for which social welfare policy must prepare.

Although some people with disabilities have had a pathology from birth, most people who end up on the long-term disability transfer rolls were of working age and employed when their pathology began to affect their ability to work.[6] Burkhauser and Daly (1995), using data from the Health and Retirement Survey, find that 81.0 percent of the cohort of men and 57.7 percent of the cohort of women aged 51 to 61 in 1992 who reported a current work-limiting health condition said that onset occurred during their worklife.[7] In general, one can imagine four paths, as illustrated in Figure 1, that such workers may take following the onset of a health condition.

The *work path* encompasses public programs that provide or encourage rehabilitation to overcome work limitations caused by a pathology. It also includes more direct labor market intervention through the creation of specific government sector jobs for people

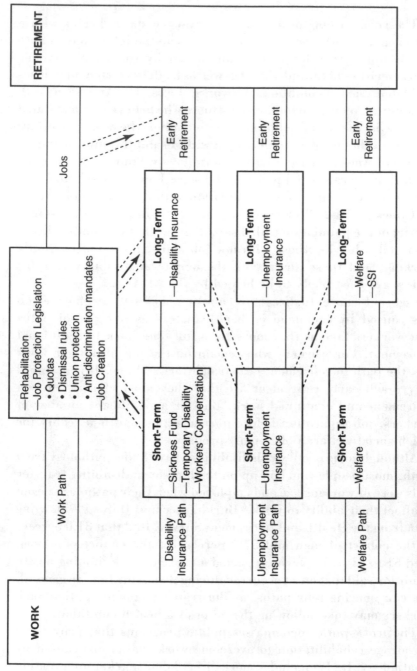

Figure 1 Social Welfare Protection System

with disabilities, subsidies to those who employ such workers, job quotas, and job protection legislation such as dismissal rules or antidiscrimination legislation requiring accommodation for workers with disabilities. The ADA clearly falls into this category of public policies in its attempt to end job discrimination. Work path policies attempt to maintain those with disabilities on the job and in the labor market, either through the carrot of subsidies or the stick of mandates.

In the early 1970s vocational rehabilitation was the primary mechanism for assisting workers with disabilities to stay in the work force in the United States. But after its rolls increased by over 40 percent between 1970 and 1975 – from .87 to 1.24 million – cuts in funding over the next decade resulted in dramatic drops in the population served, so that by 1985 they stood at .93 million. Since then the population served has remained stable at about 1 million. The Comprehensive Employment and Training Act of 1973 (CETA) provided public service jobs for workers with social disadvantages as well as those with disabilities. By 1980, over 1 million such jobs existed. This program ended in the early 1980s and was replaced by the Job Training Partnership Act (JTPA), which primarily funds direct training. JTPA funds cannot be used for public-service jobs. Anderson, Burkhauser, and Raymond (1993) find workers with disabilities are underrepresented among JTPA trainees.

In the United States, rehabilitation and job programs are secondary to transfer payments as a means of helping people with disabilities.[8] In the 1990s, antidiscrimination laws – such as the Americans with Disabilities Act – supported by cultural pressures to incorporate and accommodate diversity have emerged as major tools to keep people with disabilities in the work force. The view that people with disabilities have a legal right of access to government-funded services and facilities flows out of the civil rights movement of the 1960s and was first codified into law by the Rehabilitation Act of 1973. The Americans with Disabilities Act of 1990 is a significant extension of that principle into the private sector.

The *disability insurance path* encompasses traditional disability insurance-based transfer programs. Such programs include short-term sickness programs that mandate employers to provide replacement of lost wages during the first few weeks of sickness or directly provide such replacement through short-term social insurance.

After some period, workers receiving short-term benefits are eligible to move to a long-term disability insurance program. Often acceptance into this program requires meeting both health and employment criteria. This path eventually merges with Social Security retirement programs.

In the United States many firms have short-term sick leave as part of their fringe benefit package, but many firms do not. There are no government short-term sickness programs and eligibility requirements for long-term disability benefits include a five-month period of not working with the expectation of no substantial gainful activity for at least one year.[9] The relatively strict nature of the disability test in this program is one reason that a substantial number of people with disabilities in Table 1 did not receive disability transfer payments in 1988 despite not working during the entire year. In the United States, for those who drop out of the work force, the disability insurance path is the most common public program path taken by those with disabilities.

The Social Security Disability Insurance rolls increased rapidly during the first half of the 1970s and continued to increase substantially until 1978 when acceptance rates into the program began to fall. This administrative retrenchment was reinforced by legislative changes, principally the 1980 amendments to the Social Security Act. Among other things, these amendments required Social Security administrators to reevaluate current beneficiaries. This, together with an even further decline in acceptance rates to less than 30 percent in 1982, led to a decrease of 6 percent in the disability insurance population in the midst of the deepest American recession since the Great Depression. (For a fuller discussion of disability policy history see Weaver, 1986.)

But retrenchment was accomplished at the cost of a careful process that could survive the political firestorm it generated. First the courts and then Congress intervened to restrict the ability of program administrators to remove beneficiaries from the rolls. (See Berkowitz, 1987, and Derthick, 1990, for detailed discussions of this period of disability policy history.) The consequences of these legal and administrative reactions were not immediately felt. During the longest period of economic growth in United States history, 1983–1989, disability insurance rolls increased only modestly. But the administrative restrictions imposed by Congress and the courts in 1984 began to have an effect in the recessionary years of the 1990s, as the disability insurance rolls once again began to increase dramatically. The 1991 and 1992 increases in the rolls exceeded anything seen by the disability insurance program since the early 1970s, when the disability transfer system was considered out of control. In 1990, 5.4 million persons received either Social Security Disability Insurance or SSI benefits. By 1992, 6.3 million were on the rolls, an increase of over 15 percent. At the same time the acceptance rate for disability insurance benefits increased to almost 48 percent in 1992, higher than any other annual rate since 1972 (U.S. Department of Health and Human Services, various years).

The *unemployment insurance path* encompasses the short-term unemployment benefits that seek to replace lost wage earnings due to cyclical economic downturns. At some point longer term unemployment insurance becomes available, often at a lower replacement rate. This also merges with the Social Security retirement system at older ages. Disentangling exits from a job because of a health condition and exits from a job because of economic forces is in practice a difficult and often controversial task, especially because these exits can be influenced by the rules established by a country's social welfare system.

In periods of economic downturn and firm "downsizing," the entire social welfare system attempts to ameliorate the consequences of a loss of employment. How much pressure economic forces place on the disability transfer system depends on disability program generosity and accessibility compared to alternative government programs. This pressure is greater in the United States, which provides substantially more generous and longer lasting transfer benefits to those labeled as disabled than to those who are unemployed or poor, than in countries that have attractive alternatives to disability cash transfers.

In the early 1980s, United States unemployment insurance benefits were not extended as the recession deepened, and major retrenchments in disability acceptance policy kept the disability insurance rolls low. In the recession of the early 1990s, unemployment benefits were extended, but the easing of the eligibility criteria for disability insurance by the courts and the Congress in the 1980s, as well as changes in the definition of *mental disorders* by the

Social Security Administration itself, allowed a major increase in the overall disability insurance rolls in 1991 and 1992.

The *welfare path* encompasses the set of means-tested programs that serve as a safety net for workers without jobs who are not eligible for disability- or unemployment-based social insurance programs. Such programs can be universal, subject only to a means test and/or linked to an inability to work either because of ill health, poor job skills, or child rearing. This track can continue past retirement age for those not eligible for Social Security retirement benefits. The Food Stamp program comes closest to being a general income-tested program in the United States. Supplemental Security Income (SSI) is a means-tested program for those aged 65 and over, and it is available for younger people with a disability. Other examples of federal categorical means-tested programs are Aid for Families with Dependent Children (AFDC) and Women, Infants and Children, both of which are aimed at helping children.

It is on the welfare path that the social welfare system of the United States varies most from Western European countries. In the United States there are no universal social safety nets that provide a basic income to all citizens. Hence, a program like SSI, which in principle restricts eligibility to those under age 65 living in low-income households, faces much greater applicant pressure during declines in economic conditions than do the disability transfer programs in Western European countries. During economic downturns SSI program administrators face the same pressures to allow unemployed workers onto the SSI blind or disabled rolls as do SSDI administrators. Retrenchment in policy during the early 1980s resulted in a fall in the SSI adult blind and disabled population. But disability policy changes brought on by legislative and court actions in 1984 led to modest increases in the rolls over the remainder of the decade and to rapid expansion in the recessionary years of the early 1990s.

The simplified social welfare system pictured in Figure 1, and the role disability policy plays within it, provides a framework for considering the degree to which the ADA will increase employment among people with disabilities and offset the rise in the long-term disability transfer population.

MAINTAINING PEOPLE WITH DISABILITIES IN THE WORK FORCE

When a pathology begins to affect one's ability to work, important job-related decisions must be made by both the worker and his or her employer. These decisions will be influenced by the social institutions of the country. The relative rewards of continued movement along the work path versus entry onto an alternative path will be considered by the worker. In like manner, an employer's willingness to accommodate the worker will also be influenced by the social institutions and legal mandates within which the firm must operate.

This is not to suggest that all workers can or will transform themselves into candidates for disability transfer benefits. Rather it recognizes that those with some work limitations who are having difficulty with their current job or who are no longer working will be influenced by the relative rewards provided by the disability insurance, unemployment insurance, and welfare paths in deciding whether to try to remain in the labor force or to apply for transfer benefits.

Nor does it suggest that all people with disabilities have the ability to continue to work. Some have work limitations so severe that continued employment is impossible and a movement onto the transfer rolls is inevitable. But for others who experience the onset of a pathology that affects their ability to work, the length of time they stay on the job depends on the social institutions that are in place as well as their specific pathology and their particular job and employer. It is this subset of the population with disabilities that public policy can influence to either stay on the job or join the "purely" pathology-driven candidates for disability transfer or welfare programs.

In the United States, where welfare benefits are low and difficult to obtain for households without children, unemployment insurance benefits are of relatively short duration, and little is available in terms of rehabilitation and job protection or accommodation, the number of applicants for disability transfers will be relatively large. Disability transfer applicants will increase as replacement rates increase, as the period over which benefits can be received length-

171

ens, and as the probability of acceptance onto the disability rolls grows. It is not a surprise, given these characteristics of the United States social welfare system, that substantial applicant pressure was put on our disability transfer system during the economic downturn of the early 1990s.

In contrast, in European countries, where disability insurance path benefits are far more generous than in the United States, disability application pressure is less severe during economic downturns because all persons who sustain a work-limiting health condition are required to receive rehabilitation. Following rehabilitation, it is government policy to provide jobs in the public sector if private sector jobs are unavailable. For instance, in Germany, a combination of lower replacement rates, relatively more generous unemployment benefits, and a quota system deflect much of the pressure on the disability transfer system. (See Daly, 1994, for a comparison of work and transfer experience in the United States and Germany in the 1980s.)

THE AMERICANS WITH DISABILITIES ACT OF 1990

In the spirit of the Civil Rights legislation of the 1960s, the ADA attempts to provide people with disabilities the same access to employment as people without disabilities. Title I of the Americans with Disabilities Act of 1990 requires employers to make reasonable accommodations to workers with disabilities unless this would cause an undue hardship on the operation of business. This policy thrust also follows civil rights legislation of the 1960s in extending protection from employment discrimination to those with disabilities. On 26 July 1992, all employers of 25 or more workers were subject to the ADA. On 26 July 1994, its coverage was extended to all employers of 15 or more workers. But, when considering the actual influence of this act on the work of people with disabilities, it is important to recognize when it is most likely to be used and by whom.

It is unlikely that any of the 3.47 million recipients of Social Security Disability Insurance or SSI in 1992 will return to work as a result of ADA or any other current prowork policies. Despite some efforts to encourage those on the rolls to reenter the work force by extending the period of eligibility for Medicaid and Medicare benefits and allowing labor earnings during a transitionary period before ineligibility occurs, only a tiny percentage of those who go into these programs ever return to the work force.

Hennessey and DyKacz (1993) compared recovery termination rates (those who leave the program because they are judged able to engage in substantial gainful activity) of Social Security Disability Insurance beneficiaries entitled in 1972 and 1985 and found that, after four years, 7.7 percent of new beneficiaries in 1972 recovered but only 3.9 percent of new beneficiaries in 1985 recovered after four years.

Bound (1989; 1991) showed that the prognosis is not much better for those who apply for Social Security Disability Insurance benefits but are rejected. Using data from the 1978 Survey of the Disabled, he found that fewer than 30 percent of rejected applicants in the 1970s were employed in 1978 and only about two-fifths of that 30 percent were working full time.

Such data suggest that once the transition process to official disability has reached the point of either acceptance or rejection for disability transfer programs, a return to work is unlikely. Thus, current groups of the doubly disadvantaged, who are already on the disability insurance or welfare paths and whose income is dominated by transfers, are unlikely to return to the work path because of the ADA.

But the same is also likely to be the case for those who have applied for entrance to the disability insurance or welfare paths and have been turned down. The legal process to official disability can be a long one. Both those who succeed and those who fail to gain entrance to the disability rolls have already traveled a long road. To be eligible for benefits, a worker must not have performed any substantial gainful activity for at least five months and must be expected to not do so for at least a year. But lack of work for at least five months is only the beginning of the process for denied beneficiaries.

A combination of reductions in disability determination staff from 13,302 in 1986 to 11,168 in 1991 and the growth in applications fueled by the recession of the early 1990s has increased the time needed to process claims from 64 days in 1989 to 91 days in April 1992. Access time is estimated to be 213 days in fiscal year 1993 (Beedon, 1993). But this is only the first step in the elimination process and it does not include delays in a final determination caused by the appeals process. Those who are denied benefits at every step can spend several years before possible appeals are exhausted.

For workers with disabilities who do not work throughout this process, a return to work may be quite unlikely, even if they are ultimately rejected by the system (see Parsons 1991 for a fuller discussion). Hence, deciding to remain on the job after a health condition first begins to affect performance may bear little resemblance to the decision to work of those who have long since left the job they held when their work impairment first began. For those who have already left the work path it will be difficult to return, even with the ADA. The hope provided by the ADA is that intervention at the point a health condition first starts to affect job performance will delay job exit, as well as application for disability benefits. The ADA will actively reduce transfer dependency by reducing the likelihood that the onset of a pathology will lead down an incline onto the transfer paths.

Does Accommodation Prolong Work?

As we have discussed, it is likely that the ADA will do little for those already on the disability transfer rolls. But Table 1 shows that the majority of working-age people with disabilities are not in these programs and could have their work life extended by the ADA.

The first effective date for the employment provisions of the ADA was 26 July 1992, so it is far too early to determine its influence on accommodation. But an important new data set begun in 1992 provides a first glimpse of how workers with disabilities in 1992 were accommodated when their health condition first began to affect their ability to work.

Table 3 uses data from the Health and Retirement Survey (HRS) to show the accommodation experience of a random sample of men and women aged 51–61 in 1992. As before, we define the population of people with disabilities using a self-report work limits question. Like the PSID, the HRS asks respondents, "Do you have any impairment or health problem that limits the kind or amount of paid work you can do?" Because only one wave of data has been collected, we are unable to distinguish short-term from long-term

Table 3

Employment and Accommodation of Persons Impaired During Their Work Life[a,b]

	All Persons	Men	Women	No High School Degree	High School Graduate
Employed at the time of impairment[c]	998	561	437	356	642
Percent accommodated by initial employer[d]	23.0	21.5	24.9	21.1	23.9
Percent accommodated who are currently working[e]	47.3	50.3	43.9	34.3	52.9
Percent not accommodated who are currently working	32.9	38.9	28.7	17.6	40.9
Ratio of work probabilities[e] $100 * [(A - B)/B]$	.44	.29	.53	.95	.29

[a]The sample Ns represent the actual number of observations in the data.
[b]The reported percentages are weighted to adjust for families' unequal selection probabilities under the Health and Retirement Survey sample design.
[c]Employed at the time of impairment includes all those individuals who report that they were employed when their health began to limit their work.
[d]This category includes all of those individuals who were accommodated by their employer at the time the impairment occurred.
[e]This category calculates those individuals who are currently working divided by whether they were accommodated or not. The current job may be with the initial employer or any subsequent employer.
Source: Health and Retirement Survey Alpha Release Tape.

health problems. Thus, our sample of people with disabilities from the HRS includes all individuals who answer yes to the work limits question. Although all of these people had a health condition that affected their ability to work in 1992, the onset of those conditions and their employers' responses to them predate the implementation of the ADA. In this pre-ADA sample nearly one person in four was accommodated by his or her employer at the time health first began affecting the person's ability to work. Women were slightly more likely to be accommodated than men. High school graduates were slightly more likely to be accommodated than those with less than a high school education.

More important for those who hope that accommodation will prolong work life, nearly one-half (47.3 percent) of those who were accommodated by their employers were working in 1992 whereas fewer than one in three (32.9 percent) of those not accommodated were working in that year. Men were more likely to be working than women and high school graduates more likely than those with less education.

The last row of Table 3 shows the current employment of those accommodated relative to those not accommodated. Those who were accommodated were 44 percent more likely to be working than those not accommodated, with the highest percentages among women and those with less than a high school education.

These results are consistent with those reported in Burkhauser, Butler, and Kim (1995), which used data from the 1978 Survey of Disability and Work to trace the ability of workers to continue with their employers following the onset of a health condition that affected their ability to work. They found that 30 percent of men with disabilities in 1978 had been accommodated by their employers at the time they experienced a work-limiting health condition. By simulating the results of their hazard model for an otherwise average worker who is accommodated, they estimated that the worker would continue on the job another 7.5 years. For the same worker who was not accommodated, they estimated a continued tenure of 2.6 years. The results from these two pre-ADA samples suggest that accommodation can prolong work life following the onset of a health condition.

THE POWER OF POLICY INTERVENTION

Early indications are that accommodation can extend employment for people with disabilities. But the dimensions of this impact must be put in perspective. The median age at onset of the health condition that limited work in the HRS sample in Table 3 was age 49. Age 62 is the earliest age of eligibility for Social Security benefits. Hence, even if accommodation nearly triples work life as reported by Burkhauser, Butler, and Kim (1995) to 7.5 years, this will not keep the average worker in the work force to early Social Security retirement age.

In addition, the Burkhauser, Butler, Kim (1995) results, as well as the ones reported in Table 3, probably represent the upper limit of the effect of ADA-enforced accommodation for at least two reasons. It is unlikely that prior to the ADA employers randomly chose who they accommodated. In the absence of the ADA a profit-maximizing firm would be more likely to accommodate those whose

Table 4

Distribution of ADA Title I Charges Received
26 July 1992–31 August 1993

Violations	Number	Percent of Total[a]
Discharge	7,024	49.0
Failure to Provide Reasonable Accommodation	3,216	22.4
Hiring	1,871	13.1
Harassment	1,428	10.0
Discipline	1,039	7.2
Layoff	706	4.9
Rehire	552	3.9
Benefits	524	3.7
Wages	516	3.6
Promotion	508	3.5

[a]This list adds up to more than 100 percent because individuals can allege multiple violations.
Source: ADA Compliance Guide Monthly Bulletin (1993).

chance of success per dollar spent on accommodation was highest. If successful, the ADA, which requires accommodation unless it imposes an undue hardship on the employer, is likely to widen the scope of accommodation to workers with more significant conditions and lower expected success rates. (See Chirikos, 1991, for a review of the literature on accommodation prior to the passage of the ADA.) A second, and potentially more important, concern is whether the law will significantly increase accommodation, especially for the doubly disadvantaged who were left behind in the last economic recovery and who were less likely to be accommodated prior to the ADA.

In the first 13 months after its enactment, from 26 July 1992 through 31 August 1993, 14,334 complaints alleging discrimination in employment under Title I of ADA were filed with the Equal Employment Opportunity Commission (EEOC). The distribution of the alleged violations is reported in Table 4. It is important that the great majority of charges were brought by employees against their current employer. Only 13.1 percent involved people with disabilities seeking new employment. And the two most common violations concerned discharge and failure to provide reasonable accommodation. This provides further evidence that the ADA will be more effectively used to ensure continued work with a current employer than to secure work with a new employer.

O'Meara (1989) documents a similar allegation pattern with respect to charges filed with the EEOC under the Age Discrimination in Employment Act (ADEA) of 1967. O'Meara reports that 76 percent of the allegations of violation under the ADEA between 1978 and 1983 resulted from terminations.

Although no data are currently available on the characteristics of the workers who brought allegations to the EEOC under the ADA, it is likely that they will be similar to plaintiffs in ADEA cases. Schuster and Miller (1986) found that during the early 1980s most ADEA plaintiffs were white, male professionals and managers. As we saw in Table 2, among those with disabilities, current employment is much greater for nonblacks and those with at least a high school education. Therefore, even though the ADA will extend legally enforceable civil rights to all people with disabilities, those workers with the negotiating strength and access to the legal system required to secure employer compliance with ADA mandates will likely be disproportionately white, male, highly educated professionals and managers. The doubly disadvantaged may remain outside the impact of ADA.

Increasing an individual's ability to fight civil rights violations is appropriate regardless of his or her age, race, gender, or economic status. But the ADA is likely to be most effective in extending the employment of those whose disabilities are most easily accommodated and who possess the strongest education, training, and marketable skills. As we saw in Table 2, and as Burkhauser, Haveman, and Wolfe (1993) and Daly (1994) have demonstrated, using multiyear data from an income distribution perspective, this elite subgroup of those with disabilities is also the group that after the economic recovery of the late 1980s moved closest to labor earnings parity with those without disabilities. In the absence of additional federal support, the impact of the ADA on the doubly disadvantaged who were left behind by economic recovery in the 1980s is likely to be minimal and its effect on current disability transfer recipients nil.

CONCLUSIONS AND POLICY CONSIDERATIONS

The recession of the early 1990s has once again shown how sensitive the long-term disability transfer population is to economic conditions. Social Security Disability Insurance rolls increased by nearly 20 percent between 1989 and 1992. SSI disability rolls increased by 25 percent over the same period. The causes for such a rapid increase in the long-term disability transfer population are rooted more in economic factors than in changes in the health of American workers. In response to the treatment of disability transfer recipients during the retrenchment period of 1978 to 1983, Congress and the courts significantly increased access to the disability insurance and welfare paths out of the labor force. When the recession of the early 1990s struck, the number of applications to disability transfer programs soared and so did the number of new beneficiaries.

Title I of the Americans with Disabilities Act of 1990 mandated that employers accommodate qualified workers with disabilities. Preliminary research suggests that accommodation at the moment that a health condition first begins to affect one's ability to work will help prolong work life. But between 1989 and 1992, people with disabilities were more likely to travel the disability insurance and welfare paths. In 1992, 1.3 million people applied for Social Security Disability Insurance benefits and .6 million were awarded benefits. In that same year the adult population on the blind and disabled SSI program increased by 344,000 or 9.4 percent. By comparison, in the first 13 months of the ADA's existence, July 1992 to August 1993, 14,334 charges were filed with EEOC. Even though those numbers do not provide a systematic comparison of the relative importance of the ADA, their orders of magnitude suggest more will be needed to keep people with disabilities on the job.

The longest recovery of the post-World War II period in the United States ended in 1989. If the 1990s are a period of slow economic growth, then it is likely that people with disabilities will repeat their experiences of the early 1980s, as reported by Burkhauser, Haveman, and Wolfe (1993) and Daly (1994), and will be disproportiately hurt by the recession. However, a prolonged recovery from the recession of 1990–1992 is likely to mean that, for most people with disabilities, economic integration will recur. Therefore, in general, people with disabilities have the same interest in policies that improve general economic growth as people without disabilities. But for the doubly disadvantaged, whose economic well-being has not risen with economic recovery and who are least likely to be aided by the ADA, no current policies are likely to bring economic integration.

What Can Be Done

The policy options to be sketched here are not meant to represent a specific legislative agenda, but rather to provide a sample of the kind of creative pro-work changes in government policy that would increase the likelihood of employment for people with disabilities. Some are marginal, others radical. Unlike the ADA, all would directly affect the government budget. But each is likely to affect the doubly disadvantaged at least as much as the ADA.

Direct Government Subsidies for Accommodation Prior to passage of the ADA, Section 190 of the Internal Revenue Code permitted businesses to deduct up to $35,000 for expenses incurred in removing physical barriers to access by handicapped and elderly individuals. In a revenue-neutral move following passage of the ADA, Section 190 deductions were reduced to a maximum of $15,000, but an "access credit" was enacted that enables small businesses to claim a credit against taxes for one-half of their first $10,000 of eligible costs of complying with the ADA. This extremely modest credit was expected to result in an annual revenue loss to the Treasury of less than $10 million. (See Schaffer, 1991, for a fuller discussion.) This is a trivial government expenditure when compared to transfer payments or even current rehabilitation pro-grams. A more controversial strategy for increasing accommodation would be for the United States to follow the example of European countries where employers who provide accommodation and train-ing to workers with disabilities receive generous government-funded reimbursements. Making government, rather than employers, pri-marily responsible for financing the costs of accommodation would shift public policy from the stick of ADA mandates to the carrot of accommodation tax credits.

The Earned Income Tax Credit Expansion of the Earned Income Tax Credit (EITC) was the single most important piece of welfare legislation passed in the first two years of the Clinton Administration. It will effectively raise the hourly wages earned by a minimum wage earner with children in 1996 from $4.25 per hour to $5.95 per hour. (See Burkhauser, Couch, and Glenn, forthcoming, for a fuller discussion.) Expanding EITC eligibility to people with disabilities who live in low-income households would increase their reward for staying on the work path. This would target government funding to those with disabilities and poor job skills whose current productivity in the private sector is not great enough to command wages sufficient for their families to reach a minimum living standard.

Education and Job Training The EITC is an effective method of providing low-wage workers who live in or near poverty with greater income until they acquire the education, skills, and training to earn higher wages on their own. For those with disabilities and low job skills who are capable of work, transfer payments tied to wages offer a pro-work alternative to SSI. But, in the longer run, the road to higher wages for the doubly disadvantaged is the same as for those without disabilities but with poor job skills. As the Clinton administration plans its new job and welfare policies, it needs to recognize that most people with disabilities are capable of work and should have the same access to job programs and the same responsibility to leave the welfare rolls as other Americans.

Rehabilitation More substantive policy changes would shift current American disability policy from one primarily driven by transfers to one where a return to work was the primary goal. For instance, one such change would require all Social Security Disability Insurance or SSI applicants to go through a temporary benefit phase in which they were evaluated for rehabilitation, as is done in Sweden and Germany. Linking rehabilitation to the transfer program is especially important given the drop in age and the changing mix of conditions of new beneficiaries.

What We Need to Know

It is beyond the scope of this chapter to specify the optimal mix of policies and programs to best integrate people with disabilities into society. Providing accommodation will certainly extend the work life of those with disabilities. But accommodation was provided to a large minority of workers with disabilities before the passage of the ADA and it remains to be seen how much more accommodation will be provided because of the ADA.

To answer that question, and more generally to determine how people with disabilities will fare over the next decade, investments in a new generation of data on people with disabilities are critical. Because disability is a process of transition for most people, it is important that the data be multiperiod. The new Health and Retirement Survey under the leadership of the National Institute on Aging is a major advance in this direction. It combines excellent data on socioeconomic variables with excellent information on a respondent's health and the workplace. But it is limited to a cohort of men and women aged 51–61 in 1992. Hence, even though it will become the most important data source for following the transition into disability and retirement for older workers in the 1990s, it will not capture the experience of younger workers. It is critical that multiyear data be collected on younger cohorts. Without such data, it will be difficult to capture the influence of accommodation on the whole population.

Researchers will, however, be able to monitor the overall economic well-being and work experiences of people with disabilities using nationally representative cross-sectional data from the Current Population Surveys and multiyear data like the PSID and SIPP. The CPS and PSID have been used to evaluate the population with disabilities since the 1970s and will continue to provide some evidence of how they have fared in the 1990s. The SIPP has detailed disability questions that focus on physical, ADL (activities of daily living), and IADL (instrumental activities of daily living) limitations and allow researchers to describe the level and degree of impairment among those with disabilities. The next step is to add supplementary disability modules, like those in the SIPP, to the CPS and PSID so that researchers can begin to track the changing causes and conditions.

Table A-1

Definition of Disability for Cash Benefits

Program	Purpose of Definition	Definition — Cash Benefits
Disability Insurance (OASDI)	Entitlement to benefits to partially replace past earnings.	INABILITY TO WORK. Inability to engage in substantial gainful activity by reason of a medically determinable physical or mental impairment that is expected to last 12 months or result in death. The impairment must be of such severity that the individual cannot, after taking account of his age, education and work experience, do his previous work or any other work that exists in the national economy.
Private long-term disability insurance	Contractual entitlement to benefits to partially replace past earnings.	OWN OCC/ANY OCC. Often, for first two years, inability to do own occupation. Then inability to do any suitable occupation.
Private short-term disability insurance	Contractual entitlement to benefits to temporarily replace earnings.	OWN JOB. Inability to perform own job.
U.S. Civil Service disability	Federal employees' entitlement to disability pension.	OCCUPATIONAL. Because of disease or injury, unable to render useful and efficient service in the employee's current position or in a vacant position in the same agency at the same pay level for which the individual is qualified for reassignment.
Railroad retirement disability annuity	Railroad workers' entitlement to monthly annuity based on disability.	TOTAL AND PERMANENT DISABILITY (same as OASDI). Occupational disability (for workers with 20 years of service and current connection with railroad job) is inability to perform the worker's regular railroad job.
Veterans' Compensation	Veterans' entitlement to compensation for disability caused during military service – ranging from 10 to 100 percent disability.	A rating board of the Department of Veterans' Affairs determines each individual's disability rating on a case by case basis.
Supplemental Security Income (adults)	Entitlement to means-tested cash assistance.	INABILITY TO WORK. (same as disability insurance – OASDI).
Supplemental Security Income (children)	Entitlement to means-tested cash assistance.	Comparable to INABILITY TO WORK. Same as disability insurance – OASDI, modified with individualized functional assessment based on age-appropriate functioning.

Table A-1 (CONT.)

Program	Purpose of Definition	Definition
		Civil Rights Protection
Americans with Disabilities Act	To determine who is protected by the non-discrimination and public accommodations provisions of ADA.	BROAD. Individual with a physical or mental impairment that substantially limits one or more major life activity; a record of such an impairment; or being regarded as having such an impairment.
		Eligibility for Services
Federal and State programs. Vocational Rehabilitation (VR)	To determine who is eligible to receive VR services.	SERVICE NEED. Individual with a physical or mental disability that is a significant impediment to employment and requires VR services to prepare for, enter, engage in or retain gainful employment. SERVICE DELIVERY. If accepted for services, individualized written rehab plan (IWRP) lists goals and individual services to be provided.
Private employment based disability insurance – VR	To determine who might be offered employer-financed VR services (which are not part of contractual employee benefit agreement).	COST/BENEFIT. Employer- or insurer-financed VR services are at the discretion of the employer/insurer and are provided based on cost recovery potential of the employee to return to work. SERVICE DELIVERY. At the discretion of the employer/insurer, subject to agreement of the worker.
Medicaid – institutional care	Eligibility for Medicaid-financed institutional care, or community-based alternative.	ADL LIMITATION. Needs assistance with activities of daily living (ADLs) or medical assessment of need for institutional care. Depends on the state plan.
Clinton Health Care Reform Plan	Eligibility for home and community-based care under the proposal.	ADL LIMITATION. Requires assistance to perform three of five ADLs: eating, bathing, dressing, toileting and transferring; or severe cognitive or mental impairment, or severely disabled child under six years of age.
Special Education – Part B	Eligibility of children aged 3 to 21 for special education services.	TYPES OF DISABILITIES. Categories include mental retardation, hearing, speech or vision impairment, serious emotional disturbance, orthopedic or other health impairment, deaf-blind, multi-handicapped, or severe learning disability. SERVICE DELIVERY. Individualized education plan (IEP) describes services the school system is obligated to provide the student.

Table A-1 (CONT.)

Program	Purpose of Definition	Definition
		Eligibility for Services (cont.)
Special Education, Early Intervention – Part H	Eligibility of infants and toddlers for early intervention services (aged 0 to 3 years)	DEVELOPMENTAL DELAY in cognitive, physical, communication, social, emotional, or adaptive development, or child with diagnosed conditions with high probability of developmental delay. SERVICE DELIVERY. Individualized Family Service Plan (IFSP) describes services and supports that the state is obligated to provide the family.
Medicaid – EPSDT	Eligibility of children for Medicaid financed services	ASSESSMENT OF NEED. Any medically necessary treatment that is diagnosed under the EPSDT provisions of Medicaid is a covered service that will be financed by Medicaid.
U.S. Census (STP)	Data collection – estimate prevalence in the population for statistical purposes	FUNCTIONAL LIMITATIONS. Difficulty with (and/or unable to): see, hear, speak and be understood, carry 10 lbs., climb stairs, walk a quarter mile.
U.S. Census (SIPP) HRS	Data collection – estimate prevalence in the population for statistical purposes	ADLs. Difficulty (or need assistance) with: getting around inside or outside the home, getting in or out of a bed or chair, taking a bath or shower, dressing, eating, and using the toilet.
U.S. Census (SIPP) HRS	Data collection – estimate prevalence in the population for statistical purposes	INSTRUMENTAL ACTIVITIES OF DAILY LIVING. Difficulty (or need for assistance) with: going outside the home, keeping track of money or bills, preparing meals, doing light housework, and using the telephone.
U.S. Census (SIPP) PSID HRS	Data collection – estimate prevalence in the population for statistical purposes	WORK LIMITATION. A physical, mental or other health impairment that limits kind or amount of work respondent can do or prevents work at a job or business.
National Health Interview Survey (NHIS)	Data collection – estimate prevalence in the population for statistical purposes	MAJOR ACTIVITY LIMITATION. Because of a chronic health condition, limitation in (or inability to perform) major activity – which is play for young children, school for school-age children, work for working age adults.

Source: Reno (1994). Materials provided to the National Academy of Social Insurance (NASI). Panel on Disability Reform.

REFERENCES

Aarts, L., R. V. Burkhauser, and P. de Jong. 1982. "A Cautionary Tale of European Disability Policies: Lessons for the United States." *Regulation* 15, no. 2: 75–86.

"ADA Employment Bias Complaints to EEOC Top 11,000." 1993. *ADA Compliance Guide Monthly Bulletin* 4, no. 11.

Anderson, K. H., R. V. Burkhauser, and J. E. Raymond. 1993. "The Effect of Creaming on Placement Rates under the Job Training Partnership Act." *Industrial and Labor Relations Review* 46, no. 4: 613–624.

Bazzoli, G. J. 1985. "Evidence on the Influence of Health." *Journal of Human Resources* 20, no. 2: 214–234.

Beedon, L. E. 1993. "Changing Social Security Disability Insurance." AARP Public Policy Institute Working Paper 9302. Washington, D.C.: AARP.

Bennefield, R. L., and J. M. McNeil. 1989. "Labor Force States and Other Characteristics of Persons with Work Disabilities 1981 to 1988." *Current Population Reports*, Special Series no. 160: 23. Washington, D.C: Bureau of the Census.

Berkowitz, E. 1987. *Disability Policy: America's Programs for the Handicapped*. New York: Cambridge University Press.

Bound, J. 1989. "The Health and Earnings of Rejected Disability Insurance Applicants." *American Economic Review* 81, no. 5: 1427–1434.

———. 1991. "Self-Reported versus Objective Measures of Health in Retirement Models." *Journal of Human Resources* 26, no. 1: 106–138.

Bound, J., and T. Waidman. 1992. "Disability Transfers, Self-Reported Health, and the Labor Force Attachment of Older Men: Evidence from the Historical Record." *Quarterly Journal of Economics* 107, no. 4: 1393–1419.

Burkhauser, R. V., J. S. Butler, and Y. W. Kim. 1992. "The Importance of Employer Accommodation on the Job Duration of

Workers with Disabilities: A Hazard Model Approach." *Labour Economics* 3, no.1:1-22.

Burkhauser, R. V., and M. Daly. 1995. "Employment and Economic Well-Being Following the Onset of a Disability: The Role for Public Policy," Cross-National Studies in Aging Program Project Paper No. 22, All-University Gerontology Center, The Maxwell School. Syracuse, NY: Syracuse University. March.

Burkhauser, R. V., K. A. Couch, and A. J. Glenn, forthcoming. "Public Policies for the Working Poor: The Earned Income Tax Credit Versus Minimum Wage Legislation," In *Research in Labor Economics* 16, ed. Solomon W. Polachek. Greenwich, Conn.: JAI Press, Inc.

Burkhauser, R. V., R. H. Haveman, and B. L. Wolfe. 1993. "How People with Disabilities Fare when Public Policies Change." *Journal of Policy Analysis and Management* 12, no. 2: 251–269.

Burkhauser, R. V., and P. Hirvonen. 1989. "United States Disability Policy in a Time of Economic Crisis: A Comparison with Sweden and the Federal Republic of Germany," *Milbank Quarterly* 67, no. 2: 166–194.

Chirikos, T. N. 1991. "The Economics of Employment." *Milbank Quarterly* 69 (Supplement 1-2): 150-182.

Chirikos, T. N., and G. Nestel. 1984. "Economic Determinants and Consequences of Self-Reported Work Disability." *Journal of Health Economics* 3, no. 2: 117–136.

———. 1991. "Occupational Differences in the Ability of Men to Delay Retirement." *Journal of Human Resources* 26, no. 1: 1–26.

Daly, M. C. 1994. "The Economic Well-Being of Men with Disabilities: A Dynamic Cross-National View." Unpublished Ph.D. dissertation, Syracuse University.

de Jong, P., M. Herweijer, and J. deWildt. 1990. *Form and Reform of the Dutch Social Security System.* Deventer, Netherlands: Kluwer Law and Taxation Publishers.

Derthick, M. 1990. *Agency under Stress: The Social Security Administration in American Government.* Washington, D.C.: Brookings Institution.

Frick, B. 1990. "Interne Arbeitsmärkte und betriebliche Schwerbe-hindertenbeseahäftigigung: Theoretische Analysen und empirische Befunde," Ph.D. dissertation, Trier University.

Haveman, R. H., and B. L. Wolfe. 1990. "The Economic Well-Being of the Disabled, 1962–1984." *Journal of Human Resources* 25, no. 1: 32–55.

Hennessey, J., and J. M. Dykacz. 1993. "A Comparison of the Recovery Termination Rates of Disabled Worker Beneficiaries Entitled in 1972 and 1985." *Social Security Bulletin* 56, no. 2: 58–69.

Hill, M. S. 1992. *The Panel Study of Income Dynamics: A User's Guide*. Beverly Hills, Calif.: Sage Publications.

Jones, N. Lee. 1991. "Essential Requirements of the Act: A Short History and Overview." *Milbank Quarterly* 69 (Supplement 1–2): 25–54.

Laplante, M. 1991. "The Demographics of Disability." *Milbank Quarterly*, 69 (Supplement 1-2):55-80.

McNeil, J. M. 1993. "Americans with Disabilities: 1991–92," *Current Population Reports*, Household Economic Studies P70-33. Washington, DC: Bureau of the Census.

Myers, R. J. 1982. "Why Do People Retire from Work Early?" *Aging and Work* 5: 83–91.

———. 1983. "Further Controversies on Early Retirement Study." *Aging and Work* 6: 105–109.

Nagi, S. 1965. "Some Conceptual Issues in Disability and Rehabilitation." In *Sociology and Rehabilitation*, ed. M. B. Sussman. Washington, D.C.: American Sociological Association.

———. 1969. *Disability and Rehabilitation: Legal, Clinical and Self-Concepts of Measurement*. Columbus: Ohio State University Press.

———. 1991. "Disability Concepts Revisited: Implications to Prevention." In *Disability in America: Toward a National Agenda for Prevention*, ed. A. M. Pope and A. R. Tarlove, Appendix A. Washington, D.C.: National Academy Press.

O'Meara, D. 1989. "Protecting the Growing Number of Older Workers: The Age Discrimination in Employment Act." *Labor Relations and Public Policy Series* No. 33. Philadelphia: Industrial Relations Unit.

Parsons, D. O. (1980). "The Decline in Male Labor Force Participation." *Journal of Political Economy* 88: 117–134.

————. 1982. "The Male Labor Force Participation Decision: Health, Reported Health, and Economic Incentives." *Econometrica* 49: 81–91.

————. 1991. "The Health and Earnings of Rejected Disability Insurance Applicants: Comment." *American Economic Review* 81, no. 5: 1419–1426.

Reno, V. 1994. Preliminary status report of the Disability Policy Panel convened by The National Academy of Social Insurance.

Schaffer, D. C. 1991. "Tax Incentives." *Milbank Quarterly* 69 (Supplement 1-2): 293–312.

Schuster, M., and C. P. Miller. 1986. "An Evaluation of the Age Discrimination in Employment Legislation." Final report of the NRTA-AARP Andrus Foundation, February 18, All-University Gerontology Center, The Maxwell School, Syracuse University.

U.S. Department of Health and Human Services, Social Security Administration. Various years. *Annual Statistical Supplement.* Washington: U.S. Government Printing Office.

Weaver, C. 1986. "Social Security Disability Policy in the 1980s and Beyond." In *Disability and the Labor Market: Economic Problems, Policies, and Programs*, ed. Monroe Berkowitz and Ann Hill, pp. 29–63. Ithaca, N.Y.: ILR Press.

NOTES

1. The American with Disabilities Act of 1990 consists of five titles and offers civil rights protection across a wide front for people of all ages with disabilities. This chapter focuses on the importance of Title I (employment) on people of working age with disabilities. See Jones (1991) for a review of the ADA.
2. Since 1968, the PSID has interviewed annually a representative sample of some 5000 families. At least one member of

each family was either part of the original families interviewed in 1968 or born to a member of one of these families. Table 1 uses data from the 1988 and 1989 waves of the PSID to represent the working-age (18 to 61) noninstitutionalized U.S. population of household heads and their spouses in 1988. For a more complete discussion of these date, see Hill (1992).

3. The PSID does not ask about the health of all household members. Hence, this sample will exclude adults aged 18 to 61 who live in a household in which they are neither a head nor a spouse. It is likely that a disproportionate percentage of such people will have a work limitation. The choice of "working-age" is somewhat arbitrary. We chose age 18 because that is generally the age of high school graduation. We chose age 61 because it is the last year before eligibility for Social Security retirement benefits.

4. Bennefield and McNeil (1989) report that estimates from the CPS are lower than estimates from both the Survey of Income and Program Participation (SIPP) and the National Health Interview Survey (NHIS).

5. Burkhauser, Haveman, and Wolfe (1993) use a two-pronged definition of *disability* that includes both individuals who report that their health limits their ability to work full time and individuals who receive disability-related transfers. They do not report the proportion of their disability population that meets each of the two criteria. To obtain an estimate of the number of working-age people in their sample who were included based on the health-constrained work criterion, we used information from an earlier paper by Haveman and Wolfe (1990) in which they report the proportion of individuals with disabilities who meet each of the criteria. We assume this proportion remained constant between 1984 – the last year examined by Haveman and Wolfe (1990) – and 1988. In 1984, 62 percent of the population with disabilities as defined by Haveman and Wolfe (1990) and Burkhauser, Haveman, and Wolfe (1993) were considered disabled by the health-constrained work criteria. Thus, we estimate the prevalence of health-constrained work in 1988 as 62 percent of the disability population (9.9 percent of the working age population) or 6.2 percent.

6. After-government income is based on actual income data from the PSID. Before-government income is a "counterfactual," which makes the strong assumption that behavior does not change in the absence of government. This is clearly only an approximation of what would actually occur in the absence of government. Hence, our before-government values are best thought of as a means of showing to whom current benefits go, given current government policy, rather than as a measure of what would actually occur in the absence of government. To adjust for families of different sizes, family income was adjusted by using the equivalence scale in the official poverty measures.

7. In 1992, 57 percent of those receiving Social Security Disability Insurance were aged 50 to 64. Of those receiving such benefits for the first time in 1992, 51 percent were aged 50 or over (U.S. Department of Health and Human Services, 1993).

8. To the degree that death before age 61 is more likely for those with disabilities whose onset was at birth or before age 18, this older cohort-based population will overstate the average age of onset. Even after adjusting for such biases, it is likely that the great majority of people with disabilities had work experience before onset of their disability.

9. Burkhauser and Hirvonen (1989), for instance, show that, in 1985, 25 people were in supported work or vocational rehabilitation programs for every 100 persons receiving disability transfer benefits in the United States. This was a decline from over 40 per 100 in the 1970s. In contrast, Western European countries like Sweden, which uses rehabilitation and job creation programs as their principal mechanism for responding to the needs of people with disabilities, had a ratio of 30 per 100 in 1985. Germany, where medical and vocational rehabilitation as well as a mandated job quota system are the primary policy tools for assisting those with disabilities, had a ratio of 45 per 100 in 1985.

10. In Sweden and Germany there is a deliberate effort to rehabilitate workers who continue in a short-term sickness program. In addition, there are restrictions on the ability of employers to discharge a worker with disabilities.

Implications for Income Maintenance Policy

Edward D. Berkowitz

EDITOR'S NOTE

One of the desired outcomes of the ADA is an increase in the employment of people with disabilities. Yet our nation's primary response to disability has been retirement rather than work. It is ironic that, just as the ADA mandate goes into effect, the rolls of income maintenance support programs (SSI and SSDI) have swelled. As Berkowitz notes, "Rising numbers of people seek tickets out of the labor force, just as a major new law is providing a new source of tickets into the labor force."

Berkowitz asks the key question for reforming our nation's social welfare policy so that the goals of the ADA can be met. How do we construct a system so that work replaces retirement as the nation's primary response to disability? He proposes reforms in the nation's SSI/SSDI programs that would promote rehabilitation, permanent health insurance benefits, and employment as the first line of response to disability. Intervention must begin before an individual is on the rolls, not afterward, he argues. He calls for enhanced federal incentives to businesses for employing people with disabilities and concludes that our nation will not likely achieve the desired outcomes of the ADA without fundamentally altering its income maintenance programs.

Edward D. Berkowitz is professor and chair of the Department of History at the George Washington University. Berkowitz has written widely on social welfare policy including a watershed analytic history of federal disability programs, Disabled Policy *(1987). He is the author of* America's Welfare State *(1991),* Social Security and Medicare: A Policy Primer *(1993), and* Mr. Social Security: The Life of Wilbur J. Cohen *(1995).*

ADA[1]

In thinking about the Americans with Disabilities Act (ADA), it helps to separate the passage and implementation of the act. During congressional debate, it was only natural for proponents, hoping to attract the votes necessary for passage, to portray the legislation in positive terms. In particular, they sought to counteract the charge that the act would be needlessly intrusive. As a consequence, they promised that the act, far from exemplifying excessive government regulation, would, in fact, save the taxpayers' money. In making this claim, the proponents followed a long tradition in social welfare policy of transforming apparent expenditures into long-term investments that would pay future dividends (Berkowitz, 1991).

The dividends from ADA, it was implied although never explicitly stated, would come from reductions in expenditures in Social Security Disability Insurance (SSDI) and Supplemental Security Income (SSI). These were the nation's most important and most costly income maintenance programs for people with disabilities. In 1990, when the ADA was enacted, they provided over $38 billion for approximately 6,374,000 people with disabilities (Koitz, Kollman, and Neisner, 1992, pp. 64–65). Trends indicated that both benefit programs had been steadily expanding since 1982 (Berkowitz, 1993; Burkhauser, Haveman, and Wolfe, 1993).

In this chapter, I argue that progress in stemming the enrollment and the costs depends upon using the positive features of the ADA and making fundamental changes in SSI and SSDI. If we are to allow the ADA to set the tone for our disability policy, then we must change the other social welfare programs that affect people with disabilities. In particular, we must find ways to prevent people from entering the disability rolls. We must create a climate in which people with disabilities expect to work and employers expect to hire them. The only way to do that is to change the rules for awarding SSI and SSDI benefits.

This chapter, it should be emphasized, focuses exclusively on the relationship between ADA, on the one hand, and SSI and SSDI, on the other. It uses the programs administered by the Social Security Administration as a case study of the inconsistency between the ADA and the nation's income replacement programs. In viewing policy through this lens, I do not mean to distort the purpose of the ADA. As the other chapters in this book make abundantly clear, the primary purpose of ADA is not to reduce the size of the SSI or SSDI rolls, any more than the primary motivation for passing ADA was to reduce social welfare expenditures.

The chapter chronicles the early stages in the implementation of the ADA, focusing on the promises made during the legislative debate. It then describes historic patterns and recent developments in SSI and SSDI, highlighting the volatility in the number of people on the rolls. Next, the discussion turns to previous efforts to reform the SSI and SSDI programs so as to encourage program beneficiaries to work and explains the reasons for the failure of those efforts. Finally, the essay suggests ways in which SSI and SSDI could be changed to promote the goals of the ADA.

IMPLICIT PROMISES

The first task is to delve selectively into the legislative history of the ADA. When one studies the legislative record, one finds repeated references to the ways in which the act, if passed, would reduce the costs of income maintenance programs. Simply put, the act would help people with disabilities to get jobs. Once people with disabilities obtained jobs, they would no longer need either welfare (SSI) or social insurance (SSDI) payments. In other words, passage of ADA would help to reorient the nation's social welfare policy. SSI and SSDI condition aid to people with disabilities on the total inability to work. ADA would emphasize the entrance of people with disabilities into the labor force.

In reporting on the bill in 1989, the Senate Labor and Human Resources Committee highlighted the testimony of Sandra Parrino, the chair of the National Council on Disability. Parrino said that it was "contrary to sound principles of fiscal responsibility to spend billions of Federal tax dollars to relegate people with disabilities to positions of dependency on public support." She referred to the "unwanted dependency" of people with disabilities on "social welfare." In taking this position, Parrino also reflected the sentiments of key members of the Bush administration, including the attorney general and the president himself.[2] The House Education and Labor Committee quoted Justin Dart, a former member of the National Council on Disability and an influential proponent of the ADA, as saying that, "We are already paying unaffordable and rapidly escalating billions in public and private funds to maintain ever-increasing millions of potentially productive Americans in unjust, unwanted dependency." The implicit promise in Parrino's and Dart's remarks was that passage of ADA would end the dependency and save the government money.[3]

Because the ADA had never been tried, no one knew whether it would, in fact, reduce social welfare costs. Previous laws, even the influential Section 504 of the Rehabilitation Act of 1973, lacked the sweep of the proposed new law. Proponents of ADA did know, however, that people wanted to be reassured about the low costs and positive effects of the new law and hastened to provide that reassurance.

The final version of the legislation included an elaborate preamble that suggested the need for a sweeping civil rights law aimed at people with disabilities. In keeping with the promises made, this statement of "findings and purposes" listed "full participation" and "economic self-sufficiency" among the "proper goals" of the nation's disability policy. "Unfair and unnecessary discrimination and prejudice" cost the country "billions of dollars in unnecessary expenses resulting from dependency and nonproductivity."[4] Presumably, the new law, by reducing the unfair and unnecessary discrimination, would also reduce the amount of money spent for dependency and nonproductivity.

Achievement of this ambitious goal required that more people with disabilities enter the labor force. Figures about the labor force participation rate of people with disabilities were difficult to obtain. Methodological issues concerning how to define and count the number of people with disabilities complicated the calculations (GAO, 1993, pp. 25–26). By one authoritative account, of the 7.9 million people with "severe work limitation" in 1990, only 12.3 percent were in the labor force and of those 2.7 percent or 213,000 people were unemployed. The remaining 6,914,000 people of working age with severe work limitation were not in the labor force.[5] The great majority of those people, approximately 6,034,000, were on either SSDI or SSI (Koitz, Kollman, and Neisner, 1992, pp. 64–65). One test of ADA would be to see if it would cause more people with a chronic illness or an impairment to find and hold jobs.

As a politically salient test of ADA's effectiveness, therefore, one could imagine a sequence in which the act made employers more aware of the abilities of people with disabilities and more aware of the consequences of the economic costs and legal penalties of discriminating against such people. That would cause a reduction in the unemployment rate for people with disabilities and might induce more people with disabilities to enter the labor force. Policy makers intended SSI or SSDI payments only for those who could demonstrate a total inability to work. As more people with disabilities entered the labor force or were expected to enter the labor force, therefore, the number of people on either SSDI or SSI should fall.

To be sure, many variables intervene in the process. For example, if the number of people with disabilities rises for demographic or health-related reasons, the disability rolls will rise. A long chain of evidence links the rate of disability to the aging of the population (Fries and Crapo, 1981). An unexpected event, such as the recent AIDS epidemic, increases the rate of morbidity and eventually of disability in the population. Furthermore, disability programs, although explicitly not designed to be a substitute for unemployment compensation, often function as exactly that. Hence, a rise in unemployment might cause a rise in the rolls, as it did between 1970 and 1975. In addition, low levels of education or a lack of support services induce people to seek either SSI or SSDI, simply for lack of a better alternative.

Despite these very real problems, the ADA sent a signal to the nation that people with disabilities could and should work. Title I stood at the heart of the ADA's employment strategy. Section 102 stated that, "No covered entity shall discriminate against a qualified individual because of the disability of such individual in regard to job application procedures, the hiring, advancement, or discharge of employees, employee compensation, job training, and other terms, conditions and privileges of employment."

This broad statement raised a host of further questions. The act defined a *qualified individual* as one "who with or without reasonable accommodation can perform the essential functions of the employment position that such person holds or desires." Businesses were expected to provide reasonable accommodation unless such an accommodation would pose "an undue hardship on the operation of the business" (Jones, 1990).

The section had the repetitive quality of legal prose, and for all that the terms were defined at considerable length, the section was also rather vague. To be sure, the nation had experience with Section 504 of the Rehabilitation Act of 1973, which uses many of the same terms. Despite that fact, concepts such as "essential functions" of a job and "undue hardship" would need to be defined first by regulation and later by case law. Nonetheless, the general expectation for the new legislation was clear: If one could reduce discrimination in the workplace, then one could raise the labor force participation rate of people with disabilities. If the labor force participation rate rose, then the number of people on the disability rolls would fall.

INCONCLUSIVE BEGINNINGS

Despite these hopes and expectations, legislators responsible for Social Security Disability Insurance and Supplemental Security Income never held hearings on the law. It fell into the bailiwick of committees concerned with civil rights, energy, transportation, labor law, and services for people with disabilities. In the House of Representatives, four major committees conducted hearings and issued reports on the ADA. Nonetheless, the House Committee on Ways and Means, responsible for much of the nation's income maintenance legislation, never reported on the law. The fit between ADA and the nation's income maintenance programs was never discussed publicly or placed in the public record.

In the period between July 1990 and July 1993, officials in the EEOC wrote regulations to govern Title I of the ADA, and the employment section of the law went into operation. Early results of the law's effectiveness in reducing or stemming the growth of the disability rolls are inconclusive. Still, there has been a disturbing rise in both the SSDI and SSI rolls between 1990 and 1992. For example, the number of people on SSDI and SSI fell between 1978 and 1984. Between 1990 and 1992, this number has increased dramatically.

Enforcement depended on people being willing to file a complaint with the Equal Employment Opportunity Commission. By the middle of 1993, the EEOC had received more than 11,000 charges of discrimination, nearly half of which concerned not people looking for a job but rather people discharged from a job. Whether this pattern would persist was not known (National Council on Disability, 1993, p. 36). The EEOC itself brought attention to the problems of discharges in November 1992 when the government filed its first lawsuit under the ADA. The case concerned a Chicago man who lost his job after his employer discovered he had brain cancer (Lewin, 1992).

ADA AND THE RHETORIC OF POLICY

If it was difficult to detect tangible results in the early period, the act nonetheless transformed the way in which policy makers talked about disability. The Ways and Means Committee asked the National Academy of Social Insurance to undertake a study on Rethinking Disability Policy. This study began in the summer of 1993. In the past the members of such a study group might have considered SSDI and SSI exclusively. In 1993 it became obligatory to mention the ADA. The National Academy promised a review of disability programs "that is mindful of the program costs and of the empowerment goals embodied in the Americans with Disabilities Act of 1990." Jerry Mashaw, the Yale law professor appointed to chair the group, said that, "This is a critically important time to be rethinking disability policy. The Americans with Disabilities Act emphasizes inclusion and independence as it bans discrimination in public accommodations and private employment."[6]

The official literature of the Social Security Administration (SSA) also explicitly referred to the Americans with Disabilities Act. In a booklet intended for wide distribution to people with disabilities, the SSA, which was responsible for administering both SSDI and SSI, noted that, "The enactment of the Americans with Disabilities Act (ADA) is a major step in the continued progress toward full empowerment for people with disabilities. Our mission to encourage employment and productivity is in keeping with the mandate provided by the ADA" (Health and Human Services, 1991).

Agency leaders, such as Gwendolyn King, the Bush administration's commissioner of Social Security, spoke of new goals of disability policy that were consistent with the objectives of the ADA. "I believe," said Gwendolyn King, "that the Disability Insurance and Supplemental Security Income programs should not be viewed exclusively as maintenance measures, as keeping disabled Americans at a barely visible status quo. I believe our programs should, in every case possible, be used as a leg up, as a stepping stone to a higher plane."[7] Louis Enoff, who became acting commissioner upon King's departure in September 1993, told an international conference that, "In the future, we have to build assumptions into our economic planning that people with impairments will be in the work force, and we must provide incentives for employers to promote this objective and disincentives for employers who fail to promote this objective." Enoff mentioned the ADA as a "positive first step."[8] And Robert Ball, commissioner of Social Security between 1962 and 1973 and still very much involved in Social Security policy making, asserted to a congressional subcommittee in April 1993 that, "There is no doubt in anyone's mind, certainly not in the minds of people with disabilities, particularly the younger ones – that a lifetime of receiving benefits from the government is vastly inferior to a lifetime in which they can contribute, as other people do, through regular jobs and work and so be a part of the community."[9]

HARD REALITIES: SSDI AND SSI IN OPERATION

Talk of this sort continued the process of reassurance that had begun during the congressional deliberations. It expressed future goals of disability, rather than current realities. As the ADA began operations, nothing in the performance of SSDI or SSI suggested that ADA had begun to change the nation's approach to disability. In fact, the income maintenance programs were expanding at disturbing rates.

Here some brief background on SSDI and SSI becomes necessary. SSDI began in 1956 as an extension of Social Security or old-age and survivors insurance. Before this date, retirement protection under Social Security was linked either to the death of a wage earner or to a worker's reaching the sanctioned retirement age of 65. SSDI operated similarly to Social Security in that it emphasized the orderly withdrawal of people from the labor force. People paid for SSDI as they did for Social Security, through a payroll tax assessed on them and on their employers. Between 1956 and 1972, SSDI benefits came to resemble other Social Security benefits. Like the other benefits, SSDI featured family protection, and entitlement to SSDI also enabled the beneficiary (but not his or her family) to receive Medicare. The only difference was that a two-year waiting period applied between eligibility for benefits and eligibility for Medicare.

Supplemental Security Income, legislated in 1972, operates as a welfare, rather than a social insurance program. This means that the program is financed through general revenues, instead of payroll

201

taxes. It also requires applicants to pass a means test – prove they are poor – before they receive aid. In an analogous fashion with SSDI, SSI recipients receive health insurance in the form of Medicaid.

As legislated in 1972, SSI included federal payments to the states for welfare grants to the elderly, the blind, and the "permanently and totally disabled." In 1974, during the program's first full year of operation, the elderly made up the majority of the SSI caseload. This changed by 1987. By 1991, disabled adults and children accounted for 71.4 percent of the people on SSI (Koitz, Kollman, and Neisner, 1992, p. 65).

Although separate programs, SSI and SSDI share a common procedure for determining disability and a common definition of disability. A person seeking SSDI, SSI, or increasingly, a combination of both, applies for them at an office of the Social Security Administration. Once the Social Security claims representatives and the claimant have gathered sufficient information to complete the application, the claims representatives send the file to a state disability determination office. Disability examiners in this office, working with the aid of vocational and medical consultants, act as the primary gatekeepers of both the SSI and SSDI programs. They are employees of state governments, because the state governments, rather than the federal governments, run the disability determination offices.

Both the SSDI and SSI laws define *disability* as the inability to engage in substantial gainful activity by reason of a medically determinable impairment (or impairments) expected to result in death or last at least 12 months. For an adult, a person has to be unable to do any work that exists in the national economy, for which that person is qualified by virtue of age, education, and work experience. Neither of the programs pays partial benefits based on the severity of disability. Instead, benefits vary in SSDI by family size and average predisability earnings and in SSI by such factors as state standards of need and the beneficiary's other income sources.

As a practical matter, the Social Security Administration asks the state disability determination offices to follow a five-step procedure in determining disability. In the first step, the examiners check to see if the applicant is currently working and making more than $500 a month, defined as the "substantial gainful activity" amount.

If so, the application is denied. (Few cases are rejected in this manner, because presumably the field offices have already checked to see if the applicant is working before they send the files to the disability determination office.) In the second step, the state disability examiners decide whether the applicant has a severe impairment. If not, the application is denied. In the third step, the state disability examiners attempt to ascertain if the impairment is included on a list of impairments defined to be disabling by the Social Security Administration. If the impairment is listed and if it can be expected to last at least 12 months, then the person receives benefits. If the impairment is judged to be equivalent of one of the disabling impairments, then the person also receives benefits. (Most benefits are awarded in this step, either for "meeting" or "equaling" the listings.)

If a decision cannot be reached on medical factors alone, the examiners proceed to examine the applicant's residual functional capacity. In the fourth step, they determine if the person's impairment prevents that person from meeting the demands of "past relevant work." If not, then benefits are denied. If so, examiners proceed to the fifth and final step in which they attempt to ascertain if the impairment prevents the applicant from doing other work.

Here vocational factors come into play. The Social Security Administration has developed an elaborate series of rules to reach a decision based on a person's age, education, work experience, and residual functional capacity. One might consider the case of a person whose maximum sustained work capacity is limited to sedentary work and who is 50–54 years old, has less than a high school education, and has no skilled work experience. According to the SSA rules, such a person would be considered disabled and given benefits. The assumption is that such a person should not have to work. But if that person's employment experience includes skilled work, then the rules dictate that the person be denied benefits. In 1991, nearly 32 percent of the benefits granted by the state agencies were based on these sorts of vocational considerations (Health and Human Services, 1992, p. 2).

If a person is denied SSDI or SSI benefits by the disability determination office, the system permits substantial avenues of appeal. The person has the right to ask the state agency to reconsider its decision. If still denied, the person might seek a hearing in which he or she presents the case in front of an administrative law judge (ALJ). The state offices have only a file, a paper record of evidence, to consider. The administrative law judge has the opportunity to see the applicant and to ask him or her questions. Between the time of the applicant's initial application and the hearing before the administrative law judge, the applicant's condition might have worsened. Over half of the applicants retain some sort of legal representative to argue their case before the ALJ (in 1980, 41 percent of the applicants were accompanied by a legal representative; Health and Human Services, 1992, p. 29). For these reasons, among others, ALJs reverse a substantial number of the decisions made by the state agencies. In fiscal 1991, the administrative law judges approved benefits in 66 percent of the cases they heard (Health and Human Services, 1992, p. 29).

If denied by the administrative law judge, the applicant can still pursue the case through the Appeals Council of the Social Security Administration and then through the federal courts. At the end of fiscal year 1991, 22,381 individual SSI and SSDI cases were pending in the court system, as well as an additional 100 "class action" suits (a case filed on behalf of an entire group of individuals; Koitz, Kollman, and Neisner, 1992, p. 5).

THE GROWTH OF SSDI AND SSI

The early period of the ADA's implementation coincided with a time of rising concern over the growth of the SSDI and SSI rolls. Between 1980 and 1991, the number of SSDI disability recipients (workers only) grew by 13 percent; between 1985 and 1991 the number grew by 21.6 percent. Between 1980 and 1983, there was an absolute decline in the number of SSDI worker recipients; then the rate began to rise. After 1989 it rose at a rapid rate (Koitz, Kollman, and Neisner, 1992, p. 64; see Table 1).

Between 1980 and 1991, the number of people with disabilities receiving SSI rose by a spectacular 55.2 percent. Between 1979 and 1991, the number of disabled children on the SSI rolls more than doubled. In 1979, disabled children accounted for 5.1 percent of all of the people on the SSI rolls. In 1991, disabled children made up 8.6 percent of the total SSI caseload. Between 1991 and 1992, the number of disabled children on SSI increased by an

Table 1

DI Worker Recipients, 1960–1992
(in thousands)

Calendar Year	DI Recipients[a]	As a Percent of 1980 Recipients
1960	455	16
1965	988	35
1970	1,493	52
1971	1,648	58
1972	1,833	64
1973	2,017	71
1974	2,237	78
1975	2,489	87
1976	2,670	93
1977	2,837	99
1978	2,880	101
1979	2,871	100
1980	2,859	100
1981	2,777	97
1982	2,604	91
1983	2,569	90
1984	2,596	91
1985	2,657	93
1986	2,728	95
1987	2,786	97
1988	2,830	99
1989	2,895	101
1990	3,011	105
1991	3,195	112
1992 (Feb.)	3,230	113

[a]End-of-year. Excludes family members of disabled worker recipients.
Source: Social Security Bulletin, spring 1992, and *Annual Statistical Supplement*, 1991.

estimated 42 percent. In those same years, the number of disabled adults grew, going from 2.1 million in 1979 to 3.2 million in 1991, but not nearly so rapidly (Koitz, Kollman, and Neisner, 1992, p. 65).

As these and other statistics imply, if one looks at the annual number of people annually admitted to the SSDI rolls between 1980 and 1991, one discovers a drop between 1980 and 1982, a rise between 1982 and 1986, leveling off between 1986 and 1989, and then a steep rise between 1989 and 1991. The rate of people admitted to the SSI rolls follows a roughly similar pattern, with a deeper drop in 1982 and a sharper rise between 1989 and 1991 (see Figure 1). Beginning in 1989, more people were admitted to the SSI rolls than to the SSDI rolls. The growth in both SSI and SSDI continued in 1992 and presumably into 1993.[10]

Although the programs tend to grow at roughly the same rates, they serve substantially different clienteles. Statistical snapshots taken of the SSDI and SSI caseloads in December 1992 illustrate the differences between the two programs. SSDI contains few people less than 17 years of age. The largest single group of disabled workers is between 50 and 59. The age distribution of SSI beneficiaries is far more even, with nearly equal numbers of beneficiaries who are less than 17, in their 20s, in their 30s, and in their 50s. SSI beneficiaries therefore tend to be younger than those on SSDI. Mental impairments and mental retardation account for more than half of the SSI caseload, particularly at the younger ages. Impairments related to the circulatory, respiratory, and musculoskeletal systems account for the bulk of SSDI beneficiaries. Both of the caseloads are getting younger (the average age of newly awarded DI recipients dipped below 50 for the first time in 1985), and both contain growing numbers of people with mental impairments.[11]

Surges in the rate of growth of the programs have occurred often in their histories. SSDI experienced rapid growth between 1970 and 1975. The number of SSDI awards per 1,000 insured workers, defined as the incidence rate, rose from 4.9 in 1970 to a record level of 7.3 in 1975. The termination rate, which measures those who either recovered, died, or reached the normal retirement age, declined from 15.9 percent in 1970 to 13.3 percent in 1975. In 1972, Congress raised the level of all Social Security benefits, includ-

Figure 1

SSI-Disability Recipients, Number and Percentage Distribution of Adults and Children, 1974–1991 (in thousands)

Calendar Year	Disabled Adults		Disabled Children	
	Number[a]	Percent of SSI Recipients[b]	Number[a]	Percent of SSI Recipients[b]
1974	1,639	41.0	71	1.8
1975	1,879	43.5	128	3.0
1976	1,935	45.7	153	4.1
1977	2,012	47.5	175	3.6
1978	2,052	48.6	197	4.7
1979	2,066	49.8	212	5.1
1980	2,106	50.8	229	5.5
1981	2,111	52.5	230	5.7
1982	2,080	53.9	229	5.9
1983	2,150	55.1	236	6.1
1984	2,250	55.9	249	6.2
1985	2,368	57.2	265	6.4
1986	2,516	58.9	280	6.6
1987	2,641	60.2	289	6.6
1988	2,740	61.4	290	6.5
1989	2,858	62.2	296	6.5
1990	3,023	62.7	340	7.1
1991	3,215	62.8	439	8.6

[a]Includes blind recipients.
[b]Percentages do not add across to 100 percent because the table does not show SSI "aged" recipients.
Source: SSA, Dec. 1991.

ing SSDI, substantially, and instituted a system that linked future benefit increases to the rate of inflation as measured by the Consumer Price Index. The combination of rising disability rolls and rising benefits caused SSDI benefit payments to triple between 1970 and 1975. In 1978 the number of disabled workers receiving SSDI reached a level that would not be exceeded until the next surge in 1989 (Berkowitz, 1987).

Rising expenditures fueled congressional concern over the program in the period between 1975 and 1980 and led to remedial legislation in 1980. This legislation, as interpreted by the Reagan administration, produced considerable administrative tightening in the program. In 1975, more than one-half of all applications received in the SSDI program resulted in benefits being awarded at the initial level of consideration. In 1981, slightly over a quarter of all applications were successful at the initial level of consideration. A process of expanded review of people already on the rolls caused a sixfold increase in the number of people terminated because of "recovery." *Recovery* meant simply removal, rather the receipt of a job. By the fall of 1984, the Social Security Administration had reviewed about 1.2 million disability beneficiaries and informed about 490,000 of them that they would be removed from the rolls (Berkowitz, 1987; Derthick, 1990).

The tightening of the rolls in the early 1980s caused Congress to reconsider its 1980 actions and pass new legislation in 1984. This new legislation made it more difficult for the Social Security Administration to remove someone from the SSI or SSDI rolls unless it could prove that the person's condition had improved medically. The new legislation produced what program administrators describe as a "looser adjudicative climate." Combined with the deterioration in the economy at the end of the 1980s, it set the stage for the recent surge in the disability rolls. Applications for disability benefits rose by an average of more than 10 percent per year in 1990 and 1991. The rate of the acceptance of applications also rose and the termination rate fell to its lowest level ever in 1991. Analysts ascribed most of the rise in the SSDI rolls to the sharp increase in applications (Health and Human Services, 1992).

The reasons for the volatility in the SSDI and SSI rolls are complex. In SSDI, workers apply for benefits based on their assessment of their physical condition, of the value of the benefits relative to the amount of money they feel they can earn, and of their sense of whether or not they can get on the rolls. The economy and the more subtle "disjuncture between the rhythms of chronic disease and the rhythms of work" affect their earnings (Yelin, 1993, p.

153). High levels of unemployment or layoffs increase the value of Social Security benefits relative to their earnings. The sense of whether or not a claim will be successful depends in part on the signals that disability claims assessors receive from the Social Security Administration, the Congress, and the courts. A rise in applications leads to increased backlogs, which raise the acceptance rate. As Robert Ball has remarked in a recent congressional testimony, backlogs produce "a lowering of adjudicative standards" that make it "much easier to process allowances than disallowances."[12] Rising disability rolls, in turn, often induce Congress to tighten the program, which lowers the acceptance rate.

The courts, still another factor involved in the administration of the programs, play a particularly important role in the level of people on Supplemental Security Income rolls. In February 1990, for example, the Supreme Court ruled against the government in the *Zebley* case. The Court agreed with a lower court decision that SSA was discriminating against children in its use of the first three steps of the disability determination process. Therefore, the court ordered the SSA to contact the families of nearly half a million children who applied for SSI. The agency's planning called for 50 percent of those contacted to respond; however, the response was greater than anticipated.[13] In 1990, the Social Security Administration also undertook a major outreach effort to inform people of their rights under SSI.

By the end of 1992, SSDI and SSI appeared to be approaching another in a long series of crises that marked the programs' histories. Acting in response to a report from the trustees of the Social Security Disability Insurance trust funds late in 1992, the Department of Health and Human Services and the Congress commissioned special studies to determine the reasons for the programs' growth. In April 1993, the trustees advised that the DI trust fund would be depleted in 1995. They recommended changes in Social Security financing to keep the disability insurance trust solvent through 2020. Congress held hearings on these recommended changes (Health and Human Services, 1992).

THE DILEMMAS OF REFORM

It appears that the ADA and the nation's major income maintenance maintain separate existences. Despite good will and interest on both sides, few tangible links unite SSDI and SSI, on the one hand, and the ADA, on the other. The history of the ADA reflects, in part, the economic boom of the 1980s and societal worries about labor shortages. Members of Congress agreed to the legislation with the understanding that people with disabilities would provide a major new source of productive labor. By the time the ADA was passed and put into operation, however, the boom was over, and the economy had begun to deteriorate. The deterioration fueled a major expansion of SSI and SSDI for reasons related to the internal political dynamics of those programs, dynamics that had nothing to do with the ADA.

The resulting irony has become a common feature of America's disability policy. People in the disability rights movement and in the Equal Employment Opportunity Commission work hard to implement a law dedicated to the participation of people with disabilities in the labor force. Other people in the labor force and in law offices across the country put equal, if not greater effort, into proving the inability to engage in substantial activity. Rising numbers of people seek tickets out of the labor force, just as a major new law is providing a new source of tickets into the labor force.

In trying to devise a way out of this dilemma, one has to remember that all of the people on SSI or SSDI have proven their inability to work to the satisfaction of a state disability determination office, an administrative law judge, or a federal judge. Terminations due to recovery stand at historically low levels. Meanwhile, the Social Security Administration received more than 2 million SSI and SSDI claims in 1992.[14]

Title I of the ADA has a large reach in that it applies to all businesses with more than 15 employees as of 26 July 1994. At the same time, the rules of dispute resolution under ADA require time-consuming determinations of individual situations that make it unlikely that the ADA could ever handle the millions of people who apply for SSI or SSDI.

The manual that employers receive to explain the regulations governing Title I emphasizes individual assessments. The manual asserts, for example, that whether a function is essential to a particular job can be determined only by a careful consideration of that job. As for "reasonable accommodations," the manual states that "every reasonable accommodation must be determined on an individual basis. A reasonable accommodation always must take into consideration two unique factors: the specific abilities and functional limitation of a particular applicant or employee with a disability and the specific functional requirements of a particular job" (U.S. Equal Employment Opportunity Commission, 1992, p. III-6). Similarly, "whether a particular accommodation will impose an undue hardship must always be determined on a case-by-case basis. An accommodation that poses an undue hardship for one employer at a particular time may not pose an undue hardship for another employer or even for the same employer at another time" (U.S. Equal Employment Opportunity Commission, 1992, p. III-12).

The ADA steadfastly resists the notion of universal standards, even to the point of internal contradiction, as indicated in the following passage from the manual:

> Even if a modification meets the standards required under Title II or III, further adaptations may be needed to meet the needs of a *particular* individual. For example, a restroom may be modified to meet standard accessibility requirements (including wider door and stalls and grab bars in specified locations) but it may be necessary to install a lower grab bar for a very short person in a wheelchair so that this person can transfer from the chair to the toilet. (U.S. Equal Employment Opportunity Commission, 1992, p. III-18)

Similarly, "any determination of a direct threat to health or safety must be based on an individualized assessment of objective and specific evidence about a particular individual's present ability to perform essential job functions, not on general assumptions or speculations about a disability" (U.S. Equal Employment Opportunity Commission, 1992, p. IV-7). In other words, a person needs to be considered independent of his or her disability; one cannot make presumptions of a person's competence based on his or her disability.

The Social Security Administration inevitably depends on what the ADA regulations might refer to as "blanket exclusions." Anyone with an impairment who meets or equals the listing and is not working and who is likely to have that impairment for 12 more months receives benefits. SSA is geared to a system of mass adjudication that depends on intensive interaction between the applicant and the system. ADA follows a different approach. It sets standards that are, in essence, expected to be self-administering. Only if the system fails does a person need to register a complaint and the EEOC need to investigate.

ADA depends first upon the good will of the employer and then upon a system of case-by-case dispute resolution that will result in highly individualized outcomes suited to the particular person and work environment. SSI and SSDI rely upon a more formal decision system that strives to treat similar people in similar manner and that will result in benefits that are uniform from person to person.

Further, if ADA were to make blanket exclusions, people with disabilities would complain that the spirit of the law had been violated. If the Social Security Administration altered its disability standards from person to person, people in economic distress would complain of capricious and discriminatory treatment. Yet, despite this fundamental dilemma, everyone concedes that employment is a preferable response to disability than retirement or a life spent outside of the labor force. How, then, might the goals of the ADA be incorporated into SSI and SSDI?

PREVIOUS EFFORTS AT REFORM

Here again some history is in order. The effort to facilitate employment of people with disabilities did not begin with passage of the ADA in 1990. Well before that date, the Social Security Administration had attempted two sorts of interventions that were designed to accomplish the goal of Title I of the ADA. The first approach consisted of the formal provision of rehabilitation services to people on the disability rolls. The second approach involved creating economic incentives for people on the disability rolls to enter the labor market. Neither of these approaches enticed many people to leave the rolls.

I have told the story of the relationship between the vocational rehabilitation program and SSDI elsewhere (Berkowitz, 1987; Berkowitz and Berkowitz, 1990). It is a story of distrust between Mary Switzer of the Office of Vocational Rehabilitation and the officials of the Social Security Administration.

It is also a story of the small rehabilitation program simply being overwhelmed by the large number of applicants for disability insurance. Original plans called for every applicant to be seen by a rehabilitation counselor to determine if that person could return to work. Subsequent plans provided elaborate screens that prevented most disability applicants from being referred for rehabilitation services.

Between 1965 and 1981, the Social Security Administration paid what amounted to a subsidy to the vocational rehabilitation program in return for services rendered to those on the disability rolls, including, after 1974, the SSI rolls. This practice came under increasing scrutiny and ended in 1981. In 1981, SSA spent $124 million on the rehabilitation services for DI and SSI recipients. In 1982, under the new system, it spent only $3.5 million. Even in the 1980s, more than 200,000 cases were referred each year to rehabilitation, but less than 2,000 were successfully rehabilitated – placed in a job – in any one year (Koitz, Kollman, and Neisner, 1992, p. 149). The GAO published a study in 1987 of people awarded disability benefits in 1983 in 10 states. The investigators found that "only 1 percent of the beneficiaries had been removed from the benefit rolls by February 1986 for working and, of these, fewer than one-third had been clients at a VR agency" (GAO, 1987, p. 19). Rehabilitation services, at least those provided by the vocational rehabilitation program, did not appear to be the answer to returning disability beneficiaries to work.

In the period after passage of the 1980 law, the Social Security Administration launched a second strategy to remove people from the disability rolls and place them in the labor force. Section 1619 introduced a new system of work incentives for people on SSI. Work would no longer be considered, in and of itself, evidence that a person should be removed from the rolls. Instead, the person retained disability status until there was medical improvement in his or her condition. Someone who chose to enter the labor force would not have his or her benefits reduced dollar for dollar. Instead, the person would continue to have some SSI benefits until his or her "countable income" exceeded the SSI benefit standard. In 1991, that meant the person's "countable" income could reach up to $406 a month and the person could still receive an SSI benefit. Furthermore, such things as impairment-related expenses reduced a person's countable income. A person who no longer received a cash SSI benefit could still receive Medicaid if his or her gross earned income "is insufficient to replace SSI, Medicaid, and any publicly funded attendant care" (Health and Human Services, 1991, pp. 48–49). In theory, then, a person could receive Medicaid for life, even if the person were working, provided no medical improvement in the condition occurred, and the worker did not earn too much money.

For SSDI recipients, the work incentive provisions operated somewhat differently. A person on the SSDI rolls could undertake a nine-month trial work period. At the end of this period, if the person now made at least $500 a month and therefore engaged in "substantial gainful activity," the person received three additional months of benefits and then cash benefits ended. For the next three years, the person could automatically be reinstated to the rolls, should his or her earnings stop or fall below the substantial gainful activity level. During this period as well, the person continued to receive Medicare. Hence anyone who tried to enter the labor force had the right to a free year of benefits and four years of Medicare (Health and Human Services, 1991, p. 36).

Although these work incentive provisions represented substantial liberalizations of the law, they failed to induce many people to leave the rolls. One reason was that they were complex and difficult for many beneficiaries to understand. Allen Jensen, who studied the effects of the work provisions on a group of SSI and SSDI beneficiaries, found that many people did not receive correct information. One 79-year-old father of a 26-year-old mentally retarded man said, "I understand that he [the son] can make about $6,000 a year working and still draw Social Security. Or is he like me and can make an unlimited amount?" The answer was that the law governing the son's earnings differed from the law that applied to the father's earnings, but no one had explained that clearly to the father. One woman, described as having a mobility impairment, told Jensen that, "they send out all this information and looking at it – even with all the education I have – after reading it totally confuses me. From page to page it totally contradicts itself" (Jensen, 1990, pp. 37, 39).

Another reason that the work incentives did not function better was a fear among many recipients that they would lose their benefits if they went to work. As an employment counselor told Jensen, the parents of a 30-year-old mentally ill person "were afraid about their son losing his disability benefits – because he had been disabled all his life and the parents had seen him try to work and had not succeeded. His father had gone through one heck of a time trying to get him on benefits and there had been a lot of screwups and he didn't want to go through all of that again" (Jensen, 1990, p. 41).

Related to the fear of losing benefits was a fundamental distrust of the Social Security Administration. As one case manager of a mental health clinic said, "We're at the mercy of these big agencies [Social Security Administration and State Income Maintenance]." An employment specialist at a private rehabilitation agency for the mentally ill noted that, "You will get conflicting stories, and you will get plain deception from Social Security. . . . Whenever a letter from Social Security comes into that household, I get a phone call before it is even opened. There is a general level of panic that hits the household. Even when the letter is fairly benign it really strikes fear . . . There is the issue that the disability check is essential for that family structure to stay afloat and to pay the rent" (Jensen, 1990, p. 46).

One of Jensen's case histories, which describes a 38-year-old woman who is a paraplegic and has a disease known as lupus, captures many of the problems and ambiguities involved in returning disability beneficiaries to work. She became disabled at age 21, "caused by a myelitis." Because she had worked since age 18, she had the minimum number of covered quarters to qualify for SSDI. She also learned at some point that she had lupus. According to Jensen, her counselor told her that,

> You have some choices. You can risk your benefits because you have guaranteed benefit now (SSDI) – a guaranteed minimum income. You can risk that and try to get back to work. But you have to consider that because of your disability it is going to take you a couple of hours to get dressed instead of one, consider your travel time and therefore sitting time. You will probably be sitting up longer than your skin can tolerate because of the Lupus.

Although the woman could have worked, she took SSDI benefits, as she explained, to protect herself from the interaction of her two impairments. She worried in particular about losing her health insurance benefits. Although she knew about a new work incentive provision that might allow her to purchase Medicare protection, she said that her husband's earnings would disqualify her from benefiting from that provision. "I earned my benefits myself before I was married so why should I be penalized for being married as to being able to buy into Medicare?" she said. As for the four years of Medicare associated with the trial work provisions, she said, "I plan on living longer than that. Until . . . the health insurance problem is fixed for me, going back to work is a moot point." Here, then, was a woman undone by the disincentives and complexities of the system (Jensen, 1990, pp. 90–91).

Even as the work incentive features of the Social Security disability programs remain in place, the Social Security Administration has tried new approaches. The latest effort consists of an elaborate experimental project known as Project Network. In this experiment, a group of people will voluntarily participate in active case management and another group of people will act as a control group. Four different types of case management will be investigated. In one, SSA employees in field offices will themselves act as the case managers. In another, state vocational rehabilitation officials will assume the role of case managers; private rehabilitation counselors will serve this function for a third group of SSI and SSDI beneficiaries. The fourth type of case management involves what SSA describes as "the referral manager model," in which SSA employees will refer beneficiaries to selected public and private agencies in the community. Pilot sites across the country have already been selected, contractors chosen, and results should be available by 1995.[15]

Although the experiments will yield much useful data, they also demonstrate the difficulties of this type of social research. In Richmond, Virginia, where the "vocational rehabilitation outstationing model" is to be tested, for example, the local Social Security office sent out 3,000 postcards asking for volunteers to participate. The office received 300 responses. Of those, half came in for interviews, and an unknown number will end up as participants. Half of the participants will be in the control group. Those in the control group learn the disappointing news that they will not receive services. These people may, however, be referred for vocational rehabilita-

216

tion services, just as anyone on the disability rolls may be referred. The experiments will therefore not involve a randomly selected group of SSA beneficiaries but rather a highly motivated group of SSA beneficiaries.[16]

THE REALITY OF REFORM

Rehabilitation services, work incentives, and Project Network share a common approach to the problem of work disability. They all intervene *after* a person has entered the SSI or SSDI rolls. They provide incentives and services only after a person has been judged to be unable to engage in substantial gainful activity and participated in the process in which the odds of obtaining benefits have never been better than even (Koitz, Kollman, and Neisner, 1992, p. 82). In the SSDI program, the termination rate (people going off the rolls) has never been higher than 20 percent, and the "recovery" rate (people going off the rolls because of an improvement in their condition) has never been higher than 4.8 percent (and is currently on the order of .3 percent, in large part because few reviews of people on the rolls are being performed; Koitz, Kollman, and Neisner, 1992, p. 98).

The long-term prospects for improvement in the recovery rate and for a reduction in the size of the SSI and SSDI rolls, despite the implementation of the ADA, do not appear hopeful. The system faces demographic and internally generated problems. The typical SSDI recipient is in his or her late 40s. People in the baby boom cohort, the nation's largest single age cohort, are approaching that age. More people were born in 1957 than in any other year. They will turn 50 in 2007. The system is therefore entering a period of maximum demographic peril, and this peril exists independent of the economic and administrative forces that generate claims. In addition, the Social Security system is about to raise the standard retirement age from 65 to 67. Early retirements, payable in the next century, will be worth only 70 percent of full retirement benefits. Disability payments will be unaffected by the changes in retirement age. Hence, the value of a disability benefit relative to an early retirement benefit will rise and increase the pressure on the disability system (Burkhauser, 1992, p. 12).

A NEW REFORM PROPOSAL

For work to replace retirement as the nation's primary response to disability, two things need to happen. First, the employment and other provisions of the ADA need to act as a "latent" screen that keeps people from applying for SSI and SSDI benefits. In this regard, as one authority points out, employers must lean to accommodate the rhythms of chronic illness. "All else being equal," writes Yelin, "people with discretion over work activities will be less likely to stop working whether they have severe heart disease or mild back pain, whether they are employed in an auto plant or university" (Yelin, 1993, pp. 116–117). ADA must become a vehicle that facilitates, by way of positive example and implicit threat, this sort of discretion. In particular, employers need to explore the limits of reasonable accommodation through such things as job restructuring and job reassignment. We do not yet know if employers will accomplish this task. We are still at the reassuring promise, not the hard data, stage.

It seems reasonable to suggest that not much will happen in the absence of tangible financial rewards for employers to undertake the necessary accommodation. The system, as presently constituted, does provide some tax incentives, including a special tax credit, established in 1990, designed to relieve the financial pressure on smaller employers that make accommodations required by the ADA. Perhaps this strategy, a characteristic product of a fiscally stringent era when the federal government no longer has available funds to make direct grants in aid, should be expanded. If so, an employer should receive a reward for making a job transfer or a job accommodation in which the costs are indirect, such as in a reallocation of supervisory time, even though these costs are difficult to measure.

The second thing that needs to happen is for changes to be made in the SSDI and SSI programs themselves. Such changes can occur only at a time, such as in 1980 and 1984, when Congress decides to reopen the program for discussion. The present crisis in the disability programs has so far been handled sedately by means of proposed transfers in funds from one trust fund to another. Social Security proponents do not want the funding crisis in disability insurance or Medicare to become an opportunity for conservatives to dismantle the programs in a fundamental way. Conservatives know that Social Security reform can become a potent weapon that is used against them, as it was in the 1982 congressional elections. The results tend to be the perpetuation of the status quo, with only marginal adjustments in all of the Social Security programs.

At the same time, outside forces may induce change. For one thing, there may still be a fundamental discussion of access to coverage by health insurance over the next several years. Such a discussion will force policy makers to examine Medicare closely and, because Medicare, Medicaid, SSDI, and SSI are linked, the health discussion may focus new attention on the disability programs. Once the disability programs receive scrutiny, policy makers will focus on the relationship between the ADA and the programs administered by the Social Security Administration. Indeed, the process has already begun, as a careful reading of Robert Ball's recent congressional testimony indicates.

Nearly everyone concedes that, for employment incentives to be effective, the process of intervention must begin before a person enters the rolls. Hence, a fundamental reform might involve the creation of a new type of benefit, one that facilitates labor force participation rather than hinders it.

Policy makers might decide to include an age screen in the SSDI and SSI application process. For those over 50, the system might proceed as before, with retirement benefits awarded on the basis of impairment or a combination of impairment and functional limitations. Children, who constitute the fastest growing segment of the SSI rolls, should also be treated as they are now.

Those between 18 and 50, including those who become 18 while on the SSI rolls, would be scrutinized more closely. Their applications would either be rejected, accepted with full benefits, or accepted as being in "rehabilitation" status. Those in rehabilitation status would receive an unconditional lifetime entitlement to Medicare or Medicaid and perhaps an annual grant that could be used for disability-related expenditures that enable the individual to work, such as assistive technology or personal assistance services or even further training or education. Employers who hired a person on rehabilitation status might receive a discount or rebate on the Social Security payroll taxes for that employee. Employers would also not have to pay health insurance premiums for that employee, another source of potential savings.

Such a system would go a long way to reducing the disincentives created by fears of losing health insurance and create additional incentives for employers to hire people with disabilities. Those in rehabilitation status would be given government help, but the expectation would be that such people would have to work. The system would permit the sort of individual, case-by-case approach to reasonable accommodation that is encouraged by the Americans with Disabilities Act. Such a system would also face the fundamental reality that older workers, who drop out of the labor force because of a physical or mental impairment, make poor candidates for rehabilitation. Indeed, when SSDI began, it provided benefits only to those 50 years or older.

The question remains of just how states would adjudicate cases under the new system. I suggest two distinct steps. First, all applicants, regardless of age, should receive information about the ADA from the SSA. This reform should be relatively easy to implement. Perhaps a system of voluntary peer referral could also be instituted, so that people applying for disability benefits could learn how people in similar circumstances manage daily routines and cope with the problems of the workplace. Such a system could be managed through local centers for independent living organizations run by and for the people with disabilities.

As a second step, the SSA would gather information together, much as it does now, and send the file to the state disability determination office. The office would screen by age and process the applications of those above 50 or below 18 as it does now. For those below 50, the process would begin exactly as it does now. If a person with a severe impairment met or equalled the medical listing and if that impairment was expected to last a year, the person would receive benefits. Instead of proceeding to the next step of the process, in which the agency considers factors related to a person's work experience, education, and residual functional capacity, state examiners might instead put all of the remaining applicants in rehabilitation status. Such a procedure would, in fact, simplify the disability determination process.

Those on rehabilitation status would be expected to work. For such people, all waiting periods for the receipt of benefits would be waived. If a person on rehabilitation reported no substantial gainful activity (or income below the substantial gainful activity level) for a period of 3 years or if that person reached age 50, the case might be reevaluated and the person treated as he or she would be at present. For such people, the new system would have the effect of a lengthened waiting period for cash disability benefits.

As a safety net for people on rehabilitation status unable to find work, I suggest the receipt of unemployment compensation benefits. The appeal of such benefits lies in their link to labor force participation. In a social policy sense, incorporation of unemployment compensation into the system sends an important signal. Someone with an impairment who is looking for work is unemployed not disabled. As a practical matter, I realize that states, rather than the federal government, pay unemployment compensation. Special federal grants to the states, similar to the ones made for periods of extended unemployment, will be needed to facilitate unemployment compensation for people in rehabilitation status.

Creation of the system I propose depends on building a political consensus. It may be necessary to postpone discussion of such a system until the nation enters an economic boom. In such circumstances, people tend to accept the notion of employing people with disabilities more readily. Legislating such a system or a similar system also requires obtaining the good will of such key groups as state disability adjudicators, the legal profession, and the medical profession. Disability rights activists must come to regard the new system as a positive step, not as a punitive measure. People with disabilities would have to see the system as empowering and supporting their independence – not as denying them benefits to which they are entitled. Social Security proponents must come to see the system not as a way of limiting benefits for which they have worked all their lives but of providing the benefit of independence. Ways will need to be found to keep those on rehabilitation status from overloading the hearing and appeals system with requests to be changed to regular benefit status.

As this discussion makes clear, implementing the new system will require substantial lead time. In addition, the new system will have to be sold as, at best, revenue neutral rather than as a means of reducing the number of people and the cost of the disability rolls. Such a system might well cause the rolls to rise.

The big losers under this sort of system would be unemployed people in rehabilitation status, who would receive less than they do at present. Such a benefit cut might be difficult to legislate. Undoubtedly, many would appeal the decision, as they do at present: the longer the appeal process, the less likely a return to work. Hence, the system would depend on the latent screening effect of the ADA to dissuade such people from applying in the first place. Special care would also need to be taken to preserve the rights of certain classes of SSI recipients, such as those people with developmental disabilities who have never worked. Perhaps the system should be implemented only in SSDI and another system, similar to the present, 1,619 provisions, should govern SSI.

CONCLUSION

One cannot anticipate all of the contingencies nor can one legislate for Congress. We have to recognize that a law such as ADA has many purposes, only one of which is to reduce the dependence of people with disabilities and increase their independence. The implication of this purpose is a reduction of those on the SSI/SSDI roles. However, we need to understand that most on the SSI and SSDI rolls have legitimate reasons for being there. And those on SSI and SSDI, as Elizabeth Boggs has recently pointed out, may not account for the major portion of those who can most benefit from Title I of the ADA. She argues that "those with disabilities not severe enough for Social Security's definition, but who are unemployed or underemployed because of simple discrimination or because of discrimination combined with the need for 'reasonable accommodation' should be the primary focal populations for the employment mandate of the ADA." She points to the 1 million recipients of general assistance and the recipients of food stamps as groups that include many people who might benefit from Title I.[17]

Elizabeth Boggs's comments point out the complexity of social policy in this area and underscore the need for further research. I am persuaded, however, of the need for reform of SSI and SSDI. As matters stand, the nation's two major income maintenance programs for people with disabilities and its civil rights law operate completely independent of one another. A crisis in one hardly touches the other. This situation needs to change, and it will change only if the country chooses to embrace the ADA and if the country elects to make fundamental changes in the income maintenance programs. The time for reassurance has passed. It is now a time for facing hard realities in order to alter outcomes.

NOTES

1. The author would like to acknowledge the helpful comments of Jane West, Marty Ford, Susan Parker, Elizabeth Boggs, Virginia Reno, Alexander Vachon, Alan Jensen, Joe Delfeco, Doris Brennan, and Richard Burkhauser in the preparation of this chapter.
2. Sandra Parrino quoted in "U.S. Senate, August 30, 1989. The Americans with Disabilities Act of 1989," *Senate Report* 101–116 (August 30, 1989): 17.
3. Dart quoted in House of Representatives, *Report 101-485-Part 2*, "The Americans with Disabilities Act of 1990," p. 44.
4. Public Law 101-336, the Americans with Disabilities Act of 1990.
5. The definitional problems of work disability are daunting. Because the U.S. Bureau of the Census defines *severe work limitation* as not working at all or receiving Medicare or Supplemental Security Income, one would not expect to find a high labor force participation rate among people in this category. An estimated 14.2 million people of working age have some form of work disability – a limitation in work due to chronic illness or impairment. See U.S. Department of Education, 1992.
6. Based on press releases obtained from the National Academy of Social Insurance.
7. Gwendolyn King quoted in *Social Security Courier* (October 1992), privately obtained.
8. Louis Enoff, unpublished remarks made at a conference on disability policy sponsored by the International Social Security Association, Rotterdam, the Netherlands, October 1992.
9. Testimony of Robert Ball, "Reallocation of a Portion of the Social Security Contribution Rate from the Old-Age and Survivors Insurance Trust Fund to the Disability Insurance Trust Fund," 22 April 1993, before Subcommittee on Social Secu-

rity, Committee on Ways and Means; obtained from Robert Ball's office.

10. I have gathered these statistics from Social Security Administration data as interpreted by Jane L. Ross, associate director, Income Security Issues, General Accounting Office, "Social Security: Rising Disability Rolls Raise Questions That Must Be Answered" (22 April 1993), privately obtained, and Koitz, Kollman, and Neisner, 1992.

11. I am indebted to Virginia Reno for illustrating these trends for me. She supplied me with data from the National Academy of Social Insurance study of disability.

12. Testimony of Robert Ball, "Reallocation of a Portion of the Social Security Contribution Rate from the Old-Age and Survivors Insurance Trust Fund to the Disability Insurance Trust Fund" (22 April 1993); mimeo, privately obtained.

13. Personal communication from Susan Parker to Jane West (19 August 1993).

14. I am grateful to Virginia Reno of the Social Security Administration for highlighting some of these statistics for me.

15. "Project Network Description," unpublished planning document obtained courtesy of the Social Security Administration.

16. I base this paragraph on an observer's notes, privately obtained, from an SSA briefing on Project Network held on 4 June 1993.

17. She made these points in a private communication to Jane West, 18 September 1993.

REFERENCES

Berkowitz, E. D. 1987. *Disabled Policy: America's Programs for the Handicapped*. New York: Cambridge University Press.

———. 1991. *America's Welfare State*. Baltimore: Johns Hopkins University Press.

———. 1993. "An American Perspective on Disability Programs." Discussion paper prepared for International Social Security Association. Mimeo.

——— and M. Berkowitz. 1990. "Labor Force Participation among Disabled Persons." *Research in Labor Economics* 11: 181–200.

Burkhauser, R. V. 1992. "Disability or Work: Handicap Policy Choices." Maxwell School Policy Studies Paper 5. Mimeo.

————, R. H. Haveman, and B. L. Wolfe. 1993. "How People with Disabilities Fare When Public Policies Change." *Journal of Policy Analysis and Management* 12, no. 2: 251–269.

Derthick, M. 1990. *Agency under Stress: The Social Security Administration in American Government.* Washington, D.C.: Brookings Institution.

Fries, J. F., and L. Crapo. 1981. *Vitality and Aging: Implications of the Rectangular Curve.* San Francisco: W. H. Freeman.

General Accounting Office. 1993. *Vocational Rehabilitation: Evidence for Federal Program's Effectiveness Is Mixed.* GAO/PEMD-93-19. Washington, D.C.: GAO.

————. 1987. *Social Security: Little Success Achieved in Rehabilitating Disabled Beneficiaries.* HRD 88-11. Washington, D.C.: GAO.

Health and Human Services. 1991. *Red Book in Work Incentives: A Summary Guide to Social Security and Supplemental Security Income Work Incentives for People with Disabilities.* Social Security Administration. Publication 64-030. Washington, D.C.: Government Printing Office.

————. 1992. *The Social Security Disability Insurance Program: An Analysis.* Report pursuant to a request from the Board of Trustees of the Federal Old-Age and Survivors Insurance and Disability Insurance trust funds. Mimeo.

Jensen, A. C. 1990. "Consumers' Experiences with Work Incentive Policies in the Supplemental Security Income and Social Security Disability Insurance Programs: An Exploratory Study." Study Supported by the National Foundation for People with Disabilities. Mimeo.

Jones, N. 1990. "The Americans with Disabilities Act: Major Distinctions between the Senate and House Versions as Passed." *CRS General Distribution Memorandum* (June 5).

Koitz, D., G. Kollman, and J. Neisner. 1992. "Status of the Disability Programs of the Social Security Administration." *CRS Report for Congress*. Washington, D.C.: Government Printing Office.

Lewin, T. 1992. "U.S., in Job Case, Files First Lawsuit under New Disabilities Law." *New York Times* (7 November): 6.

National Council on Disability. 1993. *ADA Watch – Year One: A Report to the President and the Congress on Progress in Implementing the Americans with Disabilities Act* (5 April 1993). Washington, D.C.: Government Printing Office.

U.S. Department of Education. 1992. "National Institute on Disability and Rehabilitation Research, People with Work Disability in the U.S." *Disability Statistics Abstract*, 4. Washington, D.C.

U.S. Equal Employment Opportunity Commission. 1992. *A Technical Assistance Manual on the Employment Provisions (Title I) of the Americans with Disabilities Act*. Washington, D.C.: EEOC.

Yelin, E. 1993. *Disability and the Displaced Worker*. New Brunswick, N.J.: Rutgers University Press.

The Intersection with Workers' Compensation

Christopher G. Bell

EDITOR'S NOTE

Two scenarios are gradually emerging as employers and employees navigate the sometimes conflicting and sometimes reinforcing requirements of these two sets of mandates. The undesirable scenario yields extensive litigation and hefty settlements resulting in more injured workers leaving the work force. The desirable scenario yields the ADA reasonable accommodation requirement reinforcing rehabilitation and return-to-work services provided under workers' compensation resulting in continued employment of injured workers. In some cases an injured worker must choose between utilizing the workers' compensation system, where the incentive is to maximize lost work capacity in order to gain compensation, or the ADA, where the employee must demonstrate work capacity despite an impairment to retain employment. Bell analyzes requirements of the two sets of mandates, noting that the workers' compensation system is grounded in the assumption that impairments cause work limitations whereas the ADA is grounded in the assumption that people can work despite impairments.

Christopher G. Bell is a partner in the management, labor, and employment law firm Jackson, Lewis, Schnitzler, and Krupman in Washington, D.C. Bell was acting associate legal counsel for ADA services and a principal advisor to Chairman Evan J. Kemp, Jr., at the U.S. Equal Employment Opportunity Commission in Washington, D.C., where he led the development of the EEOC's ADA regulations and Technical Assistance Manual. Bell provided technical assistance to the White House, the Senate, and the House of Representatives during the ADA's legislative consideration. In 1983 he coauthored Accommodating the Spectrum of Individual Abilities *for the U.S. Commission on Civil Rights, which provided a conceptual foundation for the ADA, and* The Workers' Compensation–ADA Connection *(1993). Portions of this chapter have been published elsewhere.*

INTRODUCTION

The ADA is widely acknowledged as far-reaching landmark legislation; however, few who worked on its enactment foresaw the breadth and depth of its potential impact on workers' policy and practice compensation. Although not a single line in the ADA or its legislative history mentions workers' compensation, there was never any doubt that many injured workers could be "individuals with disabilities" protected by the ADA. Nonetheless, at the time the legislation was being crafted – during 11 congressional hearings and 5 committee mark-up sessions – virtually no attention was paid to how it might affect the workers' compensation system, injured workers, or employer practices relating to workers' compensation.

Many in business view the ADA as being superimposed on a workers' compensation system already in crisis. Workers' compensation costs have skyrocketed over the past decade and the trend continues. According to Richard N. Victor, the executive director of the Workers' Compensation Research Institute, workers' compensation is the fastest growing labor cost, reaching approximately $70 billion in 1993.[1] In some states, employers have faced a 300 percent increase in workers' compensation medical costs during the past decade.[2] And disability costs nationwide are expected to reach $200 billion by the year 2000.[3] Many in business saw the ADA as one more costly federal regulation allowing injured workers to make one more claim against employers. In contrast, others saw the ADA as consistent with the goals of speedy recovery and early return to work of injured workers. In this view, the ADA could be a profit center for business, allowing it to reduce benefit costs by bringing injured workers back to work sooner. Early implementation provides evidence that both scenarios are emerging.

This chapter examines the interaction between the ADA and workers' compensation laws. The first section analyzes how workers' compensation laws and the ADA overlap by examining the key elements of each as well as potential implementation conflicts and opportunities. The next section explores early evidence found in EEOC charge data, court cases, and interviews with members of the bar. It analyzes the degree to which injured workers may be using the ADA and what the potential impact of that usage may be on ADA enforcement generally. The final section of the article explores the potential impact of the interplay between workers compensation and the ADA, including consideration of the role injured workers might play in shaping how the ADA will be viewed by the general public and its political representatives.

THE POTENTIAL OVERLAP BETWEEN THE ADA, WORKERS' COMPENSATION, AND INJURED WORKERS

Overview of Additional Rights Granted to Injured Workers by the ADA

The ADA can grant additional rights to injured workers above and beyond whatever rights or benefits they may be entitled to under workers' compensation law. The ADA prohibits employment discrimination against a "qualified individual with a disability"[4] in all aspects of the employment relationship including recruitment, hiring, compensation, training, discharge, and benefits.[5] Many injured workers will satisfy the ADA's definition of a *qualified individual with a disability* protected from discrimination because of a work-caused disability. An employer is required to provide a reasonable accommodation to enable an otherwise qualified individual with a disability to perform the essential functions of his or her job unless the specific accommodation would impose an undue hardship on the employer's business.[6] Of particular relevance to injured workers, reasonable accommodation may include job restructuring, part-time or modified work schedules, provision or modification of equipment, and where necessary, reassignment to a vacant position.[7]

The ADA prohibits "limiting, segregating, or classifying" a qualified disabled worker in a manner that adversely affects employment opportunities.[8] An employer is prohibited from asking job applicants on an application form or in an interview medical or disability-related questions, including whether an applicant has ever been injured on the job or filed a workers' compensation claim.[9] Nor can an employer refuse to hire or return to work an individual with a disability on the basis of an unsubstantiated concern of further workers' compensation claims.[10]

Victims of disability discrimination in violation of the ADA may be hired or reinstated and may receive back pay as well as compensatory and punitive damages.

Overview of Rights and Remedies under Workers' Compensation

All 50 states have workers' compensation laws, which vary greatly in their provisions, benefits, and procedures. In general, these laws

230

provide a worker suffering an occupational illness or injury with specified medical and wage loss benefits without the worker having to successfully sue his or her employer. The worker gains these benefits without having to prove fault by an employer. In return, the worker gives up the right to sue the employer for negligence and receive a potentially greater award of damages from a jury.

To receive benefits, the worker must be employed by a covered employer and sustain an injury or illness that rises within the scope of employment. Unlike the ADA, benefits may be received for even a minor, transitory injury or illness, such as a slight sprain or a laceration with no resulting loss of work.

Three broad categories of benefits are provided: (1) medical and related expenses; (2) disability benefits including compensation for lost wages, and (3) death benefits. The benefits vary from state to state.

Medical benefits include total coverage of expenses, without copayments or deductibles for medical, psychiatric, rehabilitation, and nursing care. Many states also provide some coverage for vocational rehabilitation.

Disability benefits are computed using a medical loss theory, wage loss theory, or some combination of the two. Both theories attempt to provide compensation for an approximation of lost earnings or earning capacity. Medical loss benefits compensate a worker for the medical injury itself, regardless of whether there is actual loss of earnings or earning capacity. Certain medical injuries are considered to be presumptively compensable disabilities benefit and a specified amount of benefits is set forth on a statutory schedule, such as a specified dollar amount for the loss of a hand or eye. Workers' compensation disability benefits also may use a formula to determine compensation for lost earnings based upon an employees's average weekly wage and the number of weeks of incapacity. Jurisdictions usually have a maximum and minimum benefit average, between 50 and 66 percent of the employee's average weekly wage up to a set maximum dollar amount. Disability benefits may be paid out based upon the duration and severity of the disability.

Disability is usually characterized as either partial or total and either temporary or permanent. Temporary partial disability usually means a worker has sustained a minor injury such as a sprain or mild fracture resulting in a temporary inability to return to the worker's usual job but not from all gainful employment. Temporary total disability refers to a medical condition that precludes all gainful employment for a temporary but undetermined period of time. A permanent partial disability is a medical condition that is irreparable but ultimately not a complete bar to employment. For example, a worker might lose an eye. During an initial hospitalization and recovery period, the worker might be completely incapacitated. After reaching maximum medical improvement, the worker may be able to return to gainful employment but not necessarily the job he or she had at the time of the injury. Compensation for permanent partial disabilities is usually made on the basis of a predetermined schedule.

Permanent total disability refers to a medical condition that is irreparable, and even after reaching maximum medical improvement, the worker is not expected to be able to perform gainful employment. Permanent total disability benefits may be a scheduled loss, such as loss of sight in both eyes, or may be assessed on the basis of a variety of factors including age, education, training, skills, employment history, and the nature and severity of the injury. All jurisdictions provide compensation to survivors for a worker who is killed as a result of a job-related accident or illness, and many jurisdictions provide benefits for disfigurement.

The level of benefits an injured worker may receive is not intended to fully compensate the worker for all economic losses. Wage loss payments can be quite low in comparison to actual wages or the worker's needs. This fact may create an added incentive for injured workers to look to the ADA to provide additional compensation in the form of back pay, as well as compensatory and punitive damages.

Moreover, workers' compensation statutes do not require an employer to provide reasonable accommodation, assess a worker's ability to perform "essential" job functions or otherwise analyze its obligations under the ADA, when determining the ability of an injured worker to resume employment. However, many workers' compensation statutes have provisions that prohibit discrimination and retaliation against a worker for filing a claim or receiving benefits. Most jurisdictions also have a second injury or subsequent injury fund designed to remove financial disincentives in hiring employees with a disability. Without a second injury fund, if a worker suffered increased disability from a work-related injury because of a preexisting condition, the employer would have to pay the full cost. The second injury fund provisions limit the amount the employer must pay in these circumstances and provide for the balance to be paid out of a common fund.

A majority of workers' compensation claims are not contested. Most jurisdictions have an administrative agency that administers the statute. Uncontested claims are paid. Contested claims are subject to informal proceedings, then usually some form of formal hearing before a hearing officer with appeal to an administrative appeals board. Questions of law are then appealable to the state judiciary.

SPECIFIC ADA PROVISIONS AND THEIR POTENTIAL INTERPLAY WITH INJURED WORKERS AND WORKERS' COMPENSATION PRACTICES

The ADA's potential overlap with workers' compensation occurs in the following areas: definition of *disability*; qualified individual with a disability; restrictions on medical examination and inquiries; reasonable accommodation and undue hardship; enforcement, remedies, and settlements.

Definition of Disability

An injured worker must have a "disability" as defined by the ADA to be protected. Having a "disability" is different from having a compensable injury for workers' compensation purposes. *Disability* is defined in three ways by the ADA:

1. Any person who has a physical or mental impairment that substantially limits one or more of the individual's major life activities.[11]
2. Any person who has a "record of" a substantially limiting impairment.[12]
3. Any person who is "regarded as" having a substantially limiting impairment, regardless of whether the person is in fact disabled.[13]

The ADA's definition of *disability* is both narrower and broader than the typical definition of a compensable injury under most workers' compensation laws. Under the ADA, a work-caused injury must substantially limit a person's major life activities, presently, in the past, or as perceived by an employer. Major life activities include caring for oneself, performing manual tasks, walking, seeing, hearing, speaking, learning, and working.[14] Other common daily activities such as sitting, standing, bending, reaching, grasping, concentrating, reasoning, and basic socialization skills are also included. Thus, the ADA is narrower in coverage than workers' compensation statutes in that a work-caused injury must also substantially limit a major life activity.

Minor, nonchronic impairments of short duration with little or no permanent or long-term impact will not constitute an ADA-covered disability.[15] This includes common workplace injuries such as a broken leg or sprained joints.[16] However, according to the EEOC, even a temporary condition, such as a broken leg, can become a disability if it takes significantly longer to heal than normal and during that time the individual is unable to walk or if the impairment heals but leaves a permanent limp that substantially limits the individual's ability to walk.[17] An injured worker limited only in the ability to perform one particular job for one particular employer is not "disabled" for ADA purposes. Rather, the worker must be disabled from a class of jobs or broad range of jobs in many classes.[18]

An injured worker also may have a "record of" a disability and be protected. An injured worker has a "record of" a disability when he or she has recovered in whole or in part from an impairment that had substantially limited a major life activity in the past. For example, according to the EEOC, an injured worker who had been unable to work for one year because of a workplace accident would probably have a record of a disability. If an employer refused to hire or return this person back to work because of that record, this would violate the ADA if the worker was qualified for the position sought. Note, however, that a mere record of having filed a workers' compensation claim does not give a person a "record of" a substantially limiting impairment.[19] Rather, the workers' compensation record must indicate that the occupational injury or illness resulted in an impairment that substantially limited one or more major life activities.

The ADA definition of *disability* is broader than workers' compensation definitions in that an injured worker can be "regarded as" having a disability. In other words, the individual may have no current or past "disability" but still be protected by the ADA because of the subjective perception of an employer that the worker has a disability. When an employer perceives an injured worker to be significantly restricted in the ability to perform manual tasks or any other major life activity, the injured worker is regarded as having a disability by the employer.[20] This is true whether or not the worker is, in fact, substantially limited by the impairment.

The "regarded as" part of the ADA's definition of *disability* is expansive and depends upon the attitude of the employer, not the nature of the injury. Many injured workers potentially may be protected by the ADA as a result of an employer's fears concerning the risk of future injury, increases in workers' compensation premiums, or the cost of accommodation. These common employer concerns about injured workers create ADA coverage when it is shown that as a result, an employer took an adverse employment action because it regards an individual to be substantially limited in any major life activity such as performing manual tasks or performing a class of jobs.[21]

Case law developed under the ADA and its precursor, the Rehabilitation Act, continues to be more favorable to employers in limiting claims by persons, including injured workers, who profess to have a disability. Courts are interpreting both laws to exclude from disability status persons who merely are unable to perform or are regarded by an employer as being unable to perform one job for one particular employer.[22] A growing number of courts are construing the Rehabilitation Act not to cover "temporary" or perceived "temporary" disabilities.[23] This will have the effect of excluding many injured workers from ADA protection.

Qualified Individual with a Disability

The ADA requires that one simultaneously have a disability and be qualified. Theoretically, these twin standards put a potential ADA claimant in a difficult catch-22; if he or she emphasizes the severity of limitations resulting from disability, the claimant may leave the impression of not being qualified for the job. On the other hand, a claimant who emphasizes ability may defeat his or her claim to having a disability. However, having a disability and being simultaneously qualified are not necessarily contradictory states of being. For example, an individual is protected from discrimination based on a past record of a disability, such as a history of severe back problems as well as being perceived as having a more severe disability than one actually does. Stigma and bias that block the path to employment of a qualified person can be readily addressed by the ADA while bypassing the law's catch-22. Reasonable accommodation also can turn an unqualified person with a disability into a qualified individual with a disability by reducing or eliminating the effects of the individual's functional limitation without affecting disability status. However, where an individual cannot be effectively accommodated and the job's essential functions require the use of impaired physical or mental functions, the individual is not likely to be qualified.

A current employee in such a circumstance might well file for permanent total disability benefits under workers' compensation emphasizing his or her inability to perform on the job while at the same time seeking reasonable accommodation. Claiming to be permanently and totally disabled, however, may undercut a plaintiff's claim to be a "qualified individual with a disability," able to perform the essential functions of a job in spite of a disability. Two courts have used the sworn factual statements on applications for long-term disability insurance benefits as a basis for finding plaintiffs were not qualified to perform the essential functions of their jobs.[24]

To avoid this problem, some individuals with disabilities have asserted that their only disability stems from an employer's perception that they are not qualified for a position because of an impairment. This emphasis on being qualified rather than having a disability also has doomed claims as some courts have concluded that such individuals do not have a disability.[25]

Restrictions on Medical Examinations and Inquiries

The ADA severely restricts disability-related medical inquiries and examinations in ways that affect common workers' compensation practices. Before a job offer is made, an employer may not inquire about an applicant's disability status or medical history. Inquiries concerning past on-the-job injuries or workers' compensation claims are expressly prohibited.[26] This includes inquiries of third parties about an applicant's workers' compensation history.

An employer may condition a job offer on the satisfactory completion of a medical examination or medical inquiry provided such examination or inquiry is made of all applicants for the same job category and the results are kept confidential with a few narrow exceptions.[27] An employer may choose to require all postoffer candidates to complete a medical history questionnaire and selectively require a medical examination of those candidates whose medical history justifies a more thorough medical evaluation concerning a particular issue.[28] Postoffer medical examinations and inquiries do not have to be job-related and questions concerning past workers' compensation claims and on the job injuries are expressly permitted.

A job offer may be withdrawn only if the medical examination reveals that the individual is either (1) unable to do the essential functions of a job even with reasonable accommodation or (2) the individual would pose a direct threat to his or her own health or safety or the health or safety of others that cannot be eliminated or acceptably reduced by reasonable accommodation.[29]

Medical examinations and inquiries of current employees are required to be job-related and consistent with business necessity.[30] Accordingly, return-to-work physical examinations must be narrowly tailored to ascertain whether the injured worker can safely perform the essential functions of his or her job with or without reasonable accommodation.

During the EEOC's ADA rule making, concerns were expressed by business and employer groups concerning the need for medical information to process workers' compensation claims and meet the requirements of second injury funds. These concerns were addressed in the rule making by expressly permitting employers to use medical information garnered during postoffer or postemployment medical examinations for workers' compensation purposes.[31]

In order to withdraw a job offer on health or safety grounds, an employer must show that the individual poses a high probability of substantial harm to health or safety and that the risk of substantial harm cannot be eliminated or reduced below the direct threat level by a reasonable accommodation.[32] This is a very stringent standard that employers will not be able to meet in most circumstances when attempting to screen for potential future injury. In fact, medical science will rarely have the data to demonstrate that there is a "high probability" that something bad will happen. Moreover, such claims cannot be speculative or based on future risk. Only the current abilities of the individual to safely perform essential job functions can be assessed.

The following examples were derived from the EEOC's *Technical Assistance Manual*. They demonstrate how the direct threat standard applies to common injured worker scenarios.

1. An applicant for a laborer job has had no back pain or injuries in his previous jobs, which require heavy lifting. But, a back x-ray reveals a back anomaly. The company doctor worries that there is a slight chance that the applicant could develop back problems in the future. The threat of future back injury is too slight to meet the direct threat standard, according to the EEOC.
2. A significant risk would exist for an individual with a back anomaly who has a history of repeated back injuries in similar jobs and whose back condition has been aggravated further by injury and where there are no accommodations that would eliminate or reduce the risk.
3. A physician's evaluation indicates that an employee has a disk condition that might worsen in 8–10 years. This is not a sufficient indication of imminent potential harm.[33]

Reasonable Accommodation

Unlike workers' compensation, the ADA requires an employer to make reasonable accommodation to the known physical or mental limitations of an individual with a disability who is qualified for a job. The concept underlying reasonable accommodation is a deceptively simple one. Making adjustments in the work space, schedule, or tools used can enable a person with medically-based functional limitations perform a job successfully. Of necessity, however, reasonable accommodation must be tailored to the specific abilities and limitations of the individual as well as the particular demands of the job. The ADA, therefore, simply provides a list of nonexclusive examples of reasonable accommodations. A reasonable accommodation under the ADA means:

(i) Modifications or adjustments to a job application process that enable a qualified applicant with a disability to be considered for the position such qualified applicant desires; or

(ii) Modifications or adjustments to the work environment, or to the manner or circumstances under which the position held or desired is customarily performed, that enable a qualified individual with a disability to perform the essential functions of that position; or

(iii) Modifications or adjustments that enable a covered entity's employee with a disability to enjoy equal benefits and privileges of employment as are enjoyed by its other similarly situated employees without disabilities.[34]

The statute and regulations provide the following nonexclusive list of examples:

(i) Making existing facilities used by employees readily accessible to and usable by individuals with disabilities; and

(ii) Job restructuring; part-time or modified work schedules; reassignment to a vacant position; acquisition or modification of equipment or devices; appropriate adjustment or modifications of examinations, training materials, or policies; the provision of qualified readers or interpreters; and other similar accommodations for individuals with disabilities.

Many employers have offered injured workers "light duty" jobs as a means of expediting return to work. Companies have saved considerable dollars in workers' compensation costs as a result of return-to-work programs utilizing light duty. According to the EEOC, an employer is not required by the ADA to create light duty jobs.[35] However, if an employer has established a light duty position, it may be required to transfer an injured worker as a reassignment to a vacant position. If the position is a temporary one, an employer is not required to make it permanent. In addition, a lighter duty position may be created by job restructuring if the heavy duty task a worker cannot do is a marginal rather than an essential job function. Some have argued that transferring tasks to other employees can be a form of reasonable accommodation. Although it is clear that job restructuring can include transferring or eliminating marginal tasks, the courts have not been very receptive to assigning coworkers or employing additional persons as an accommodation.[36]

The EEOC has interpreted the ADA to include additional unpaid leave as a form of reasonable accommodation subject to the undue hardship limitation.[37] This means that an employer applying a neutral leave policy to terminate a disabled employee may be required to make an exception to that policy as a form of reasonable accommodation. The amount of additional unpaid leave that would have to be provided is not specified in the EEOC's regulations. Moreover, in a recent article in the fall 1993 issue of the *Labor Lawyer*, Peggy Mastroianni and David Fram, two EEOC ADA policy officials, state that an employer also would be required to hold an employee's job open until he or she returned unless an employer can prove it would be an undue hardship to do so.

Some decisions under the ADA and the Rehabilitation Act provide employers with some authority to deny such an accommodation request.[38] On the other hand, presence at the workplace may not be an essential function for every job. Working at home or out of the office may be feasible in some cases.[39] The courts have yet to grapple with the interplay between the ADA and the Family and Medical Leave Act (FMLA), which entitles an employee with a "serious health condition" up to 12 weeks of unpaid leave with continuation of benefits and job restoration. Many injured workers will have rights under the FMLA, including rights to intermittent and reduced leave, that may undercut somewhat the employer argument that presence on the job is per se an essential function.[40]

Reassigning an employee who can no longer do a job because of a disability is also a form of reasonable accommodation.[41] For this to occur, there must be a vacant position to which the employee can be reassigned and the employee must be qualified to perform the position. An employer is not required to create a new job.[42]

Some claim that communication between an employer and an injured worker frequently breaks down when a workers' compensation claim is contested. Increased potential for ADA liability arises when this occurs. Because failure to consult with the person with a disability requesting accommodation results in denial of an employer's "good faith" defense to liability for compensatory and punitive damages, good communication between employer and employee is essential to the provision of reasonable accommodation.

Providing reasonable accommodation is an interactive process between an employer and a person with a disability requesting it. The EEOC has suggested steps that can be taken when an employee is unable to suggest a reasonable accommodation that an employer is willing to provide.[43]

Undue Hardship

An employer does not have to provide a reasonable accommodation that would impose "significant difficulty or expense" on the employer in relation to its business and the resources available to provide the accommodation.[44] An accommodation is not required if it is "unduly costly, extensive, substantial, or disruptive, or would fundamentally alter the nature or operation of the business."[45] In determining whether the cost of an accommodation would pose an undue hardship, the EEOC has apparently instructed its investigators to consider the amount of money an employer would save in workers' compensation related expenses if an injured worker is returned to work with reasonable accommodation rather than remaining out of work on benefits.[46]

Enforcement, Remedies, and Settlement

As noted earlier, workers' compensation is intended to be the exclusive remedy for workplace injuries. In return for giving up a right to sue his or her employer for damages, the worker is relieved of having to prove the employer was at fault and receives a specified certain sum. The ADA, in contrast, provides for hiring or reinstatement plus back pay. Future pecuniary and nonpecuniary compensatory and punitive damages are capped at between $50,000 to $300,000 depending upon the size of the employer.[47] The prevailing plaintiff also may receive court costs and attorneys fees.[48] Even though some state courts have held that an injured worker who receives benefits under workers' compensation law is barred from suing the employer for disability discrimination based on the work-caused injury, state workers' compensation laws cannot bar ADA claims.[49]

The ADA also may affect the settlement of workers' compensation claims. When a workers' compensation claim is settled, an injured worker typically receives a lump sum benefit in return for signing a general release, waiving all claims against the employer. It is far from certain whether a general workers' compensation release not mentioning release of ADA claims would bar a later lawsuit by an injured worker under the ADA. The issue has yet to be authoritatively addressed by the courts, but it is likely that an ADA waiver will be held to a "knowing and voluntary" standard.[50] The failure of a workers' compensation release to expressly waive ADA rights may make the release ineffective in barring any later ADA lawsuit. In addition, an employer will have to provide additional monetary consideration for the waiver of the ADA claims to be effective.

HOW THE ADA AND WORKERS' COMPENSATION OVERLAP TO CREATE BOTH POTENTIAL LITIGATION AND OPPORTUNITIES FOR COST CONTAINMENT

The ADA and workers' compensation have differing philosophical underpinnings. The ADA rests on the premise that disability does not necessarily mean inability to work; it protects from discrimination the able person with a disability. To qualify for ADA protection, a person must be simultaneously disabled yet able. As with other civil rights laws, the ADA prohibits discrimination because of prejudice, myths, bias, or stereotypes against qualified persons with disabilities. In addition, reasonable accommodation is required to remove barriers to employment caused by the interaction between functional limitations resulting from a medical impairment and the workplace.[51] The theoretical focus of the ADA, therefore, is on eliminating unnecessary barriers preventing workers with disabilities from working. In theory, if not always in practice, an applicant or employee pursuing an ADA claim is seeking work.

The goal of workers' compensation is also to eliminate barriers to return an injured worker to work by paying for medical expenses and providing compensation while the worker is recovering, until he or she is able to return to work. However, in contrast to an ADA claim, an injured worker filing a claim for benefits may be seeking time-loss benefits on the basis of inability to work. Appropriately, the workers' compensation system, in assessing benefits, focuses on inability, what a worker is no longer able to do because

242

of on-the-job injury. An employee may have to prove that he or she cannot work at the old job or occupation because of a work-caused injury or illness to receive benefits. For example, in California, an employee is entitled to benefits if a workplace injury precludes him or her from engaging in his or her usual and customary occupation or the position in which he or she was engaged in at the time of the injury. Or, a worker may need to prove only that he or she has a disability for which a specified amount of benefits are statutorily provided based upon presumptive medical loss or loss of work capacity. Unlike the ADA, workers' compensation rests on the premise that impairments are the cause of work limitations. An employer is not required by workers' compensation law to look at the "essential functions" of the job or to consider whether a reasonable accommodation might enable the individual to perform the job in question.

A potential conflict arises because the workers' compensation law appropriately focuses on lost capacity to award benefits whereas the ADA focuses on remaining ability to prevent discrimination. If an employer makes placement decisions based only upon work restrictions without focusing on work abilities, it may inadvertently violate the ADA.[52] Unlike workers' compensation, the ADA affirmatively requires an employer to focus on ability and consider reasonable accommodation. Even though workers' compensation law encourages employers to return injured workers to productive employment, it does not require them to do so or to consider accommodation.

Therefore, in a workers' compensation claim, the employer argues that the worker is able to return to work and is accordingly not entitled to benefits while the injured worker argues that he or she is too disabled to work and is entitled to benefits. In contrast, in an ADA proceeding, an injured worker argues that she was disabled but able to work with reasonable accommodation whereas an employer argues that the worker is not disabled or, alternatively, if the worker is disabled, is too disabled to work, even with reasonable accommodation.[53] Therefore, in an ADA claim, the employer and injured worker reverse their traditional workers' compensation arguments.

Making inconsistent claims in competing forums creates potential pitfalls for both worker and employer. As noted earlier, courts are already beginning to dismiss ADA and Rehabilitation Act discrimination claims based upon injured worker's assertions that they cannot work in application for workers' compensation and long-term disability benefits. An employer may also be caught in the same contradiction. Although it does not appear to have happened yet, there is no reason why an employer's evidence that a worker is medically able to return to work made in a workers' compensation proceeding cannot be used against the employer in an ADA lawsuit in which the employer claims the worker is not a qualified individual with a disability able to perform essential job functions.

However, the difference in legal standards between a benefits statute and a civil rights statute can result in a determination that an employee who is simultaneously permanently and totally disabled for workers' compensation purposes is also a "qualified individual with a disability" protected from disability discrimination and entitled to reasonable accommodation by the ADA.[54]

Given this interplay between the ADA and workers' compensation, the basic types of ADA/injured worker charges can be accurately predicted. Two basic types of such charges are likely – one by those who seek a return to work and the other by those who seek to maximize benefit payments. The first type will be filed by injured workers who believe they have been denied employment because of a present, past, or perceived workplace injury or predisposition to injury. These individuals would rather work than receive compensation benefits. In this category are three discharge-related workers' compensation scenarios:

- The injured worker, after recovery from medical treatment, requests to return to the former job, but the employer offers only modified duty, fearing reinjury if full duty is performed.
- The injured worker, following recovery from medical treatment, requests a different position or modified duty on account of disability, but the employer offers only the former unmodified position.
- The injured worker, following treatment, requests either the old job, modified duty, or reassignment but is terminated as unable to work due to disability.[55]

ADA charges will also be filed by applicants for employment with histories of prior workplace accidents and compensation claims as well as applicants whose job offer has been withdrawn because a preemployment medical examination reveals a medical condition that the employer fears will cause future injury.

The second type of charge will likely be filed by injured workers who do not wish to return to work but would rather receive the maximum amount of benefits possible. To such individuals, the ADA becomes a second avenue for relief. These workers may file a workers' compensation claim and an ADA charge, knowing that in many instances the employer will settle both claims in one settlement, the amount of which is increased by the existence of the ADA charge. This occurs because an employee's release of his or her claims under the ADA will be legally effective only if the employee receives money in addition to benefits to that he or she was entitled to under workers' compensation law.

Potential conflicts and contradictions exist between the ADA and workers' compensation that likely will spawn litigation. However, both mandates are also likely to support return-to-work initiatives. Return-to-work programs save scarce dollars and reduce the potential for ADA liability. It has long been recognized that proper disability management programs, including return-to-work programs, help injured workers to recover more quickly and save employers many more dollars than such efforts cost. Professionals in the field of rehabilitation were quick to recognize that the ADA's prohibition against discrimination and mandate for reasonable accommodation could do much to strengthen return to work efforts.[56] Anecdotal evidence gained by the author suggests that this awareness is also extending to employers and their counsel. An individual responsible for workers' compensation and benefits at Lockheed reported that his company had always supported return-to-work and modified-work programs for injured workers. Prior to the ADA, however, managers and supervisors were reluctant to provide modified work for an injured worker, citing productivity concerns. After the ADA, the company trained managers in their ADA responsibilities to accommodate and told them they simply had no choice but to provide reasonable accommodations. The ADA made the return-to-work and modified-work programs even more appealing to the company.

In a similar vein, the head of a nurses union reported that the ADA had made a significant difference for her members. Before the ADA, she said, hospitals would simply fire any nurse with physical restrictions. Now, in contrast, the union has been successful in securing accommodation for injured and ill members, because employers fear ADA liability if the nurses are discharged. A Florida workers' compensation defense attorney reported that the ADA has made it much easier to talk her clients into bringing injured workers back to work. Although she has not seen a lot of ADA litigation in Florida, she believes that the mere fear of potential ADA liability has made many of her clients sit up and listen when she talks about modified work. Another workers' compensation defense attorney reports that he counsels his employer clients that it is far cheaper to bring a worker back to work with accommodation, even if there is some risk of future workers' compensation claims, than to oppose accommodation. He stresses that the employer can save on time-loss payments under workers' compensation as well as the much greater potential for ADA liability. His belief is that, in the long run, ADA will result in reduction of workers' compensation costs if employers respond appropriately in their own economic interest. The biggest barrier, he believes, is the anger and frustration that many employers feel when they believe an injured worker is committing fraud and malingering. In such circumstances, it may be very difficult for employers to set aside their emotional desire to get the employee out of the workplace and analyze the case under the ADA to see if such a response is defensible.

THE POTENTIAL IMPACT OF THE ADA ON WORKERS' COMPENSATION REFORM

Efforts to reform workers' compensation and reduce costs sometimes have unforeseen ADA consequences. For example, California recently radically overhauled its workers' compensation system to reduce benefits and expenses for vocational rehabilitation. As amended, the California Labor Code requires employers to inform injured workers of their ADA rights and provide them with written notification of whether the employer will or will not provide modified or alternative work. The conflict between the reform law and the ADA is this: The ADA may require modified or alternative work as a form of ''reasonable accommodation'' unless the employer

246

can demonstrate that the accommodation would pose an undue hardship. However, the California reforms do not mandate modified or alternative work. The result will be that many California employers will blithely issue notices to injured workers denying them, in writing, what the ADA is requiring. These "no accommodation" notices will be, in many cases, a written admission of ADA liability that will be Exhibit Number 1 for the plaintiff in an ADA jury trial.

The California reform law also contains other ADA-related provisions harmful to employers. The state workers' compensation agency is required to publish a pamphlet informing workers of their rights under the ADA and the State Fair Employment and Housing Act (which also prohibits disability discrimination) as well as the workers' compensation law. Employers must provide this pamphlet to injured workers who have been out of work for at least 90 days. Together with the "no accommodation" notices, an employer is effectively telling an injured worker, "I will not give you a reasonable accommodation, and if you don't like it, you can sue me. Here's a booklet that tells you just how to do that." This provision also will likely be used by plaintiffs' attorneys to argue that the exclusive remedy clause of the workers' compensation law does not bar discrimination claims by injured workers under the state Fair Employment and Housing Act. Exclusive remedy provisions in state law cannot bar claims brought under a federal law such as the ADA.

Finally, the new reform law will encourage rehabilitation counselors to identify possible modified or alternative work with the same employer that previously has failed or refused to provide it. The law encourages rehabilitation counselors to build an ADA case against the employer by showing how modified or alternative work could have been provided to the injured employee but was not. This investigation, which is for rehabilitation purposes, must be paid for by the employer. It will likely be Plaintiff's Exhibit Number 2 in an ADA trial.

Other states have attempted workers' compensation reforms that have negative ADA implications. For example, Louisiana has eliminated or tightened up on compensable claims in certain categories such as heart attack, carpal tunnel syndrome, horseplay at the work site, and accidents occurring when a worker is intoxicated by alcohol or illegal drugs. Other states limit workers' compensation awards for workplace stress claims by imposing more stringent eligibility requirements. It is possible that some of these disability specific restrictions may be subject to challenge under Title II of the ADA as a state program that discriminates on the basis of disability in its eligibility criteria. Appellate courts in Oregon and Pennsylvania have suggested that such restrictions do violate the ADA.[57]

Florida and Oregon have enacted "preferred worker" programs, providing employers who hire injured workers with reduced workers' compensation premiums. Providing preferential treatment for injured workers does not violate the ADA. However, concerns have been raised as to how an employer is to determine, in advance of making a job offer, that an applicant is an injured worker when the ADA prohibits such preoffer inquiries. The EEOC has made clear in its Enforcement Guidance on "Preemployment Disability-Related Inquiries and Medical Examinations under the Americans with Disabilities Act of 1990" that inquiries for the purpose of providing "affirmative action" are lawful under the ADA.

THE ROLE OF INJURED WORKERS IN ADA ENFORCEMENT

EEOC ADA Charge Statistics

It is difficult to document the percentage of ADA charges or lawsuits filed by injured workers. Neither the EEOC nor the federal courts keep such data. Unfortunately, the EEOC charge data collection system does not inquire of charging parties whether their impairment arose out of employment or whether a workers' compensation claim is pending.[58] Early evidence suggests, however, that injured workers are playing a significant role in ADA enforcement. It will take several years before a sufficient number of court decisions have been reported to assess the role injured workers are playing in any statistical sense; as of July 1994, the Bureau of National Affairs indicated that only 124 ADA court decisions had been reported.[59]

However, a number of trends relating to injured workers can be seen from the ADA charges filed with the EEOC through 31

July 1994. The 31,242 ADA charges filed during the first two years Title I has been in effect demonstrate three key trends.

First, current employees, not applicants, are filing the predominate number of charges. This trend is indicated by the high percentage of discharge claims (50 percent) and the low percentage of hiring claims (11.3 percent).

Second, if "back impairment" is used as a rough proxy for injured worker claims, the data continue to suggest that injured workers are filing a significant percentage of ADA charges. Back impairment is the disability most often claimed by ADA charging parties (19.9 percent) and 46 percent of the bad back claims concern discharge.

This is a significant statistic in light of the high percentage of work-caused back injuries reported in surveys of occupational injuries and illnesses. It is estimated that strains of the lower back, spine, and various sprains accounted for 36 percent of worker injury costs for claims submitted in 1992 according to a study by the ITT Hartford Insurance Group.[60] According to the 1992 Bureau of Labor Statistics Report of Occupational Illness and Injuries, back injuries and illness accounted for 28 percent of all reported occupational incidents causing lost work days. According to the National Institute for Occupational Safety and Health, back pain accounted for 500 million lost work days in 1988 based on 22 million cases; about 12 percent of workers with back injuries stopped working or changed jobs.[61]

There are likely many workplace injuries other than back problems that lead workers to file ADA charges. According to OSHA, 147,000 cases of so-called ergonomic hazards injuries, such as carpal tunnel syndrome, were reported in 1988, accounting for 52 percent of all reportable illnesses.[62] Since December 1993 the EEOC has been tracking the number of charges from individuals claiming to have a "cumulative trauma disorder," a category that would include carpal tunnel syndrome. Through 31 May 1994, 127 such claims have been filed.

A third trend revealed by EEOC charge data is that the majority of persons filing ADA charges do not have what the public might perceive as "traditional" disabilities, such as mobility impairments, deafness, and blindness. Fully 24.6 percent of all the charges fall within a category denominated "other" because they do not fit within the EEOC's extensive list of common impairments. How many individuals in the "other" category may be injured workers is not known.

Response of the Bar

Even though EEOC charge data suggest that employers may be seeing a number of ADA claims filed by injured workers, few employers report receiving such charges or any ADA charges for that matter. Many large employers and management attorneys report being surprised at the lack of ADA-related activity in their area.

A manager at Pacific Bell reports relatively few ADA charges at his company, and other than saber rattling, the manager has yet to see much connection between injured workers and the ADA. A workers' compensation defense attorney reported that claimants' attorneys are asserting a right to reasonable accommodation as a part of mandatory vocational rehabilitation services required by the California workers' compensation statute. These assertions are made in correspondence that reference the ADA, but litigation is not proceeding. As she put it, they know the ADA acronym but not the substance.

A workers' compensation defense attorney acknowledged that he knows of the ADA but needed to learn much, much more about it. He said he has seen very little, if any, reference to ADA by claimants' attorneys in the San Diego, California, area. However, he noted that, because his practice is exclusively in the area of workers' compensation, large ADA cases would be turned over to the larger law firms that do big, civil defense work.

On the other side of the country, a management employment lawyer in Baltimore, Maryland, likewise reports little ADA activity although he characterized his city as a "hot labor center." He said even his biggest employers in the city only have two or three ADA charges. He believes that injured workers will drive ADA enforcement but he thinks it will take two to three years to happen. One explanation he cites is the lack of familiarity of the workers' compensation claimants' bar with the ADA. Most such attorneys, who will be the first lawyers to come into contact with injured workers, are small practitioners with volume practices that do not involve much court work. Many of these lawyers express a desire to see "model" ADA court papers that they can simply alter to fit the facts of their claim before they will get involved. In this attorney's view, it will take some big jury verdicts with a lot of publicity to get the claimants' bar involved. His views are shared by many other management attorneys who note that the ADA's complexity causes many plaintiffs' lawyers to shy away from bringing ADA lawsuits.

There are anecdotal signs, however, that the claimants' bar is becoming more interested in the ADA, at least in some parts of the country. In Florida, many claimants' attorneys reported at a statewide workers' compensation conference that they were learning the ADA. Several indicated that, although they had been referring claimants with potential ADA claims to other plaintiff employment lawyers, they were acquiring copies of pleadings to begin to undertake such representation. Some claimants' attorneys are worried that failure to advise their clients about potential ADA claims will result in legal malpractice liability. These attorneys are preparing to advise clients on whether they have a valuable ADA claim. By and large, however, the consensus among management attorneys is that the claimants' bar has a long way to go before it is as knowledgeable about the ADA. Some have expressed the belief that if and when Congress removes the caps limiting recovery of compensatory and punitive damages, the incentive for ADA litigation will be high enough to tempt the workers' compensation claimants' bar to get involved.

INJURED WORKERS AND LITIGATION UNDER DISABILITY DISCRIMINATION LAWS

The potential for ADA litigation to arise out of the workers' compensation system was dramatically demonstrated by a case brought under state law just prior to the effective date of the ADA. An injured worker with carpal tunnel recovered a large jury verdict against her employer under a state disability antidiscrimination law similar to the ADA. Janice Goodman was a 56-year-old microfilmer with The Boeing Company when she developed carpal tunnel syndrome giving her increasing pain in her hands and arms. Despite repeated requests to her employer, she was not given a rotation of tasks nor an appropriate reassignment. She sued under the

Washington state fair employment law for failure to provide reasonable accommodation, harassment, and negligent infliction of emotional distress. The jury awarded her $1,126,000, less $37,000 for wage loss benefits, for a net award of over $1,088,000.

In *Tuck* v. *HCA Health Services of Tennessee*,[63] the United States Court of Appeals for the Sixth Circuit affirmed an award of $26,755 in back pay under Section 504 of the Rehabilitation Act and a state disability discrimination law to a nurse terminated by her hospital employer because her on-the-job back injury prevented her from being able to perform essential patient-lifting duties. The nurse had a history of back injuries, resulting ultimately in extensive back surgery, including the removal of a disk. After being out on workers' compensation benefits for approximately 11 months, she was released by her doctor to return to work, with restrictions. It was not disputed by the plaintiff that she could not perform the essential functions of lifting, supporting, and repositioning patients. The hospital attempted to accommodate her by reassigning her to the progressive care unit, a small ward with only 14 beds and three nurses on duty. As an accommodation, the other two nurses agreed to help the plaintiff with her heavy duties if she would help them perform their lighter duties. One night, a nurse called in sick, leaving only the plaintiff and one other nurse to care for 14 patients. The plaintiff was unable to pitch in on the heavy duties of her job. Although the hospital had agreed to permit her eight weeks under this restricted duty program, she was fired because of the hospital's view that she still could not perform the essential functions of her nursing job. The Court of Appeals disagreed and ruled in her favor. The court noted that there was no indication that she had been warned or counseled about performance problems. The court found that the hospital had been advertising to fill a variety of nursing positions in different wards some of which, in the court's view, plaintiff was able to perform but she was not offered a reassignment. The court also found it significant that four months after her discharge, the plaintiff gained employment in another health care facility in a job that was allegedly as physically demanding as the job she was discharged from. Finally, the court noted that the duty to prove that the plaintiff could not be accommodated fell to the hospital, and it had failed to meet its burden.

252

A reverse scenario is playing out in New York, where police officers have challenged a requirement that they perform light duty. In charges filed with the EEOC, the officers contend that they are being denied long-term disability benefits because their municipal employer is requiring them to perform light duty work within their medical restrictions.

That injured workers now may have a right to reasonable accommodation has led one employer to contest a court's award of permanent total disability benefits under state workers' compensation law. In *Trans Mart, Inc.* v. *Brewer*, 1993 WL 383019 (Ala. Civ. App., 1993), the Alabama Court of Civil Appeals rejected an employer's argument that an award of permanent total disability benefits was improper because it failed to take into account the impact of the ADA on employment practices, making it more likely that the claimant could be gainfully employed. The court concluded that the ADA was intended to outlaw discrimination not to reduce the rights or benefits of injured workers.

A few ADA-related claims have surfaced with respect to employer inquiries. For example, at least six ADA charges have been filed against Rockwell International, Inc., of Troy, Michigan, for allegedly disqualifying applicants based upon the results of a nerve conductivity test used to detect the presence of or susceptibility to carpal tunnel syndrome. The charges assert that offers of employment were withdrawn based on the test results that were not "job-related and consistent with business necessity."[64] The Minnesota Supreme Court rejected an employer's efforts to deny workers' compensation to an injured worker who allegedly gave false answers on a job application concerning previous injuries because the court found the questions did not concern the essential functions of the job as required by the Minnesota Human Rights Act.[65]

CONCLUSION

Congress did not foresee the impact ADA would have on injured workers and workers' compensation. Some overlap is inevitable, as both workers' compensation and the ADA reflect different approaches to the problem of disability. Potential conflict arises because of the workers' compensation system focus on inability rather than remaining ability. Preliminary evidence suggests that discharged injured workers are making use of the ADA's protections. On the other hand, the ADA also supports efforts at returning injured workers to work with proper disability management programs. Such programs have the potential to cut benefit costs and reduce ADA liability.

The degree to which the ADA and workers' compensation conflict may have important implications for the future of the ADA. If employers increasingly adopt ADA-consistent practices to promote accommodation and return to work resulting in reduction in workers' compensation costs, there will be a growing political and economic consensus that the ADA works. Under this scenario, ADA becomes so enmeshed in positive workers' compensation cost containment practices that employers see the ADA as enhancing profits rather than generating losses.

The political and economic consensus supporting the ADA could be gradually eroded by a torrent of frivolous charges and lawsuits filed by workers with minor, trivial impairments. Employers may be hit with large jury verdicts by juries who understand little about this complex law but feel that, on balance, employers are usually rich and unfair. A large volume of high-dollar ADA awards against employers on behalf of individuals the public does not consider to have a disability could set the stage for amendments to curb the reach of the ADA.

At this juncture, evidence supporting both views can be found. Frivolous and nonfrivolous ADA claims are being made and litigated. Jury verdicts and court decisions are beginning to emerge. The scope of the ADA's impact on workers' compensation – and vice versa – will not be fully known for years to come.

NOTES

1. "Workers' Comp: 'Fastest Growing Labor Cost'," *Daily Labor Report*, Bureau of National Affairs (20 May 1993): A-19.
2. Donald E. Shrey and Robert E. Breslin, "Employer-Based Disability Management Strategies and Work Return Transition Programs," in *Americans with Disabilities Act: Access and Accommodations*, ed. Nancy Hablutzel and Brian McMahon (Paul M. Deutsch Press, 1992), p. 142.

3. Ibid.
4. 42 U.S.C. § 12111(8) (1992); 29 C.F.R. § 1630.2(m) (1993). For purposes of the ADA, a "disability" is a mental or physical impairment that substantially limits the individual in any major life activity, including working. The ADA protects an applicant or an employee with a disability if he or she is "qualified." A "qualified individual with a disability" is a person with a disability who satisfies job prerequisites, such as education and experience, and who can perform the "essential functions" of a job with or without a reasonable accommodation.
5. Ibid., § 12112(a); § 1630.4.
6. Ibid., § 12112(b)(5)(A); § 1630.9.
7. Ibid., § 12111(9); § 1630.2(o).
8. 42 U.S.C. § 12112(b) (1992).
9. Ibid., 12112(d)(2)(A); 1630.13(a); and 1630.13 App.
10. Ibid., 1630.2(r) and App.; 1630.15(a) App.
11. Ibid., § 12102(2)(A); § 1630.2(g)(1).
12. Ibid., § 12102(2)(b); § 1630.2(g)(2).
13. Ibid., 12102(2)(C); § 1630.2(g)(3).
14. Ibid., § 1630.2(i) (1992).
15. Ibid., § 1630.2(j) App.
16. Ibid., § 1630.2(j) App.
17. See EEOC, *Technical Assistance Manual on the Employment Provisions (Title I) of the Americans with Disabilities Act* (Washington, D.C.: EEOC, January 1992), p. IX-2; hereafter TAM.
18. Ibid., § 1630.2(j)(3).
19. TAM, p. IX-2.
20. See, e.g., Cook v. Rhode Island; 10 F.3d 17 (1st Cir. 1993); E. E. Black, Ltd., v. Marshall, 497 F. Supp. 1088 (D.Haw. 1980).
21. TAM, p. IX-3.
22. E.g., Welsh v. City of Tulsa, 977 F.2d 1415 (10th Cir. 1992); Byrne v. Board of Educ., School District of West Allis–West Milwaukee, 979 F.2d 560 (7th Cir. 1992); Maulding v. Sullivan, 961 F.2d 694 (8th Cir. 1992); Dailey v. Koch, 892 F.2d 212 (2d Cir. 1989); Forrisi v. Bowen, 794 F.2d 931, 934 (4th Cir. 1986); Jasany v. United States Postal Service, 755 F.2d

1244 (6th Cir. 1985); Fuqua v. Unisys Corp., 716 F. Supp. 1201 (D.Minn. 1989); Elstner v. South Western Bell Telephone Co., 659 F. Supp. 1328 (S.D.Tex. 1987) *aff'd*, 863 F.2d 881 (5th Cir. 1988); and Tudyman v. United Airlines, 608 F. Supp. 739 (D.Cal. 1984).

23.   E.g., Evans v. Dallas, 861 F.2d 846, 852–853 (5th Cir. 1988); Grimard v. Carlston, 567 F.2d 1171, 1174 (1st Cir. 1978); Paegle v. Dept. of Interior, No. 91-1075 (D.D.C. 8 February 1993); Visarraga v. Garrett, No. C-88-2828, 1992 U.S. Dist. LEXIS 9164, p. *13 (N.D. 16 June 1992); Saffer v. Town of Whitman, No. 85-4470, 1986 WL 14090 at *1 (D.Mass. 2 December 1986); Stevens v. Stubbs, 576 F.Supp. 1409 (D.Ga. 1983).

24.   August v. Offices Unlimited, Inc., 981 F.2d 576 (1st Cir. 1992); Reigel v. Kaiser Foundation Health Plan of North Carolina, cite other cases.

25.   Jasany v. U.S. Postal Service, 755 F.2d 1244 (6th Cir.1985); Forrisi v. Bowen, 794 F.2d 931 (4th Cir. 1986).

26.   42 U.S.C. § 12112(d) (1992); 29 C.F.R. § 1630.13 (1993).

27.   Ibid., 12112(d)(3) (1992); § 1630.14 (1992).

28.   EEOC, "Enforcement Guidance: Preemployment Disability-Related Inquiries and Medical Examinations under the Americans with Disabilities Act of 1990" (19 May 1994), p. 41.

29.   42 U.S.C. § 12112(d)(3) (1992); 29 C.F.R. § 1630.14(b) and 1630.15 (1992).

30.   42 U.S.C. § 12112(d)(4) (1992); 29 C.F.R. § 1630.14(c) and 1630.15 (1993).

31.   Shrey and Breslin, "Employer-Based Disability Management Strategies and Work Return Transition Programs," p. 141.

32.   42 U.S.C. § 12113(b) (1992); 29 C.F.R. § 1630.15(b)(2) (1993).

33.   See, generally, TAM, Chapter 4, "Establishing Nondiscriminatory Qualification Standards and Selection Criteria."

34.   29 C.F.R. § 1630.2(o)(1) (1993).

35.   However, the Department of Labor has recently ruled that failure to provide a light duty position to an injured employee violates Section 503 of the Rehabilitation Act of 1973. OFCCP v. Cissell Mfg. Co., No. 87-OFC-26 (Dept. Labor 14 February 1994).

36. See Reigel, M.D. v. Kaiser Foundation Health Plan of North
    Carolina, No. 93-556-CIV-5-F (29 June 1994), slip op. at 24
    ("[R]equiring the Medical Group to either permanently assign
    an existing physician assistant to work with plaintiff to per-
    form the physical aspects of her position or hire a new assistant
    to do the same cannot be considered a reasonable accommoda-
    tion. The [ADA] does not require an employer to hire two
    individuals to do the tasks ordinarily assigned to one."); John-
    ston v. Morrison, Inc., 849 F. Supp. 777, 780 (N.D.Ala. 1994)
    (Restaurant not required to assign another employee to help
    food server during her panic attacks as this would eliminate
    essential job functions); See also Gilbert v. Frank, 949 F.2d
    637, 644 (2d Cir. 1991) (employer not required to assign
    coworker to do physically demanding tasks employee no longer
    able to do); Treadwell v. Alexander, 707 F.2d 473, 478 (11th
    Cir. 1983) (assigning additional employees to cover plaintiff's
    physically demanding duties was an undue hardship); Cole-
    man v. Darden, 595 F.2d 533, 540 (10th Cir.), cert. denied,
    444 U.S. 927 (1979) (under the Rehabilitation Act, an
    employer may be required to have someone assist the disabled
    individual to perform the job, but the employer is not required
    to have someone perform the job for the disabled individual).
37. 29 C.F.R. § 1630.2(o) App.; H. Rep. 101-485, Pt. 2, 101st
    Cong., 2d Sess. 64 (1990).
38. See, e.g., Jackson v. Veterans Admin., 22 F.3d 277, 280
    (11th Cir. 1994) (Rehabilitation Act does not require a federal
    agency to accommodate periodic, unanticipated absences of
    probationary employee); Carr v. Reno, 23 F.3d 525, 531 (D.C.
    Cir. 1994) ("An essential function of any government job is
    an ability to appear for work [whether in the workplace or,
    in the unusual case, at home] and to complete assigned tasks
    within a reasonable period of time. . . . To require an
    employer to accept an openended 'work when able' schedule
    for a time-sensitive job would stretch 'reasonable accommoda-
    tion' to absurd proportions and imperil the effectiveness of
    the employer's public enterprise"); Larkins v. Ciba Vision
    Corp., 1994 WL 370138 *14 n. 5 (N.D.Ga.) (ADA does not
    require employer to accommodate employee totally disabled
    from working); Beauford v. Father Flanagan's Boy's Home,

831 F.2d 768, 771 (8th Cir. 1987), *cert. denied*, 485 U.S. 938 (1988) (Rehabilitation Act does not protect employee who is no longer able to do his or her job due to physical and emotional ailments arising out of pressures of work); Matzo v. Postmaster General, 685 F. Supp. 260, 263 (D.D.C. 1987), *aff'd without opinion*, 861 F.2d 1290 (D.C. Cir. 1988) (regular attendance is an essential function); Stevens v. Stubbs, 576 F. Supp. 1409, 1415 (N.D.Ga. 1983) (Rehabilitation Act "does not protect absenteeism or employees who take excessive leave and are unable to perform the prerequisites of their jobs").

39. See Langon v. HHS, 959 F.2d 1053 (D.C. Cir. 1992) (Rehabilitation Act may require federal agency to consider accommodating a computer programmer with multiple sclerosis by allowing her to work at home); EEOC v. AIC Security Investigation, Ltd., 820 F. Supp. 1060, 1065 (N.D.Ill. 1993) ("To be sure, attendance is necessary to any job, but the degree of such, especially in an upper management position . . . where a number of tasks are effectively delegated to other employees requires close scrutiny. . . . What is material is that the job gets done").

40. The FMLA has many implications for workers' compensation. The interplay between workers' compensation, FMLA, and ADA is discussed, generally in Christopher G. Bell, "Integrating ADA and FMLA into Workers' Compensation and STD Policies and Practices," *ADA Policy and Law* 2, no. 5 (May 1994): 11–14.

41. 42 U.S.C. § 12111(9)(B); but see Reigel, M.D. v. Kaiser Foundation Health Plan of North Carolina, *supra* (ADA does not require reassignment citing pre-ADA Rehabilitation Act case law).

42. Maged v. Federal Reserve Bank of Philadelphia, 776 F. Supp. 200, 204 (E.D.Pa. 1991); EEOC, TAM, § 9.4.

43. U.S.C. sec. 1981 a(a)(3).

44. 42 U.S.C. § 12111(10) (1992); 29 C.F.R. § 1630.2(p) (1992).

45. 29 C.F.R. Part 1630, App. at 413 (1992).

46. Letter from Evan J. Kemp, Jr., chairman, EEOC to Christopher G. Bell dated on or about 17 March 1993.

47. The Civil Rights Act of 1991 "provides a limitation on the sum of punitive damages and compensatory damages for future pecuniary losses, emotional pain, suffering, inconvenience,

mental anguish, loss of enjoyment of life, and other nonpecuniary losses." The limitation on the amount of damages (caps) is based on the size (number of employees) of the respondent. The limitations are stated as follows:

15–100 employees, $50,000
101–200 employees, $100,000
201–500 employees, $200,000
501 employees or more, $300,000

EEOC, "Enforcement Guidance: Compensatory and Punitive Damages Available under Section 102 of the Civil Rights Act of 1991" (14 July 1992), pp. 4–5.

48. 42 U.S.C. § 2117(b); 42 U.S.C. § 1981a(b)(2).
49. See, e.g., Langridge v. Oakland Unified School Dist., 25 Cal.App.4th 664, 31 Cal.Rptr.2d 34 (Cal. App. 1994).
50. See Wittorf v. Shell Oil Co., 1994 WL 150810 (E.D.La.) (there is no reason why the "knowing and voluntary" standard should not apply to the ADA); Callicotte v. Carlucci, 698 F. Supp. 944 (D.D.C. 1988) (employee with chronic alcoholism and depression did not knowingly and voluntarily waive Rehabilitation Act claim when agreeing to probation and last chance agreement in lieu of termination).
51. See, generally, Christopher G. Bell and Robert L. Burgdorf, Jr., "Orienting Principles of Handicap Discrimination Law," Chapter 5 in *Accommodating the Spectrum of Individual Abilities* (Washington, D.C.: U.S. Commission on Civil Rights, 1983).
52. Richard Pimentel et al., *The Workers' Compensation–ADA Connection: Supervisory Tools That Cut Costs and Reduce ADA Liability* (Chatsworth, Calif.: Milt Wright and Associates, 1993), p. 8.
53. Bolton v. Scrivner, Inc., 836 F. Supp. 783, 788–89 (W.D.Okla.1993).
54. Tuck v. HCA Health Services of Tennessee, 7 F.3d 465 (6th Cir. 1993).
55. John H. Geaney, "Where ADA and Workers' Compensation Clash," *New Jersey Law Journal* 133: 1, 32.
56. See, generally, Shrey and Breslin, "Employer-Based Disability Management Strategies and Work Return Transition Programs," pp.139–167.

57. Hershey Chocolate Co. v. Workmen's Compensation Appeal Board, 1994 WL 32137 (Pa.Cmwlth.); Way v. Meyer, Inc., 1994 WL 47053 (Or.App.).

58. The author wrote to the EEOC chairman Evan J. Kemp, Jr., to request that this information be collected during the charge filing process but he declined to do so for administrative reasons.

59. Special Report, "Greater Activism, Awareness Mark ADA as Law Extends to Small Employers," *Daily Labor Report*, Bureau of National Affairs (26 July 1994), p. C-6. Although not expressly stated, BNA is apparently referring to court published rulings in ADA lawsuits. Jury verdicts, non-published orders, and out of court settlements would not be included in this number.

60. "Sprains Most Costly Worker Injuries, Study Says," *Daily Labor Report*, Bureau of National Affairs (23 September 1993), p. A-16.

61. "NIOSH Study Identifies Back Pain as Major Problem for U.S. Workers," *Daily Labor Report*, Bureau of National Affairs (5 May 1993), p. A-4.

62. 57 Federal Register 34192.

63. 7 F.3d 465 (6th Cir. 1993).

64. "Carpal Tunnel Test Spurs Charges of ADA Employment Discrimination," *Disability Compliance Bulletin* 4, no. 4 (1 September 1993): 10.

65. Huisenga v. Opus Corp., 1992 Minn. LEXIS 366, (Minn. Sup. Ct. 1992).

III:
Public Accommodations and
Transportation

Inclusion in
Public Accommodations

Andrew I. Batavia

EDITOR'S NOTE

Likely the most far-reaching provision of the ADA, the public accommodations mandate, requires over 5 million private businesses to become accessible to and usable by people with disabilities. Offering a new market to businesses and increased opportunities to participate in the economy to people with disabilities, this mandate has the potential to generate a notable contribution to the nation's economy. Batavia's comprehensive examination of implementation reveals sporadic progress nationwide, with the private sector, the disability community, and government agencies assuming stances ranging from stubborn resistance or inattentiveness to innovative problem solving. Recommending further policy clarification, targeted technical assistance, certification of model state and local building codes, ongoing monitoring of compliance, aggressive federal enforcement, and continued partnership between the disability community and the business community, Batavia looks forward to a long-term future of accessible and inclusive commerce.

This chapter was written in 1994. Some important developments have occurred since that time, including the resolution of several court cases and expanded implementation efforts by various federal and state agencies. But the general conclusions and recommendations of this chapter continue to apply.

Andrew I. Batavia, J.D., M.S., served as special assistant to Attorney General Thornburgh at the U.S. Department of Justice when the regulations for Title III of the ADA were promulgated. In that capacity he helped oversee the Justice Department's national ADA implementation effort and helped to draft the regulations. He has also served as executive director of the National Council on Disability, associate director of the White House Domestic Policy Council, research director for disability and rehabilitation research at Abt Associates, and associate director of the National Rehabilitation Hospital Research Center. He is a founding associate editor of the Journal of Disability Policy Studies *and a member of the faculty of Georgetown University Medical School. Batavia currently serves as legislative assistant to Senator John McCain (R-Ariz.), chief sponsor of Title IV of the ADA. The views expressed in this chapter are solely those of Mr. Batavia.*

INTRODUCTION – PHILOSOPHY AND GOALS OF TITLE III OF THE ADA

In the United States, there are approximately 5 million places of public accommodation, such as restaurants, theaters, hotels, grocery stores, shopping malls, banks, dry cleaners, gas stations, professional offices, amusement parks, private schools, day care centers, and health spas.[1] Title III of the ADA[2] was designed to ensure access for all people with disabilities to such places, as well as to commercial facilities such as office buildings. As such, it is arguably the most far-reaching public access law in history (Burgdorf, 1991; Parmet, 1993).

Congress, in debating Title III, recognized that individuals with disabilities require access to private sector facilities and services to have the same opportunities as other citizens. However, Congress also found that it would be inefficient and unfair to impose the burden of access on businesses when the costs are great compared with their ability to meet those costs. This conflict between basic individual rights and reasonable social obligations was resolved through a well-balanced set of statutory provisions implemented by regulations promulgated by the U.S. Department of Justice (DOJ) and the Architectural and Transportation Barriers Compliance Board (Access Board).

The goals of Title III are twofold: In the short run, places of public accommodation must be accessible to the extent not unduly burdensome to covered entities; in the long run, as new buildings are built, old buildings are modified, new technologies become available, and economic circumstances change, the country must become accessible. This short- and long-term perspective offers the appropriate framework by which to assess implementation. With an initial effective date of 26 January 1992, certain progress toward short-term objectives should be discernable even now. The jury will be out for years in determining whether the long-term goals are met. This chapter considers how Title III is being implemented and whether the goals of Title III are being achieved.

Thus far, the implementation effort has been a story of considerable, though mixed, success. It has involved both investigatory discretion and rigorous enforcement by government agencies, innovative accommodation and stubborn resistance by the business community, and gentle prodding and hardball negotiating by the disability community. In the short run, progress is occurring sporadically throughout the country. In the long run, the vast majority of places of public accommodation and commercial facilities will be accessible to people with disabilities, if public and private enforcement remains active and reasonable.

REQUIREMENTS OF TITLE III

The goals of Title III are achieved through a very specific statutory scheme implemented through in-depth regulations and guidelines.

Statutory Scheme

Under Title III, owners, lessors, lessees, and operators of places of public accommodation (except for religious organizations and private clubs) are prohibited from discriminating on the basis of disability.[3] This means that an individual with a disability may not be denied, due to his or her disability, an equal opportunity to participate in and partake of the goods, services, facilities, privileges, advantages, or accommodations of a covered entity in the most integrated setting appropriate to the needs of that individual. Unlike Titles I or II, which have qualifications requirements, persons with disabilities need not demonstrate that they are qualified to participate in the public accommodation (Parmet, 1993).

Title III lists 12 categories of covered places of public accommodation: places of lodging; establishments serving food or drink; places of exhibition or entertainment; places of public gathering; sales or rental establishments; service establishments; public transportation terminals, depots, or stations; places of public display or collection; places of recreation; places of education; social service center establishments; and places of exercise.[4] Unlike the employment requirements of Title I, entities are covered regardless of size or number of employees.

All covered entities must make reasonable changes in their policies, practices, and procedures to accommodate the needs of people with disabilities unless the entity can demonstrate that the modifications would fundamentally alter the nature of its products, services, or benefits.[5] Auxiliary aids and services must be provided to individuals with visual or hearing impairments or other individuals with disabilities, unless such provision would result in an "undue burden" (i.e., it is significantly difficult or expensive).[6]

Physical barriers in existing facilities must be removed, if such removal is "readily achievable"[7] (i.e., easily accomplishable and able to be carried out without much difficulty or expense).[8] If it is not, alternative methods of providing the services must be offered by the public accommodation, if such alternative methods are readily achievable.[9] These requirements have been in effect for over three years, so evidence of their effects should now be available.

All new construction in places of public accommodation, as well as in commercial facilities, must be accessible.[10] Elevators are generally not required in buildings with fewer than three stories or fewer than 3,000 square feet per floor, unless the building is a shopping center, mall, or professional office of a health care provider.[11] The effective date for new construction requirements was 26 January 1993.

Alterations of existing facilities must also be accessible.[12] When alterations to primary function areas are made, an accessible path of travel to the altered area (and the bathrooms, telephones, and drinking fountains serving that area) must be provided to the extent that the added accessibility costs are not disproportionate to the overall cost of the alterations. The statute specifically requires DOJ to determine what costs are disproportionate, which the department subsequently determined is anything above 20 percent of the cost of the alterations project.[13]

To reduce the burden of improving access, a tax credit equal to 50 percent of expenses between $250 and $10,250 is available to eligible small businesses (with gross receipts of no more than $1 million or 30 or fewer full-time employees in the previous year).[14] This credit may be carried forward up to 15 years and back up to 3 years, and may be claimed each year that a business makes an ADA-required accessibility expenditure. All businesses may deduct in one year, rather than capitalize over several years, barrier removal expenses up to $15,000.[15]

The attorney general may bring a civil action in a U.S. district court if he or she has reason to believe that there is a pattern or practice of discrimination under Title III or if there is discrimination that raises an issue of general public importance. In addition, a private individual may bring suit for injunction relief, including an order to alter facilities to make them accessible. Monetary damages may be awarded to an aggrieved individual if requested by the attorney general. However, punitive damages are not permitted.[16]

DOJ REGULATIONS AND GUIDELINES

One major aspect of implementing Title III was the promulgation of interpretive regulations in a timely manner by the DOJ and publication of ADA Accessibility Guidelines (ADAAG) by the Access Board. These regulations were published by both agencies in the *Federal Register* on the statutory deadline of 26 July 1991, one year after the signing of the ADA.[17] The DOJ has also published and updated a Title III *Technical Assistance Manual,* clarifying its regulations and offering specific examples of what is required. Although the specific contents of those regulations and guidelines are beyond the scope of this chapter, certain problems pertinent to the implementation process are discussed in the section on government monitoring and enforcement.

TECHNICAL ASSISTANCE ON TITLE III

DOJ Activities

The public access section of the Civil Rights Division of the DOJ, which has primary responsibility for investigating and litigating Title III complaints, has encouraged voluntary compliance by providing education and technical assistance to industry and the general public. It has conducted these activities both through speeches and presentations by DOJ staff and through grants to nonprofit organizations. The access section has produced handbooks, manuals, and fact sheets; provided speakers for conferences; responded to thousands of calls to its information hotline; and awarded $6.5 million in technical assistance grants (DOJ, 1993).

In 1993, the public access section expanded its outreach program through several direct mailings in addition to its general distribution of technical assistance materials. Information was sent to 15,000 architects and contractors, 500 service providers for AIDS, and 5.9 million businesses. Grants have been awarded primarily to address the specific needs of certain target audiences. For example,

DOJ grants have targeted the needs of older Americans, museums, architects, interior designers, people with cognitive disabilities, people with mental disabilities, people speaking any of 12 different languages, librarians, mediators, retail shops and other covered entities, police, and "911" emergency operators (DOJ, 1993).

NIDRR Activities

The National Institute on Disability and Rehabilitation Research (NIDRR) has funded 10 regional Disability and Business Technical Assistance Centers (DBTACs) to provide ADA information to people with disabilities and covered entities in different parts of the country. The DBTACs offer technical assistance on all aspects of the ADA, and therefore it is difficult to discern precisely how much of their services relate directly to Title III. However, several DBTACs have indicated that Title III occupies a majority of their time and effort (see the section on private sector monitoring).

GOVERNMENT MONITORING AND ENFORCEMENT OF TITLE III

A variety of federal entities have been involved in monitoring or enforcing Title III, including the DOJ, the National Council on Disability (NCD), the General Accounting Office (GAO), and two committees of Congress.

DOJ Complaints and Investigations

The public access section of the DOJ has received complaints under Title III from individuals in every state, the District of Columbia, and Puerto Rico. It is currently investigating over 1,200 complaints, which have been made by every category of entity covered under the ADA. However, it is not investigating all complaints it receives, apparently because of lack of staff. Approximately 65 percent of complaints have been in the area of barrier removal, 25 percent have involved policies and procedures, and 15 percent have concerned auxiliary aids and services (DOJ, 1993).

The DOJ attempts to resolve most complaints through informal or formal settlement agreements. However, it has the authority to file civil actions and seek monetary damages and civil penalties and has used this authority as leverage to achieve voluntary compliance. Typically, it will have an investigator contact the covered entity accused of a violation to determine whether there is, in fact, a Title III obligation and whether it has been satisfied. If a violation is found, the covered entity is given an opportunity to correct it before any legal action is taken.

At the time of this writing, the DOJ has filed four ADA lawsuits, intervened in a fifth lawsuit, and participated by filing an amicus ("friend of the court") brief in support of five other lawsuits. Most of these have been Title II cases involving discrimination by state and local governments rather than private entities covered under Title III. However, a few Title III cases have been filed by the DOJ and many have been settled informally out of court.

The DOJ obtained its first consent decree resolving the case of *U.S.* v. *Venture Stores, Inc.* on 26 May 1993. In this case, a firm that operates more than 90 discount department stores in 8 states was challenged for its policy of requiring customers to present a driver's license to pay for merchandise with a personal check. This policy discriminated against those individuals with disabilities that prevent them from obtaining a driver's license, such as blindness and high-level quadriplegia. The consent decree requires the firm to accept state ID cards for check cashing.

Subsequently, a consent decree was obtained in *United States* v. *Allright Colorado, Inc.* Allright, a company that owns and operates over 100 parking lots and garages in Denver, which intentionally failed to comply with Title III's accessible parking space requirements, agreed to pay a $20,000 civil penalty, to add over 400 accessible parking spaces with appropriate signage, and to adopt enforcement policies to ensure that people with disabilities are able to benefit from the new accessible parking.

The department's other cases have not been resolved at this time. In *Pinnock* v. *International House of Pancakes*, the DOJ intervened in a private action challenging the constitutionality of the ADA. The case involves failure to undertake readily achievable barrier removal and provide auxiliary aids and services. In *U.S.* v. *Morvant* and *U.S.* v. *Castle Dental Center*, the DOJ challenged the practice of refusing to provide dental treatment to individuals who have tested positive for HIV. The department argued that there is no scientific or medical justification for excluding persons with HIV or AIDS from dental treatment solely on the basis of their HIV-positive status.

In addition, the DOJ has resolved some Title III conflicts through formal settlement agreements, which are signed by the department and the respondent and include provisions for enforcement. Its first formal settlement agreement, in March 1993, required the Municipal Credit Union to install a permanent ramp at its entrance, to inform its customers that this entrance is now accessible, to post appropriate signage, and to instruct its staff to provide requested assistance to individuals with disabilities. It must be emphasized that a settlement agreement is not an admission of guilt, and some businesses that choose to settle may not have had a legal obligation under the ADA.

In July 1993, the DOJ and the Inter-Continental Hotel in New York City entered into a formal settlement agreement whereby the hotel chain would make numerous changes to its facility and procedures over a five-year period, including removal of barriers in all public areas and 21 guest rooms. Among the changes that the hotel would undertake under this agreement are to provide television decoders, telephone handset amplifiers, visual smoke alarms, door knock and telephone indicators in 35 guest rooms, making elevator modifications to ensure access for persons with visual impairments, and room assignment modifications to ensure accessible rooms for those who request them.

Also in July 1993, the DOJ entered into formal agreements with the Quality Hotel Downtown in Washington, D.C., and Sardi's Restaurant in New York City. The Quality Hotel agreement resolved a complaint that hotel staff did not permit a guest to use a motorized scooter as a mobility device to get to his room. The hotel agreed to pay $10,000 in damages and require all hotel employees to undergo training on the ADA. The Sardi's settlement, resolving a complaint that the restaurant's restrooms were inaccessible to wheelchairs, resulted in the installation of an accessible bathroom and signage indicating its location.

In March 1994, the DOJ entered into a symbolically important formal agreement with the owners and operators of the Empire State Building to remove architectural barriers. The agreement mandates modifications to the lobby, entrance, and observation decks, including the installation of automatic doors, accessible ticket counters, and accessible observation periscopes. However, it does not require that privately leased office space be made accessible. Under the agreement, the Justice Department may seek civil penalties if the owners do not comply. Attorney General Janet Reno stated that "[n]o persons with disabilities should ever be denied the chance to view the wondrous historic sites that this country offers. Our Department's continued vigorous enforcement of the ADA will ensure that many more historic sites will become accessible."[18]

Finally, DOJ has resolved many Title III complaints through informal agreements in which the covered entity voluntarily agrees to make specified modifications, sometimes after extensive negotiations with DOJ attorneys. In the area of barrier removal, for example, a national retail chain agreed to provide accessible parking at its stores throughout the country and a rental car company agreed to provide accessible parking at a major airport. The vast majority of complaints are resolved through such informal agreements (DOJ, 1993).

DOJ Certification Applications

The ADA authorizes the DOJ to certify that state or local building codes meet or exceed the ADA's minimum accessibility requirements. Compliance with a certified code constitutes rebuttable evidence of compliance with the ADA. The public access section of DOJ issued its first response to a request for certification by the State of Washington on 20 May 1993. This letter, which was not a formal determination of equivalency or nonequivalency, provided technical assistance in the form of a side-by-side comparison of the Washington code and ADA requirements.

In response to a request from the Council of American Business Officials, the DOJ is reviewing the 1992 revision of the American National Standards Institute (ANSI) standard for accessible and usable buildings and facilities. If this is certified, it should expedite the certification of local and state building codes that are based on it. However, it will still not offer a guaranteed "safe harbor" for the construction industry. The DOJ recently began compliance reviews of new construction and alteration projects that are in the planning phases.

National Council on Disability

In its ADA Watch Project, the NCD[19] monitored the first year of ADA implementation, and developed 22 findings and 16 recommendations (NCD, 1993). Although its report addressed the ADA generally rather than focusing on specific titles, it did document several exemplary approaches to complying with Title III requirements. In one particularly effective effort, the America West Arena in Phoenix established 14 wheelchair sections at different locations and price ranges, a dog park for service animals, assistive listening access for people with hearing impairments, and a brochure on stadium access (NCD, 1993).

NIDRR Technical Assistance Centers

In conducting research for this chapter, the author asked the NIDRR regional DBTACs how Title III was being implemented in their regions. The following are their specific responses of those DBTACs that responded.

Region IV – Southeast DBTAC (Ala., Fla., Ga., Ky., Mo., N.C., S.C., Tenn.) Approximately 40 percent of our average of 800 telephone and written inquiries per month relate to Title III compliance issues. Analysis of these inquiries shows that many places of public accommodation have taken some steps toward voluntary compliance, but those steps and the actual benefits to customers with disabilities vary widely. Businesses seem to be most aware of, and comfortable with, removal of physical barriers, as opposed to communication barriers; however, obstacles still remain.

Removal of communication barriers is presenting the most resistance, especially among professionals such as doctors, attorneys and bankers. Their general attitude is one of resentment when informed of their ADA obligations to provide effective communication, especially when interpreters are the solution. In general, ADA compliance continues to be a back burner issue, especially for the small business community. The 1996 Olympics (in Atlanta) will be the single most important event to demonstrate to the world our commitment to ADA compliance and enforcement.

Region V – Great Lakes DBTAC (Ill., Ind., Mich., Minn., Ohio, Wis.) The Great Lakes Region in general has demonstrated a "good faith" effort to comply with Title III of the ADA. The primary factor which has contributed to this is the presence of a large number of advocacy groups within the disability community who have developed collaborative relationships with the business community and are actively involved with education and technical assistance efforts. The business community has responded positively to ADA in the majority of situations. It appears that compliance has been achieved more rapidly in areas where Statewide Business Organizations became involved early on and have continued to promote ADA with their membership on both a state and local basis. Initial resistance was overcome primarily through promotion of creative approaches to compliance and the support of local business groups in educating their memberships. The majority of Title III barriers which continue to exist in the region are located within rural areas. Contributing factors appear to be related to the limited availability of technical assistance by qualified individuals, limited financial resources and attitudinal barriers.

Region VI – Southwest DBTAC (Ark., La., N.Mex., Okla., Tex.) Our DBTAC receives its greatest number of inquiries on Title III issues. Most of the technical assistance provided involves barrier removal issues. In providing assistance on Title III, we find that the greatest barrier to access is still attitudes. We often have to explain the reason why certain technical requirements are necessary. Many callers request justification for the changes they must make as they do not understand what providing access for certain types of disabilities truly means. Promoting sensitivity to disability is a necessary component of everything that we do. Our approach to solving any conflicts that arise as we provide assistance is to simply educate all callers concerning their rights and responsibilities under the law and let them decide how they should resolve the conflict.

We do encourage voluntary compliance through education and hope that by providing callers with the information and the reasons why certain changes must be made that any conflicts will be resolved in a nonadversarial manner. The demand for technical assistance is tremendous; we respond to more than 1,000 requests in an average month. Still, we feel that there remains much to be done. The level of voluntary compliance is extremely low; many businesses are still not aware that they are covered under the Act, and those that do, most seem to have adopted a "wait and see" attitude. Successful implementation of the ADA depends on how well compliance is "institutionalized" at all levels of our society. For this to occur, much more needs to be done to promote the ADA as many in our society are unaware of its existence. A dedicated, comprehensive education and enforcement effort must also be undertaken to assure compliance.

Region VIII – Rocky Mountain DBTAC (Colo., Mont., N.Dak., S.Dak., Utah, Wyo.) Many public accommodations and especially small businesses believe their Title III barrier removal requirements are dependent on the number of employees they have (like the Title I Employment provisions). In addition, private companies are not learning that generous tax credits and tax deductions are available to offset the costs they incur to remove barriers from existing facilities. Typically, businesses will make changes for one of two reasons: 1) to increase their "bottom line" or profits, or 2) to reduce their chances of a lawsuit. Unfortunately, the general lack of knowledge and misleading ADA publicity obscures the many benefits businesses can realize from the ADA. As a result, business people are deciding to wait until court cases occur, at which time they will react. This defensive posture does not embrace either the spirit or the letter of the law and runs contrary to the fact that the ADA is a "win-win" proposition.

Congressional Monitoring – The GAO Study

The congressional committees with oversight responsibility over the ADA's implementation – primarily the Senate Subcommittee on Disability Policy of the Committee on Labor and Human Resources and the House Subcommittee on Select Education and Civil Rights of the Committee on Education and Labor – have expressed an ongoing interest in Title III. The House subcommittee had the foresight to request a long-term evaluation by the General Accounting Office of whether the main objectives of the ADA are being achieved, including whether access to goods and services had increased and discrimination has decreased since the act passed. Much of the preceding discussion of Title III implementation has focused on process – whether the regulations were published on time, whether technical assistance is available, and whether policy issues have been adequately resolved. Although process is essential and success is unlikely without a well-devised implementation plan, the ultimate criteria by which historians and social scientists will judge the ADA will be its substantive outcomes – whether discrimination decreases, whether access to places of public accommodation increases, whether public attitudes toward people with disabilities as equal citizens improve. In assessing such outcomes, anecdotal evidence such as that presented previously is useful, but we also need more systematic evaluations based on sound scientific methodology.

This is why the congressionally sponsored GAO study is so important. At the time of passage of the ADA, virtually no hard "baseline data" existed on the extent of accessibility in places of public accommodation in this country. Even though extensive anecdotal evidence of discrimination and poor access were presented at congressional hearings and in press stories, based largely on testimony accumulated through the Congressional Task Force on Empowerment chaired by Justin Dart, this important documentation could not serve as an adequate basis for a scientific evaluation of ADA outcomes. In the context of Title III, what was needed was a carefully controlled longitudinal study of the same businesses before and after ADA enactment.

The first stage of the GAO study involved visits by the investigators to 231 randomly selected businesses with at least 25 employees and gross receipts of $1 million[20] (as well as government facilities) to evaluate specific access features using the minimum accessibility standards of ADAAG. Eight different types of businesses were visited. The study was conducted in 11 different cities, which were chosen specifically because they were relatively old and in states without strong laws protecting people with disabilities. In addition, owners or managers and people with disabilities were interviewed concerning accessibility issues.

The first visits and interviews were held in early 1992, several months before the first applicable ADA requirements went into effect. The primary finding was somewhat surprising. The researchers found that, at the time of their visit prior to the implementation of the ADA, "most businesses and government facilities we observed had established access consistent with the accessibility standards on most features." Of the 416 different accessibility features assessed in 231 establishments, 67 percent of the observed features were consistent, on average, with the ADAAG standards; this ranged from 92 percent for the most accessible to 40 percent of features for the least accessible (GAO, 1993).

Other findings were more predictable. Survey respondents with disabilities found most of the identified barriers were in 7 of 19 types of establishments: restaurants or bars; hotels, motels, and inns; theaters, concert halls, and stadiums; office buildings; service establishments such as laundromats, dry cleaners, barber and beauty shops, and travel agencies; auditoriums, convention centers, and lecture halls; and sales or retail establishments such as bakeries, grocery stores, clothing stores, and shopping centers. Fewer barriers were found in banks; medical offices, lawyers' and accountants' offices; terminal depots; museums, libraries, and galleries; parks and zoos; schools and day care centers; social service centers; gymnasiums, health spas and other places of recreation; government buildings; and bus, rail, and other public transportation systems (GAO, 1993).

The study did find that some important barriers to access exist. These include doors that were too heavy to open easily; insufficient number of assistive devices for deaf people in hotel rooms; inaccessible showers or tubs in hotel rooms; inaccessible toilets in hotel rooms; inaccessible sinks in hotel rooms; table legs or pedestals prohibiting full entry; high service counters; lack of raised numbers on elevator door jambs; restrooms or stalls too small; pay phones without text telephones (TTYs or TDDs); pay phones without amplication systems; pay phones that are not wheelchair accessible; and water fountains that are not wheelchair accessible (GAO, 1993).

Surprisingly, the study did not include stairs – the barrier that many people envision when they think about inaccessible facilities

– in the list of important barriers (GAO, 1993). This is probably because the study examined only larger businesses, which may be less likely to have entry barriers than smaller businesses. Whether or not small facilities are more likely to have accessibility barriers is a research question that should be investigated. However, anecdotal evidence suggests that they are.

The author of this chapter surveyed a two-block area on Connecticut Avenue in Washington, D.C., within a mile of the White House, and discovered 21 small businesses with one step at the entrance, the removal of which would almost certainly be readily achieved unless the business was financially marginal. This constituted almost half of the businesses surveyed. This large percentage of facilities with a single step was consistent with his experience and that of many of his colleagues throughout the country as wheelchair users and suggests that a study examining smaller businesses would reveal that this is a prevalent barrier.

Finally, the GAO study found that many owners and managers were not adequately aware of the ADA or its requirements just prior to implementation. Only 31 percent of those interviewed indicated that they were familiar with the ADA. Forty-seven percent reported that they did not know that they were legally required to remove barriers before the effective date of 26 January 1992. This lack of awareness by a large proportion of people responsible for compliance with the ADA is particularly disturbing considering that they were interviewed 18 months after the passage of the law and in the month prior to the effective date of implementation (GAO, 1993). The researchers pointed out that these results were consistent with the Gallup Organization (1992) and Buck Consultants (1992) surveys.

Following the collection of baseline data during the first phase of the GAO study, the researchers collected additional data in August 1992 and April 1993 from other businesses in the same cities (GAO, 1994). Their principal findings over the 15 months of the study were that barrier removal efforts had increased, but half of the businesses still had done nothing and half had no plans to do anything. The accessibility of facilities had increased slightly, though seven important types of barriers continued to present problems (GAO, 1994).[21]

Another important finding of the second phase of the study was that there was a significant increase in familiarity with the ADA over the 15-month period (GAO, 1994). The most frequently reported sources of information about the ADA were corporate headquarters and the media. Interestingly, the researchers found that approximately 35 percent of the barriers removed did not have to be removed under the ADA, suggesting that knowledge of specific requirements of Title III may still be lacking.

Although we cannot conclude definitively from the GAO study that Title III compliance is increasing (because the study did not consider such issues as whether removal of the specific barriers were readily achievable), its findings concerning the accessibility of facilities and the knowledge of the ADA strongly suggest that compliance had increased during the period of the study. Whether it will continue to increase, and at what rate, are questions that still must be considered.

The GAO researchers concluded that, although businesses have begun to respond to the ADA, the continued presence of barriers and lack of plans to remove them and the inappropriateness of some barrier removal plans suggest the continuing need for education and outreach (GAO, 1994).

PRIVATE SECTOR MONITORING

For the ADA to be implemented successfully, it will require the active participation of all affected persons and entities. Recognizing this, organizations representing people with disabilities and covered entities have been monitoring implementation of Title III. This section discusses monitoring and enforcement activities of a few key groups.

Disability Advocacy Groups

Prior to the first effective implementation date, the United Cerebral Palsy Association (UCPA) conducted a Public Accommodation Access Survey in 11 cities – Atlanta, Boston, Birmingham, Dallas, Denver, Detroit, New York, Oklahoma City, Pittsburgh, San Francisco, and Washington, D.C. In January 1992, teams of people with disabilities and UCPA affiliates in each city surveyed between five and eight places of public accommodation randomly selected from certain preselected categories of everyday use (e.g., grocery stores, banks, retail stores, restaurants, hotels, movie theaters, fast food chains, and museums).

The stated purpose of the survey was to determine whether America was "ready for the ADA." Survey teams visited the selected sites with access checklists reflecting Title III requirements concerning approach and entry, interiors, customer service, amenities, and site-specific factors (e.g., accessible counters at banks). Overall, on a four-point A–D grade scale, almost all of the surveyed cities ranked B – basically barrier free. The most significant barriers identified were inaccessible entries (e.g., steps, heavy doors), lack of accessible parking spaces, inaccessible rest rooms, and inadequate telecommunications devices for people with hearing or speech impairments.

Hotels and retail stores were most likely to be graded A, which UCPA concludes is a response to the growing disability market. However, it is not clear why these types of public accommodations would respond more strongly to positive market forces than banks and theaters. Consistent with this market orientation theory, almost all businesses surveyed ranked A in customer service. Even though the small number of businesses surveyed does not allow us to confidently generalize UCPA results to the entire country, the survey was important for four reasons:

1. The survey represented the first attempt to determine the extent of access throughout the country, thereby demonstrating a methodology by which access can be assessed and establishing the capacity to carry it out.

2. It yielded results that, although not necessarily statistically valid and reliable for purposes of broad generalization, could be used to corroborate the results of other studies (such as the GAO study discussed earlier). As one of the few national access studies ever conducted, it offers some of the best baseline data available.

3. The survey facilitated a dialogue between the disability community and the business community. Such communication in identifying problems and suggesting solutions can be helpful to the implementation effort. One manager of a Birmingham

hotel was reported as saying that the survey saved him $1500 in consultants' fees.

4. Finally, and perhaps most important to the implementation effort, the survey focused national attention on Title III and its effective date. It was covered by the *New York Times*,[22] NBC's *Today Show*,[23] ABC's *Business World*,[24] ABC national news,[25] and Voice of America broadcasts,[26] as well as numerous local papers and stations.

Another disability organization that has been monitoring ADA implementation is the National Organization on Disability (NOD), which commissioned Louis Harris and Associates to conduct a survey in June 1993 on awareness of the ADA and attitudes toward accommodating the needs of people with disabilities (Harris and Associates, 1993). Almost three years after the law was passed, only 41 percent of respondents were aware of the ADA. On the other hand, only 5 percent of respondents stated that we are moving "too fast" in requiring that workplaces, transportation, and public buildings are accessible to people with disabilities.

Regulated Businesses

The Building Owners and Managers Association (BOMA), which represents the office building industry, has been active in monitoring and facilitating the Title III implementation effort. It has distributed thousands of its booklets, *Opening Doors* and *The ADA Answer Book*, informing its members of their rights and obligations under Titles I and III of the ADA. In monitoring Title III implementation, BOMA has identified several problem areas.

First, as suggested already, the certification of a local building code does not guarantee that a building will be in compliance, thus leaving significant uncertainty. In this regard, BOMA has advised its members to make a "good faith" effort to comply, including full documentation of a comprehensive assessment of the facility, the identification and prioritization of barriers, an assessment of the resources of the party responsible for barrier removal in determining whether removal was required, and a multiyear plan to implement changes.

Second, it is often unclear who has the primary obligation for barrier removal – the owner or the tenant? Although the regulations and guidelines indicate that this issue must be resolved through an analysis of the lease, many leases are ambiguous or unclear as to this allocation. This issue will presumably be resolved over time as new model leases are developed with the ADA in mind (BOMA International, 1993).

BOMA concludes that

> Title III of the Americans with Disabilities Act has been in effect for over 18 months now. While property owners and managers have sought to understand the law and taken extensive efforts to comply, much confusion continues over questions of interpretation, implementation and enforcement. A great deal of misinformation has been in circulation from self-professed ADA "experts," who sometimes mislead building owners and managers on what is needed to comply with the law. Consequently, a good deal of frustration continues to be expressed in the real estate industry over numerous issues, technical as well as general. (BOMA, 1993)

Another major private sector association that has been tracking Title III is the National Federation of Independent Business (NFIB), which represents small businesses throughout the country. A strong opponent of passage of the ADA, NFIB has indicated that it was not opposed to the intent of the law (citing that small businesses employed approximately 60 percent of individuals with disabilities who were working prior to ADA enactment), but it objected to what it refers to as "vague and punitive language of the Act" and the potential for "open-ended liability – never knowing if they have made the accommodations necessary to cover any of the 600 plus disabilities."[27]

With respect to Title III implementation, NFIB has stated that

> The typical small business owner takes home less than $40,000 annually. Because of this, most small business owners are not easily able to retain legal counsel and certainly can not afford to go to court. One court case is enough to bankrupt a small business. On a positive note, NFIB members are doing all that they can to comply with the law to the best of their ability. . . .
> In complying, our members have displayed creativity. For example, we have a member who sells stained glass. Her busi-

ness is three steps up a hill, which made building a ramp impossible. In order to meet public accommodation requirements, she put together a sample kit of all her stained glass products and brings the kit to customers with disabilities.[28]

PRIVATE SECTOR ENFORCEMENT OF TITLE III

Throughout the country, local disability groups have been mobilizing to ensure the strict enforcement of Title III. In Austin and Houston, Texas, members of ADAPT crawled up the stairs of places of public accommodation and placed "ADA Violator" stickers on the windows of inaccessible businesses.[29] Several businesses are reported as agreeing to enhance their accessibility in response to these tactics. Similarly, members of Disabled in Action picketed the Empire State Building because its 86th Floor Observatory, as well as other aspects of the building, are inaccessible to people with mobility impairments (Mandell, 1992).

Other groups have used less militant approaches. The Montgomery, Maryland, chapter of Self Help for Hard of Hearing (SHHH) has been questioning local theater managers as to whether they are in compliance with the ADA requirement to provide assistive listening devices to its members (Murdoch, 1993). It found a wide variation in theater accessibility and attitudes, ranging from full compliance with excellent sound quality to refusal to comply without a court order. The chapter's president, Barry Kasinitz, stated that "We are optimistic that we can bring down the barriers without lawsuits and public demonstrations. We would prefer that businesses open their doors to us because we convince them that it's in their own best interest" (Murdoch, 1993).

Although not the preference of most, people with disabilities and disability groups may bring private lawsuits to obtain court orders to stop discrimination under Title III of the ADA. However, because monetary damages cannot be awarded, potential plaintiffs have had difficulty attracting attorneys to pursue such cases. Despite this lack of financial incentives, a few private cases have been filed, primarily by attorneys with disabilities on their own behalf or by attorneys serving people with disabilities on a pro-bono basis (i.e., free of charge).

For example, Marc Fiedler, a Harvard-trained attorney with a spinal cord injury, established the Disability Rights Council of

Greater Washington (D.C.) to pursue private sector enforcement of the ADA, particularly Title III. Individually or with attorneys contributing their time and expertise to the council, he has brought actions against a national theater chain, clothing store chain, department store, and record chain. These suits have resulted in settlements in which the defendants have agreed to make certain modifications.

Similarly, Charles Weir, an assistant city attorney in San Antonio who was paralyzed in a diving accident, has filed at least 15 cases against businesses in Austin. With respect to his actions against several fast food chains, a medical clinic, and a car dealership, he stated that

> I know it would appear that I'm a crusader, but I don't think of it in those terms. . . . Because most of the companies in this country never felt a moral obligation to make their businesses accessible to the disabled, the U.S. Congress provided them with a legal obligation. . . . Many of those same companies have chosen to ignore that legal obligation.[30]

Some disability organizations have also implemented enforcement campaigns. For example, Advocacy, Inc., in Austin, Texas, began Phase I of its ADA litigation campaign in the summer of 1993 by filing 53 lawsuits throughout Texas, 40 of which were Title III cases (Advocacy, Inc., 1993). It targeted a different industry each week, focusing on large companies and chains. The objective of the campaign was to obtain voluntary compliance to the greatest extent possible, and in fact, 68 businesses came into compliance without litigation. In one particularly creative initiative, the organization negotiated an agreement with the Texas lottery whereby all 15,131 lottery retailers in the state would have to become accessible or lose their right to sell lottery tickets (Advocacy, Inc., 1993).

The vast majority of alleged Title III violations are resolved out of court soon after an informal complaint is made or a formal complaint is filed in court. This is largely because the cost of making the necessary modification is often substantially less than the cost of litigating (including legal fees, court costs, and lost productivity). For example, the International House of Pancakes agreed to install a ramp at one of its Philadelphia restaurants in response to a complaint asserting that ramping the five-inch step was readily achievable.[31]

Despite the strong incentive to settle, some cases have been litigated to legal resolution by a judge or jury. A comprehensive analysis of key Title III cases that have been decided by the courts is beyond the scope of this chapter. However, one case is worthy of particular attention because it addresses the sensitive issue of whether safety may be used as a defense to a Title III claim.

In *Anderson* v. *Little League Baseball*,[32] a federal judge invalidated a general policy of the national little league banning coaches in wheelchairs from sitting in the coaches' box (Tom, 1993). The court found that the league's policy, which applied generally to all coaches who use wheelchairs regardless of disability or specific safety circumstances, does not satisfy the narrow exception that an individual may be prevented from participation "where such an individual poses a direct threat to the health and safety of others."

PUBLIC ACCOMMODATIONS ISSUES REQUIRING ATTENTION

In this early stage of Title III implementation, several issues are proving problematic and require additional attention from the responsible government agencies or the private sector or both. They fall into the areas of process and policy issues and are as follows.

Process Issues

Regulatory Clarification Some of the findings and recommendations of the NCD's *ADA Watch* report have particular relevance to Title III (NCD, 1993). Finding no. 14 states that "Covered entities are looking for the greatest degree of certainty of being in compliance with the ADA that the federal government can provide." This finding pertains to all of the titles, but it is particularly relevant to criticisms of Title III regulations that do not offer clear guidance.

The DOJ regulations were drafted with fairly strict adherence to the specific language of the ADA and its legislative history. This approach has implications for implementation. For example, like the statute, the regulations offer no specific formulas for defining the key terms *readily achievable and undue burden,* as elements of the business community requested. Instead, the DOJ chose to maintain the statutory definitions (presented in the section on the requirements of Title III) and provide clarification through a number of examples.[33]

Although the DOJ had the discretion to do this and may have thereby avoided legal problems, the resulting case-by-case analysis has increased the level of uncertainty during implementation with respect to compliance (Romano, 1993; McKee, 1993). It is clear that ramping a single step is almost always readily achievable and ramping a large flight of stairs typically is not. However, situations between these extremes are largely uncertain, depending on the specific economic circumstances of the covered entity. Similarly, it is often unclear when the obligation to provide auxiliary aids or services is applicable to a specific covered entity.

Technical Assistance In addition to increased policy clarification, the NCD's recommendations call for more targeted technical assistance (NCD, 1993). The technical assistance activities of the DOJ and NIDRR have been largely successful with respect to those entities that are aware of the ADA and particularly those that wish to comply. However, as surveys have demonstrated repeatedly, many covered entities still appear to be unaware that they have obligations under the law. Private sector monitoring activities further suggest that many entities that are aware are resisting compliance due to a lack of understanding as to why a specific modification is required. Clearly, further targeted technical assistance with respect to Title III is needed.

Ongoing Monitoring The GAO and UCPA studies have provided a good first step in scientifically assessing progress in making places of public accommodation accessible. However, they examine only a very limited number of geographic sites and, therefore, can serve as only broad indicators of such progress. On the other hand, monitoring activities by local advocacy groups have addressed a broader range of geographic areas, but have offered largely anecdotal evidence rather than more rigorous systematic analysis. What is needed is an expansion of the more scientific approach to more geographic areas. Local disability and business organizations can play an important role in systematically observing and documenting progress in implementing Title III.

Enhanced Enforcement It is somewhat disconcerting that the DOJ is not examining every complaint that is filed. Even though this may be an inevitable consequence of having limited resources to address a large number of complaints, it is little consolation to those who are so frustrated with impediments to access that they have filed complaints. There are two obvious responses to this substantial problem. The DOJ can increase its enforcement resources or increase the efficiency of its enforcement activities. It has started to achieve the former by increasing the staffing of its compliance section. With respect to increasing efficiency, more still needs to be done. One important area that will substantially improve compliance is the certification of model and local building codes (as discussed in the next section).

State and Local Building Codes A substantial problem relates to the implementation of the ADAAG, which was published in the *Federal Register* as an appendix to the DOJ Title III regulation. The ADA allows the DOJ to certify state and local building codes as being substantially equivalent to the ADAAG.[34] These codes are often based on model codes, which in turn are typically based on the American National Standards Institute (ANSI) standards. At the time of this writing, no code has been certified. Consequently, it is reported that there has been little local enforcement of the ADAAG by the estimated 67,000 code enforcement entities around the country that have adopted the model codes.[35]

Without local enforcement of the ADAAG, there is no compliance "safe harbor" for any business, architect, developer, or anyone involved in the design and construction of buildings. There are a number of subtle but important differences between the ADAAG and the model codes.[36] For example, the ADAAG requires permanently installed assistive listening systems in all newly constructed assembly areas with a capacity of 50 or more persons. If local code officials are not reviewing plans or inspecting with this requirement in mind, a business could unknowingly subject itself to a legal complaint when an individual with a hearing impairment attends an event in the assembly area.

Some states have adopted laws that adopt the ADAAG. In Arizona, for example, state law not only adopts ADAAG, but also mandates all local building code officials to adopt them as well. The state attorney general is then required to seek certification of substantial equivalency from the DOJ. When the state code is certified and the local jurisdictions have complied with the state mandate, the problem of the standards being enforced at the local level will be largely resolved. This process should eliminate most of the frustration and litigation that was feared when the ADA passed.

The DOJ certification of building codes is a cumbersome and time-consuming process. There are virtually hundreds of these state and local codes throughout the country, and it will be some time before a substantial number of them have been certified. Certification of the ANSI standards should help, but additional approaches to streamline the certification process and offer greater certainty to builders would be valuable.

Policy Issues

Relationship between Title III and Other Laws Despite extensive discussion in the DOJ regulations and guidelines, there is still considerable misunderstanding of the boundaries of Title III of the ADA and how it differs in coverage with other laws such as the Rehabilitation Act, the Fair Housing Act, and Title II of the ADA. For example, it appears that some tenants with disabilities believe that the ADA (rather than the less stringent Fair Housing Amendments) applies to their apartment buildings. Further educational efforts in clarifying such distinctions would be valuable for those covered entities that address issues affected by the various laws.

Auxiliary Aids and Services As compared to the barrier removal and new construction requirements of Title III, covered entities tend to be even less certain about the requirements to offer auxiliary aids and other services. They are particularly confused with respect to providing such aids and services to individuals with hearing or communication impairments. In addition, there has been some resistance to accommodating these individuals, in part due to cost considerations. Such resistance has been very strong at professional offices, such as those of doctors and lawyers. Additional technical assistance is needed in this regard, particularly with respect to tax relief available to covered entities.

Alterations Projects It appears that some covered entities do not fully understand the extent of their obligation to make the adjoining areas of their building alterations fully accessible. Every time that a significant alteration project is seriously contemplated, an analysis must occur to determine whether the alterations requirements of Title III apply to the project. These requirements are essential because they offer the only means by which old buildings are likely to become accessible over time. It is likely that understanding of these requirements will improve over time as a result of technical assistance efforts by the DBTACs, BOMA, and other organizations.

Licensing Courses and Exams Accommodating the needs of people with disabilities in licensing courses and exams has been one of the areas of substantial resistance to Title III compliance. This may be a result of the costs involved, such as the fees of certified sign language interpreters. Several lawsuits have already been brought in this area.[37] Technical assistance and information on tax relief available would be helpful to avoid these conflicts.

Recreational Activities Another area in which there has been some resistance is making recreational activities accessible. This may be a result of stereotypes and other social attitudes that people with disabilities do not engage in active forms of recreation or exercise. Educational efforts are needed to eliminate these misperceptions and inform covered entities how to make their facilities accessible. Some elements of the theater industry have been fairly responsive in complying with Title III, although others have made changes only after threats of legal action.

Removal of Barriers As suggested already, the decision of the DOJ not to specifically define the requirements for barrier removal more precisely has contributed to the "wait and see" attitude on the part of some covered entities. As case law develops, this uncertainty should be diminished and compliance should be enhanced. However, many situations are clear that they require barrier removal immediately, and enforcement should be particularly rigorous in these cases. For example, removal of a single step to a place of public accommodation is almost always readily achievable. The most important factor in ensuring removal of "readily achievable" barriers will be the active involvement of people with disabilities at the local level informing covered entities of their obligations (Kamin, 1992; Megan, 1993).

Smoking in Public Places An emerging issue under Title III is whether smoking in a public place constitutes discrimination against people with certain disabilities, such as individuals with environmental illness and respiratory impairments. On 25 May 1993, a number of groups with high sensitivities to secondhand smoke, including people with asthma, held a press conference at the San Francisco office of the American Lung Association arguing that the ADA gives them the right to a smokeless public environment (Moore, 1993).

This issue was raised at length in the hearings for the DOJ regulations, but the department ultimately chose to leave it for the courts to decide. Throughout the country, ADA cases have been filed against restaurants, bars, and other public accommodations requesting that smoking be banned (Brooks, 1993). This controversy has been fueled by a recent report by the Environmental Protection Agency finding that secondhand smoke is a Class A carcinogen (Kessler, 1993).

Health Insurance Another major question is how Title III, which applies to insurance companies and HMOs, will affect access to health insurance. This issue will be complicated further if and when Congress passes a health reform law. The question then will be how the reform law interacts with the ADA in its treatment of people with disabilities (Batavia, 1993). As a result of a general insurance provision in Title V, the ADA offers conflicting messages on insurance practices affecting people with disabilities. The ADA appears to say inconsistently that insurers may continue to treat people with disabilities different than nondisabled people but may not do so in a manner that discriminates against people with disabilities.[38]

The preamble to the DOJ regulations attempts to clarify this apparent inconsistency, based on language from the congressional reports.[39] It clarifies that, under the ADA, insurers may no longer treat people differently on the basis of disability unless their differential treatment is justified by sound actuarial principles or reasonably anticipated experience. Unfortunately, this preamble language was not incorporated directly into the language of the regulations.[40] Without this specific regulatory language, some will assume *erroneously* that insurers may continue to conduct business as usual, denying coverage or raising rates without justification. Access to insurance will require close ongoing monitoring, and additional clarification may be needed.

Right to Die It appears that the ADA may play a key role in one of the major medical ethics issues of our time – whether a hospital may withdraw life support treatment when the patient's family opposes such withdrawal. At least one district court has found that Section 302, providing that "[n]o individual shall be discriminated against on the basis of disability in the full and equal enjoyment of . . . services" prohibits the hospital from denying ventilator services to an anencephalic (i.e., no cerebral cortex) infant whose mother demands continued treatment.[41] The appeal of this case, and others likely to follow, will have profound implications for medical ethics and economics, as well as how the ADA is perceived by the public.

Conclusions

Significant progress has been made with respect to the process of implementing Title III of the ADA. Regulations and guidelines were published on time, a major technical assistance program was established and implemented, and a substantial enforcement effort has been undertaken in both the public and private sectors. In this regard, implementation must be thus far considered a success. It is less certain whether these efforts have translated into success in achieving the short-term goals of Title III – compliance and increased accessibility. Other than information from formal complaints, court cases, and a few studies, most of the evidence on compliance with the Title III is anecdotal.

The evidence suggests that compliance – and progress toward a fully accessible nation – is mixed. Some businesses have been very responsive to the new requirements prior to the effective date. Many have implemented necessary modifications only after being informed of alleged violations or threatened with legal action, and others are doing nothing until they receive such intervention. Title III imposes little penalty for those covered entities that choose not to comply or to wait until a complaint is brought against them. A few entities have chosen to contest the lawsuits, claiming no obligation or that they have satisfied their obligation. Many are still unaware of their Title III obligations, despite extensive educational and technical assistance efforts.

Several strategies are suggested by this analysis:

- First, the DOJ should continue to clarify its policy, particularly with respect to those areas that are definitionally unclear or have been misunderstood by the public;
- Second, the DOJ and NIDRR should further target their educational and technical assistance efforts to inform covered entities of their Title III obligations;
- Third, the DOJ should complete certification of model, state, and local building codes as soon as possible to increase the efficiency of the Title III implementation effort;
- Fourth, in addition to the ongoing federal monitoring effort, state and local governments and organizations should undertake joint efforts to systematically assess compliance levels throughout the country;
- Fifth, based in part on this national assessment, federal enforcement efforts should be targeted at those industries and businesses that are ignoring their obligations or refusing to comply;
- Sixth, the DOJ should investigate all formal complaints and more aggressively bring legal actions for monetary damages against those businesses that resolutely refuse to comply after being fully informed of their obligations and having adequate opportunity to respond;
- Finally, and most important, people with disabilities should continue to work closely with businesses in their communities

to inform them of their obligations and how they can most efficiently and effectively meet them.

Title III will not implement itself. It will require the ongoing vigilance of all involved parties: architects, builders, building inspectors, contractors, designers, owners, lessors, lessees, government officials, and people with disabilities. Every time a building is constructed or altered to be inaccessible, it will remain inaccessible for generations, imposing opportunity costs on our nation for that duration. Every time a service is denied to a person with a disability, it delays that individual's opportunities and ability to participate on an equal basis. Conversely, every time a building or service is made accessible, it confers expanded opportunity permanently.

ACKNOWLEDGMENTS

The author thanks Irene Bowen, Barbara Bode, Randy Dipner, Pat Going, Robin Jones, Shelley Kaplan, Caroline Steinbower, Susan Castle-Webb, and Jane West.

REFERENCES

Advocacy, Inc. 1993. ADA Litigation Program: Phase I, Austin, Texas (Summer).

Batavia, A. I. 1993. "Health Care Reform and People with Disabilities." *Health Affairs* 12, no. 1 (Spring): 40–57.

BOMA International. 1993. "The ADA: Update on Key Issues." Unpublished document available through BOMA International, Washington, D.C.

Brooks, S. 1993. "First ADA Case Is Filed on Secondhand Smoke," *Restaurant Business Magazine 1993* 92, no. 6 (10 April): 28.

Buck Consultants. 1992. *ADA – The Americans with Disabilities Act.* Secaucus, N.J.: Author.

Burgdorf, R. L., Jr. 1991. "Equal Access to Public Accommodations." In *The Americans with Disabilities Act: From Policy to*

Practice, ed. J. West, pp. 183–213. New York: Milbank Memorial Fund.

Department of Justice. 1993. *DOJ Enforcement Fact Sheet*. Washington, D.C.: Author.

Gallup Organization. 1992. *Baseline Study to Determine Business' Attitudes, Awareness and Reaction to the Americans with Disabilities Act*. Princeton, N.J.: Author.

General Accounting Office. 1993. *Americans with Disabilities Act: Initial Accessibility Good but Important Barriers Remain*. Washington, D.C.: Author.

————. 1994. (Title Forthcoming) Washington, D.C.: Author.

L. Harris and Associates. 1993. "Questions on Americans with Disabilities Act: Prepared for the National Organization on Disability." Unpublished survey statistics available through NOD.

Kamin, B. 1992. "Disabled Work to Break down Barriers That Set Them Apart from Illinois Art and Culture." *Chicago Tribune* (28 June): 1C.

Kessler, B. 1993. "Woman Fighting for Breathing Space; Law, EPA Report May Aid Effort to Make FW Nightclub Smoke-Free." *Dallas Morning News* (1 May): A1.

Mandell, J. 1992. "Thousands of New York's Stores and Restaurants Are Closed to the Disabled Due to One Unnecessary – and Illegal – Step at the Door." *Newsday* (12 February): 56.

McKee, B. 1993. "The Disabilities Labyrinth; Small Firms Want to Comply with the New Federal Anti-Bias Law, but Vague Rules Make It Tough." *Nation's Business* 83, no. 4 (April): 18.

Meadley's Litigation Reports on the ADA. Wayne, Penn.: Meadley Publications Inc.

Megan, K. 1993. "Day-Care Centers May Be Put in Bind; Suit May Affect How Day-Care Centers Deal with Disabled." *Hartford Courant* (24 May): A1.

Moore, T. 1993. "Asthmatics to Use Disability Law to Battle Smoking." *San Francisco Chronicle*: A18.

Murdoch, J. 1993. "Hearing-Impaired Put Theaters to Test; Group Is Touring Movie Houses to Check Compliance with Disability Law." *Washington Post* (15 July): M1.

National Council on Disability. 1993. *ADA Watch: Year One*. Washington, D.C.: Author.

Parmet, W. E. 1993. "Title III: Public Accommodations." In *Implementation of the Americans with Disabilities Act: Rights and Responsibilities of All Americans*, ed. Lawrence O. Gostin and H. A. Beyer, Chapter 10. Baltimore: Paul H. Brookes Publishing Co.

Romano, M. 1993. "ADA Round Two Begins; Americans with Disabilities Act." *Restaurant Business Magazine* 92, no. 8 (20 May): 66.

Tom, D. 1992. "Paraplegic Coach Fights for Policy Change." *USA Today* (10 July): 12C.

United Cerebral Palsy Associations. 1992. *National Survey Results Look at America's Readiness for ADA Access*. Washington, D.C.: Author.

NOTES

1. "Final Regulatory Impact Analysis of the Department of Justice Regulation Implementing Title III of the Americans with Disabilities Act of 1990," U.S. Department of Justice (8 April 1992). Analysis prepared in consultation with Dr. Gregory S. Crespi.
2. The Americans with Disabilities Act of 1990, Pub. L. 101-336; 42 U.S.C. 12101 *et seq* (July 26, 1990).
3. ADA, Section 302.
4. ADA, Section 301 (7).
5. ADA, Section 302(b)(2)(A)(ii).
6. ADA, Section 302(b)(2)(A)(iii).
7. ADA, Section 302(b)(2)(A)(iv).
8. ADA, Section 301 (9).
9. ADA, Section 302(b)(2)(A)(v).
10. ADA, Section 303 (a)(1).

11. ADA, Section 303 (b).
12. ADA, Section 303 (a)(2).
13. These requirements are the major provisions of Title III that are addressed in this chapter. For purposes of focus, some other significant provisions are not addressed, such as those on transportation (ADA, Section 304).
14. 26 I.R.C. 44 (1990).
15. 26 I.R.C. 190 (1990).
16. ADA, Section 308.
17. *Federal Register* 56, no. 144 (26 July 1991): p. 35544.
18. "Justice Department Settlement Ensures Access to Empire State Building by People with Disabilities," DOJ press release (March 3, 1994).
19. The NCD is an independent federal agency that advises the president and the Congress on disability policy.
20. The study was limited to these relatively large businesses, those with fewer than 25 employees and receipts of less than $1 million were not subject to enforcement until later.
21. These were (1) not enough signs with raised print or braille, (2) lack of required number of assistive devices for the deaf in hotel rooms, (3) inaccessible showers or tubs in hotel rooms, (4) inaccessible toilets in hotel rooms, (5) inaccessible sinks in hotel rooms, (6) pay phones without TTYs or TDDs, and (7) pay phones without amplification systems.
22. January 27, 1992.
23. January 24, 1992.
24. January 26, 1992.
25. January 27, 1992.
26. February 7, 1992.
27. Based on a written statement presented by Caroline Steinbower of NFIB.
28. Ibid.
29. "Disabled Texans Protest Lack of Access to Buildings," *Houston Chronicle* (27 July 1993): A-11.
30. *Meadley's Litigation Reports on the ADA* 1, no. 1 (February 1993): 7.
31. For a comprehensive update on ADA cases that have been settled (or resolved in court), see *Meadley's Litigation Reports on the ADA.*

32. No. CIV-92-1282-PHX-EHC, D.Ariz.
33. There are four factors: nature and cost of the action, financial resources of the parties, the impact of the operation on the site, and the effect of the action on profitability.
34. ADA, Section 301(b)(1)(A)(ii).
35. Conversation with Susan Webb, former member of the Access Board.
36. The model code groups and the American National Standards Institute standards, on which most model codes are based, are in the process of being updated consistent with ADAAG. The 1992 version of the ANSI standards is very close to meeting the ADAAG requirements. However, as ADAAG is still evolving to include guidelines for state and local government entities, children's facilities, recreational facilities, and other situations, ensuring that the model codes are substantially equivalent in a timely manner is extremely difficult if not unrealistic.
37. U.S.A. v Becker C.P.A. Review D.D.C. Civ. No. 92-2879.
38. On the one hand, Sections 501(c)(1) and (2) state that the ADA "shall not be construed to prohibit or restrict [insurers, HMOs, and other entities that administer benefit plans] from underwriting risks, classifying risks, or administering such risks that are based on or not inconsistent with State law." Similarly, Section 501(c)(3) states that the ADA does not prohibit or restrict "a person or organization covered by this Act from establishing, sponsoring, observing, or administering the terms of a bona fide plan that is not subject to State laws that regulate insurance." On the other hand, Section 501(c) states that these sections "shall not be used as a subterfuge to evade the purposes of title I and III."
39. Department of Justice, "Nondiscrimination on the Basis of Disability by Public Accommodations and in Commercial Facilities," *Federal Register* 56, no. 144 (26 July 1991): 35544, pp. 35562–35563.
40. 28 C.F.R. Section 36.212.
41. In the Matter of Baby K, No. 93-68-A6, E.D., Va.

Toward Accessible Transportation

Rosalyn M. Simon

EDITOR'S NOTE

The ADA resolved the decades-old transportation policy debate between those advocating accessibility of the generic transportation system and those advocating a separate system of vans and taxis – paratransit. The resolution requires an accessible generic system with paratransit available only for those who, because of their disability, are unable to use the generic system. In her examination of implementation, Simon reports that the policy resolution may exist only on paper, as paratransit services grow steadily to meet increasing demand and utilization of increasingly accessible fixed-route systems remains low. With paratransit costs anticipated to be as much as $1 billion per year in 1997 when full compliance is required and available funds for public transportation shrinking, the pressure on transit systems may serve to limit fixed-route transportation for the general public. Simon recommends increased technical assistance to transit systems to assist them in developing paratransit eligibility determination programs, more education for people with disabilities about the requirements of the law and expanded training for bus operators about their new responsibilities under the law.

Rosalyn M. Simon is director of Project ACTION of the National Easter Seal Society. Project ACTION is a national research and demonstration program funded by the U.S. Department of Transportation to promote accessibility and cooperation between the disability and transit communities. Simon received her Ph.D. in disability transportation policy and special education from the University of Maryland. She has worked for the both the Washington, D.C., Metropolitan Area Transit Authority and the Mass Transit Administration of Baltimore to administer accessible transportation policies and promote utilization of accessible fixed-route systems.

INTRODUCTION

Despite the enactment of several federal laws and a series of implementing regulations over the past two decades, the provision of public transportation for people with disabilities has been varied and uneven. Disagreements between the disability community and the transit industry over the method of accessible transportation service delivery created prolonged tension and brought little resolution. The debate was framed in terms of rendering the existing standard transportation system (e.g., fixed route buses and subways) accessible or supporting a separate paratransit system that provided door to door or curb to curb service in small vans and taxis. Since the 1970s, federal policy fluctuated between the notion of accessible transportation as a civil right and the cost of making public transportation systems accessible. The result was confusion for all affected parties and a thwarting of the delivery of uniform accessible transportation services (Katzmann, 1986).

The enactment of the ADA sought to resolve the transportation policy debate by standardizing the delivery of accessible public transportation services. Under previous transportation regulations implementing Section 504 of the Rehabilitation Act of 1973, public transit systems could provide either accessible fixed route or paratransit services. The ADA requires the provision of both accessible fixed route service for people with disabilities, including wheelchair users, and complementary paratransit service for individuals whose disabilities prevent them from using accessible fixed route service.[1]

The passage of the ADA signaled a major change in federal policy with significant impact on public and private transportation providers. The ADA exceeds previous federal legislation governing the provision of accessible transportation in its coverage, intent, and potential impact on service delivery. The law sets standards for the design and delivery of accessible bus service, specifies requirements for accessible rail service, establishes accessibility standards for vehicles, and extends transportation access to the private sector. Unlike earlier accessible transportation policies, which were limited to individuals who were physically unable to access fixed route services, ADA incorporates disability as previously defined in Section 504 and covers a wide range of temporary and permanent impairments, as well as a series of infectious diseases and conditions. The law protects all individuals who have, have had a record of, or are regarded as having physical or mental impairments that substantially limit one or more major life functions. Underlying the policy is a mandate to bring people with disabilities into the mainstream with an assurance of accessible transportation delivery in the most integrated setting possible. Therefore, emphasis is placed on service delivery to individuals with disabilities in the same vehicles and facilities as the general riding public. Paratransit or other special transportation services, are not viewed as a standard for accessible transportation service delivery, but rather as a necessary accommodation or "safety net" allowable to ensure transportation equity for persons with disabilities who cannot use accessible fixed route systems.[4]

OVERVIEW

Significant progress has been made in implementing the ADA transportation requirements in the four years since the law's enactment. Fleet accessibility has grown. Rail station facility access has increased. Paratransit service delivery has been expanded and even at this early juncture, service quality has been greatly improved. Private providers are becoming aware of their accessible transportation responsibilities, as are over-the-road bus companies. The law appears to have facilitated improved relationships between the disability community and the transit industry. General awareness of the law among public transit operators appears high as most systems are actively involved in efforts to meet statutory and regulatory requirements.

However, a number of implementation problems have emerged as transportation providers attempt to translate ADA policy into practice. Although the ADA resolved the accessible transportation debate at the policy level by guaranteeing individuals with disabilities a civil right to the same public transportation available to the general public, the issue of separate versus integrated accessible transportation remains at the implementation level. Ironically, contrary to the notion of service delivery in the most integrated setting, it appears that many riders with disabilities prefer using paratransit instead of fixed route (National Easter Seal Society (NESS), 1993; Access to the Arts, 1994; GAO, 1994). The status of bus fleet accessibility has increased nationwide, but fixed route systems are not yet perceived as viable transportation options by many riders with disabilities. Increased numbers of people with disabilities are using public transportation, but local paratransit usage far exceeds accessible fixed route. Costs and complex economic, political, and operational concerns surrounding ADA complementary paratransit service are nearly unanimously cited as major barriers to implementation (NESS, 1993; Hartman and Kurtz, 1993). Paratransit costs are more expensive than anticipated, and resources are limited. Many transit systems lack the financial capacity necessary for full compliance (Hartman and Kurtz, 1993). Cooperative relationships between representatives of the transit industry and the disability community have been forged, but more than 200 complaints and 4 class action lawsuits have been filed against transit systems by individuals with disabilities for failure to comply with ADA. Research suggests that implementation is progressing but is clouded by a lack of funding mechanisms, operational problems surrounding ADA complementary paratransit requirements, and limited technology (NESS, 1993; Hartman and Kurtz, 1993).

In this chapter, I will examine ADA implementation in transportation from six vantage points: (1) the requirements of the law, (2) federal efforts to implement the law, (3) public fixed route bus systems, (4) paratransit systems, (5) rail systems, and (6) over-the-road bus systems. I present conclusions about progress to date and offer recommendations to improve implementation in the future. Data sources for this article are primarily three studies. The first is a 1993 survey of 554 public fixed route operators (with 288 respondents) sponsored by the National Easter Seal Society (NESS, 1993). The other two research initiatives were sponsored by Project ACTION. One study interviewed more than 70 individuals representing the disability community, the transit industry, and state and local governments on their perceptions of ADA implementation in transportation (Hartman and Kurtz, 1993). The other study surveyed 1,500 bus operators and 3,000 consumers regarding their attitudes toward public transit accessibility since the ADA (Access to the Arts, 1994).

REQUIREMENTS OF THE LAW

Statutory requirements for public transportation are delineated in Title II of the ADA; requirements for private transportation operators are detailed in Title III.[5] The U.S. Department of Transportation (DOT) regulations promulgated pursuant to Titles II and III were published on 6 September 1991 and amended on 30 November 1993.[6] To enforce the prohibitions of discrimination, statutory and regulatory provisions impose strict deadlines for compliance and provide for sanctions on federal transportation funding if deadlines are not met. Access requirements extend beyond vehicles and system infrastructure to cover maintenance, personnel training, information services, and communication systems. These requirements represent a significant change in the most fundamental aspects of how mass transit systems administer their programs of accessible transportation. In recognition of the magnitude of program change in transportation, the ADA provides for phased-in compliance until 1997. The effective dates of transportation statutory and regulatory requirements are displayed in Table 1.

Fixed Route Systems

Public fixed route operators began implementing ADA's vehicle acquisition requirements 30 days post enactment. The legislation requires the purchase or lease of accessible vehicles and demonstration of "good faith efforts" in acquiring used vehicles. In compliance with this mandate, rapid, light, commuter, and intercity rail systems must have at least "one car per train" accessible by 1995.[7] In meeting this requirement, "good faith efforts" must be undertaken to locate accessible vehicles before purchasing or leasing inaccessible vehicles. Although ADA does not require transportation providers to purchase new vehicles or retrofit existing buses, rail cars, or historic vehicles, it may be necessary to retrofit in order to achieve one car per train by 1995.

Effective October 1991, ADA regulations require that operators be proficient in accessibility equipment operation and serve passengers in a courteous and respectful manner.[8] To comply with this requirement, operators are required to provide boarding and securement assistance upon the request of the passenger (even if it is necessary leave their seats), to announce stops at all major intersections and transfer points, or upon passenger request, and to assist persons with visual impairments to identify buses at stops serving multiple bus routes. To ensure safe and reliable vehicle operation, bus operators are accountable for mandatory maintenance and operating procedures when lifts malfunction during service as specified in the final rule.[9]

Table 1
ADA Transportation Timetable

Date	Requirements
26 August 1990	Public transit vehicles ordered after this date must have lifts and other features for people with disabilities
26 January 1992	Alternative service (paratransit) must begin to be provided to individuals with disabilities who cannot use the regular transit system. ADA Paratransit Plans due to DOT
26 July 1992	Joint Paratransit and Key Station Plans due to DOT
May 1993	Office of Technology Assessment Study Report issued
26 July 1993	Key stations required to be accessible
May 1994	Over-the-Road Bus Regulations to be issued*
26 July 1994	Detectable warnings required on rail platforms
26 January 1995	One rail/AMTRAK car per train accessible
26 July 1996	Over-the-Road Bus Regulations effective for large operators*
26 July 1997	Over-the-Road Bus Regulations effective for small operators* Full compliance with ADA Paratransit Requirements

*Implementation has been postponed.

Complementary Paratransit Service

To ensure public transportation equity for persons with disabilities who cannot use accessible fixed route systems, the law requires the provision of comparable complementary paratransit service. Comparability is defined according to six minimum service criteria:

service area, hours and days of service, response time, fares, trip purpose restrictions, and capacity constraints. Effective 26 January 1992, operators have five years, until 1997, to phase in all six ADA complementary paratransit service criteria to meet full compliance.

Service Criteria Paratransit, identical to the fixed route service in terms of days and hours of service operation, must be provided to origins and destinations within 3/4 mile corridors on either side and within a 3/4 mile radius at the ends of each fixed bus route and around each rail station on the line. Reservation systems must be established to accept and provide requests for "next day" service and advance reservations up to 14 days. Complementary paratransit fares may not exceed two times the regular passenger fixed route fare; reduced and other fare discounts do not apply. Trip restrictions or priorities are prohibited, and operators may not limit service to eligible users. In addition to personal care attendants, who may accompany the passenger at no charge, each qualified paratransit user is entitled to at least one paying travel companion. Eligibility affords paratransit users nationwide reciprocity. At full compliance, operators must have sufficient capacity to fulfill all requests for rides by eligible users.

Eligibility The ADA is a civil rights statute, not a transportation or social service program statute. The ADA clearly emphasizes nondiscriminatory access to fixed route service, with complementary paratransit acting as a safety net for people who cannot use the fixed route system. Under the ADA, complementary paratransit is not intended to be a comprehensive system of transportation for individuals with disabilities.[10]

Eligibility for complementary paratransit service, to be determined for each trip requested, is based on one's functional ability to use the fixed route service at the time of the requested trip. To ensure that ADA complementary paratransit service is provided to and available for persons with disabilities who cannot avail themselves of fixed route, three statutory categories of eligibility are established: (1) riders who cannot independently board, ride, or disembark an accessible fixed route vehicle; (2) riders who can board, ride, or disembark an accessible fixed route vehicle but for whom an accessible vehicle is not available at the time or place of travel; and (3) riders who, due to the combination of a disability-related condition and environmental barriers, cannot reach the bus or rail stop.

Operators are required to establish a process for determining ADA complementary paratransit eligibility, which strictly limits ADA eligibility to individuals in the specified regulatory categories and includes administrative appeals procedures to ensure due process rights for applicants denied eligibility. Public systems were required to submit initial plans to the FTA on 26 January 1992, and annual updates each successive year until 1997, detailing plans for phasing in service criteria. Plans are to be developed in consultation with people with disabilities according to specified public participation guidelines. If meeting the service criteria by 1997 will result in an undue financial burden or making measured progress is unobtainable, the entity may request an undue financial burden waiver in conjunction with submission of the annual plan. The regulations specify allowable expenses that may be included in calculating requests for undue financial burden waivers. If paratransit is provided to ADA noneligible passengers, costs must be apportioned so that only expenses attributed to service delivery to eligible consumers are counted. Plan approvals and waiver determinations are under the authority of the U.S. Depatment of Transportation's Federal Transit Administration (FTA).

Key Rail Stations

Any facility used in providing public transportation constructed or altered after 26 January 1992 must be accessible to individuals with disabilities, including wheelchair users. Key stations in rapid, light, or commuter rail systems must be made accessible to and useable by persons with disabilities. *Accessibility* is defined according to standards designated by the Architectural and Transportation Barriers Board, which address accessible routes, signage and identification signs, rail to platform height, lighting and illumination, automatic fare collection systems, detectable warnings for platform edges, public address systems, text telephones (TTYs), visual display systems, escalators, and elevators. Unless granted a time extension, key rail stations were required to be accessible by 26 July 1993. Where extraordinarily expensive structural changes are necessary to meet compliance, such as elevator installation or platform modifications, the FTA has authority to grant rapid and light rail systems 30-year extensions, providing two-thirds of all key stations are accessible within 20 years. The FTA may grant 20-year extensions to commuter rail stations. Key station compliance plans were to be submitted to the FTA by 26 July 1992.

Over-the-Road Bus Systems

One of the most contentious issues surrounding the enactment of the ADA was the accessibility of over-the-road buses (OTRBs), buses with a high passenger deck located over the baggage compartment. OTRB systems are private bus companies that usually provide intercity, tour, and charter service. They may be the only public transportation available in some rural areas. The contention centered around the costs and financial impact on OTRB companies of acquiring accessibility. To ensure the promulgation of sound regulatory policy in light of uncertainty regarding the potential financial impact on the industry, Congress directed the U.S. Office of Technology Assessment (OTA) to study the issues and present recommendations (Robinson, 1993). Released in May 1993, the OTA study defines an accessible OTRB as one that allows boarding by persons with disabilities with minimal assistance from the operator and passengers to remain with their mobility aids while riding the vehicle and has the following components:

- access to on-board or stationed-based level changing devices;
- a door wide enough to accommodate persons with disabilities using mobility aids;
- two securement positions;
- internal and external systems to communicate with persons with sensory impairments;
- an accessible restroom or operational procedures to allow use of accessible restroom facilities; and
- personnel adequately trained in equipment use and service delivery to persons with disabilities.

The OTA study recommends that fixed route operators of OTRB service purchase 100 percent accessible vehicles and demand responsive systems provide enough accessible OTRBs to meet the demand. Retrofitting is not recommended as a requirement, rather accessibility is phased in as vehicles are purchased or leased. Reservation systems, serving all riders, may allow passengers to notify systems of accessibility needs in advance. OTA calculated accessibility costs at $18,000–$40,000 per vehicle over its 20-year lifetime, which represents approximately 1 percent of vehicle capital and operating costs. Installation of an accessible restroom represents the most expensive proportion of vehicle accessibility. OTA speculates that a significant financial impact may be borne by fixed route OTRB systems, and rural communities could experience service reduction. Although OTA acknowledges that physically assisting passengers to board vehicles does not meet ADA requirements, it notes that the practice may continue until vehicle accessibility is achieved. The DOT, in conjunction with the Access Board, must issue final regulations and accessibility standards for OTRB accessibility to be effective for large OTRB operators in 1996 and small operators in 1997. The president of the United States has the authority to delay implementation for one year.

FEDERAL EFFORTS TO IMPLEMENT THE LAW

Within the U.S. Department of Transportation, primary responsibility for ADA implementation rests with the Federal Transit Administration. ADA paratransit and key station plans are reviewed at the regional level. The Office of Grants Management provides technical assistance, training, oversight, and contractor assistance to the FTA regional offices. Recommendations for paratransit plan approval or disapproval are made by each regional administrator. Disapproved plans are forwarded to the ADA Review Board, which recommends appropriate action to the FTA administrator. Final decisions regarding plan approval, key station extensions, and undue financial burden waivers rests with the FTA administrator. The DOT's Office of Civil Rights and the FTA's Office of Civil Rights monitor compliance and investigate complaints. The Access Board has responsibility for developing minimum guidelines and providing technical assistance on accessibility.

Project ACTION

To facilitate ADA compliance, FTA sponsors training activities and funds technical assistance and research initiatives. Project ACTION (Accessible Community Transportation in Our Nation) is a national research and demonstration program funded through a cooperative agreement between the Federal Transit Administration and the National Easter Seal Society. Each year, Project ACTION funds local demonstration projects and research activities to improve transportation for persons with disabilities, assist transportation providers in implementing the ADA, and promote cooperation between the transit industry and the disability community. Project ACTION's local demonstration program focuses on several key areas of concern to the disability community and the transit industry to improve transportation accessibility: identifying persons with disabilities in the community and their transportation needs, developing effective marketing and outreach programs and strategies, developing consumer travel training and transit personnel training programs, assisting private transportation providers, developing and applying appropriate technology to eliminate critical barriers to transportation and accessibility, and developing ADA implementation projects. Since the initial local demonstration funding cycle in 1991, Project ACTION has funded 60 model programs and research initiatives for a total of $4.5 million. Project resources and products are disseminated nationwide through Project ACTION's National Institute for Accessible Transportation (NIAT) and through regional and national conferences. In June 1994, Project ACTION sponsored the first national policy conference on ADA implementation in transportation, which attracted more than 300 representatives of the disability community, transit industry, and state, local, and federal government.

FIXED ROUTE BUS SYSTEMS

Despite concerns about the costs of accessibility, fixed route bus systems are gradually becoming accessible as vehicle acquisition is proceeding as the law intended.

Bus Fleet Accessibility Has Increased Since the Passage of the ADA

After more than three years of purchasing 100 percent accessible vehicles, the national state of accessibility has improved. Prior to enactment of the ADA, in 1990, approximately 70 percent of public fixed route operators reported purchasing some proportion of accessible buses. Over one-fourth did not initiate accessible bus purchases until ADA became law (NESS, 1993). From 1991 to 1993, there was a 27 percent increase in first-time purchases of accessible buses by transit systems. Most transit systems implemented ADA vehicle purchase policies in 1992. In that same year 37 systems still had not yet begun to purchase 100 percent accessible buses. By 1995 all public fixed route transit systems should be purchasing only accessible buses (NESS, 1993).

As intended by the law, fleet accessibility has improved gradually. Today, more than 50 percent of the 52,500 national bus fleet is accessible (NESS, 1993). In 1989 only one-third (36 percent) of the nation's bus fleet was accessible (American Public Transit Association (APTA), 1989). Accessible buses accounted for approximately 39 percent of total bus fleets in 1990, 46 percent in 1991, and 52 percent in 1992 (NESS, 1993). These figures reflect an annual increase in accessible buses of 17 percent and a growth of the proportion of accessible buses to total bus fleet size of 16 percent since ADA took effect. According to APTA (1993) approximately 100 public transit systems have already reached 100 percent accessibility. Projections indicate that by 1995, 123 additional public operators' bus fleets will become fully accessible. Given the annual growth rate, by 1997 more than 70 percent of public transit operators' bus fleets will become 100 percent accessible (NESS, 1993). Nationwide, fleet accessibility should be completed between 2001 and 2005 (NESS, 1993).

Expenditures for Accessible Fixed Route Bus Service Are Generally in Line with Projections

Accessible fixed route bus service costs are primarily capital expenditures for vehicle purchases. In 1991, the total unit price for a lift/securement package ranged from $14,000–$16,000 per vehicle (U.S. Department of Transportation, 1991). Since becoming standard features on buses, costs for lift/securement systems have not increased significantly. In 1994 dollars, lift/securement systems add approximately an additional $17,000 to an average vehicle price, which ranges from $200,000 to $275,000 dependent upon the options selected (Don Smith, Lift-U, personal communication 19 January 1994). The DOT's regulatory impact analysis (1991) projected accessible bus purchases nationwide at $42–$58 million per year. FTA is currently reporting annual capital expenditures to purchase accessible buses at $50 million (GAO, 1994). No transit system reported increased operating costs due to lift maintenance or longer dwell times because of expanded accessible fixed route bus service (Hartman and Kurtz, 1993). Anticipating the additional costs of fixed route accessibility, the Intermodal Surface Transportation Efficiency Act of 1991 (ISTEA)[11] increases the federal capital share from 80 to 90 percent for the vehicle-related equipment compliance costs of ADA.

Accessible Fixed Route Bus Ridership by Persons with Disabilities Is Minimal

Findings do not provide a precise comparison between accessible fixed route bus ridership and fixed route ridership because most transit systems do not yet differentiate between these data. However, even though firm conclusions cannot be drawn regarding ridership by persons with disabilities, low lift utilization suggests that accessible fixed route bus service has not yet penetrated the lift user market (NESS, 1993; Access to the Arts, 1994). Transit operators report that ridership by persons with disabilities is relatively small (Hartman and Kurtz, 1993; GAO, 1994). Several reasons may account for this low accessible fixed route ridership, such as limited fixed route accessibility, consumer perception of service unreliability, consumer preference for paratransit, environmental barriers, and operator attitudes (NESS, 1993; Hartman and Kurtz, 1993; Access to the Arts, 1994). Due to the lack of uniform accessibility in many fixed route systems, accessible service is not frequent enough or available on enough bus routes to make linked trips. As a result, in many communities accessible fixed route service has not yet become a viable travel alternative for persons with disabilities.

Many consumers seem to prefer paratransit over fixed route service and appear hesitant to depend on accessible fixed routes (NESS, 1993; Access to the Arts, 1994). One out of two individuals with disabilities who are public transportation users agreed that transportation for people with disabilities should be provided using small buses and vans (Access to the Arts, 1994). A majority (75 percent) of people with disabilities who use public transportation nationwide perceive accessible fixed route bus service as unreliable and poorly maintained (Access to the Arts, 1994). Lack of pedestrian accessibility also deters fixed route usage by people with disabilities, particularly in suburban areas where sidewalks may not exist. Many people with disabilities still encounter difficulty or are unable to reach boarding locations because of inaccessible street conditions and missing curb cuts (NESS, 1993; Hartman and Kurtz, 1993). Transit systems report that state and local government entities often appear unresponsive regarding compliance with ADA guidelines for pedestrian accessibility, especially curb cuts (NESS, 1993). The requirement that personal care attendants, who ride at no charge on paratransit, pay full passenger fares when accompanying passengers with disabilities on fixed route systems was also identified by consumers as a deterrent to fixed route ridership. Negative attitudes and actions of bus operators serve to create reluctance among persons with disabilities to use fixed route service (NESS, 1993; Access to the Arts, 1994).

Bus Operators Are Resisting DOT Service Delivery Requirements

Accessible fixed route transportation, as a viable alternative to paratransit, is under fire as a significant percentage of consumers with disabilities express dissatisfaction with bus operators' negative attitudes and actions. Critics quickly point out operators' failure to announce stops and "passing up" of passengers using wheelchairs. Often implied in the many expressions of malcontent with operator behavior is the allegation that transit systems have not yet adequately trained drivers to provide ADA-quality fixed route service (NESS, 1993).

In several local communities, transit systems report driver resistance to making stop announcements. Apparently vehemently

opposed to the rule, bus operators in several systems have disman-
tled microphones and other components of internal public address
systems. Drivers claim that passengers with disabilities do not
appreciate the announcements and other passengers are annoyed
by the service. More than one-fourth (29 percent) of bus operators
surveyed by Access to the Arts (1994) believe that stop announcements are unnecessary. Failure to announce stops engendered litigation against the Southeastern Pennsylvania Transportation
Authority (SEPTA) in Philadelphia by the National Federation of
the Blind in 1992.[12] The case was settled out of court with SEPTA
agreeing to enforce the stop announcement policy. Although several
systems have initiated training and disciplinary processes, operator
behavior and compliance concerns have appeared to generate interest among transit systems in microcomputer technology to automate
stop announcements (Hartman and Kurtz, 1993).

Accessible Fixed Route Bus Service Presents Operational Challenges and Safety Concerns

In many local communities, accessible fixed route bus service has
not yet become routine service delivery, and transit systems are
experiencing myriad operational problems. Even though lift technology has greatly improved in recent years and does not present
the proportion of problems as in the past, it has been at the heart
of a number of complaints. With the newer generation of lifts,
research indicates that most problems associated with lift malfunction are usually due to operator error and infrequent use (Williams,
Sanchez, and Soper, 1987). One of the first ADA transportation
lawsuits, filed in Philadelphia against Southeastern Pennsylvania
Transportation Authority (SEPTA), involved nonworking lifts
("Lift Maintenance," 1993). Disabled in Action, a disability advocacy group, and five individuals with disabilities filed suit in October
1993 for failure to maintain lifts in operating condition and not
ensuring that drivers allow passengers with disabilities to board.[13]
SEPTA claimed that a significant proportion of their fleet is composed of vehicles equipped with older generation lifts for which
budget constraints preclude replacement. A settlement agreement
was reached in March 1994 that delineated a comprehensive program of preventive maintenance, procedures to inform and accom-

modate passengers with disabilities, replacement bus service when lifts malfunction during service, requisite levels of accessible fixed route and driver responsibilities, consumer complaint procedures, progressive disciplinary procedures for bus drivers, and compliance monitoring. Failure to provide accessible fixed route buses as required by the ADA was the primary complaint in a class action suit filed by individuals with disabilities against the Regional Transit Authority in New Orleans in December 1993.

In transporting passengers who use mobility aids, universal securement continues to raise safety concerns. Although the regulations stipulate that transit systems should use a securement system to ensure that the wheelchair remains within the securement area, securement of three-wheeled scooters and other nontraditional mobility aids is still difficult and, in some cases, impossible. According to the regulations, transit systems cannot refuse to transport passengers using mobility aids that cannot be properly secured, which raises serious safety, insurance, and liability concerns. Although transit systems may require that wheelchairs and other mobility devices be secured, passenger restraint systems are optional. Four point passenger restraint systems appear to be nearly unanimously disliked by consumers and operators because the process is time consuming, cumbersome, and hinders passenger independence. Consequently passengers often refuse to use four point passenger restraint and securement systems (Hartman and Kurtz, 1993).

A related safety concern – standees on lifts – that emerged as a point of contention between the transit industry and the disability community, ultimately resulted in a clarification of the Final Rule.[17] Consistent with the rule, most transit systems allow individuals who cannot use the steps to enter and leave the bus by using the lift. However, concerns about passenger safety created a reluctance among transit systems to allow standees to use lifts on buses that are not equipped with handrails. Because evidence was unavailable to substantiate such transit system safety concerns, disability advocates argued that restricted lift use violates one's civil right to public transportation. A revised Final Rule allows standees to use lifts without restriction except for one model vehicle with an arcing lift that may be hazardous to standees.

COMPLEMENTARY PARATRANSIT SYSTEMS

Analysis of initial ADA paratransit plans and first year updates indicates that 116 systems report full compliance with ADA paratransit provisions by the end of 1993 and most transit systems project full compliance in 1996 (GAO, 1994). Compliance with service criteria prohibiting capacity constraints appears to be the greatest challenge to transit systems, largely because of the difficulty in predicting demands and concerns about cost. Transit systems have exhibited particular difficulty with developing eligibility policies and procedures. In many plans, problems were identified with estimating demand, providing consistent budget information, and conducting adequate public participation (EG&G Dynatrend, 1993). Problems in rural areas seem to be affecting the design of service delivery. At this juncture, only two transit systems, Richmond, Virginia, and Suffolk County, New York, have petitioned the FTA for undue financial burden waivers. In both cases, final decisions are pending. However, because transit systems have five full years to phase in compliance, it is highly likely that FTA will deny these requests ("FTA Unlikely to Approve," 1994).

Paratransit Operating Costs Are a Major Barrier to ADA Implementation

Since the inception of accessible transportation policy, costs have been the most critical issue in the debate regarding the method of providing service (Petty, 1987). Consistent with projections, paratransit costs may be the most expensive compliance costs of the ADA rule, and have emerged as a major implementation concern:

> Annual costs for implementing the ADA rule's criteria for complementary paratransit services could impact substantially on urban systems of all sizes (U.S. Department of Transportation, 1991, p.II-27).

Declining ridership, annual decreases in federal funding, and dwindling state and local budgets have made the past several years financially difficult for public transit systems (Hartman and Kurtz, 1993). Sometimes cited as an "unfunded federal mandate," the ADA presents requirements, without additional funds, that transit systems are expected to comply with under existing budgets. Although transit systems expressed full agreement with the civil rights principle of the law, the lack of designated federal funds has produced serious concerns about the reality of implementation, particularly complementary paratransit services (NESS, 1993).

Transit systems have now begun to realize the potential financial impact of the ADA; capital expenditures were generally anticipated but paratransit costs are already consuming a larger than expected portion of their budgets. More than one-half of public transit systems responding to a national survey about ADA implementation identified costs as the major barrier to ADA implementation in transportation (NESS, 1993). In paratransit operations, capital costs are relatively minor and usually federally and state subsidized; operations costs are more significant. According to FTA, operating costs represent 86 percent of paratransit costs (GAO, 1994). Variables that influence the costs of operations include driver salaries and benefits, maintenance, training, eligibility determinations, as well as the administrative expenses of reservations and scheduling. Given the labor-intensive aspect of the service, the manner of providing paratransit becomes a key determinant in controlling costs.

Evidence suggests that public operators benefit substantially from contracted arrangements with private providers, yet direct operation is the most common method of paratransit service delivery (NESS, 1993). Although a more expensive proposition for public operators because of higher union wages, 39 percent of transit systems reported directly operating all or some portion of their own paratransit programs (NESS, 1993). A review of ADA plans revealed that paratransit operations are not encouraging privatization as expected ("Use of Private Sector," 1994).

Higher driver wages and the additional costs of the service criteria raise per passenger trip costs. Before the ADA became effective, 160 systems reported one-way paratransit trip costs ranging from $10.55–$15.82 (RIA, 1991). However, per passenger trip costs are expected to increase substantially by virtue of the ADA service criteria and increased administrative responsibilities. The FTA is reporting aggregate paratransit costs at full compliance to be $700 million annually, $600 million of which represents operating costs (GAO, 1994). Other estimates for full compliance range from $900 million to $1 billion annually (NESS, 1993).

Several transit systems report that their paratransit operating budgets will triple to meet compliance (Strandberg, 1992). According to the GAO (1994), paratransit costs will increase more than 100 percent by 1996. The rise in costs is expected to be even greater in the largest urban systems, although small urban and rural systems often have a greater dependence on federal operating assistance to keep their systems running (Rahall, 1993). Transit operations, including paratransit, are heavily financed by local funding sources and supported by state and federal assistance. Federal operating assistance, increasingly in short supply, now faces the possibility of further reduction. Although the administration's proposed fiscal year 1995 budget increases the transit capital formula program, Section 9 operating assistance is decreased by 25 percent, from $802 million to $600 million ("President's '95 Budget Plans," 1994). Reducing federal operating assistance funds may result in greater difficulty for transit systems in meeting the requirements of complementary paratransit services.

Paratransit Planning and Budgeting Has Not Been Coordinated

Processes for planning and budgeting paratransit services at different levels of government were not coordinated. Public sector operating budgets are often decided no more than a few months before the budget year begins; therefore, funding availability is unpredictable (Hartman and Kurtz, 1993). Because operating funds remain uncertain from year to year, many paratransit plans were developed and approved locally and at the federal level with little attention to fiscal capacity to fund the plans. As a result, most transit systems have little confidence that resources will be available to fund their plans within the required time frames.

"A lot of transit authorities are setting up plans to comply with ADA, but they don't have much money [to implement them]" ("FTA Unlikely to Approve," 1994, p. 2).

The FTA's review of plans is primarily regulatory and does not examine the funding sources for services. As the date for full compliance approaches, financial pressure will increase. Pressure to meet compliance will be enhanced because 1996 is an election year. As 1997 approaches, requests for undue financial burden waivers will increase (NESS, 1993; GAO, 1994). The combination of political and financial pressures may result in a head-on collision between costs and civil rights.

Funding Paratransit May Affect the Equitable Distribution of Public Transportation Services

The high cost of paratransit may eventually decrease the availability of public transportation. Paratransit is becoming a disincentive to fixed route expansion, as transit systems admit limiting the expansion of fixed route service because of the corresponding paratransit service area implications (Hartman and Kurtz, 1993). Moreover, because the additional costs of paratransit operations must be assumed under existing operating budgets, transit systems have expressed concern about the possible financial impact of paratransit on their overall operations (EG&G Dynatrend, 1993). Without increased funding many transit systems may have to displace seniors, raise fares, reduce service areas, or decrease or eliminate service (Rosenbloom, 1993). Providing paratransit at the expense of reduced availability of public transportation is a trade-off that may not be well received by the general riding public. The increased costs of accessibility, aggravated by a lack of federal funding, has created serious problems, difficult choices, and high frustration for transit operators.

Transit Systems Face Complex Problems in Determining Paratransit Eligibility

Determining ADA paratransit eligibility at the local level has emerged as a major concern as transit systems grapple with the political reality of making objective assessments of paratransit need as opposed to the demands and preference of consumers. Section 504 paratransit criteria varied from system to system; most were liberal, allowing use by people with disabilities and senior citizens. As a result, paratransit became extremely popular with and depended upon by many persons with disabilities and senior citizens. Designed to serve individuals whose disabilities prevent them from using accessible fixed route, federal paratransit eligibility guidelines are provided to ensure that the resources available are provided to the persons who actually need them.

According to the ADA functional definitions and stringent DOT eligibility requirements, fewer persons with disabilities may be found eligible to use paratransit services; able-bodied senior citizens who do not have disabilities may be considered ineligible. Although the rules specify minimum levels of required services, costs may preclude transit systems from continuing to serve current paratransit users who do not meet the eligibility criteria. Federalizing the eligibility categories provides transit systems with the requisite tools to make determinations and reduces some of the local political pressure; however, determining paratransit eligibility is still very complicated and politically sensitive. One's functional ability to use accessible fixed route service resists precise measurement and requires some level of subjective judgment, as it is difficult to fit individuals with disabilities neatly into one of three eligibility categories on a trip by trip basis. To further complicate the task, consumers have raised the issue that the eligibility determination process represents a return to the medical model approach to disability.[18] At the same time, however, transit systems report difficulty in achieving an adequate level of consumer participation in the determination process (Access to the Arts, 1994).

Most systems doubt that the political process will support eligibility decertification decisions in the face of pressure from previously certified individuals. To avoid such decisions, at least for the short term, many systems are "grandfathering" all current users, a practice that serves only to increase demand and constrain capacity. A transit system in Tucson, Arizona, which reported a 33 percent increase in paratransit ridership, grandfathered all current users because they were "apprehensive because of the possibility of lawsuits" (NESS, 1993).

Paratransit Demand Is Rising

Since initial predictions of paratransit usage, transit systems are reporting notable increases in paratransit demand that exceed estimates projected in their paratransit plans. When pre-ADA paratransit demand exceeded capacity, transit systems would implement restrictions to suppress ridership. Under the ADA, not only is this practice considered discriminatory, but by 1997 transit systems must comply with requirements that specify that all requested rides must be provided. Transit systems report that rising demand will continue to constrain capacity and prevent full ADA compliance. Lenient certification procedures, increased visibility, improved service quality, client dumping by health and human service agencies, and consumer ridership patterns have served to increase paratransit demand.

Transit systems reported increases in paratransit ridership from 23 million riders in 1990 to 25 million riders in 1991, to 26 million in 1992 (NESS, 1993). Paratransit ridership increased 13 percent between 1990 to 1992. Persons with disabilities accounted for 54 percent of total paratransit ridership in 1990 and 58 percent in both 1991 and 1992. Senior citizens represented 32 percent of paratransit ridership in 1990 and 28 percent in both 1991 and 1992. Other riders, identified as personal care attendants, escorts, or nondisabled children and adults, accounted for approximately 14 percent of paratransit ridership in 1990, 1991, and 1992. (These figures should be interpreted with caution since the data are not complete (NESS, 1993).)

Lenient Certification Lenient certification provides a partial explanation for increased demand. Rather than tightening eligibility, in most cases, revised certification procedures have loosened eligibility for ADA paratransit service. Systems in Birmingham–Jefferson County, Alabama, and Louisville, Kentucky, changed their paratransit eligibility procedures from physician certification to service provider and applicant self-certification, which had little effect on decreasing eligible paratransit users. Instead, applications for paratransit increased and denial rates decreased.

The Transit Authority of River City (TARC), Louisville, Kentucky, initiated its ADA paratransit service in October 1992. Fleet capability was increased from 18 to 72 vans through multiple local contracts. Paratransit eligibility is determined through applicant self-certification. Questionable or difficult determinations are referred to a local rehabilitation agency to conduct functional assessments. Approximately 85 applicants have been referred to date, at a cost of $105 per assessment. Frail elderly persons, many of them displaced aging agency clients, constitute the largest portion of the new applicants. Recent data indicate that applicants are being determined ADA-eligible at a rate of 200 per day, which has doubled ridership. March 1992 monthly ridership data indicate 17,255 total paratransit trips; ridership for March 1993 was reported at 30,760, representing a 56 percent increase within a one year period. According to transit staff, increased visibility through increased capacity, passenger marketing through word of mouth, and client displacement by human service agencies account for the increased demand (T.Morris, TARC, personal communication, 6 May 1993).

Improved Service Improved service quality has been cited as a factor influencing rising paratransit demand. ADA complementary paratransit service requires improved levels of service that exceed pre-ADA paratransit services (Rosenbloom, 1993). Improved service seems to have attracted new riders who were unwilling or uninterested in using the pre-ADA paratransit. Pioneer Valley Transit Authority, Springfield, Massachusetts, reported that extending paratransit service hours to include evenings and weekends to meet the requirement of the service criteria produced "a deluge of requests." Since hours were increased in April 1992, 10,239 trips were provided to 992 eligible users during the extended hours (*Union News*, 5 February 1993). Birmingham–Jefferson County Transit Authority, Alabama, accredited an expanded paratransit service area and improved an advance reservation requirement, resulting in an increase in ridership (Rosenbloom, 1993).

Client Dumping Client "dumping" or "shedding" by health and human service agencies may have contributed to increased demand. Primarily funded by the U.S. Department of Health and Human Services (DHHS), human services transportation evolved to meet the transportation needs of persons with disabilities and senior citizens when accessible public transportation was not yet available (Davis, Jr. et al., 1982). For the most part, such services were limited to agency clients and program beneficiaries. Now that paratransit responsibility has been legally transferred to the designated public agency and as a cost-saving measure, some health and human service agencies are eliminating client transportation services. The practice of client dumping may increase paratransit demand on public transit systems (GAO, 1994).

Consumer Reluctance to Use Fixed Route Service To further compound the situation, current paratransit users are not making the transition to fixed route services. The DOT regulatory language suggests that comparatively small numbers of persons would be eligible for ADA paratransit and demand would decrease over time: "[paratransit] impact should be reduced over time as fixed route systems become more accessible."[19] Contrary to such regulatory assumptions, growing fleet accessibility is having little impact on consumer transition from paratransit to fixed route service. Consumers with disabilities, who may agree with the civil rights principles of the ADA, may not necessarily want to use fixed route service. According to a transit staff person, "Consumers with disabilities [who are unwilling to give up paratransit] claim that the vocal independent wheelchair users who fought for lifts on buses were a minority and do not represent the majority of consumers with disabilities" (NESS, 1993).

Seniors May Be Displaced by Persons with Disabilities

Before the ADA, most transit systems designed their paratransit programs to serve "the elderly and handicapped." Age (usually 65 years and up) was a frequent qualifier for eligibility. As a result, able-bodied senior citizens were the primary users of paratransit and continue to represent significant proportions of paratransit ridership. However, given the financial constraints facing most transit systems, there is little incentive to continue to serve senior citizens who are not ADA-paratransit eligible. Senior citizen paratransit ridership declined 11 percent from 1990 to 1992. Findings of a recent AARP study (Rosenbloom, 1993), suggest that 33 percent of current senior paratransit users will be displaced by persons with disabilities. One in five transit systems reported non-ADA-eligible seniors will be displaced through rigorous screening during the eligibility process (Rosenbloom, 1993). Muncie [Indiana] Transit will keep seniors on their paratransit rolls but give preferential treatment to persons with disabilities over senior riders. Sacramento and Duluth Transit changed their certification process to eliminate age as a criteria for paratransit service. Others will utilize more indirect strategies to limit service to seniors, such as decreasing service areas.

Paratransit Requirements Spawn Litigation

As predicted, ADA compliance is being tested at the local level through litigation (Weisman, 1992). Two class action lawsuits were recently filed against transit systems by consumers with disabilities for failure to provide comparable complementary paratransit as required by the ADA. Consumers with disabilities in New Orleans charged the Regional Transit Authority (RTA) with failure to provide both the level of paratransit service approved in their plan and accessible fixed route service.[20] RTA, which chose to provide paratransit under Section 504, is one of the few remaining transit systems that still does not have lift-equipped fixed route vehicles.

In the Twin Cities metropolitan area, the governor activated 200 members of the Minnesota National Guard to drive paratransit vehicles during a recent service breakdown due to a contract change. The new contractor for Metro Mobility, Minnesota's Regional Transit Board's paratransit service, initiated service in October 1993 with a shortage of 150 drivers, which caused a virtual collapse of the system and stranded thousands of paratransit users. After the situation was declared an emergency, National Guard drivers provided a short-term solution during the transition. Several consumers without access to transportation during this period have sued the transit agency and the contractor for not receiving paratransit services.[21]

RAIL SYSTEMS

Thirty-seven rail properties submitted ADA key station plans to the FTA designating 708 key stations nationwide. Although all transit systems did not meet the required deadline, rail station accessibility has increased since the passage of the ADA.

Time, Technology, and Budget Constraints Deter Key Station Accessibility

Approximately 40 percent of the 37 key station plans submitted to FTA in July 1992 missed ADA accessibility deadlines (*TD Safety Report*, 1993). Time extensions were requested for 399 key stations; 284 were granted. Key station accessibility is expensive and a lack of capital funding is problematic for many rail properties. Key station accessibility requirements place additional financial liability on rail operators, which must be absorbed within existing capital budgets. Moreover, ADA's stringent time frames were unrealistic for many transit systems in light of lengthy mandatory local level solicitation and procurement procedures. In such cases, it was simply impossible to meet the 26 July 1993 completion date. Capital costs for key station accessibility represent a one-time expenditure. Generally, station to station modifications vary in costs and complexity, but the total cost for key station accessibility is estimated to be approximately $907 million (FTA, personal communication, 2 February 1994).

Detectable Warnings Emerge as the Most Controversial Issue in Key Station Accessibility

"Platform edges bordering a drop-off and not protected by platform screens or guard rails shall have a detectable warning. . . . Detectable warnings shall consist of raised truncated domes. . . . and shall be 24 inches running the full length of the platform drop-off."[22]

The DOT rules requiring the installation of detectable warnings on rail platform edges sparked controversy in the disability community and the transit industry. Although not opposing the need for tactile strips, many transit systems raised concerns about the safety, maintenance, and durability of the existing technology and its application to rail platforms. Transit systems also questioned the wisdom of making large financial investments in technology, such as detectable warnings, that has had limited field testing in actual use. The key concern for most disability advocates is the safety of rail passengers who are blind or otherwise visually impaired. Originally required by 26 July 1993, a recent modification to the DOT rule extended the completion date for the installation of detectable warnings to 26 July 1994 to allow transit systems additional time to address unresolved technical issues. Under an equivalent facilitation clause in the ADA regulations, transit systems may request DOT approval to use altenative technology to meet ADA requirements. In the summer of 1994, following months of negotiations with DOT, the Washington Metropolitan Area Transit Authority (WMATA) was granted a four to six month extension to test alternative forms of detectable warning technology. After testing and selecting a particular technology, WMATA will seek a DOT equivalent facilitation determination. If such a determination is granted, the agency has 12 to 18 months to complete the installation of the approved technology.

OVER-THE-ROAD BUS SYSTEMS

DOT and the Access Board have initiated the OTRB rule-making process. In October 1993, DOT published an *Advanced Notice for Proposed Rulemaking* (NPRM), soliciting comments regarding the applicability of regulations established for private operators of OTRBs.[23] Following this notice, a joint DOT/Access Board workshop was held to solicit public comments from interested parties. The initial schedule projected the publication of an NPRM in early spring 1994 with final regulations to follow in May 1994. As of August 1994, an NPRM was not yet published. The disability community is urging DOT to make regulations for OTRBs consistent with the rules for other private operators "primarily" in the business of providing transportation, which specify that accessible vehicles should be purchased unless their systems, when viewed in entirety, provide a level of equivalent accessible service.

CONCLUSIONS

Requiring both accessible fixed route service and comparable paratransit, the ADA is already having a significant impact on the nation's transportation systems. Now that DOT regulatory policy and enforcement governing the provision of accessible transportation is in place, implementation has largely shifted to the nations' transportation providers. Implementation is moving forward and has generated a heightened awareness of ADA and accessibility issues in transportation.

ADA Implementation Is Moving Forward

Public bus, rail, and paratransit systems are more accessible to persons with disabilities and increased travel options exist. An individual with a disability has one out of two chances to board a lift-equipped bus, as more than 50 percent of the national bus fleet is accessible. Fleet accessibility should largely be completed within the next 7–10 years. Almost one-half of the nations' key rail stations should now be in compliance with ADA accessibility requirements. Most private providers are cognizant of their ADA responsibilities. The federal government has begun the rule-making process to ensure that over-the-road buses are accessible to persons with disabilities. After four years of implementation, significant strides have been made in improving transit accessibility nationwide. However, as implementation proceeds, financial uncertainties have become apparent as transit systems confront the costs of implementation with limited financial resources.

Transit Systems Lack Adequate Finances To Implement ADA Fully, Particularly Complementary Paratransit Services

Obtaining the financial resources to meet ADA paratransit requirements is the greatest challenge facing public transit systems (GAO, 1994). At this time of dwindling state and local budgets and reductions in federal operating assistance, transit systems are expected to absorb the additional costs of ADA's accessibility requirements within their existing budgets. To generate finances to comply with ADA requirements, transit systems are considering raising fares and reducing service. This strategy may be ineffective, however, because in some instances fare increases have resulted in decreased ridership, which in turn serves to further reduce operating revenue ("Hearings Begin," 1994). Financing facility access in key stations is also a challenge in many transit systems, particularly the older rail properties. Limited capital resources, compounded by stringent time frames, has delayed key station compliance.

Limited Technology Is Affecting Implementation

As experience with implementation grows, transit systems are recognizing that technology to meet accessibility requirements needs modification, raises safety concerns, or has not been field tested. Technology concerns have been raised regarding detectable warnings, universal securement, and passenger restraint systems.

Paratransit Demand and Funding Are on a Collision Course

Just as federal resources dwindle and paratransit costs increase, paratransit demand has expanded. Despite the "mainstreaming" intent of the ADA, many individuals with disabilities seem to prefer using paratransit over fixed route systems. Generally, individuals with disabilities who use public transportation are not making the transition to fixed route services. To avoid the political confrontations, transit systems, for the most part, are "grandfathering in" existing paratransit users. Increased visibility and improved paratransit services may be attracting new users. Lenient certification procedures and "dumping" by health and human service agencies may also be serving to increase ridership. Transit systems have three years remaining to meet full compliance. Ridership trends demonstrate that paratransit usage is steadily on the rise. If such a trend continues until 1997, it will be virtually impossible for transit systems to meet the ADA requirement to eliminate paratransit capacity constraints. Increased transit system requests for undue financial burden waivers are likely to result. In addition to limiting transportation accessibility for people with disabilities, failure to reach ADA compliance by 1997 without FTA-approved waivers, may result in the loss of federal financial assistance.

Political Tensions May Be Imminent

As the election year approaches, paratransit costs, eligibility, and service denial may become political issues. Transit systems are reticent to determine ADA paratransit eligibility because most transit staff perceive themselves as ill-prepared to make judgments about an individual's functional ability. Transit systems are reluctant to disqualify applicants for ADA eligibility. Paratransit service denial to seniors may also be a political concern. The ADA is intended to guarantee access to transportation to people with disabilities, not to limit transportation services to other individuals. The rules establish minimum guidelines, and transit systems have the option of serving individuals who do not meet the eligibility criteria. Determinations of who to serve, however, have funding implications because the costs of paratransit service delivery to non-ADA-eligible passengers cannot be included in requests for undue financial burden waivers. Denial of paratransit to seniors also has the potential to create discord between the disability and aging communities.

RECOMMENDATIONS

Given the preceding conclusions, recommendations to facilitate implementation should address how to build the financial and technical capacities of transit systems, how to encourage alternative service delivery models, how to encourage effective communication and behavior change, how to develop effective partnerships, and how to improve data collection systems. Toward these ends, I offer the following recommendations.

Develop Funding Mechanisms

The major factor inhibiting implementation is a lack of funding. Transit systems have conducted the formal ADA planning process for meeting compliance; however, without additional resources they will not be able to fund the planned services. Transit industries are critical of the lack of funding authorization accompanying a federal mandate of such magnitude. The absence of federal financial support causes transit systems to reallocate existing resources and commit additional monies to meet their responsibilities under the law, both of which are difficult propositions given the status of most state and local budgets. Funding is needed to support implementation.

Coordinate Public and Human Service Transportation Programs

It is likely that many of the same individuals who are eligible for ADA paratransit are also eligible for client transportation services provided by health and human service agencies. Given today's financial environment, transit systems are concerned that health and human service agencies are "dumping" their clients on to the public paratransit provider, which constrains capacity and increases costs. To address such concerns, strategies should be designed to develop statewide coordination of public and health and human service transportation programs. Developing such arrangements should be cost effective because they could eliminate duplication, reduce per trip costs, and ultimately relieve the demand on the public paratransit provider.

Develop Integrated Service Delivery Models

As transit systems seek innovative solutions to addressing paratransit demand, integrated service delivery models should be examined. Rather than viewing accessible fixed route and paratransit as parallel modes, opportunities to integrate these services, such as paratransit feeder systems, service routes, or using paratransit vehicles during off-peak hours to provide fixed route service, should be explored.

Enhance Technical Assistance for Transit Systems

Despite the level of prescriptiveness, the DOT rules do not provide sufficient operational guidance to assist transit systems in determining ADA paratransit eligibility. Recognizing the need for assistance, the FTA is currently sponsoring training in this area nationwide. However, model programs and guidance in evaluating functional skills to use accessible fixed route services are critical to successful eligibility determination programs. To facilitate implementation, additional guidance is needed to assist transportation providers with critical issues of eligibility determination. In general, technical assistance availability should be enhanced to facilitate paratransit compliance in the remaining three critical years of the five-year phase-in period.

Accelerate Research Activities

Demand for technological advancement in accessible transportation is increasing. The DOT and the Access Board should give priority to and increase research and demonstration efforts to improve accessible transportation delivery.

Facilitate Communication and Training

Little attention has been given to the complexity of behavior change required by affected parties in response to ADA policies. The ADA dictates new roles for some consumers with disabilities and seniors who are frequent paratransit users, as well as highly diverse new roles for bus operators. The rules attempt to force behavior change of these key affected parties, who were most likely absent from discussions and negotiations during the DOT rule-making process. As a result, some consumers and operators are resisting change as they strive to maintain the status quo. For many persons with disabilities, using accessible fixed route service represents a radical departure from the norm, until very recently, as many did not perceive fixed route service as a realistic travel alternative. In addition, myriad factors still impede fixed route usage.

The role of bus operators has become increasingly complex as they assume greater front-line responsibility for ADA service delivery. Detailed regulations define new roles for and increase demands on bus operators. Given their critical role in service delivery, it is essential that bus operators be knowledgeable of ADA rules and regulations for equipment operation, maintenance procedures, and service delivery to persons with disabilities. Before consumers and operators can be expected to comply with policies that require such significant changes in behavior, communication through information sharing and training is essential. Mechanisms are needed to enhance the development and dissemination of such information and training programs. Moreover, transit systems should begin to identify incentives for improving bus operator behavior such as rating accessibility equipment operation proficiency in roadeo competitions or forging alliances with state licensing departments to include these skills in state requirements for commerical drivers licenses.

Track Accessible Fixed Route Ridership through Improved Data Collection

To obtain a definitive picture of ADA implementation in public transit systems, improved data collection systems are needed to assess accessible fixed route ridership and to disaggregate accessible fixed route costs and funding sources. These data could be included as a part of FTA annual reporting requirements for recipients of federal financial assistance.

Forge Local Level Partnerships to Improve Pedestrian Accessibility

Transit systems and consumers with disabilities should forge partnerships with state and local governments to improve pedestrian accessibility and remove environmental barriers. At this juncture, major responsibility for implementing transit accessibility is in the hands of the transit industry. Resolving problems related to pedestrian accessibility and environmental barriers will require the participation of state, local, and federal governments, consumers with disabilities, senior citizens, and other affected parties.

REFERENCES

Access to the Arts. 1994. "Attitudes of Public Transit Personnel and People with Disabilities toward Public Transit Accessibility." Preliminary report. Washington, D.C.: Project ACTION.

American Public Transit Association. 1989. *1989 Transit Passenger Vehicle Fleet Inventory: A–Z*. Washington, D.C.: Author.

————. 1993. *1993 Transit Fact Book*. Washington, D.C.: Author.

Davis, F.W., Cunningham, L. F., Burkhalter II, D.A. and LeMay, S. 1982. Human Service Transportation At the Crossroads. *Transportation Research Record #850*. Washington, D.C.: Transportation Research Board.

EG&G Dynatrend. 1993. *Implementation of the Complementary Paratransit Provisions of the Americans with Disabilities Act of 1990 (ADA)*. Burlington, Mass.: Author.

Federal Transit Administration. 1993. *National Transit Summaries and Trends for the 1991 Section 15 Report Year*. Washington, D.C.: U.S. Department of Transportation.

"FTA Unlikely to Approve Financial Hardship Waivers for Paratransit." 1994. *TD Safety Report* (9 February): 2.

General Accounting Office. 1994. *Americans with Disabilities Act: Challenges Faced by Transit Agencies in Complying with the Act's Requirements*. GAO/RCED 094-58. Washington, D.C.: U.S. Government Printing Office.

Hartman, R. J., and E. M. Kurtz. 1993. "ADA Stakeholders Forum: Taking the Pulse in Representative American Communities." Unpublished report. Washington, D.C: Project ACTION.

"Hearings Begin This Week on Huge Transportation Plan." 1994. *Urban Transport News* (3 March): 36.

Katzmann, R. 1986. *Institutional Disability: The Saga of Transportation Policy for the Disabled.* Washington, D.C.: Brookings Institution.

"Lift Maintenance Hit in Precedent Setting Lawsuit." 1993. *TD Safety Report* (27 October): 1.

National Easter Seal Society. 1993. "National Accessible Fixed Route Bus System Survey." Unpublished manuscript. Washington, D.C.: Author.

Petty, L. 1987. "Section 504 Transportation Regulations: Molding Civil Rights Legislation To Meet Realities of Economic Constraints." *Washburn Law Journal* 26, 558–600.

"President's '95 Budget Plans Bear Transit Wins and Losses." 1994. *Urban Transport News* (17 February): 26.

Rahall, N. J. 1993. "Not by Highways Alone." *Roll Call* (8 March).

Robinson, B. 1993. "Impact of the Americans with Disabilities Act on the Bus Service." *TR News* 168: 22–23.

Rosenbloom, S. 1993. *The Impact of the Americans with Disabilities Act Transportation Requirements on Older Americans: Will Older Persons Lose Mobility?* Washington, D.C.: American Association of Retired Persons.

Strandberg, K. W. 1992. "ADA: The Intent, Impact and Implementation." *Mass Transit* 19: 24–31.

"Use of Private Sector Lacking, ADA Guru Finds." 1994. *TD Safety Report* (19 January): 4.

U.S. Architectural and Transportation Barriers Compliance Board. 1993. *Access America,* vol. 2. Washington, D.C.: Author.

U.S. Congress, Office of Technology Assessment. 1993. *Assessment to Over-the-Road Buses for Persons with Disabilities.* Washington, D.C.: U.S. Government Printing Office.

U.S. Department of Transportation. 1991. "Final Regulatory Impact Analysis Assessing the National Compliance Costs of the Department of Transportation's Final Rule Implementing the Americans with Disabilities Act of 1990 Surface Transportation Accessibility Requirements." Washington, D.C.: Office of the Secretary.

Weisman, J. J. 1992. "Paratransit May Cost Double Fare: FTA a Weak Link in ADA Compliance." *EPVA Action* (June): 10–11.

Williams, E. A., C. A. Sanchez, and C. L. Soper. 1987. "Wheelchair Accessibility Systems Maintenance Cost Study." Technical report 64F333/DMT-157 Urban Mass Transportation Administration, Washington, D.C.

NOTES

1. 49 CFR Part 27 (1986).
4. *Federal Register* 56 (1991): 45601.
5. 28 CFR Part 36.
6. 49 CFR Parts 27, 37, 38 (1991).
7. 49 CFR Part 37, Subpart D.
8. 49 CFR Part 37.173 (1991).
9. 49 CFR Part 37.163 (1991).
10. *Federal Register* 56 (1991): 45601.
11. Intermodal Surface Transportation Efficiency Act of 1991. P.L.102-240 23 USC 120.
12. Hardin v. Southeastern Pennsylvania Transportation Authority (SEPTA)., No. 91-CV-7434.
13. James v. Southeastern Pennsylvania Transportation Authority (SEPTA) No. 93-CV-5538 (E.D.Pa. Oct. 20, 1993).
17. *Federal Register* 58 (1993): 63092.
18. Prior to a paradigm shift with the onset of the Disability Rights Movement of the 1970s, disability was viewed as a medical problem, people with disabilities as sick. Decisions surrounding service delivery and community living were made by health and human service providers, instead of the individual with a disability.
19. *Federal Register* 56 (1991): 45745.

20. Tubre v. Regional Transit Authority (RTA) No. 93-4124 (E.D.LA. Dec. 15, 1993).
21. Lijewski v. Regional Transit Board, No. 3-93 Civil 768 (D.Minn. Nov. 15, 1993).
22. *Federal Register* 56 (1991): 45713.
23. *Federal Register* 58 (1993): 52735.

IV:
Impact on People with Disabilities

People with Psychiatric Disabilities

Leonard S. Rubenstein

EDITOR'S NOTE

Although people with psychiatric disabilities are protected by the ADA, the act has generated little progress in changing public attitudes or widely accepted stereotypes of mental illness. However, it is being used effectively to challenge "business as usual" in several arenas. In the area of professional licensing, the ADA has challenged the assumption that a history of treatment for mental health problems or psychiatric disability renders an applicant suspect.

Rubenstein invokes the ADA to challenge the disparity in health insurance coverage for mental and physical illness. Although the impact of the ADA on employment is yet to be determined, it will likely be less for people with psychiatric disabilities than for others, one reason being that the body of knowledge and experience in providing work accommodations for people with psychiatric disabilities falls short of that for people with physical and communication disabilities. Rubenstein looks to the ADA for continued challenges to a society that often accepts discrimination against people with psychiatric disabilities as "nothing more than common sense."

Leonard S. Rubenstein is executive director of the Bazelon Center for Mental Health Law, a nonprofit public-interest law center in Washington, D.C. A graduate of Harvard Law School, Rubenstein is an adjunct professor at Georgetown University Law Center. Rubenstein has served as attorney for adults and children with mental disabilities, obtaining precedent-setting federal court decisions establishing legal rights to appropriate care, fair treatment, and protection against abuse. Cofounder of the Washington Legal Clinic for the Homeless, Rubenstein has been a member of the American Bar Association Commission on Mental and Physical Disability Law, president of the ACLU of Virginia, and a member of the national ACLU board.

INTRODUCTION

The ADA confronts a world that views discrimination against people with psychiatric disabilities as natural, reasonable, and just. Even as attitudes about mental illness in matters such as insurance coverage are beginning to change, the idea that people with psychiatric disabilities are entitled to equality in social life remains foreign both in public opinion and in law. Despite episodic antistigma campaigns, discrimination in the workplace, in commerce, and in social institutions is considered nothing more than, as one commentator put it, ordinary common sense (Perlin, 1992). This must be so in a society whose most dehumanizing epithets – deranged, crazy, insane – signal mental illness.

In such a world, the ADA's inclusion of people with psychiatric disabilities has taken society by surprise, demanding changes in attitudes and behavior in a world unaccepting of and unprepared for people with psychiatric disabilities. Indeed, the fact that people with psychiatric disabilities were included in the ADA at all is a testament not only to the unity of the disability rights movement and the courage and tenacity of members of Congress who refused to abide the rank hostility of others, but to the very lack of visibility of mental disability in a law principally concerned with physical access (Rubenstein, 1993).

So the ADA carries a lot of freight for people with psychiatric disabilities, seeking nothing less than to transform a world that is not quite ready for it. Some have expressed skepticism whether any civil rights law can bear so heavy a load. The ADA's burden of change for people with psychiatric disabilities is complicated by the very invisibility of the disability. For them there is no equivalent to the physical changes to the environment that not only make the world accessible but, as important, expose the public to people with physical disabilities going about the business of life. Despite evidence of success among people with mental illness, including elites, and the high prevalence rate of mental illness in the general population, psychiatric disability remains associated with personal tragedy, violence and failure.

Given so great a task, what difference has the ADA made for people with psychiatric disabilities? What is the status of implementation on their behalf? After just five years, it may even be presumptuous to try to assess the ADA's impact. We have had no sweeping pronouncements from the courts; indeed, there have been only a handful of relevant decisions. Nor can we point to startling, assumption-challenging examples for people with mental illness that have characterized public attention to physical disability in the wake of the ADA. Such examples range from sensational achievements, like a one-handed major league pitcher throwing a no-hitter, to more routine but ultimately more profound changes, like people with physical disabilities using public transportation. Neither the sensational nor the routine achievements of people with mental illness have yet been publicly discovered or embraced.

Given the current pervasiveness of prejudice toward people with mental illness challenge, though, a rapid turnabout in attitudes, law, or social practices could hardly be expected. We must, in fact, adjust our scales of measurement to look at whether the ADA has begun to make inroads into commonly accepted practices regarding people with psychiatric disabilities and whether it has increased recognition of the very existence of discrimination. In this chapter, I will focus on three issues that may help us think about these more modest inquiries.

- Has the ADA begun to become a vehicle to challenge conventional attitudes about people with psychiatric disabilities or who are perceived to have such disabilities?
- Has the ADA begun to open opportunities in the workplace for people with psychiatric disabilities?
- Has the ADA accelerated the process of integration of people with psychiatric disabilities in the mainstream structures of society?

THE IMAGE OF PSYCHIATRIC DISABILITY AND ITS SOCIAL USES

Despite apparent progress in understanding conditions like depression and bipolar disorder, despite almost a century of Freud's influence on Western culture, despite the proliferation of confessional talk shows, people remain secretive about treatment for mental health problems. When people seek treatment at all, they want reassurance about confidentiality, particularly from employers. They do so because of the continued association of mental or emotional problems with serious personal or character defects. Many people will not reveal mental health problems because they reasonably fear being judged on the basis of their psychiatric problem, not their abilities or character.

We want to believe – and the ADA certainly says – that the determination of a person's ability to engage in an occupation or to gain a social benefit should be made on the basis of skills or abilities, not diagnosis or a record of having undergone treatment. Treatment for a mental health problem or a mental disorder, of itself, does not permit conclusions about character, skills, trustworthiness, or other traits thought necessary for a particular benefit or job. Impaired judgment or erratic behavior may in some circumstances be associated with a psychiatric condition, but for the purposes of everyday life, what is relevant about the person is the impaired judgment or erratic behavior, not the diagnosis. It follows that we ought to be concerned about behavior and qualifications, not psychiatric treatment or diagnosis.

The ADA tackles this type of stereotyping of people with disabilities by prohibiting the use of medical history as a surrogate for assessment of job qualifications. Title I of the ADA contains an elaborate set of rules that deprive the potential employer of information about a person's medical history or disability until after a preliminary offer of employment has been made;[1] the employer is permitted to inquire only whether the person possesses the qualifications for the job, whatever they may be. As a result, many employers have removed questions from their employment applications like "are you now or have you ever been" in mental health treatment.

Licensing agencies of all kinds, from those allowing people to drive a car to those charged with regulating professionals, however, still routinely inquire into a person's treatment for mental health problems rather than asking directly about the person's conduct or behavior. A person's disclosure of treatment for a psychiatric condition often brings about intrusive and humiliating investigations, as though treatment for a mental health problem is an indication of bad character. These intrusions have been so common and routine that, until the ADA came along, they went unquestioned along with the many other humiliations attendant to having undergone mental health treatment. For example, every year, tens, perhaps hundreds of thousands of the nation's elite – physicians, lawyers, and other professionals – file applications for professional licenses with state agencies. The applications typically demand information about instances of mental health treatment, often going back decades, and demand a waiver of confidential medical records.

The ADA immediately raised the question whether licensing agencies can continue to rely on these stereotypical, discriminatory questions in professional licensing, particularly when they are assessing character and fitness. The controversy has also spawned the most important litigation concerning people with psychiatric disabilities (or perceived psychiatric disabilities) under the ADA.

Consider the following questions drafted by the National Conference of Bar Examiners which, until recently, were used in about 30 states:

- Have you ever been treated or counseled for any mental, emotional, or nervous disorder or condition?
- Have you ever voluntarily entered or been involuntarily admitted to an institution for treatment of a mental, emotional, or nervous disorder or condition?

The questions reinforce the worst stereotypes about psychiatric disability – that mental health treatment or a psychiatric diagnosis, totally apart from the person's behavior, poses a serious question about a person's competence to act as a professional. At the heart of these stereotypical attitudes is the belief that people with mental disorders in general lack certain characteristics necessary for professionals, such as reliability, good judgment, and trustworthiness.

The most a person's psychiatric records could reveal are past behaviors that, if repeated, might affect the practice of law. But character committees typically do not ask about the very behaviors they are purportedly most concerned about, such as whether the applicant has neglected work, been unreliable, or failed to live up to responsibilities. No medical records or inquiries into treatment are required to ask about these behaviors.

The legal question under the ADA is whether authorities are entitled to seek information about a person's mental health history as part of the licensing process. To deny these agencies the information represents a frontal attack not only on common stereotypes about people who have undergone treatment for a mental health problem but on the authorities' perception of their duty to the public.

The first challenge to inquiries about mental health treatment in professional licensing came in the District of Columbia, which hosts – along with New York and California – the greatest concentration of lawyers in the United States. In response to a request to

strike the inquiry, the District of Columbia Court of Appeals[2] eliminated all questions about a person's history of mental health treatment, retaining only questions about psychiatric hospitalization
and drug and alcohol treatment within the past five years. It issued
no opinion explaining its decision, though its counsel in the matter
described his recommendations (Reischel, 1992).

The decision in the District of Columbia stimulated further interest and controversy. Some bar examiners attacked the District of
Columbia decision as an affront to the duty of bar examiners to
learn about psychiatric history (Pobjecky, 1992). On the other
hand, the American Psychiatric Association Work Group on Disclosure adopted *Recommended Guidelines Concerning Disclosure and
Confidentiality*, recommending that residency programs and licensing agencies focus on work impairment rather than on history of
psychiatric treatment (American Psychiatric Association, 1992). It
did not take long before these concerns found their way into the
courts, as challenges to questions about mental health treatment
in the contexts of medical and legal licensing were filed.

In the fall of 1993, the Civil Rights Division of the United States
Department of Justice, the most influential interpreter of Title II
of the ADA (covering the activities of public entities, including
licensing agencies) filed a brief amicus curiae in the case of *Medical
Society of New Jersey* v. *Jacobs*, in the United States District Court
in New Jersey.[3] The brief was the department's first application
of the Americans with Disabilities Act to mental disability. The
question in the case was whether physicians seeking renewal of
their medical licenses must disclose psychiatric illness, drug or
alcohol dependence, and physical, mental, or emotional conditions
resulting in termination or a leave of absence from practice during
the preceding 12 years.[4]

The Justice Department reviewed the ADA's approach to qualification standards,[5] acknowledging at the outset the legitimacy of the
concern that motivated the licensing agency to impose the requirement in the first instance: protection of the public. Therefore the
department agreed that an essential eligibility criterion for licensing
a physician is the "ability to safely and competently practice medicine." The problem, the Justice Department argued, was the way
the Board of Medical Examiners went about this task. Rather than
focusing on the relevant question – the ability to practice medicine

safely – it asked questions about disability as a trigger for further screening and inquiry. No similar burden of providing private and intrusive information is placed on people without disabilities or, for that matter, on people with physical disabilities.

The brief attacked the central premise underlying reliance on the disability-based inquiries, that there exists a connection between information about particular disabilities and fitness to practice medicine. It stated flatly that "Diagnosis or treatment for a mental disorder or substance dependency provides no basis for assuming that these disabilities will affect behavior."[6] Moreover, the department reasoned, even if, as the Board of Medicine argued, some disabilities do have some affect on behavior, it remains the behaviors, not the disabilities, that are the legitimate concern of the board. And those behaviors can be identified by asking relevant questions about them rather than about disability:

> The Board may obtain sufficient information to assess fitness to practice surgery or medicine through questions that focus on behavior rather than status. Nothing in the ADA prohibits the Board from asking applicants or licensees about past conduct or behavior that may evidence an incapacity to practice medicine or surgery. Such conduct or behavior, whether it results from mental illness, substance dependency, or other factors (such as irresponsibility or bad moral character), is a much better indicator of suitability as a physician than an applicant's diagnosis or treatment history.[7]

This analysis also sheds light on the provision of the department's *Technical Assistance Manual* that permits public entities to consider factors related to disability in determining whether the individual is qualified.[8] The department restricted consideration to "any inappropriate behavior associated with that disability."[9] In other words, the behavior associated with disability must be discovered through inquiries about behavior, not disability. As the brief explained:

> Thus, the Board may inquire generally about any leaves of absence or terminations from employment in the past but may not focus the inquiry on those leaves of absence and terminations occasioned by physical or psychiatric illnesses or conditions. Similarly, the Board may inquire about personal

behavior, including whether the applicant uses drugs or alcohol and the frequency of use. The Board may ask applicants whether there is anything that would currently impair their ability to carry out the duties and responsibilities of a physician. Such a question, along with other questions about conduct and behavior, are a permissible means of ascertaining an applicant's fitness. In contrast, asking about an applicant's history of diagnosis and treatment for mental disorders or substance dependency treats a person's *status* as an individual with a disability as if it were indicative of that individual's future *behavior* as a physician. By focusing on the disability itself, instead of focusing on relevant factors that may be associated with the disability, the Board cannot accurately assess a licensee's fitness to practice medicine and may discriminate against a qualified individual with a disability.[10]

Finally, the Justice Department addressed the administrative burden that results if disability can no longer be used as a trigger or shortcut to further an investigation about behavior. This burden is not a legitimate excuse under the ADA, because "the use of mental or physical disability as a 'red flag' to conduct further investigation of a person for unfitness is precisely the sort of conclusory jump which the ADA was enacted to combat."[11]

The United States District Court in the *Jacobs* case adopted the Justice Department's reasoning. Although the court denied the plaintiff's motion for a preliminary injunction on other grounds, it did find substantial merit in the challenge to the questions about history and treatment. In an opinion issued on 5 October 1993, the court focused on the extra burdens the questions placed on qualified individuals with disabilities because affirmative answers to the questions triggered inquiries not made of individuals who do not have disabilities. Central to the court's reasoning was the recognition that "it has been held to be fundamental that an individual's status cannot be used to make generalizations about that individual's behavior."[12] Even to the extent the questions have some utility in identifying people with problems worthy of investigation, the court held, the evil is the singling out of people with disabilities for these additional investigations.

Finally, the court also accepted the Justice Department's view that alternative, nondiscriminatory means are available to screen out incompetent or misbehaving physicians. As the court explained:

> The Court is confident that the Board can formulate a set of questions that screen out applicants based only on their behavior and capabilities. For example, the Board is not foreclosed by Title II from screening out applicants based on their employment histories; based on whether applicants can perform certain tasks or deal with certain emotionally or physically demanding situations; or based on whether applicants have been unreliable, neglected work, or failed to live up to responsibilities.[13]

This case was just the first foray into an area fraught with controversy precisely because it challenges widely accepted stereotypes that are entrenched in people's minds and so deeply embedded in practice. *Jacobs* was followed in 1993 by *In re Underwood*,[14] where the Supreme Court of Maine held that questions about mental health treatment during the 10 years preceding applications for admission to the bar violated the ADA. In 1994, the American Bar Association, while not citing the ADA, urged bar examiners to narrow mental health inquiries and in 1995, a federal court held that questioning bar applicants whether thay had been treated or counselled for a mental or emotional disorder violated the ADA.[15] Additional reforms are sure to follow.

EMPLOYMENT

Access to Work

The centerpiece of the ADA is and remains opening employment opportunities to people with disabilities. But the ADA encountered a world where, for people with psychiatric disabilities, scant attention had been paid to its dual approach of nondiscrimination and reasonable accommodation. In 1990, it did not take two hands to count the number of articles on reasonable accommodation for people with a psychiatric disability (Mancuso, 1990). Research on efforts of people with psychiatric disabilities to obtain or maintain jobs were numerous, but usually focused on variables like symptomology, functional status, age, diagnosis, extent of work skills, and other characteristics of the person. I am unaware of any study that considered either the impact of discrimination (or, for that matter, reasonable accommodation) on access to employment.

Real world dilemmas, such as the consequences to an employee of disclosure of a disability, the kinds of accommodations needed and desired by workers, the impact of psychotropic medications on work performance, the reaction of other employees to accommodations for persons with psychiatric disabilities, received little, if any, consideration. Even the emerging field of psychiatric rehabilitation was slow to conceptualize its task in ADA terms, focusing almost exclusively on preparing the individual for work rather than preparing the workplace for the individual.

To exacerbate the problems, Congress assigned enforcement of Title I of the ADA to an agency only marginally equipped to handle it. Even without ADA enforcement responsibilities, the Equal Employment Opportunity Commission, the federal agency responsible for receiving and processing employment of discrimination under the ADA, had in the past suffered from chronic understaffing and lack of strong leadership. The agency has been overwhelmed by the enormous new responsibilities it has been assigned under the ADA. Despite a strong commitment by the agency's new leadership, these factors, combined with field investigator's lack of familiarity with psychiatric disability (U.S. Congress, Office of Technology Assessment, 1994), has rendered the EEOC's investigations of complaints of psychiatric disability difficult. The first cases to reach the courts, moreover, do not signal any identifiable trend.

In view of the blank slate on which the ADA's prohibition of employment discrimination on the basis of psychiatric disability was written, we are hardly in a position to measure its impact where it really counts – in the workplace. Reports of major changes in workplace practices, personnel policies, or attitudes about persons with a history of treatment for a psychiatric condition remain sketchy at best. Indeed, anecdotal evidence suggests that many employers and employees still remain entirely unaware that the ADA applies to persons with psychiatric disabilities. In addition, the nation's largest disability agency by far – the Social Security Administration – has paid scant attention to the impact of the ADA on the work disincentives in the disability benefit programs it administers.

Having said that, the ADA has, for the first time, brought extraordinary attention to questions about psychiatric disability and the workplace. About 10 percent of the charges of employment discrimination filed under the ADA alleged psychiatric disability. The charges have not yet generated any further guidance on the meaning of discrimination or the contours of reasonable accommodation for people with psychiatric disabilities but surely will in the months and years to come. More important, enactment of the ADA has ended the vacuum of attention paid to people with psychiatric disabilities in the workplace. A slew of federal agencies, business organizations, and foundations have focused attention on psychiatric disability and the workplace. The products of these efforts have so far remained primitive in the sense that they do little more than outline the law, provide anecdotal suggestions, and report survey data. Some do not take the employer's very real concerns into account; others give short shrift to employer obligations.

Nevertheless, they are a start. Investigations of psychiatric disability in the workplace and the technology of reasonable accommodation, together with advice for employers and consumers, have appeared (Zuckerman, Debenham, and Moore, 1993, Mancuso 1993), along with consumer guides (Bazelon Center, 1992) and traditional legal analyses (Edwards, 1992; 1993; Haggard, 1993; Parry, 1993). Some studies have begun to look at the effects of taking psychotropic medication on work performance (U.S. Congress, Office of Technology Assessment, 1994).

The ADA has also encouraged the National Institute for Disability and Rehabilitation Research (NIDRR), the federal government's principal disability research agency, to pay greater attention to psychiatric disability, a subject it largely ignored in the past. NIDRR sponsored a conference on Strategies to Secure and Maintain Employment for Persons with Long-Term Mental Illness (NIDRR, 1992), which not only brought the issues to the fore but demonstrated how little attention had been paid to them in the past. NIDRR also directed one its grantees, the Center for Psychiatric Rehabilitation at Boston University, to engage in ADA-related projects. NIDRR sponsored research on educating state rehabilitation counselors on the ADA and psychiatric disabilities. It funded an employer group, the Washington Business Group on Health, to provide information to employers that would enable them to develop job qualifications relating to the emotional requirements of work and to accommodate the needs of people with psychiatric disabilities in the workplace. Similarly, the federal Center for Mental Health

Services has provided funding to consumer-run organizations such as the National Empowerment Center to provide technical assistance on employment matters under the ADA. Congress published a major study of the federal role in promoting work for people with psychiatric disabilities (U.S. Congress, Office of Technology Assessment, 1994). The report reviews not only the impact and potential of the ADA on employment for people with psychiatric disabilities but also activities intended to fulfill the ADA's promises of nondiscrimination and reasonable accommodation.

Thus, implementation of Title I with respect to people with psychiatric disabilities has just begun. Given the lack of knowledge and experience in addressing workplace questions, and even conceptual issues concerning the meaning of discrimination and reasonable accommodation, it is not surprising that implementation has yet to reach the shop floor or the office. Anecdotal evidence suggests that the greatest impact of the ADA so far is in accommodating current employees, rather than new hires. That is a reasonable place to start, as employers face, through their own work force, the meaning and challenges of the ADA. In time, we will be able to see whether the resource material that is just becoming available to employers and workers will be converted into changes on the job.

Employee Benefits

Probably the most frequently asked question about the impact of the ADA on people with psychiatric disabilities is whether it will rectify discriminatory features of employer-provided health plans that typically require higher copayments and deductibles, annual and lifetime caps on benefits, and fewer services for mental health care than for physical health care. The debate on this question has been muffled by the far louder public discussion of health care reform, but it has not been drowned out. So far, the ADA has not touched the status quo.

From the day of enactment, the impact of the ADA on insurance, particularly employer-provided health plans, has been the subject of much head scratching, debate and controversy. In Section 501(c) of the ADA, Congress exempted from the ADA "bona fide" health insurance plans based on "underwriting risks, classifying risks, or administering such risks that are based on or not inconsistent with

State law.''[16] Congress additionally provided, however – in exquisitely opaque language – that these plans could not be used as a "subterfuge" to "evade the purposes of the ADA.''[17] On 8 June 1993, the Equal Employment Opportunity Commission issued an Interim Guidance on the application of the ADA to disability-based distinctions in employer-provided health insurance (EEOC, 1993). Although the guidance does not carry the force of law, it represents the EEOC's current interpretation of the ADA and has survived its first judicial test in a case involving limitations on coverage of AIDS in a self-insured health insurance plan.[18] The Interim Guidance interprets the ADA to place limits on an employer's ability to exclude coverage for disabilities, but authorizes discriminatory coverage of mental health treatment in health insurance policies.

The Interim Guidance establishes first that, as an employee benefit and a term and condition of employment, health benefits are subject to coverage by the ADA. It then holds that if certain health coverage is limited or excluded based on a disability-based distinction, the employer must show that the health insurance plan is bona fide and not a "subterfuge." The concepts of "disability-based distinction" and "subterfuge" will prove critical in applying the ADA to mental health coverage.

Disability-Based Distinction The first key provision of the Interim Guidance regarding mental health coverage defines *disability-based distinction*, the threshold for applying the ADA at all. The Interim Guidance provides that a benefit provision is disability-based if it meets any of the following three criteria: "it singles out a particular disability (e.g., deafness, AIDS, schizophrenia), a discrete group of disabilities (e.g., cancers, muscular dystrophy, kidney diseases), or disability in general (e.g., noncoverage of all conditions that substantially limit a major life activity)." The EEOC then reasons that discriminatory features of mental health coverage under the ADA do not fit within any of the three prongs of this definition because curbs on mental health benefits are not based on a disability but on a multiplicity of conditions, some of which are disabilities and some are not.

The EEOC explains further:

> For example, a feature of some employer provided health insurance plans is a distinction between the benefits provided

for the treatment of physical conditions on the one hand, and the benefits provided for the treatment of "mental/nervous conditions" on the other. Typically, a lower level of benefits is provided for the treatment of mental/nervous conditions than is provided for the treatment of physical conditions. Similarly, some health insurance plans provide fewer benefits for "eye care" than for physical conditions. *Such broad distinctions, which apply to the treatment of a multitude of dissimilar conditions and which constrain individuals both with and without disabilities, are not distinctions based on disability.* Consequently, although such distinctions may have a greater impact on certain individuals with disabilities, they do not intentionally discriminate on the basis of disability and do not violate the ADA.[19] (emphasis added)

In other words, according to the EEOC, because the exclusion or limitation of coverage for a range of mental health treatments affects people with disabilities and those without, the exclusion is not one based on disability and hence does not violate the ADA. The reasoning here is suspect. The fact that an exclusion is overbroad should not immunize it from the ADA, so long as the exclusion is intended to restrict or eliminate coverage for people with disabilities (Giliberti, 1994).

Consider, for example, an employer who seeks to eliminate coverage for HIV-related conditions but fears running afoul the ADA. Under the Interim Guidance, the employer could accomplish this task by also eliminating coverage for one or more nondisabling conditions of its choosing along with AIDS. Thus the employer could eliminate coverage for immune deficiency conditions, which would include AIDS (a disability) and allergies (presumably not disabilities). Under the EEOC interpretation, the employer would be insulated from liability because the immune deficiency exclusion would not "single out" AIDS.

A more appropriate interpretation of a disability-based distinction would include the case where the employer intentionally restricts or limits coverage for one or more disabilities in the health insurance policy, whether explicitly or hidden in a more general category. So long as treatment for specific disabilities is excluded or limited, it should make no difference that certain nondisabling conditions are limited in coverage as well. Thus limiting or excluding coverage for psychiatric disabilities would amount to a disability-based distinction; by contrast, limitations on coverage of non-disability-related mental health problems would not.

One could even argue alternatively that the ADA's definition of *disability* could reach people seeking mental health treatment who do not meet the ADA's principal definition of disability – an impairment that significantly limits a major life activity. Recall that the ADA defines *disability* to include people who are "regarded as" having a disability. As the discussion of the licensing standards shows and as the vast literature on stigma, prejudice, and stereotyping of people with mental health problems confirms, a case can be made that the reason for the exclusion of mental health coverage is prejudice against people perceived to have a psychiatric disability.

Discrimination in mental health coverage for people with psychiatric disabilities is surely to be challenged as a disability-based distinction, especially if the EEOC prevails in its current litigation on AIDS. No case making this claim has so far been brought.

Showing Subterfuge According to the EEOC's analysis, once a disability-based distinction exists, it is up to the sponsor (usually the employer) to show that the plan is not inconsistent with state law or a bona fide self-insured plan. In addition, the employer must demonstrate that the disability-based distinction is not a subterfuge to evade the purposes of the ADA. The Interim Guidance defines *subterfuge* as "disability-based disparate treatment that is not justified by the risks or costs associated with the disability."[20]

The EEOC advises that this determination will be done on a case by case basis, but provides some examples of potential justifications. These include showing (1) that the limitation or exclusion is not, in fact, "disability-based"; (2) that the disparate treatment is "justified by legitimate actuarial data, by actual or anticipated experience and that condition with comparable actuarial data or by actual or reasonably anticipated experience, and that conditions with comparable actuarial data and/or experience are treated in the same fashion"; (3) that the disparate treatment is necessary for the fiscal soundness of the plan; (4) that the limitation or exclusion is necessary to prevent an "unacceptable change" in coverage or premiums (e.g., significant increase in copayments or deductibles or limitation in scope of coverage); or (5) that the treatment sought has no value.

These criteria appear quite open-ended and no doubt will lead to a great deal of litigation over justifications for disability-based distinctions in health plans. Although some lawyers have argued that the defenses place too high a burden on the employer (District of Columbia Bar Task Force), the defenses may in fact have the opposite effect, legitimating many disability-based distinctions, especially those that save a great deal of money for the plan.

Significantly, the EEOC places the burden of proving these points on the employer, recognizing that employees have no access to the necessary data. Indeed, the lack of access to actuarial data has proven a significant obstacle even to analyzing insurance contracts. Private insurers will not release the information and state insurance regulatory agencies protect it from public view as proprietary data.

These matters are likely to be litigated in cases before juries in *Mason Tenders* and other cases. Though not directly affecting mental health benefits, they surely will have a dramatic impact on the effort to challenge limitations and exclusions of mental health coverage in health insurance plans that are sure to follow.

INTEGRATING PEOPLE WITH PSYCHIATRIC DISABILITIES INTO COMMUNITY LIFE

The overarching and ambitious vision of the ADA is to integrate people with disabilities into the life of the community. The rhetoric of the ADA is most stirring in addressing this vision. The findings and purposes section that "society has tended to isolate and segregate people with disabilities, and despite improvements, such forms of discrimination against individuals with disabilities continue to be a serious and pervasive social problem;"[21] that "individuals with disabilities continually encounter various forms of discrimination, including . . . segregation";[22] that individuals with disabilities are

> a discrete and insular minority who have been faced with restrictions and limitations, subjected to a history of purposeful unequal treatment, and relegated to a position of political powerlessness in our society, based on characteristics that are beyond the control of such individuals and resulting from stere-

otypic assumptions not truly indicative of the individual ability of such individuals to participate in, and contribute to, society.[23]

The House Judiciary Committee's Report on the ADA states that "integration is fundamental to purposes of the ADA. Provision of segregated accommodations and services relegate persons with disabilities to second-class citizen status."[24] True equality for people with psychiatric disabilities must include enabling them to live in normalized not specialized housing, gain access to social and support services based in the community not in institutions, and live in a legal system that bases its decisions on their abilities rather than on categorical and stereotypical assumptions denying them their humanity (Cook, 1991; Milstein and Hitov, 1993; Burnim, 1993; Rubenstein, 1993; Perlin, 1994).

The ADA, however, did little outside the domain of physical access (including transportation and communications) to explain how this vision was to come about or even consider such concrete questions as the future of institutionalization for people with mental disabilities or the use of psychiatric categories to make decisions about parental rights. The Justice Department was true to the rhetoric of the ADA by incorporating the idea of integration into its regulations under Title II of the act, but did not provide further guidance for implementation. The Justice Department regulations state:

> A public entity shall administer services, programs, and activities in the most integrated setting appropriate to the needs of qualified individuals with disabilities.[25]

This Delphic statement is enlarged upon only marginally in the explanatory materials accompanying the regulations:

> Taken together, these provisions are intended to prohibit exclusion and segregation of individuals with disabilities and the denial of equal opportunities enjoyed by others, based on, among other things, presumptions, patronizing attitudes, fears and stereotypes about individuals with disabilities. Consistent with these standards, public entities are required to ensure that their actions are based on facts applicable to individuals

and not in presumptions as to what a class of individuals can or cannot do.[26]

The Justice Department also provides a workable governing standard: an *integrated setting* means "a setting that enables individuals with disabilities to interact with nondisabled persons to the fullest possible extent."[27]

These are powerful words, and provide much to build on. Still, the absence of specific statutory language or regulatory interpretations addressing integrated services in the context of specialized programs for people with mental disabilities renders the implications of the ADA far from obvious. In the face of some prior case law under Section 504 of the Rehabilitation Act that rejects the idea that the act provided a basis for a claim to community integration,[28] the effort is far from simple.

Because of the radical change this vision requires and the lack of acceptance that such a change is warranted, implementation of Titles II and III has remained slow. Yet recognition is beginning that these titles require changes in social and governmental practices with respect to people with psychiatric disabilities and that implementing agencies have a responsibility to bring it about.

In response to enormous evidence that police agencies abuse people with psychiatric disabilities, the Department of Justice has awarded an ADA implementation grant to develop model police training programs so these agencies can learn how better to interact with people with psychiatric disabilities. The Department of Justice responded in like fashion to evidence that people with psychiatric disabilities experience discrimination in public benefit and social service programs. The department awarded a grant to document a self-evaluation process that enables agencies administering such programs to end discrimination against people with psychiatric disabilities.

The most ambitious effort to integrate people with psychiatric disabilities so far, however, has been in lawsuits seeking to transform social and mental health service systems. Advocates have urged that the rhetoric of integration be taken with utter seriousness to bring people with disabilities into communities by ending both unnecessary institutionalization and segregation.

Shortly after the ADA became effective, a court alluded to this purpose in a long-standing case that brought the closing of a large state-operated mental retardation facility and its replacement by community-based services. The state asked the court to relieve it of the obligation to provide continuing community services to former residents of Pennhurst State School on the ground that it had no constitutional obligation to do so. The court rejected the state's motion, and in the process commented:

> Further, the Commonwealth neglects to point out that in enacting the Americans with Disabilities Act of 1990, Congress affirmed that §504 [of the Rehabilitation Act of 1973] prohibits unnecessary segregation and requires reasonable accommodations to provide opportunities to include all state and local programs, regardless of the receipt of federal financial assistance.[29]

Advocates have filed cases, and in most situations await decisions, challenging discrimination or segregation in public sector activities. These cases challenge continued reliance on institutionalization for people with psychiatric disabilities, and the failure to develop adequate community-based services in the place. It is too soon to know their outcome, but it cannot be doubted that the ADA provides a powerful conceptual basis for integrating people with psychiatric disabilities into communities.

CONCLUSION

It is far too soon to judge implementation of the ADA on behalf of people with psychiatric disabilities by traditional measuring rods for antidiscrimination laws, such as employment rates, accommodations made available, and the like. Indeed, we are not yet even collecting the data by which comparisons or measurements of quantitative change can be made. We lack even some cruder measures, such as the number of cases successfully resolved.

In the absence of these measures, one's assessment of the impact of the ADA on people with psychiatric disabilities in the first two years of implementation depends entirely on the kind of questions one asks. If the question is whether the ADA changed deeply entrenched attitudes, opened the workplace, and integrated people into communities, the answer must be ''no.'' Enforcement is still at its most primitive stage; even knowledge of the ADA's coverage of people with psychiatric disabilities is not widespread. The lead enforcement agency to challenge employment discrimination has interpreted the ADA to permit discrimination in coverage of psychiatric disability in health insurance. In areas that hold the most significant potential impact – public attitudes, society's expectations about participation of people with psychiatric disabilities in social life, and obligations of social and health service systems – we see only initial concern about the problems.

When measured against the depth of an entrenched prejudice that will work to defeat everything the ADA stands for; however, the impact of the law must be considered significant. The ADA has forced attention to questions never examined in the past, such as the use of mental health information to draw conclusions about a person's character. Even though the ADA has not yet provided many answers, it has begun to draw the attention of employers, trainers, academics, advocates, and the federal government to questions of discrimination against and accommodations for people with psychiatric disabilities in the workplace. In addition, the law has forced attention to the categorical nature of discrimination in social programs.

Enactment of the ADA has also brought a proliferation of obvious accommodations for people with physical disabilities in everyday life such as in bathrooms and public telephones. Those changes reinforce an essential message of the ADA: that it is a law that asks society to adjust to the variety of individual difference (Rubenstein and Milstein, 1993). We have not yet reached such an understanding for people with psychiatric disabilities. The first years of implementation of the ADA, however, suggest that the ADA has the potential to contribute mightily to that transformation for people with psychiatric disabilities as well.

REFERENCES

American Psychiatric Association, Work Group on Disclosure. 1992. *Recommended Guidelines Concerning Disclosure and Confidentiality*. Washington, D.C.: American Psychiatric Association.

Bazelon Center for Mental Health Law. 1992. *Mental Health Consumers in the Workplace*. Washington, D.C.: Author.

Burnim, I. 1993. "Strategies for Using the ADA to Promote Community Services." Paper prepared for the National Association of Protection and Advocacy Systems, on file with the author.

Cook, T. 1991. "The Americans with Disabilities Act: The Move to Integration." *Temple Law Review* 64: 393–469.

Edwards, M. H. 1992–1993. "The ADA and the Employment of Individuals with Mental Disabilities." *Employee Relations Labor Journal* 18: 347–389.

Equal Employment Opportunity Commission. 1993. "Interim Enforcement Guidance." EEOC Notice N-915.002. Washington, D.C.: Author.

Feldblum, C. 1991. "Medical Examinations and Inquiries under the Americans with Disabilities Act: A View from the Inside." *Temple Law Review* 64: 521–549.

Giliberti, M. 1994. "The Application of the ADA to Distinctions Based on Mental Disability in Employer-Provided Health and Long-Term Disability Insurance Plans." *Mental and Physical Disability Law Reporter* 18: 600–604.

Haggard, L. K. 1993. "Reasonable Accommodation of Individuals with Mental Disabilities and Psychoactive Substance Abuse Disorders under Title I of the Americans with Disabilities Act." *Journal of Urban and Contemporary Law* 43: 343.

Mancuso, L. 1990. "Reasonable Accommodation for Workers with Psychiatric Disabilities." *Psychosocial Rehabilitation Journal* 14: 3–8.

———. 1993. *Case Studies on Reasonable Accommodations for Workers with Psychiatric Disabilities*. Sacramento: California Department of Mental Health.

Milstein, B., and S. Hitov. 1993. "Housing and the ADA." In *Implementing the Americans with Disabilities Act*, ed. L. O. Gostin and H. A. Beyer, pp. 209–222. Baltimore: Paul H. Brookes.

National Conference of Bar Examiners. *Bar Examiners' Handbook* 73:3118–3119. Chicago: NCBE.

National Institute on Disability and Rehabilitation Research. 1992. Consensus Validation Conference. Strategies to Secure and Maintain Employment for People with Long-Term Mental Illness.

Parry, J. W. 1993. "Mental Disabilities under the ADA: A Difficult Path to Follow." *Mental and Physical Disability Law Reporter* 17: 100–111.

Perlin, M. 1992. "On Sanism." *SMU Law Review* 16: 373–407.

Piltch, D., J. W. Katz, and J. Valles. 1993. "The Americans with Disabilities Act and Professional Licensing." *Mental and Physical Disability Law Reporter* 17: 556–562.

Pobjecky, T. A. 1992. "Mental Health Inquiries: To Ask or Not to Ask – That Is the Question." *Bar Examiner* 61: 31–37.

Reischel, C. L. 1992. "The Constitution, the Disability Act, and Questions about Alcoholism, Addiction and Mental Health." *Bar Examiner* 61: 10–24.

Rubenstein, L. S. 1993. "Mental Disorder and the ADA." In *Implementing the Americans with Disabilities Act*, ed. L.O. Gostin and H.A. Beyer, pp. 209–222. Baltimore: Paul H. Brookes.

Rubenstein, L. S., and L. S. Milstein. 1993. "Redefining Equality through the ADA." In *The ADA Mandate for Social Change*, ed. P. Wehman, pp. 3–18. Baltimore: Paul H. Brookes.

U.S. Congress, Office of Technology Assessment. 1994. *Psychiatric Disabilities, Employment and the Americans with Disabilities Act.* OTA-BP-BBS-124. Washington, D.C.: U.S. Government Printing Office.

Zuckerman, D., K. Debenham, and K. Moore. 1993. *The ADA and People with Mental Illness: A Resource Manual for Employers.* Washington, D.C., and Alexandria, Va.: American Bar Association and National Mental Health Association.

NOTES

1. 42 U.S.C. §12112(d)(2).
2. Admission to the bar is under the control of the highest court in each state. In the District of Columbia, that court is the District of Columbia Court of Appeals.
3. Medical Society of New Jersey v. Jacobs, No., 93-3670 (WGB), United States District Court (D.N.J.).
4. The questions included the following: Are you presently or have you previously suffered from or been in treatment for any psychiatric illness? Have you been terminated by or granted a leave of absence by a hospital, health care facility, HMO, or any employer for reasons that related to any physical or psychiatric illness or condition? (Parental leave of absence need not be disclosed.) Are you now or have you been dependent on alcohol or drugs? Have you ever been terminated by or granted a leave of absence by a hospital, health care facility, HMO, or employer for reasons that related to any drug or alcohol use or abuse?
5. The Justice Department regulations provide that the ADA prohibits discrimination against people with disabilities within the ADA in the licensing process. See 28 CFR 35.130(b)(6). Cases challenging other aspect of the licensing process have been brought (Piltch, Katz, and Valles, 1993).
6. Brief of the United States, p. 16.
7. Brief of the United States, p. 17.
8. Department of Justice, *ADA Technical Assistance Manual*, p. II-3.7200.
9. Ibid.
10. Brief, pp. 18–19, footnotes omitted.
11. Brief, p. 21.
12. Medical Society of New Jersey v. Jacobs, No., 93-3670 (WGB), United States District Court (D.N.J. October 5, 1993), Opinion, p. 16.
13. Ibid., p. 15.
14. Docket No. BAR-03-21 (Maine Supreme Judicial Court December 7, 1993).
15. Clark v. Virginia Board of Bar Examiners, 880 F. Supp. 430 (E.D., Va. 1995)

16. 42 U.S.C. §12501(c).

17. Ibid.

18. Mason Tenders District Council Welfare Fund v. Donaghey, No. 93 Civ. 1154 (JES) (S.D.N.Y.), EEOC amicus brief filed September 21, 1993. The EEOC has ruled in another case that a union's health plan that contained a $10,000 lifetime limit on reimbursement for HIV-related treatments violates the ADA. Doe v. Laborers' District Council, EEOC Philadelphia District Office, Charge Number 170930899, September 9, 1993.

19. Interim Guidance, p. 6, footnotes omitted. One of these footnotes explained that the EEOC was adopting an intentional discrimination test in deference to case law under Section 504 of the Rehabilitation Act involving challenges to health benefit plans. Alexander v. Choate, 469 U.S. 287 (1985). It should be noted that the typical limitation on mental health coverage also differs significantly from a blanket limitation in all health coverage (e.g., a limit to a certain number of hospital days) whose impact is greatest on people with disabilities. Such a blanket limitation, affecting everyone, was upheld by the Supreme Court in Alexander v. Choate, a Section 504 challenge to a state Medicaid plan's limits on hospital days.

20. Interim Guidance, p. 11.

21. 42 U.S.C. §12101(a)(1).

22. 42 U.S.C. §12101(a)(5).

23. 42 U.S.C. §12101(a)(7).

24. H.R. Rep 101-485(III), 101st Conf., 2nd Sess., p. 26.

25. 28 CFR 35.130(d).

26. 56 Fed Reg. 35557 (July 28, 1991).

27. Ibid.

28. See, e.g., Kentucky Ass'n for Retarded Citizens v. Conn., 674 F.2d 582 (6th Cir), cert. denied 459 U.S. 1041 (1982). But see Homeward Bound v. Hissom, No. 85-C-437-E (N.D.Okla. 1987).

29. Halderman v. Pennhurst State School and Hospital, 784 F. Supp. 215 (E.D.Pa. 1992).

30. Wyatt v. King, No. 3195-N (M.D. – Ala.); Jackson v. Fort Stanton Hospital and Training School, No. 87-839-JP (D.N.M.).

31. Haygood v. Texas Dept. of MHMR., No. L-93-85 (S.D. – Tex.).
32. Bosteder v. Soliz, No. 93201817A (Sup. Ct. of Thurston Co., Wash).
33. Easly v. Snider, No. 93-0224 (E.D. – Pa. 1993).
34. 609 N.E. 2d 447 (Mass. 1993).

Personal Assistance Services

Simi Litvak

EDITOR'S NOTE

Underpinning the ADA is the revolutionary notion that disability is a function of the interaction between an individual and a particular environment or situation, rather than a function of innate individual limitation. The provision of personal assistance services (PAS), services of another person to complete the tasks of daily living, demands an examination of the dimensions of that interaction.

The ADA is intended to create equal access to the goods and services of society for people with disabilities. If an individual needs PAS to experience equal access, who bears the responsibility for its provision? The business? The employer? The individual? A third party? Litvak raises these questions and concludes that, without the availability of comprehensive PAS for those who need it, the goals of the ADA will never be achieved. As an interim measure, she raises the possibility of expanding the current transportation provision that waives user fees for personal assistants who accompany people with disabilities. She looks to an expansive interpretation of the ADA as well as health care reform for progress in achieving universal access to PAS.

Simi Litvak is director of the Research and Training Center on Personal Assistance Services at The World Institute on Disability in Oakland, California. Litvak is a nationally known expert in independent living and personal assistance services. She holds a Ph.D. in rehabilitation counseling and served as a member of President Clinton's Health Care Reform Task Force.

INTRODUCTION

> The Nation's proper goals regarding individuals with disabilities are to assure equality of opportunity, full participation, independent living, and economic self-sufficiency for such individuals. (Public Law 101-336, Section 2)

Few people would dispute the values and objectives embodied in the preceding declaration from the Americans with Disabilities Act (ADA). For those who require them, few services can be as central to full participation and independent living as personal assistance services (PAS). Accordingly, the questions surrounding whether

366

the ADA requires the provision of these services, and if it does not, how and when they are to be provided and funded, emerge as central in any effort to define the place of persons with disabilities in our society.

This chapter examines the current status of personal assistance services under the ADA and analyzes issues surrounding the advisability of and responsibility for the provision of such services under a number of program authorities. The chapter also endeavors to place personal assistance services in the context of current debates over civil rights, entitlement programs, and health care reform.

WHAT ARE PERSONAL ASSISTANCE SERVICES?

In our complex society, it is hard to imagine anyone going through a day without the assistance of another person. If we eat in a restaurant, someone else cooks and serves our food; if we travel anywhere by train or bus, someone else drives it. But if we need the assistance of someone to eat the food or to "transfer" to and from the transportation vehicle, then we may be said to need personal assistance services.

Broadly speaking, PAS refers to assistance needed from another person in performing activities of daily living in such "personal" areas as dressing, toileting, and eating. People with physical or mobility disabilities may require PAS, and so too may people with sensory, cognitive, psychiatric, or communication disabilities.

Although PAS terminology is not uniformly applied to the communication assistance represented by readers who are utilized by persons who are blind or by sign-language interpreters utilized by persons who are deaf, such communication assistance comes within the PAS framework. Because this type of assistance for people with sensory disabilities is not controversial except for its cost, it will not be discussed here. In addition, there are unique sets of issues pertaining to PAS for people with psychiatric and cognitive disabilities that will not be discussed here. This chapter will focus on PAS for individuals with physical or mobility disabilities because such PAS involves a number of discrete legal, funding, and policy questions.

WHO NEEDS PAS?

The availability or unavailability of PAS materially affects the lives of an estimated 9.6 million Americans. These are people of all ages and with all types of disabilities who need hands-on, standby, or cueing assistance of another person with their daily living tasks. They include 7.8 million noninstitutionalized people, 1.5 million people in nursing homes, and .3 million people in facilities for people with mental retardation (World Institute on Disability and Rutgers University Bureau of Economic Research, 1990; LaPlante, 1991; Kraus and Stoddard, 1989). PAS users also include the 300,000 people with hearing impairments who use sign language or oral interpreters to communicate with hearing people and the unknown number of people with visual disabilities who use readers or drivers.[1] Only a small percent of these people need assistance with feeding (5 percent), dressing (20 percent), or toilet functions (12 percent), the most controversial PAS issues under the ADA (Table 1). The number of work- or school-age people living in the community needing such assistance is even smaller. Only an estimated 362,000 people in this age group need help with using the toilet and 262,000 need assistance with eating.

Lack of this assistance is a major barrier to full participation and equality of opportunity for many people with disabilities. The 1986 Louis Harris survey of Americans with disabilities found that the second most common reason given by people with disabilities for not being able to "get around, attend events, or socialize with friends outside their home" was because they "need someone to go with [them] or help [them] but don't always have someone."[2]

In many cases, the opportunity costs, though burdensome, can be endured. People find alternative means for preserving some modicum of independence, community participation, or economic activity. But in all too many cases, the absence of PAS represents an insurmountable barrier to the avoidance of institutionalization or to the ability to engage in gainful work. By and large, the persons for whom PAS are thus decisive constitute those whom society would regard as having the most significant disabilities. Although presumably few people would dispute the value of PAS to these individuals or question the legitimacy of their preference for the availability of such services over the consequences of their unavail-

Table 1

Number of People Living in Noninstitutional Settings Who Need Assistance of Another Person with Using the Toilet or Eating, by Age

Type of Activity and Nature of Assistance	All Ages		6–64		65+	
	Number	Percent	Number	Percent	Number	Percent
ADLs/IADLs[a]	7.8 million[b]	100	4.68 million[b]	100	3.12 million[b]	100
Dressing	1.528 million[d]	19.6[c]	983,000[d]	21[c]	608,400[d]	19.5[c]
Using toilet	952,000[d]	12.2[c]	362,000[d]	11.6[c]	637,000[d]	13.6[c]
Eating	436,800[d]	5.6[c]	262,000[d]	5.9[c]	184,000[d]	5.6[c]

[a]Activities of daily living/intermediate activities of daily living.
[b]Source: 1988 SIPP as reported in World Institute on Disability and Rutgers University Bureau of Economic Research (1990).
[c]Source: NHIS Survey, Home Care Supplement (1979–1980) as reported in La Plante, 1989. Data are number needing help with eating or toileting (Table 1, p. 12) divided by number needing help with a basic physical activity or IADL (Table 29, p. 39).
[d]Estimate based on using SIPP totals (a) times NHIS percentages (c).

ability, the public policy debate surrounding PAS does not hinge on these understandable sentiments. Rather, the debate revolves around the overall costs and benefits to society of making such services widely available and, in so far as their availability is deemed appropriate, on how the costs and responsibility for doing so should be allocated.

With this in mind, I turn to the Americans with Disabilities Act (ADA) to assess the extent to which it mandates or encourages the provision of PAS and the wisdom, fairness, and practicality of the arrangements it embodies.

THE ADA AND PAS

Justly called a civil rights charter for people with disabilities, the ADA opens opportunities to employment, public services, and access to public accommodations for America's citizens with disabilities. Although people who need the assistance of other persons are covered by the ADA, the extent to which the law requires employers, governmental agencies, or public accommodations to provide the services of personal assistants is key to the law's long-term impact on the lives of those needing PAS.

The ADA has three major components: Title I bars discrimination in employment on the basis of disability, and requires employers to provide "reasonable accommodations" for those employees or job applicants who, with or without such accommodations, can perform the "essential functions" of the job. Title II prohibits discrimination in the provision of services and in access to programs and facilities by governmental program operators and service providers. Title III imposes similar requirements upon "places of public accommodation"; that is, on the broad range of commercial, recreational, professional, and other entities that are defined as engaging in commerce. On balance, any nongovernmental location where goods, services, or facilities are provided to or for the use of the public is subject to the requirements of Title III. Among other provisions, Title III requires that public accommodations provide "auxiliary aids and services" in appropriate circumstances where these are necessary to meet the law's accessibility standard.

The ADA does not specify what specific measures would constitute "reasonable accommodation" or "auxiliary services." Indeed, its overall approach, utilizing a goal-oriented framework and placing considerable emphasis on the circumstances of each case, would make the fashioning of an a priori list virtually impossible. Nonetheless, from the few examples given in the statute itself, the expressions of congressional intent found in the ADA's legislative history, and the interpretive and explanatory materials set forth by the federal regulatory agencies charged with enforcing of the ADA, it is possible to suggest certain situations in which particular accommodations would be more or less likely to suffice.

PARAMETERS OF THE PROVISION OF PAS

In the employment setting under Title I, Congress clearly intended for PAS to be available to people on the job. Conference reports indicate that provision of a personal assistant for a person with a disability in performing job-related tasks (e.g., filing, reading, driving, phoning, writing, typing, setting up) can constitute a reasonable accommodation, depending upon the circumstances of the individual case. Specifically, the test for reasonable accommodation would be met if (1) providing a personal assistant for an employee does not involve undue administrative or financial hardship for the employer; (2) the functions for which the employee receives assistance are job related; and (3) the employee, not the assistant, performs the essential functions of the job (that is, no "doubling-up" on jobs).[3] In addition, the U.S. Equal Employment Opportunities Commission (EEOC), which administers Title I, has indicated that it may be a reasonable accommodation to provide personal assistance on overnight business trips in connection with specified duties related to the job (Sec. 1630.2 [o]).[4]

The provision of PAS for toileting, feeding, and dressing is not explicitly addressed either by the legislative history or EEOC interpretation or guidance. To the degree that such assistance may be indispensable to an individual's ability to work, the argument can be made that it should constitute a reasonable accommodation.[5] On the other hand, to the degree that such services can be characterized as personal rather than job-related, in so far as they would be needed whether the individual were working or not, the counterargument can likewise be made that their job-relatedness is simply too remote to require them under Title I. This issue will be further discussed later.

The regulations provide minimal guidance on the scope of PAS in relation to employment, but they are far more explicit in relation to public accommodations. In its regulations implementing Title III, the Department on Justice (DOJ) states: "A public entity is not . . . required to provide attendant care, or assistance in toileting, eating, or dressing to individuals with disabilities, except in special circumstances, such as where the individual is an inmate of a custodial or correctional institution."[6] The regulations do not define the nature of these special circumstances, leaving that determination largely to particular cases and situations that may arise over time.

Although explicitly broad limitations on PAS are delineated for the provision of "auxiliary aids and services," so too is a specific authorization. *Auxiliary aids and services* are defined to include "those aids and services required to provide effective communications." This definition encompasses readers, interpreters, writers, drivers, and facilitators for individuals with cognitive disabilities.[7] This "communications" exception to the general rule covering PAS is a specific and narrow one.

A central principle underlying Titles II and III is the assurance of the opportunity for equal participation for individuals with disabilities. Thus, public entities cannot impose or apply eligibility criteria that screen out or tend to screen out an individual with a disability. Even those who need PAS cannot be excluded from fully and equally enjoying any service. No requirement or burden can be placed on an individual with a disability that is not placed on others. This limitation prohibits any requirement for an individual with a disability to bring along an attendant as a condition of participation in the program or activity or to receive the service. Here a catch-22 arises: If one needs assistance to participate but the entity can neither require the individual to provide the assistant nor be required to furnish such assistant itself, then where does the assistance come from?

The rule is clarified, and the problem made more evident, by the regulatory provision under Title III that assistance of a "personal nature" is not required. However, if barrier removal is not readily achievable, PAS for "minimal actions" may be required as a means of modifying a policy, practice, or procedure. If PAS is provided under these conditions, it would not be considered "services of a personal nature." Two examples of minimal action are cutting up food or putting a straw in a glass.[8]

The argument for requiring public accommodations to provide services of a "personal" nature is that without such assistance many individuals will be unable to participate or enjoy the benefits of the institutions of our society. As in the employment setting, the opposing argument is that services of so personal a nature are necessitated, not by the desire to utilize a public accommodation, but by the exigencies of daily living. As such, the argument continues, it would be unfair (would represent an "undue burden," in the parlance of Title III) to require a public accommodation to meet the cost for services that are not necessitated by any of its programmatic features or facility characteristics.

Many of those interviewed for this chapter recognized that, given the many millions of accommodations of all different types covered by Title III, any broad mandate for PAS in such areas as toileting, feeding, and dressing would be unworkable. Moreover, whatever anti-ADA sentiments may now exist in certain segments of the business community would be enormously increased, with predictably adverse social and legal results, were such requirements to be adopted.

HAVE CONSUMERS COMPLAINED REGARDING PAS?

To this author's knowledge, no complaints or lawsuits regarding the unavailability of PAS in the employment setting have been formally brought before the EEOC or the courts for adjudication. It may be that people with disabilities are either frightened or unaware of the possibilities for recourse that formal complaint mechanisms and related negotiation might offer. It may also be the case, as anecdotal evidence suggests, that a number of employers are providing PAS, tacitly or expressly, to highly valued employees. Many employers are citing the "personal nature" exception to the requirement for services, even though it may not apply to Title I.

The author's survey of the regional Disability and Business Technical Assistance Centers (DBTACs), the organizations set up around the country to provide technical assistance in implementing and complying with the ADA, has yielded reports of three situations involving PAS on the job. One informant discussed the case of a person who contacted the DBTAC for advice. The individual is a person with high-level quadriplegia who obtained a $23,000-a-year job working for a large Chicago bank. This person needs assistance with eating and emptying a urine bag once a day. The employer cited the "personal nature" clause and said this type of assistance could not be provided. The bank does provide other assistance and adaptations for the employee. The DBTAC tried to intervene with the bank personnel office, pointing out that it is not an undue hardship owing to the minimal expense involved. The bank already has a nurse on staff who could possibly be called upon. In the face of continued employer resistance, the employee chose not to pursue the issue, because that person wanted the job badly and was fearful of losing it. The employee decided to pay another employee out of personal funds to obtain the needed PAS.

In the Southeast, an employee of a disability-oriented nonprofit organization asked the regional DBTAC for advice on how to negotiate with her employer to pay for PAS. Currently the employee pays herself. From this employer's standpoint the issue boils down to a question of what are work-related duties and what are not. The employer is drawing the line on eating and toileting. So far the employee has not filed suit.

The director of the Great Plains DBTAC noted that PAS is available to only 100 people in Missouri. "So asking for assistance in employment or the community seems beyond the realm of possibility. People are fighting hard to get PAS in the community and some have had to go to institutions."

It is interesting to note that in none of the reported instances so far has the employer claimed "undue hardship" regarding the provision of PAS even though PAS on the job may be more costly than other reasonable accommodations. Whether this argument would be used in litigation or has been held in reserve for use in informal negotiations is impossible to know, but the likelihood is that it would be invoked where plausible. The director of the Rocky Mountain DBTAC noted that businesses and public entities appear scared. They in fact do see PAS as one of the potentially more costly accommodations, according to the directors. They are trying to figure out how not to make PAS a covered accommodation. The director of the Northeast DBTAC indicated that the DBTAC's experience is that employers have looked carefully at the "personal services" dispensation and are using it to refuse eating and bathroom assistance.

In contrast to the employment arena, a major victory for provision of PAS in the home and community has been won in the area of access to government programs and facilities. On 31 January 1995 the United States Court of Appeals for the Third Circuit ruled that the state of Pennsylvania had violated Title II by funding services in a nursing home when the state could have provided PAS in the community. The decision in *Idell S. v. Snider* states that the ADA "make[s] clear that unnecessary segregation of individuals with disabilities in the provision of public services is itself a form of discrimination . . ."[9]

ISSUES NEEDING RESOLUTION

Even though the DOJ has not received any complaints regarding PAS, three issues have arisen in relation to public accommodations that need clarification. The first, as noted earlier, concerns what special circumstances might warrant assistance with feeding, dressing, and toileting. In addition to "custodial and correctional" facilities, there are other places where people spend a great part of their day, including schools – from day care centers to universities – shelters for battered women, and jury facilities. Some examples of the dilemma raised by this issue follow.

Students at San Francisco State University complain about the lack of PAS as a barrier to participation. Families cannot provide all the hours students need to be able to participate fully in campus life, such as social, recreational, library experiences. For example, one student who has quadriplegia receives only two hours per week of PAS from a state program. His family is expected to meet his needs that exceed this provision of service. On the other hand, another student, a strong self-advocate, receives PAS around the clock from four attendants. To date, the disability services program at SF State has not determined a policy on the provision of feeding and toileting assistance for students. Even though the program readily provides typists and dictaphones as accommodations, it does not readily provide PAS.

A related set of problems involves determination of payment responsibility, once the need for PAS is established. It is unclear who pays for attendants living in dorms. Are they residence hall workers? Currently the provision of PAS generally is at the discretion of residence halls and disabled student services.

A similar case was reported by the Southwest DBTAC. A university student needed someone to push his wheelchair. The university claimed such a request represented a need for PAS. The provision of an accessible campus was the university's obligation, and one it had met. Therefore, the university argued, the State Vocational Rehabilitation Agency should be responsible for personal help of this sort. The student, on the other hand, claimed the provision of PAS as a "program access" requirement. The dispute has yet to be resolved.

An issue arose in a day care center where no ramp was available for children in wheelchairs to enter the building. Staff would not carry the children into the center and assist in transferring them into their wheelchairs. The center said it would provide for children with disabilities only what it provides for other children. The DBTAC recommended installing a ramp and modifying the policy so that certain services would be available to children who use wheelchairs or who cannot pick up eating utensils. The case had not been settled at the time of the interview.

The second issue regards the extent to which public accommodations may be required to admit personal assistants to events free of charge. The law provides limited requirements in transportation that waive fees for personal assistants. When an assistant accompanies a person with a disability on paratransit, the assistant rides free of charge. Some argue that such a provision should be extended to all circumstances in which the presence of an assistant is necessary to access meaningful participation or full enjoyment of the public accommodation. For example, if an individual attending a baseball game needed a personal assistant for assistance in eating and toileting, that assistant should be admitted to the game free of charge. No informants reported cases involving this issue.

The third issue relates to jurisdictional disputes over which entity is responsible for payment for PAS. Such disputes are a chronic and recurrent feature of any effort to determine the availability of services, PAS or otherwise, from public program sources. In the primary and secondary school context, for example, jurisdictional disputes between special education and Medicaid regarding the authority and responsibility to pay for catheterization are common. Although such disputes are beyond the scope of this chapter, the existence of PAS funding sources outside the ADA framework inevitably complicates the analysis of ADA's potential role.

CURRENT STRATEGIES FOR MEETING PAS NEEDS ON THE JOB

Workers who need PAS for eating and toileting manage on the job in various ways. If the employer pays for the assistant, several different arrangements are possible. The individual with a disability may disguise the more personal tasks behind the more general duties of the assistant. For example, one informant is an individual with quadriplegia who holds an administrative job in a nonprofit organization. He has a half-time secretary and a half-time personal assistant who are the same person. The assistant is paid $25,000 per year (plus benefits) and provides all assistance the individual with a disability needs, including assistance with toileting, eating, driving, and running errands.

In some situations, employers have hired an employee specifically to perform PAS tasks. Several organizations reported employing a staff member whose primary job is to provide PAS to all employees who need it. Generally, these personal assistants also helped out with other tasks at the workplace as needed; for example, as relief receptionist or clerical worker. This approach tends to reduce the costs of PAS, but its cost effectiveness is dependent upon a number of employees who need PAS being concentrated in a single workplace or in locations close to each other. As such, it is an approach that best lends itself either to large employers or, ironically, to sheltered employment settings.

Just as employers are likely to provide relatively higher levels of assistance and service to their most valued employees, so too are they likely to provide disability-related assistance that might be characterized as PAS if an employee has high value to the organization; for example, an employee with a visual disability works for a large retailer in Chicago and is regularly transported to and from work by a driver. The company recently moved from Chicago proper, where the individual used the elevated for transportation, to an outlying suburb. Not wanting to lose the long-time employee, the company offered to provide transportation. The employee is 60 years old and has worked for the company almost his entire life.

In another situation, the Section 504/ADA compliance officer at San Francisco State University negotiated the provision of an assistant all day as a condition of her job. The university pays for the assistant as a reasonable accommodation. The assistant helps with bathroom and driving needs. Over time the employee's need for the assistant decreased as a result of the bathroom being made fully accessible and the provision of a teaching assistant for help with classroom duties. The cost of both the personal assistant and the teaching assistant was about $4,000 per year in 1993. How much of this sum represents add-on costs is unclear, because presumably the coordinator would have been entitled to the services of a teaching assistant even in the absence of a disability.

The California state university system has had a reasonable accommodation budget for years, established long ago at the urging of five employees with disabilities. The budget allows for provision of PAS; however, the existence of the fund is not well known. In some instances those funds have been used to provide feeding and toileting assistance.

One informant works for a state agency that provides him with personal assistance for traveling. All the assistant's expenses are paid for by the agency. "Occasionally" the employer pays personal assistant wages of $100 per day. The agency has no formal mechanism to pay personal assistants. It is the informant's sense that, if necessary, "my agency would hire an assistant for me on the job and not ask or monitor closely what that person was doing for me unless it became excessively expensive."

Although no statistics are available, anecdotal accounts indicate that people with disabilities frequently pay out of pocket for an assistant or "attendant." They may hire a coworker or someone from outside the organization. One informant spoke graphically about the problems associated with hiring a coworker:

> Prior to full-time employment . . . I held several federally funded jobs, each lasting a maximum of nine months. Finding a PA was a matter of approaching a "friendly soul" to assist me with toileting and placing and removing coats. Usually I paid them "under the table." The individuals and I worked well together but the system was frequently complicated by factors such as their need to attend staff meetings, travel, unexpected missed days, etc. In 1987, I began working full-time. Initially, I hired another employee. . . . Similar issues followed, such as scheduling conflicts. Two other disadvantages were soon discovered. The attendant was unable to accompany me on errands in town because of caseloads . . . coverage, but more importantly, I felt that the nature of the work necessitated an outside party. This would allow me to retain a sense of professionalism with the [other] employees. Currently the employee [I hired] still takes my wheelchair seatbelt and coat off every morning. Other individuals around me volunteer time

to pour coffee, place my lunch in the refrigerator, etc. My PA [from home] comes to work at noon on weekdays. [This consumer lives in a state where the user/consumer has full control over where, when, and how the assistant works and is, therefore, able to use allotted PAS hours at work.] He or she . . . accompanies me to meetings, particularly those where meals are served. This includes meetings [where] . . . travel is necessary. Although I use a power wheel chair and have a van (don't drive it), I use a manual wheel chair when driven by an attendant, and pay them mileage, which is subsidized by my organization. . . . Transportation is frequently cited as a major factor in a person with a disability's opportunity to secure and maintain employment. I feel that PAS plays an equally significant role, if not more so. . . . One problem with work and PAS is the difficulties in locating an outside person to perform the work for 1–2 hours per day. Attendants frequently want more hours than those being offered.

For those individuals who do bear the costs of their own PAS at work, federal income tax law offers some measure of subsidy. Under Section 67(d) of the internal revenue code, impairment-related work expenses incurred by workers with disabilities in order to perform their jobs are tax deductible, without regard to the threshold levels that ordinarily apply to the deduction for employee business expenses. In defining *impairment-related work expenses*, the statute refers to ''attendant care services at . . . or in connection'' with the individual's place of work. It is clear that this provision covers PAS services on the job, including services where job duties must be performed at a remote or outside location, but it is unlikely that this provision could be extended to PAS services needed at home in the context of preparation for work such as dressing.

The availability of an itemized deduction for on-the-job PAS can, ironically, represent a significant subsidy for upper-income workers. However, for low-paid individuals whose earnings are insufficient to make them liable for income taxes and for workers who cannot aggregate sufficient deductions to warrant itemization (i.e., for those workers who must use the standard deduction), the impairment-related work expense deduction is of little practical value (Mendelsohn, 1993).

Some workers with disabilities depend upon volunteer help of fellow workers. An informant reported that two managers with disabilities in government agencies receive PAS from other employers who volunteer to provide it. Both managers spend time in the field as well as in the office. Both need minimal assistance emptying urine bags and arranging and cutting food. The informant noted significant drawbacks to such informal arrangements: "Having to depend upon the kindness of others, especially people you supervise, may have a detrimental effect on the relationship between the employee with a disability and other employees."

Finally, many people simply go without feeding and toileting assistance and experience hardships. As one informant noted, "[people I know] mostly pay for it themselves, make arrangements with coworkers, hide PA tasks behind assistant duties, or mostly go without, i.e. hold their bladder, sit in wet or soiled [undergarments], go without lunch or accept medical procedures like indwelling catheters or an ileal loop bypass when this would otherwise not be necessary medically."

OTHER SOURCES OF PAS

Only 2 million of the almost 7.8 million people living in the community who need PAS received some or all PAS services from federal, state, or locally funded programs in 1988 (Litvak and Kennedy, 1991). People who need PAS have substantially lower personal incomes than the general population. Those of working age also have a sharply lower probability of working. Little private insurance coverage exists for long-term PAS. Consequently, most PAS users who live in the community live with relatives and rely on them to meet their PAS needs. People with little informal or volunteer support and high PAS needs are very likely to end up living in nursing homes. In fact older people without family support make up 90 percent of nursing home residents – most of these are women.[10]

The tax system can subsidize at-home PAS for those who pay for services out of pocket. The Child and Dependent Care Tax Credit, which is available up to a maximum of up to $2,400 a year for one qualifying dependent, and up to $4,800 a year for two or more dependents, is intended to offset the costs incurred for the care of young children or spouses and other dependents who are "incapable of self-care" when the family caregiver leaves the home to pursue gainful work. Additionally, to the extent that they can be characterized as involving nursing or equivalent care, in-home PAS expenses qualify for the medical expense deduction. Even though household maintenance services do not meet the nursing-or-equivalent test, assistance with toileting, eating, and dressing do, irrespective of the professional qualifications of the service provider (Mendelsohn, 1993).

Even though most PAS users rely on family volunteers for assistance, Nosek finds that family providers are often unsatisfactory.[11] The use of family providers can severely limit the personal and financial independence of both recipients and providers, and the stress on family relationships may increase the potential for abuse or neglect. Shifting family structures and increasing numbers of women entering the work force indicate that traditional family supports will become less available over time (Etheredge, 1987). Parents may die or become unable to assist their child with a disability. In addition, even where it is feasible for families to assist at home, it is quite awkward and often inconvenient for a family member to come to the work site or accompany a youngster to college.

Unfortunately, a simple increase in the number of people receiving PAS through the public system(s) will not solve the accommodation needs of beneficiaries. The publicly funded systems are, on balance, poorly designed for meeting the needs of persons with significant disabilities. In addition, services are unevenly distributed around the country (Litvak, Heumann, and Zukas, 1987). The PAS system is fragmented, complex, and lacks a comprehensive, coordinated policy framework. Despite a wide variety of federal and state funding sources for PAS, none of these sources has shaped the programs significantly (Litvak and Kennedy, 1991). Rather, programs have developed in response to state and local needs and priorities and advocacy efforts. They often target particular subpopulations. The funding sources a state utilizes vary from state to state. As a result programs differ in age and disability groups served. Not all disability groups are served in every state. Although most programs will serve people with physical disabilities, far fewer will serve people with cognitive or psychiatric disabilities. States vary considerably in the percentage of their potentially eligible population served by PAS programs.

Programs are usually means tested, creating a major barrier to employment and marriage for those receiving services. For example, a recipient of PAS may risk losing that service if he or she may no longer meet the low income requirement. Only a handful of programs provide PAS to people who work, and even these do not allow the assistant to accompany the individual with a disability on the job. Most programs do not allow the attendant to provide PAS outside the home except for medically related trips. Very few programs reimburse family members who serve as attendants, and some go so far as to allow only people without nondisabled spouses or other family members to become eligible for service.

Most programs are inadequate to meet the needs of consumers. They do not deliver enough hours of service or a broad enough range of services. Only a third of programs offer a comprehensive PAS package, including personal maintenance and hygiene, household maintenance, and paramedical services such as catheter assistance.

Where more than one program model exists, the determination as to what type of provider and system is best for the individual consumer is not dictated by the consumer's capacity for, or interest in, self-direction and self-management of the service. Service models also do not incorporate flexibility to respond to changing PAS needs due to the volatility of the individual's condition. What type of PAS program a particular individual is referred to depends upon the range of choices available in a particular community or within a particular program (Kimmick and Godfrey, 1991). The question of suitable program fit is both a quality of life question and an economic one. Concerns regarding liability and quality monitoring have dictated choices regarding the mode of service delivery and the design of provider training programs, while at the same time limiting consumer decision making. Generally policy makers have designed programs without attempting to differentiate among consumers in their ability to manage all or part of their PAS (Kapp, 1990).

Compounding the problems with the existing PAS programs is the major problem of assistant turnover (Litvak et al., 1990). Wages and benefits for assistants are generally poor. The wages for live-in assistants who provide PAS around the clock are even lower. Benefits, particularly for assistants not working for an agency, tend to be limited to Social Security and workers' compensation, if they exist at all.

FORGING A CONSENSUS FOR CHANGE

Little serious dispute exists regarding the value of increased PAS resources in our society. Nursing home admissions and other institutionalization would be curtailed; family and community ties would be enhanced; family providers who can work gainfully outside the home would be free to do so; and most of all, individuals with disabilities themselves would be liberated to pursue and achieve their fullest potential in independent living and employment. For those who believe that PAS, because it is so basic for so many people, represents a basic civil right, the moment for advocacy is at hand. The steady accrual of research data coupled with activism and consciousness-raising efforts at the grassroots and national levels have placed of PAS on the national agenda at just the moment when changes in our health care system, including long-term care, are imminent.

PAS is among the paramount service modalities for restoration and assurance of social vitality and economic self-sufficiency (DeJong, Batavia, and McKnew, 1992). If health care reform eventually eliminates preexisting condition exclusions, people with disabilities will be able to move freely from job to job without fear of being denied insurance coverage. If a long-term care package similar to the Clinton 1994 proposal is ever enacted, greater tax incentives will be available so that workers can deduct 50 percent of their PAS expenses from taxes owed, and those with significant levels of disability who hold lower-paying jobs will be able to receive PAS funding directly from the government without running afoul of rigid means testing.

Even with these reforms and the civil rights protections of the ADA, most people with significant disabilities will continue to face major barriers to independent living, full inclusion, and the other goals of society because of the inadequacy of PAS at home, in public accommodations, and at work. Without access to a comprehensive system of PAS for everyone who needs it, there may be no way to ensure full participation. Forging the momentum to create such a system will bring another historic landmark in the struggle for disability rights within reach.

ACKNOWLEDGMENTS

Much of the information in this chapter came from a number of informants with expertise on the ADA, including Howard Moses and Deidre Davis at the Equal Employment Opportunity Commission; John Wodatch at the Department of Justice; Laura Rauscher, Keith Williams, and Leo Canuel of the National Council on Independent Living; Pat Wright, Mary Lou Breslin, and Arlene Meyerson of the Disability Rights Education and Defense Fund; Tony Young of the American Rehabilitation Association; Wendy Wilkinson, Erica Jones, Randy Dipner, Robin Jones, Shelley Kaplan, Jim DeJong, Toby Olson, Jennifer Eckel, and Richard Dodds, directors of regional Disability and Business Technical Assistance Centers; Kirk MacGugan and Doug Martin, university ADA/504 administrators.

REFERENCES

DeJong, G., A. I. Batavia, and L. B. McKnew. 1992. "The Independent Living Model of Personal Assistance in National Long Term Care Policy: Why Has This Approach Been Largely Overlooked?" *Generations* 16, no. 1: 89–95.

Etheredge, L. 1987. "Home and Community Based Care for the Elderly." *Health Affairs* 6, no. 1: 176–189.

Kapp, M. B. 1990. "Improving the Choices Regarding Home Care Services: Legal Impediments and Empowerment." Unpublished manuscript, Wright State University School of Medicine, Dayton, Ohio.

Kimmick, M., and T. Godfrey. 1991. *New Models for the Provision of Personal Assistance Services: Final Report.* Bethesda, Md.: Human Services Research Institute.

Kraus, L., and S. Stoddard. 1989. *Chartbook on Disability in the US.* Washington, D.C.: NIDRR.

LaPlante, M. 1991. "Disability in Basic Life Activities across the Life Span." *Disability Statistics Report*, vol. 1, 1–42. San Francisco: Disability Statistics Program, University of California.

Litvak, S., et al. 1990. *Source Book of Personal Assistance Program Case Study Information, Appendix C: New Models for the Provision of Personal Assistance Services*. NIDRR Grant No. G008720134. Oakland, Calif.: World Institute on Disability.

Litvak, S., J. Heumann, and H. Zukas. 1987. *Attending to America: Personal Assistance for Independent Living*. Berkeley, Calif.: World Institute on Disability.

Litvak, S., and J. Kennedy. 1991. *Policy Issues and Questions Affecting the Medicaid Personal Care Services Optional Benefit*. Oakland, Calif.: World Institute on Disability.

Mendelsohn, S. 1993. *Tax Options and Strategies for People with Disabilities*. New York: Demos Publications.

World Institute on Disability and Rutgers University Bureau of Economic Research. 1990. *The Need for Personal Assistance*. New Brunswick, N.J.: Rutgers University.

NOTES

1. According to the Survey of Income and Program Participation (SIPP) there are 12.7 million people over 15 years old with visual disabilities. Visual limitations are defined as difficulty viewing ordinary print, even with corrective devices. There seems to be no data available to tell us the number of people with visual disabilities who need assistance, depending upon the nature of their occupations and lifestyles. The overlap between those needing assistance with household and personal tasks and those needing reading assistance is also unknown. One suspects it is high in the aging population. Finally one could assume that people with visual disabilities who do not live where there is a good transportation system will need drivers.

    The National Center for Health Statistics indicates there are 21 million people with hearing impairments. Of these approximately 300,000 are people who are "prelinguistically deaf," meaning they become deaf before the age of 3. Approximately one-third of these people are educated orally and, presumably, use oral interpreters. The other 200,000 people use sign language interpreters. Generally, people who become hearing impaired later in life tend not to be proficient in either mode of communication and must rely on real-time captioning and other technological solutions to their problems communication with hearing individuals. The overlap between those needing sign language interpreters and those needing assistance with ADLs and IADLs has not been investigated.

2. Louis Harris and Associates, "The ICD Survey of Disabled Americans: Bringing Disabled Americans into the Mainstream," (New York: International Center for the Disabled, 1986), p. 65.

3. "As with readers and interpreters, the provision of an attendant to assist a person with a disability during parts of the workday may be a reasonable accommodation depending on the circumstances of the individual case. Attendants may, for example, be required for traveling and other job-related functions. This issue must be dealt with on a case-by-case basis to determine whether an undue hardship is created by providing attendants" (Senate Labor and Human Resources Report, p. 33): House Judiciary Report, p. 41. See also EEOC and Nelson vs. Thornberg 56F F. Supp 369 (E.D.Pa. 1983).

4. "Providing personal assistants, such as a page turner for an employee with no hands or a travel attendant to act as a sighted guide to assist a blind employee on occasional business trips, may also be a reasonable accommodation." Section 1630.3(o) in EEOC Title I Regulations regarding Reasonable Accommodation, p. I-41, in the *ADA Handbook* has only two sentences: *ADA Handbook*, p. I-9, published by EEOC and DOJ in the section-by-section analysis of comments and revisions to the proposed rules.

5. The argument has several steps: (1) Employers have a far greater obligation to employees than do purveyors of public accommodations; (2) rules and regulations already acknowledge that access to lunchrooms and toilets is absolutely required for disabled employees; (3) therefore it is recognized

that functions carried out in these places are essential for employees to be able to work; (4) ergo, using the toilet and eating are essential functions for the job for which employees should receive reasonable accommodations.

6. *ADA Handbook*, DOJ Regulations for Title II (p. II-41) Paragraph (b) (8).

7. DOJ, *ADA Title III Technical Assistance Manual* (24 January 1992), p. 25.

8. The DOJ regulations state in the *ADA Handbook* (p. III-95), "Section 36.306 Personal Devices and Services."

9. United States Court of Appeals for the Third Circuit, No. 94-1234, Idell S. v. Karen I. Snider, 31 January 1995. Appeal from the United States District Court for the Eastern District of Pennsylvania (D.C. Civil Action No. 92-6054).

10. The degree of one's disability is not the key factor determining nursing home residency. More people with significant disabilities are living in the community than living in nursing homes (Pepper Commission, 1990, *A Call for Action: Final Report for Bipartisan Committee on Comprehensive Health Care* [Washington, D.C.: U.S. Government Printing Office], p. 92).

11. Margaret Nosek, "Presentation of Initial Results of Current NIDRR Funded Research," National Council on Independent Living conference, Bethesda, Md., 1990.

CONTRIBUTORS

Andrew I. Batavia is a founding associate editor of the *Journal for Disability Policy Studies* and a member of the faculty of Georgetown University Medical School. Batavia currently serves as legislative assistant to Senator John McCain (R-Ariz.).

Christopher G. Bell is a partner in the management, labor, and employment law firm Jackson, Lewis, Schnitzler & Krupman in Washington, DC. In 1983 he authored *Accommodating the Spectrum of Individual Abilities* for the U.S. Commission on Civil Rights.

Edward D. Berkowitz is professor and chair of the Department of History at the George Washington University. He is the author of *Disabled Policy* (Cambridge: Cambridge University Press, 1987), *America's Welfare State* (Baltimore: Johns Hopkins University Press, 1991), *Social Security and Medicare: A Policy Primer* with Eric Kingson (Westport, Conn.: Auburn House, 1993), and *Mr. Social Security: The Life of Wilbur J. Cohen* (Lawrence, Kans.: University Press of Kansas, 1995).

Richard V. Burkhauser is professor of economics and associate director of the aging studies program, Center for Policy Research at Syracuse University. His books include *Public Policy Toward Disabled Workers: A Cross-National Analysis of Economic Impacts* (Ithaca: Cornell University Press, 1984) with Robert H. Haveman and Victor Halberstadt and *Disability and Work: The Economics of American Policy* with Robert H. Haveman (Baltimore: Johns Hopkins University Press, 1982).

Mary C. Daly is a National Institute of Aging Post-Doctoral Fellow and adjunct professor of economics at Syracuse University. Her research includes cross-national comparisons of American and German working-age men with disabilities.

Chai R. Feldblum is associate professor of law at Georgetown University Law Center in Washington, DC and director of the Center's Federal Legislation Clinic. Her publications include

"Antidiscrimination Requirements of the ADA," in *Implementing the ADA: Rights and Responsibilities of All Americans*, edited by Lawrence Gostin and H.A. Beyer (Baltimore: Paul H. Brookes Publishing Co., 1992).

Lawrence O. Gostin is professor of law, Georgetown University Law Center and professor of public health at the Johns Hopkins School of Hygiene and Public Health. He is director of the Johns Hopkins/Georgetown University Program on Law and Public Health. Gostin has published many articles on health law, civil liberties and related subjects, and is editor of the Law and Medicine section of the *Journal of the American Medical Association (JAMA)*.

Simi Litvak is director of the Research and Training Center on Personal Assistance Services at The World Institute on Disability in Oakland, CA.

Leonard S. Rubenstein is executive director of the Bazelon Center for Mental Health law, a nonprofit public-interest law center in Washington, DC, and adjunct professor at Georgetown University Law Center. He has many publications on mental health and the law.

Rosalyn M. Simon is Director of Project ACTION of the National Easter Seal Society, the U.S. Department of Transportation's key technical assistance initiative.

Jane West, a consultant in the Washington, DC area, served as a program officer of the Milbank Memorial Fund during the project that culminated in this book. She edited *The Americans with Disabilities Act: From Policy to Practice* (New York: Milbank Memorial Fund, 1991).

Index

Note: page citations in italics refer to tables; notes are designated with n after the page number

disability insurance, 166–9, 173, 219
disability programs, 198, 219
Disability Rights Education Defense Fund (DREDF), 10, 13
disability transfers, *159*, 160, *161*, 168, 171–2, 174
Disabled in Action, 283
discrimination, 31, 58, 198, 232, 243, 276
 defined, 110
 economic costs of, 197
 in employment, 31
 in housing, 50
 and insurance companies, 110–11
 legal penalties of, 197
 and mental impairment, 340–1
 and personal assistance services, 374
 and prejudice, 197
 and psychiatric disabilities, 355
 and transportation, 306, 320
Disney Company, 39
disparate treatment, 142n102, 144n108, 354–5
District of Columbia, 14, 271, 278, 344–5
DMH. *See* Mental Health, Department of
DOJ. *See* Justice, Department of
Dole, Robert, 5
DOT. *See* Transportation, Department of
doubly disadvantaged, 154, 155, 163–4, 165, 173, 178, 181
drug tests
 and employment, 99–101, 136n49
drug use, 52
 and employment, 35–6
Dunne, John, 13
Dykacz, J. M., 173
dyslexia, 48, 73n70

Earned Income Tax Credit (EITC), 181
education, *161*, 162–3, 198
 and barriers, 279
 and disabilities, 53–5
 and discrimination, 31
 and Title III compliance, 276
 See also public awareness

Education, Department of, 16
Edwards, M. H., 350
EEOC. *See* Equal Employment Opportunity Commission
effective accommodations, 94
 See also reasonable accommodations
EG&G Dynatrend, 316, 319
EITC. *See* Earned Income Tax Credit
elevators, 267, 271, 307–8
Empire State Building, 271–2, 283
Employee Retirement and Income Security Act (ERISA), 113
 discrimination and, 43
employees
 disability-based distinctions in, 42–5
 number of, 33
 and psychiatric disabilities, 351–5
employers
 agent of, 70n34
 defined, 37–8
 financial rewards for, 218
 health benefits costs and, 114
 and personal assistance services, 373
 and workers' compensation, 229
employment, 82–151
 and accommodation, 176
employment discrimination, 37–42, 46, 200
 and psychiatric disabilities, 348–50
 See also Title I
employment opportunities, 230, 348–50
employment practices, 253
Enoff, Louis, 200–1
Environmental Protection Agency, 290
epilepsy, 34
Equal Employment Opportunity Commission (EEOC), 210
 ADA charge statistics and, 248–50
 ADA guidance and, 84, 248
 and administrative remedies, 57
 and complaints, 13–19, *15*, 32, 41, 177, 199

and reasonable accommodation,
107
and Rehabilitation Act, 85
as response to technical
assistance, 13
and Title III, 268–9, 270, 283–4
and workers' compensation,
241–2
See also court cases
Little League, 61–2, 76n106, 285
Litvak, Simi, 366–87
Lockheed, 245
long-term disability, 165, 168, 244
Louis Harris and Associates, 6–7
Louisiana, 247
lupus erythematosus, 139n79, 215

Maine, 48, 346
Mancuso, L., 348, 350
Mandell, J., 283
manifest disabilities, 94–5, 115
Marchand, Paul, 22, 23
Maryland, 250
Mashaw, Jerry, 200
Mason Tenders Welfare Fund, 124
Massachusetts, 48, 51–2, 322
Mastroianni, Peggy, 240
McCain, John, 22, 264
McGann, John, 42–3
McKee, B., 286
McKnew, L. B., 383
McNeil, J. M., 158, 163
Medicaid, 46, 172, 214, 219–20, 376
medical and related expenses, 231
medical examinations, 245
and employment, 82, 84–101
restrictions on, 236–8
Medical Examiners, Board of, 345
medical loss theory, 231
Medicare, 172, 201, 214, 216,
219–20
Megan, K., 290
Meisinger, Susan, 11
Mendelsohn, S., 379, 381
*Mental and Physical Disability Law
Reporter*, 33
mental health, 119–20, 148n131, 342
advocates for, 357
See also psychiatric disabilities

Mental Health, Department of
(DMH)
and housing discrimination, 51–2
mental impairments, 169, 206,
214–15
disability as, 35, 74n88
See also psychiatric disabilities
Michigan, 253
Milbank Memorial Fund, 4, 131n11,
131n14–15
Miller, C. P., 178
Milstein, B., 356, 359
Minnesota, 253, 324
Missouri, 374
modems, 12
modified-work programs, 245, 247
Moore, K., 350
Moore, T., 290
Morris, T., 322
multiple sclerosis, 41, 108–9,
145n117, 258n39
Municipal Credit Union, 271
Murdoch, J., 283
muscular sclerosis, 39
Myers, R. J., 157

Nagi, S., 156
National Academy of Social
Insurance, 200
National Association of Protection
and Advocacy Systems, 13
National Center for Health
Statistics, 385n1
National Conference of Bar
Examiners, 344
National Council on Disability
(NCD), 12, 25, 196, 199, 269,
273, 285–6, 296n19
National Disability Law Reporter,
33
National Easter Seal Society
(NESS), 302, 311, 312, 313,
317, 319, 320, 321, 323
Project ACTION of, 7–9, 303, 310
National Empowerment Center, 351
National Federation of Independent
Business (NFIB), 282
National Health Interview Survey
(NHIS), 24, 190n4

Rubenstein, Leonard S., 340–64
Rutgers University Bureau of
    Economic Research, 368

Sanchez, C. A., 314
Sardi's Restaurant, 271
Schaffer, D. C., 180
Schruth, Susan, 10
Schuster, M., 178
seizure disorders, 35
Self Help for Hard of Hearing
    (SHHH), 283
self-insurance health plans, 34, 43,
    121, 124
semi-quadriplegia, 49, 75n94
Senate, 21–2, 112–13
Senate Labor and Human Resources
    Committee, 114, 135n41,
    143n105, 144n107, 196, 275
Senate Labor Committee, 113,
    143n104
Senate Subcommittee on Disability
    Policy, 4, 10, 275–6
sensory disabilities, 367
service animals, 12, 106, 138n71,
    273
severe impairments, 203, 220
severe work limitations, 197, 223n5
sick days, 86–7
signage, 12, 270, 271, 307
sign language, 60, 77n107, 289, 367,
    368, 385–6n1
    See also interpreters
Silverstein, Robert, 10, 11
Simon, Rosalyn, 300–35
SIPP. See Survey of Income and
    Program Participation
smoke-free environments, 39, 106,
    108, 140n82, 290
Social Security Administration, 202,
    213, 215–16, 219, 349
Social Security Disability Insurance
    (SSDI), 154, 155, 164, 168–9,
    172–3, 179, 191n7, 381
    and income maintenance, 195–223
social welfare policies, 155, 164–70,
    195
    reorientation of, 196
social welfare protection system, *166*

Society for Human Resources
    Management (SHRM), 11, 84,
    102–4
Soper, C. L., 314
South Carolina, 56, 108–9
sovereign immunity, 31
Spartan Tool and Manufacturing
    Inc., 115–16
special treatment, 32, 46
speech impairments, 34–5
SSDI. See Social Security Disability
    Insurance (SSDI)
SSI. See Supplemental Security
    Income (SSI)
state and local governments, 121,
    221, 252
    and ADA litigation, 31, 34, 113
    and complaints, 14–15
    and litigation, 46
    and Title III compliance, 273–5
State Income Maintenance, 215
State Sides (1992), 35
Stoddard, S., 368
Strandberg, K. W., 318
substantial gainful activity, 202,
    214, 217
substantial harm, 237
subterfuge, 43–4, 113, 117–18,
    121–2, 146n119, 352, 354–5
Sullivan, Louis, 6
Supplemental Security Income (SSI),
    154, 155, 164, 169–70, 172,
    179, 195
    and income maintenance, 195–223
Supreme Court, 43, 51, 209
    See also court cases
Survey of Disability and Work, 176
Survey of Income and Program
    Participation (SIPP), 158, 182,
    190n4, 385n1
Survey of the Disabled, 173
Switzer, Mary, 212

tax credits, 11–12, 181, 218, 380
    and public accommodations,
    267–8
TDD. See telecommunications device
    for the deaf
technical assistance, 25
    effectiveness of, 10–13